LICENSING LOYALTY

THE PENN STATE SERIES IN THE HISTORY OF THE BOOK

James L. W. West III, General Editor

Peter Burke, *The Fortunes of the "Courtier":*
The European Reception of Castiglione's "Cortegiano"

Roger Burlingame, *Of Making Many Books:*
A Hundred Years of Reading, Writing, and Publishing

James M. Hutchisson, *The Rise of Sinclair Lewis, 1920–1930*

Julie Bates Dock, ed.,
Charlotte Perkins Gilman's "The Yellow Wall-paper"
and the History of Its Publication and Reception: A Critical Edition
and Documentary Casebook

John Williams, ed., *Imaging the Early Medieval Bible*

James G. Nelson, *Publisher to the Decadents:*
Leonard Smithers in the Careers of Beardsley, Wilde, Dowson

Ezra Greenspan, *George Palmer Putnam: Representative American Publisher*

Pamela Selwyn, *Everyday Life in the German Book Trade:*
Friedrich Nicolai as Bookseller and Publisher in the Age of Enlightenment

David R. Johnson, *Conrad Richter: A Writer's Life*

David Finkelstein, *The House of Blackwood:*
Author-Publisher Relations in the Victorian Era

Rodger L. Tarr, ed., *As Ever Yours:*
The Letters of Max Perkins and Elizabeth Lemmon

Randy Robertson,
Censorship and Conflict in Seventeenth-Century England:
The Subtle Art of Division

Catherine M. Parisian, ed., *The First White House Library:*
A History and Annotated Catalogue

JANE McLEOD

Licensing Loyalty

PRINTERS, PATRONS, AND
THE STATE IN EARLY MODERN FRANCE

The Pennsylvania State University Press
University Park, Pennsylvania

Library of Congress Cataloging-in-Publication Data

McLeod, Jane.
    Licensing loyalty : printers, patrons, and the state in early
    modern France / Jane McLeod.
            p.   cm.
(The Penn State series in the history of the book)
Includes bibliographical references and index.
Summary: "Explores the evolution of the idea that the rise of
print culture was a threat to the royal government of eighteenth-
century France. Argues that French printers did much to foster
this view as they negotiated a place in the expanding bureaucratic
apparatus of the state"—Provided by publisher.
ISBN 978-0-271-03768-4 (cloth : alk. paper)
ISBN 978-0-271-03786-8 (pbk. : alk. paper)
1. Printing—France—History.
2. Printers—Certification—France—History.
3. Printers—France—Social conditions—History.
4. Book industries and trade—Political aspects—France—History.
5. Censorship—France—History.
I. Title.

Z144.M39 2011
070.50944—dc22
2010039081

THIS BOOK *is dedicated to my mother and the memory of my father.*

Contents

Acknowledgments

All the people who helped make this book possible are too numerous to name. I would like to thank all the archivists and librarians in Paris, Bordeaux, Lyon, Rouen, Dijon, and Rennes who assisted me—and to give special mention to those at the Archives départementales de la Gironde, whose generous support went beyond all reasonable expectations. Special thanks are also due to the Interlibrary Loan Department at Brock University for patiently handling many orders and to the coordinator of the History Department, Heidi Klose, for technical assistance of all sorts.

I am grateful to John Bosher for inspiring my interest in French institutional history and for guiding the early stages of this work. Some of the historians whose ideas pervade the book also answered many questions and gave advice: Roger Chartier, Robert Darnton, Albert Hamscher, Elizabeth Eisenstein, Raymond Birn, and Julian Swann. Many others offered their time, expertise, and moral support: Pierre Reynard, Alan Arthur, Howard Brown, Donald Sutherland, Raymonde Litalien, Jeremy Hayhoe, Thierry Rigogne, Stephen Auerbach, Stephen Clay, Eric Wauter, and Jacob Soll. My greatest debt is to Timothy Le Goff for his knowledge of eighteenth-century France and his willingness to pass it on.

I would also like to express my gratitude to my friends and colleagues at Brock University for their help and encouragement over many years and to my editor Laura Reed-Morrisson for countless good suggestions. Research for this book was generously funded by the Social Science and Humanities Research Council of Canada, by Brock University, and by Brock University's Humanities Research Institute.

Very warm and affectionate thanks go to my husband, Hans Hansen, and to our daughters, Madeleine and Alice.

On an October afternoon in 1780, three Dijon notables met at the printers' and booksellers' guildhall to preside over a competition to fill a vacant position for a printer in their town.[1] The competition had been ordered from Versailles by Armand Thomas Hüe de Miromesnil, the keeper of the seals, who had instructed the *intendant* of Dijon to publicize it widely by putting up posters not only in Dijon but in all the towns in the area as well.[2] The inspector of the book trade in Dijon joined the three officials to oversee the candidates' performance in an examination conducted by the guild warden and two other printers. The event that occasioned the meeting of all these men was the decision of Anne Foucherot, the widow of Antoine Defay, to give up her position as printer in Dijon. She had submitted her resignation to Miromesnil, who then received a petition from her son, Antoine-Marie Defay, requesting the position. Miromesnil and Le Camus de Néville, the director of the book trade, decided to fill the vacancy by the competition. After one of the two printer-examiners declared a conflict of interest and withdrew, the examination began in earnest with the first question: "What is a printing house and what does it comprise?"

Defay passed the test. After answering some forty questions, he composed a page from a manuscript copy, proofed it, and distributed it to those present. He then repeated the exercise in different-sized fonts. His examiners deemed the pages correct and the examination complete. They then went to the door of the guildhall and called out several times to see whether there were any other candidates to be examined. There were none. By 7:00 in the evening, the meeting was over. A report of the result was sent to Versailles, where Le Camus de Néville and the masters of requests assigned to Defay's dossier could scrutinize it and advise Miromesnil on whether he should grant Defay a license to become a printer.

Officially, Le Camus de Néville had the following information to work with. First, he had Defay's own story: he was thirty-two years old and had completed his formal education, followed by an apprenticeship with his now-deceased father, who had been a printer-bookseller in Dijon. After that, he had directed the family's printing house for more than eight years.[3] His mother was sure enough of her son's knowledge of the art of printing and confident enough that her son would be chosen to succeed her that she was willing to resign her printer's license. Second, Defay provided the following documentation: a certificate of competence from the printers' guild, his baptismal certificate, and affidavits from his priest and the lieutenant of police stating that Defay had been printing since childhood, that he directed his father's printing house, and that he had always behaved in an irreproachable manner. Defay also included references from a grammarian establishing that he was educated and had studied with the Jesuits. In addition, a certificate from the prefect of the College of Dijon confirmed that Defay had completed two years of study there. Defay supplied the minutes of his printing examination, signed by the guild officers, showing that he had satisfied the requirements for obtaining printing licenses outlined by a royal decree in 1777. Defay ended his petition with the request that the king order his swearing-in before the lieutenant of police, thereby admitting him as printer-bookseller in Dijon in place of his mother. On Le Camus de Néville's recommendation, Miromesnil approved the request, and an order in council was issued by the king's privy council on 18 December 1780.[4]

The following month, the same Dijon notables assembled at an extraordinary meeting of the printers' and booksellers' guild in Dijon to hear the reading of the royal order in council admitting Antoine-Marie Defay to a printer place in Dijon. Defay then requested its registration in the Dijon guild register, and a vote was taken. Guild members unanimously agreed to register and transcribe the order in council into their minutes. Defay promised to pay the Dijon guild warden the sum of 600 livres, of which 200 would go to the guild (which already had 100 livres from him when he was accepted earlier as a bookseller) and 300 would be put into a special fund used by Miromesnil to pay the book trade inspector.

The keeper of the seals, the director of the book trade, the intendant, the lieutenant of police, the inspector of the book trade, and the guild officials in Dijon were all involved in these proceedings in accordance with the procedures for printer appointment laid out in detail by a royal order in council on 30 August 1777.[5] These procedures represent the mature development of the French monarchy's century-long policy of licensing—and consequently determining—those who would hold roughly 310 positions authorized in the realm. Licensing began in 1667 when Louis XIV's minister, Jean-Baptiste Colbert, banned all new printers in provincial towns from setting up without special approval.[6] In the following years, printers in some towns saw great advantages to be gained from royal licensing policies and made sure that the law was implemented. In other towns, the licensing requirement went unnoticed until 1704, when royal officials set quotas on the numbers of printers allowed in each town and ordered the lieutenants of police to enforce them.[7] In subsequent decades, the number of printers was forcibly reduced. By 1739—when the rules were tightened and the number of printers was again reduced—there was wide acceptance of printer licensing. In 1759 the numbers were further reduced, and in 1777 the procedures for printer appointment were clarified.

Despite the appearance of bureaucratic decision making, there was never any doubt about who would fill the vacant printer position in Dijon in 1780. It was the theatre of these two days that gave these events their meaning. The selection of a French printer was several things all at once: a guild voting to accept a colleague, the passing of a family office from one generation to the next, an event in municipal politics, an instance of royal patronage, and, finally, a harbinger of a modern bureaucratic tradition with examinations based on merit. These layered meanings all have their own histories and are part of the story of state-media relations in early modern France.[8] Printers just outside French borders have attracted the attention of many scholars who believe that the importation and sale in France of books published abroad helped prepare the way for the French Revolution—an idea that may have resonated strongly with a generation of American historians that came of age during the Cold War.[9] In contrast, political historians of eighteenth-century France have tended to regard domestic French printers as a rather subservient group and consequently of little interest.[10] *Licensing Loyalty* challenges this perception by suggesting that the relative absence of persecution of French provincial printers in the regular courts in the eighteenth century is itself a story worth telling. It reveals the very successful way in which printers managed to build multiple identities that allowed them to fit the changing economic, religious, and political realities of eighteenth-century France.

In the sixteenth and seventeenth centuries, printers were clients of a variety of political and religious bodies: the parlements, the king, the universities, the bishops and archbishops. Because it was difficult or impossible to avoid engagement with political factions, printers were vulnerable to persecution during political conflicts, and they relied on patrons for protection. During the Wars of Religion in the sixteenth century, there were Protestant printers, League printers, and many who changed sides. In the political struggles surrounding the calling of the Estates General in 1614–15, individual printers—such as Jean

Janon in Sedan, a client of the duc de Bouillon—depended on their protectors.[11] During the Fronde, relations between printers and their protectors evolved in a variety of ways. The rebel prince of Condé's printers were among several who printed *mazarinades;* other printers, however, remained loyal to the Court.[12] Later in the seventeenth century some famous Parisian printers worked for the Jesuit cause, and the printers of Port Royal also had their protectors.[13] When the Parisian publisher Guillaume Desprez, for example, was arrested in 1657 for publishing Jansenist works, he could count on supporters who used their influence with the lieutenant of police to help him escape the Châtelet's severe justice. A quick look at how Pascal's *Provincial Letters* were published shows printers and booksellers relying on powerful bishops and *parlementaires* to protect them from Jesuit pressure on Chancellor Séguier.[14] In an era when political printing could be dangerous, printers were clients of powerful factions and were accorded a high degree of protection.

Much historical writing, however, gives the impression that printers' earlier political alliances had disappeared by the eighteenth century. The standard explanation for why this happened in Paris is that the royal government imposed a series of controls during the reign of Louis XIV and subjected the city's printers to its direction. The Paris story has been well known since Henri-Jean Martin told it some forty years ago. He argued that a series of midcentury crises provoked Colbert to bring printing, publishing, and bookselling directly under the king's control.[15] Between 1643 and 1667 several crises coalesced: internal strife in an overpopulated and undisciplined book guild, quarrels between Jansenists and Jesuits, conflicts over monopolies on titles and their renewal, labor difficulties, high paper costs, the Fronde, foreign competition, pirating, and trade wars. Faced with these threats to what had been a healthy book trade, the authorities were forced, in what Martin calls *la réaction royale,* to impose supervision on the printers. Control was established in two well-known ways: by censoring works in advance of publication and by granting monopolies to favored printers. In addition, the government reduced the number of printers in Paris to thirty-six, placing all of them under the supervision of the lieutenant of police, a newly created post then held by Gabriel-Nicolas de La Reynie. By the end of the reign of Louis XIV, Parisian printers found themselves more subservient to the king than ever before.

Martin's subject was Paris; he said little about printers in the French provinces, and what he did say implies a top-down application of control to the provinces, when there was any at all.[16] The present study tells the story of the relations between printers in towns outside Paris with local authorities and with royal officials, from the reign of Louis XIV until the French Revolution. The Sun King's reign was critical in establishing royal authority over the media but, outside Paris, it was only late in the reign—especially during the tenure of Pontchartrain as chancellor—that the government began to establish its authority over printers in an unprecedented manner. Yet this development, far from consigning printers to the margins of historical interest, opened up a new era in their lives that is important to examine. Control was only possible with the considerable and active cooperation of the printers themselves. From the beginning of the eighteenth century, the establishment of the Bureau de la librairie created two-way communication between French provincial printers and royal officials that fundamentally changed—through persuasion, negotiation, bribery, and repression—the relations between printers and the government. Printers were more closely supervised through this process than in earlier centuries, but it would be wrong to suggest that they responded passively to these changes. That is the impression that printers created in their rhetoric, but we should not allow them to mislead us. What they did was create a new role for themselves as loyal agents of monarchy. Guild rhetoric and the rhetoric of absolutism coincided to create the persona of the loyal licensed printer, one that stood in contrast to disloyal outsiders who shared the ways of a disordered, immoral, and dangerous world. This dichotomy was continuously emphasized by Parisian and other licensed printers in their denunciation of the unregulated trade. The survival of feudal notions of loyalty, coupled with the ideology of absolutism, made it easy for these printers to believe their own rhetoric; their incessant appeals to fear influenced government officials who worried that an unregulated press threatened French Christian society. This idea was self-serving but very influential with French officials.

In taking on and exploiting this new identity as "pillars of monarchy," however, printers did not abandon their older identities. Instead, unconcerned about the problems of competing loyalties, conflicts of interest, or inherent contradictions, printers added yet another identity to other historic identities that they had exploited since the advent of print—as clients of patrons, as members of guilds, as members of universities, and as local businessmen.[17] Printers held onto the privileges and status offered by their previous associations and at the same time began taking advantage of those offered by their new, more intimate relationship with the developing royal administration. By 1780, when Antoine-Marie Defay was applying for his license, at least three generations of printers in his family had made careers by presenting themselves to the authorities in Versailles as loyal pillars of monarchy while keeping up their loyalties to other constituencies. Given the number of people involved in Defay's nomination as a printer, it is worth pondering who was absent from the proceedings. One missing figure was the bishop, often an important force in a provincial printer's life. Significantly, many others had a role.

Officials were aware that the king's subjects were not as unambiguously loyal as they liked to pretend, and they were also aware of printers' loyalty to nobles and bishops.[18] Consequently, the state offered privileges to printers that confirmed their special status, made them wealthy, and tied their fortunes to a strong monarchy.[19] When this failed, royal officials used repression to deter printers from being disloyal.[20] The horrific burning or execution of printers in earlier eras disappeared in the eighteenth century, but persecution did not. A number of studies have looked at the printers in the Bastille, a group that included Voltaire's publisher in Rouen and the publisher of the *Encyclopédie*, André-François Le Breton. What is clear is that spectacular court cases of printers tried in the regular courts were very rare because, from early in the eighteenth century, the infractions of licensed printers were not generally matters for the regular courts. Rather, they were handled administratively by royal officials. Chancellors or keepers of the seals, responding to information from the intendants and officials in the Bureau de la librairie, tried and punished printers directly for book trade infractions. These royal administrators not only ordered searches and seizures of books but also fined, suspended, and expelled printers and booksellers from their trades. In the second half of the eighteenth century, new officials called "inspectors of the book trade" helped royal officials implement the large body of legislation designed to control both domestic printing and the import of books from abroad.

In the history of censorship, a central idea commanding considerable support among historians is that censorship ceased to work properly in France in the eighteenth century: while under Louis XIV government control of printing and bookselling was somewhat successful, by the eighteenth century weakness had set in, either because the Enlightenment made officials more tolerant or because the government became weak.[21] The great historians of France and others more specialized in the history of censorship all say this in one way or another, as do almost all general studies and textbooks. The idea is drawn from studies of how and why the state chose the books it deemed acceptable and what controversies resulted from these choices. We are all influenced by

Denis Diderot's utter disdain for a system that he mocked by turning it on its head, saying that writers were never happier than when their books were banned, because that only gave them higher prices and more sales. Nor can we be indifferent to one of the great minds of the century, Chrétien-Guillaume de Lamoignon de Malesherbes, director of the book trade between 1750 and 1763, who famously claimed that anyone who read only what was legal was a century behind the times. Furthermore, the controversies over whether to ban some of the famous works of the Enlightenment, notably those over the *Ency-clopédie* and over Claude-Adrien Helvetius' *De l'Esprit,* suggest that the state was confused and ineffective. Research into the prior censorship mechanisms in eighteenth-century France has addressed many important questions. What were the criteria for permitting or banning titles and generally for deciding on suitable reading for the French people? What problems did the decision makers face? Was there some fundamental incompatibility between the functioning of absolute monarchy and what urban literate elites were reading and thinking? Was a developing liberalism reflected in the introduction of unofficial permissions, known as *permissions tacites,* and in the career of the well-known liberal Malesherbes as director of the book trade?[22] With the Revolution looming up in 1789, much of this interest has been teleological: a failure of censorship is needed to explain the political crises of the late *ancien regime.*

The theme of this book is different. It is not about the ways in which French officials decided what they would let the French public read. Nor is it about repression, but rather about one of the ways they tried to implement royal policy on the ground by cultivating obedience among provincial printers. Beginning with the introduction of a system of licensing printers in the provinces in 1667, French kings established and elaborated a wide-ranging set of mechanisms of communication with provincial printers and encouraged them to care about the royal government in Versailles, much as nobles were brought to care about it in the seventeenth century. The encouragement of loyalty and the enforcement of royal laws in the French provinces are central subjects in this book, making it more a contribution to the social and political history of France than to the cultural or intellectual histories that most often investigate printers. Policing the book trade in an early modern state was a difficult task when police forces were small. Even in the best policed town of the period, Paris, manpower was limited; outside the capital, the task was truly daunting. Controlling books was impossible without the cooperation of the booksellers and printers themselves, and the eighteenth-century state obtained significant cooperation from the printers, who came to see state regulation in positive terms. Cooperation from the provincial printers evolved, over time, into their active lobbying to expand their own regulation. Government officials, who arguably had their hands full in levying taxes, provisioning towns, and taming riots, nevertheless came to care deeply about book trade regulation and to fear seditious books and pamphlets. The policing of the book trade was increasingly regarded as vital to the interests of the state and therefore in need of supervision, not unlike the grain trade or the navy.[23]

The aim of this study is, therefore, to examine the government's attempts to develop a mutually beneficial relationship with France's provincial printers and to assess its success. It is the first detailed presentation of the French government's licensing policy. It offers new evidence on how both officials and printers themselves understood the issue of media control and how they influenced each other, gradually building a distinct view of the dangers of the printed word. This study also sheds new light on some larger issues, such as the extent to which French absolutism was negotiated rather than imposed, the role of lobbying behind royal legislation, and the development of bureaucracy. The following pages show that the policy was not a failure but, in fact, quite transformed the world of provincial printing by concentrating printing in the hands of a number of well-known men and women who became wealthy notables in their towns. One of the purposes of licensing was to keep authorized printing out of the hands of the poor and needy and, in this regard, it was a complete success. As a means of ensuring loyalty, however, its success was more limited; the loyalty it engendered was not resilient enough to withstand the enormous influence of the parlements over public opinion during the constitutional crises under Maupeou (1770–74) and in what has been called the Pre-Revolution (1787–89). Much of the criticism in these political struggles emanated from within the provincial towns' elites, which, by the late eighteenth century, included printers and their families. Many of these printers had especially close ties with the judicial world and could not avoid the conflicting influences of their milieu. But all through the period before 1789, printer licensing showed no sign of weakening or crumbling until the Revolution swept it away.

Chapter 1 traces the spread of printing into the French provinces following the advent of print and presents the five different identities the practitioners of the new art constructed for themselves in their communities. Chapter 2 shows how the Paris printers framed the problem of ideological control for royal officials who were faced with the challenges of the Fronde and Jansenism in the seventeenth century. It examines the first royal law—an order in council in October 1667—that reversed earlier royal efforts to encourage the proliferation of printer establishments in the French provinces and ordered the licensing of provincial printers. Chapter 3 is a study of the Bureau de la librairie, its creation, its functioning, and the activities of some of its major officials up to 1789. Chapter 4 is an analysis of the effects of an order in council issued in 1704 that set quotas on the number of printers in every French town, radically altering the lives of printers in provincial France. With the advent of licensing, printers began making written arguments evoking family, property, gender, loyalty, and protection in their petitions to royal officials in order to obtain licenses. Chapter 5 analyzes these arguments. Chapter 6 provides case studies of a few major provincial printers, revealing their close and direct ties with Versailles officials. The licensing policy improved the wealth and social status of provincial printers generally in France, as shown in chapter 7, but failed to secure the loyalty of many printers. This book is about lobbying and about the creation and propagation of the idea of loyalty in early modern France—in an era when the notion of a "free press" was only notable for its absence.

1

THE EARLY HISTORY OF PRINTERS IN
PROVINCIAL FRANCE, 1470–1660

Many stories have been told about the origins of printing in French provincial
towns. Some of the first storytellers were members of prominent eighteenth-
century printing dynasties who sought to link their ancestors to the glories
associated with the early history of printing.[1] The printing history of Rouen
presents one of these stories: the first members of the noble Lallemant family,
a dominant force in Rouen printing, sent a number of young men to Germany
to learn the new art. Another version of this story is that the generous Lallemant family paid a man to travel to Germany and Paris to learn the art of
printing before he set up the first printing house in Rouen in 1483–84. Only
more recent assessments remove the Lallemant family from any association
with the advent of print in Rouen and point instead to other names quite
unknown in the subsequent history of printing. One of these studies attributes
the first printing initiatives to two men who, after having been to Paris to train
as printers, set up business in Rouen in 1487 with two booksellers, introduc-
ing printing to Rouen some seventeen years after it was introduced to Paris.
Another places the advent of printing in Rouen in 1485, the year a Norman
printed a description of the ceremonies honoring the king's visit. This was
long before the Lallemant family—who began printing in Rouen in the later
sixteenth century—could have had any role. The story of how the Lallemant
family brought printing to Rouen resembles many claims by French nobles
that their nobility dated from the mists of time: lovely stories, but more self-
serving myths than fact.

The First Printers in the Provinces

The real story of the advent of print in the French provinces was not especially glorious, and the principal players were not ancestors of the early modern dynasties who fabricated lineages.[2] Two fellows of the Sorbonne established the first printing house in France in 1470 by bringing three German printers to Paris to print humanist texts. Lyon was the second town in France to see printing, followed by Albi and then Toulouse. Between 1470 and 1650, printers were established—at least temporarily—in more than a hundred French towns. The spread was rapid but uneven, because printing houses were often difficult to maintain. The first printers struggled financially, and much of the early spread of printing took the form of itinerant printers stopping in towns to print one or two items, usually the locally approved missal, and then moving on. By the end of the fifteenth century, printers had worked for at least some period of time in forty-seven locations within the current borders of France, and permanently established printers lived in Paris, Lyon, Caen, Rouen, Angoulême, Poitiers, Angers, and Tours.

Educational and commercial forces shaped the work of the early printers, as did the demands of the judicial world in the French provincial towns. Schools and universities supported some of the earliest permanent printing establishments in Paris, Toulouse, Bordeaux, Angers, Caen, Grenoble, Valence, Poitiers, Nantes, and Bourges. The connection with the universities in particular had considerable long-term influence over printers' identity or sense of place in their towns, because they gloried in the dignity it offered their art. Printers and booksellers vaunted this connection in repeated claims over the first three centuries of printing. It brought prestige along with numerous privileges and exemptions from municipal laws and taxes. In the major publishing centers of provincial France—Rouen and Lyon—where there were no universities, the merchants played an important role in expanding the printing and publishing industries. The first printing press in Lyon was set up in a Lyonnais merchant's son's house. Soon afterwards, Lyon merchant circles began investing heavily in the new art and were able to put up the capital needed to take advantage of the town's fairs and its commercial ties inside France and with Italian, German, and Spanish towns. The first publishers in Lyon bought paper from nearby paper mills and hired German printers; they were able to engage Franciscan, Dominican, and Augustinian monks as well as legal experts and doctors to translate the texts that were in wide demand. By the end of the fifteenth century, a number of large publishers sustained the publishing business in Lyon, and through their activities Lyon became the second-largest printing center in France. Commercial forces were also behind the development of printing in ports such as Caen and Rouen. The first printers in Rouen moved rapidly to meet the demands for printing, both in the region and further afield in Brittany and England. They exported a number of Anglo-Norman law texts, sermons in English, and other liturgical works to England, a sign of their commercial dynamism and also of the persistence of the Anglo-Norman cultural community with which the Rouennais still identified.[3] From the first days of printing until the end of the *ancien régime,* lawyers, judges, and court officials—especially in those towns that were seats of parlements—used the services of printers and were major buyers of books. The first printers to set up in Toulouse did so before 1476, and the first book published there was a legal text. In the southwest of France the spread of printing occurred in the late fifteenth century, but various attempts to run printing houses ran into repeated difficulties. Printers in the southwest tended to be nomadic and to live precarious existences.[4] Not until the second half of the sixteenth century did the demand for print increase sufficiently that prosperous printing families could be found in Bordeaux and La Rochelle.

In the first two decades of the sixteenth century, some forty-two printing houses were established in provincial France.[5] The permanent presence of a printer in a provincial town required the convergence of a number of economic, cultural, and social factors. Financial backers were necessary, among them the princes in Montbéliard, Nevers, and Chambéry, churchmen in Reims and Verdun, the commercial and municipal elite in Nîmes, and educational institutions in Douai, Bordeaux, and Tournon. In these years Paris and Lyon were the main printing towns, but Rouen, Caen, Toulouse, Rennes, Angers, and Poitiers, though well behind, were becoming significant printing centers. By one estimate, in the sixteenth century there were some 25,000 publications from Paris and 15,000 from Lyon, but only 2,569 from Rouen. Between 1550 and 1560, around 1,000 people in Paris worked in the printing and bookselling businesses, while in Lyon, the number was half that. This was an era of powerful publishers who generally hired printers to print the books. In a few cases, the printers themselves were the publishers; some of these are well known to students of humanism and the Renaissance.[6]

The first printers sought both to survive financially and to define their place in French urban society. The novelty of the new art, the diversity in printers' lives and work, and their high level of literacy made it possible for them to construct a number of identities for themselves that were both complementary and competing.

University Men

Printers embraced their identity as members of the universities. From the very beginning of printing, the printers in Paris were associated with the University of Paris, and many printers in university towns in the provinces enjoyed similar associations. In the Middle Ages booksellers had been members of the universities and it only seemed natural that, as printers forged a place for themselves in towns, they would adopt the status of medieval booksellers, with whom, of course, they shared much. The early universities served as employers and censors of printers, as they had traditionally supervised booksellers. The development of printing in Toulouse, for example, the fourth-largest printing center in France, was encouraged by the university there, especially by its faculty of law.

While the role of the universities in supervising printers declined in the seventeenth century, the relationship between the universities and printers and booksellers stayed alive but became more tenuous and contested. Compromises were made over the place of printers in university processions, the role of the rectors in approving candidates to become booksellers, and the exemptions from taxes and services that the printers and booksellers could enjoy because of their connection to universities. One benefit that printers jealously guarded was the acknowledgment that their status was above the ranks of other artisans; they repeatedly sought and obtained recognition that they were "distinct and separate from the members of the mechanical arts."[7] Printers in Paris were located in the university quarter, and one of the reform proposals in the 1660s was to confine all printing in Paris to two university buildings. When provincial licensing was introduced, the rectors of the universities were called upon to attest to the Latin and Greek abilities of the printer candidates. In the 1760s the printers in Bordeaux were outraged with the municipal government when it tried to force them to perform night watch. They went to court to have this shocking misunderstanding cleared up, and it cost them a great deal of money.[8] The Parlement of Bordeaux eventually confirmed their exemption from this onerous and degrading duty—one entirely unsuitable for university men. In Angers and Montpellier the links between the printers and the universities were very close. The connections with the universities remained useful to provincial printers until the Revolution.

Clients

Early printers had a second identity as clients of nobles and bishops. In Brittany the first presses were established by a noble at Bréhan-Loudéac and only later at Rennes in 1484.[9] Across the southwest a number of towns saw the establishment of printers under the patronage of clerics. In Angoulême, Charles d'Angoulême, Louise de Savoie, and Bishop Octavien de Saint-Gelais were the patrons of printers. In Agen the Italian bishops Antonio della Rovere (1519–38) and Matteo Bandello (1540–50), along with their entourages of lawyers, scientists, and artists from Italy, sought to promote through printing the humanism of the peninsula. In 1503 it was the bishop of Bazas, Jean III de Bonal, who brought a printer to La Réole to print manuals for priests. Over the sixteenth century, several printers in Toulouse served the region, especially its bishops and its religious orders, and would often set up temporarily in smaller towns to print what was needed.[10] Patrons played a wide range of roles in provincial printers' lives: some provided salaries, lodging, protection, and privileges. Their influence over printers' careers was often decisive.

The lives of some of these printers have been traced.[11] Claude Garnier published a number of works in Limoges between 1520 and 1530 before moving to Bazas to work for Bishop Foucauld de Bonneval, for whom he printed a breviary and life of the patron saint of the cathedral. Garnier then went to Auch, where he printed another breviary in 1533 and enjoyed for a time the protection of Cardinal François de Clermont-Lodève. He probably worked in other towns in the Midi until 1550, when his presence is again documented in Limoges. Garnier was just one of many itinerant printers in the sixteenth century for whom bishops and the courts were important clients and who began the process of making religious and legal texts available to urban elites in the smaller towns in the French provinces.

The role of print in the Counter-Reformation cannot be understood without some awareness of the bishops and other patrons who not only sought out printers, offering them incentives to operate in their dioceses, but also provided a living for printers with their orders. In Bordeaux a dynasty established by Pierre Lacourt began printing in 1616 and became the official printer of Cardinal de Sourdis, the archbishop of Bordeaux.[12] Pierre's son, Guillaume Lacourt, carried on his father's business and, by 1642, was king's printer and printer for the archbishop and for the university. In Dunkirk local officials attracted a printer to the town with offers of compensation; he, his family, and his heirs were exempted from lodging soldiers and from taxes on wine and butter.[13] The establishment of the Collège Royal in La Flèche in 1603 led to the establishment of a printer there.[14] In 1669, when one of the royal courts established to try Protestants in Castres was moved to Castelnaudary, a printer was needed there, and when this court was abolished the bishop of Saint-Papoul kept the printer on a fixed pension.[15] In Boulogne both Bishop Perrochot and the governor, Maréchal D'Aumont, played a role in attracting a printer to the town.[16] Later in the seventeenth century, when royal authorities tried to rein in this proliferation of printers, local figures—most often bishops—did their best to try to keep printers and printing houses in the smaller towns.

Nobles, too, protected printers throughout the seventeenth century. Some towns did not see permanent printers until the seventeenth century: in 1600, Charles de Gonzague, duc de Nevers, called on a Lyon printer to set up in Nevers. The duke provided the presses and fonts, paid the wages, and had the printer exempted from local taxes. Such material support was just one form of noble protection. During the Fronde, Gaston d'Orléans' clients could count on him if the police bothered them about their pamphlets against Mazarin. They benefited on occasion from the sort of sheer intimidation used by the comte de Bury when he threatened the warden of the printers' and booksellers' guild with a few strokes of the lash for seizing some *libelles* against Mazarin from his men. If the guild warden took the case to the Châtelet, de Bury warned, he would take it to the Parlement.[17] Patrons used intimidation and bribery to protect their printers, but when this failed they could resort to more indirect methods. By one account, two noble Frondeurs (the maréchals de La Mothe and Beaufort) were responsible for instigating a riot among the Parisian crowd attending the execution of a printer.[18] This unfortunate printer, named Claude Morlot, had been caught printing pamphlets against Mazarin and, for various reasons, the Parlement actually upheld the Châtelet's death sentence. Some members of the Parlement were afraid of a popular revolt if the execution went ahead. They asked for mercy but were refused. When Morlot was brought out to the gallows, he immediately began addressing the crowd by shouting that he was going to die unjustly: he had only printed attacks on Mazarin, a minor offense in his view. The crowd started throwing stones at the twelve archers surrounding him and crying, "Save him. Save him!" The archers and the executioner were forced to retreat, leaving horses and arms behind. The crowd dismantled the gallows and threw it into the river along with the cart that had carried Morlot. A leading municipal official, the *prévôt des marchands,* tried to threaten the crowd from a window, but he was barraged with stones that broke all the windows on one side of the town hall. Morlot fled to freedom. The patronage of protectors who could bring about such a turn of events was valuable.

Printers in parlementary towns developed close and important ties to the members of these superior courts fairly early in the sixteenth century. In 1535 the Parlement of Rennes authorized the printer Thomas Mestrard to do its printing, and throughout the sixteenth century it issued several decrees authorizing other printers to do the same. The presence of parlements nurtured certain dependencies. At the request of the crown attorney of the Parlement of Paris, the printer Claude Guyot in Langres moved in 1589 to Châlons, where the Parlement of Paris was in exile. Guyot was given space to set up his printing presses, and the town council provided a subsidy to pay the costs of the move. When he could not manage financially in the 1590s, he requested further sums from the Parlement.[19] After the Parlement returned to Paris, Guyot remained in Châlons and printed for the bishop. In 1608 he was drawn away to Dijon; the town government there had offered free lodging, tax exemptions, and moving expenses, and he became king's printer in Dijon.[20] The story of French provincial printing contains many such men whose careers were formed and influenced by their relations with the provincial parlements.

In the seventeenth century the demand for printing by the parlements increased enormously. The Parlement of Normandy in Rouen has been described as the "lungs" of the Rouen book trade.[21] The Parlement of Toulouse—along with the town's entrenched and powerful legal and administrative elites—played a major role in the printing world of Toulouse in the seventeenth century because it ordered books and printing and because, from an early date, it tried to regulate printers and booksellers.[22] In Bordeaux, where there were, at most, three printers in the early seventeenth century, parlementary printing was important to the leading printing family, the Millanges. Two of the printers in this family were admitted to the bar, which indicates the importance of legal printing for the family business and the close connections between the two professions. The barristers protested against Jacques Millanges' attempt to carry on the two professions but a court case decided in his favor, allowing him to continue to do so.[23]

From early on printers sought protection from the parlements when municipal authorities tried to regulate or tax them. In 1642 the *jurats* (members of the local government) in Bordeaux were pressing their claim to jurisdiction over the printers and interrogated the king's printer, Guillaume Millanges, and others for printing without their permission.[24] On the grounds that he had been sworn in by the Parlement, Millanges denied in a heated exchange that the statutes applied to him and recognized only the authority of the king and Parlement. The interrogation was dramatic, and his testimony included rude gestures as well as words. He backed down only when faced with the threat of a five-hundred-livre fine.[25] Quarrels over whether the jurats or the Parlement had jurisdiction over the printers broke out again in 1643, when the jurats summoned all the printers to find out who had printed a request made to the king on a tax matter. Millanges claimed to have done so on the orders of the Parlement. The Bordeaux printers wanted to be seen as privileged, above the kind of supervision that the jurats deemed necessary for other trades. They saw themselves as the king's printers, the printers for the Parlement, and adjuncts of the university. Their privileged position brought tax exemptions and, more important, assured recognition of their high status, quite above that of other Bordeaux artisans. The printers' powerful sense of station made it difficult for the jurats to exercise control over them; it strengthened alliances between the Parlement and the printers and curtailed the ability of town authorities to police the trade.

Patronage—whether from nobles, bishops, parlements, or the king, who sustained a number of king's printers—was an important part of printers' success. In Paris one of the principal publishers was Sébastien Cramoisy, a client of Richelieu who was closely allied with the Jesuits. He made a fortune printing schoolbooks and devotional literature in the context of the Counter-Reformation.[26] Cramoisy was named king's printer in 1633 and then the official printer of the archbishop of Paris and of several religious orders. At his death he left property worth the enormous sum of 360,000 livres. Another printer and publisher, Antoine Vitré, was probably the most active printer in Paris in this period. He began his career selling news sheets and slanderous attacks on public figures but, after being arrested for this activity, seems to have gone resolutely over to the side of the authorities, possibly denouncing his previous collaborators along the way. He then set up his own printing house and prospered spectacularly, becoming king's printer for oriental languages in 1630 and printer for the French clergy in 1633. Vitré was confident of the support of Chancellor Séguier, on whom Richelieu relied for both propaganda and censorship.[27]

Businessmen

Printers were businessmen and businesswomen and—in this third identity—they shared the concerns of other tradesmen and merchants in early modern France. In addition to running printing houses themselves, many directed publishing operations that might employ the labor of other printing houses; many also engaged in retail and wholesale bookselling. After Paris, Lyon was the largest publishing center of France.[28] A number of factors explain the growth of the printing industries there. The town was large, with a population of 60,000 by the mid-sixteenth century. While there was no university and no parlement, Lyon did have a judicial elite, an archbishop, and important religious institutions that bought large numbers of books. Its commercial fairs also made for easier access to the credit that merchants needed to ship books long distances. The demand for print in the town was influenced by the combined effects of municipal and private patronage, the need for educational books, and a strong Italian presence that promoted the art, literature, and religious sensibility of the Italian Renaissance. As printing expanded, so did demand, and sixteenth-century Lyon publishers produced books for many French towns—Paris, Bordeaux, Toulouse, Aix-en-Provence, Cahors, Saintes, and Nantes—and often for distant international markets, including the cities of Frankfurt, Antwerp, Basel, Geneva, Venice, Florence, and Pisa, as well as Spain and England.[29] Large merchant publishers were the dominant force behind many publishing ventures, and some made quite spectacular careers. Publishing flourished in Rouen and Troyes, too. The latter developed as a publishing center early, because printers there had the idea of offering cut-rate printing for the Paris market and then began specializing in popular literature, the *bibliothèque bleue*—saints' lives, adventure stories, and plays—much of it distributed throughout the countryside by peddlers.[30] But in most other provincial towns, publishing was limited; booksellers sold books published in Lyon, Paris, or abroad.

Lyon continued in the seventeenth century as a major publishing center selling locally produced works—particularly judicial and theological books, which were published not only for French markets but also for more distant ones in Spain and Italy. Just as Cramoisy was a dominant force in Parisian publishing, the Cardon brothers—Horace and Jacques—overshadowed their peers in Lyon. Sons of a Spanish noble captain, they came from Italy and bought into the publishing firms of Rouillé and Giunta. They made profits from publishing major works of Spanish theology, bringing out some 250 titles between 1600 and 1620. Horace was in constant contact with the Jesuits. He amassed an enormous fortune and became a police commissioner in 1601. Naturalized in 1605, he became active in municipal politics as the director of public charity. He was elected an alderman in 1610–11 and subsequently ennobled. When Horace and his brother slowly pulled out of their publishing business, which they left behind by 1635, one of those who took it over was the ancestor of one of largest printers in Paris, Laurent Anisson, who eventually crushed his rivals and became the last great publisher of the Counter-Reformation in Lyon.[31] But the dynamism of the early publishing business suffered setbacks during the Thirty Years' War, which restricted access to markets in Germany. War with Spain also hurt the trade in Lyon. Business recovered after the war ended, and Lyon publishers revived their links with Germany, Italy, and Spain, but by the late 1670s, competition from northern Europe was increasing.[32]

Guildsmen

Printers in some towns began appealing directly to the king for privileges and honors, and this led them to adopt a fourth identity: that of guildsmen.[33] In the sixteenth century, the king began granting printers privileges and exemptions from duties and taxes and, in general, encouraged the making and sale of *bons livres* by approving guild statutes drawn up by fledgling printing and bookselling guilds.[34] Printers in Rouen and Lyon obtained the registration in their towns of the Edict of Gaillon (1571) that recognized the privileged and corporate status of printers and permitted them to supervise their own recruitment.[35] The Bordeaux printers and booksellers drew up statutes in 1608 and their Paris counterparts did the same in 1618; the latter were often used as a model by printers in other towns. In Orléans, there was a guild from 1618 on and, in Reims, from 1626. In Rennes and Toulouse, the printers and booksellers sought and obtained guild statutes in 1623 and 1620. The Rennes statutes of 1623 were written as a "precaution against the abuses being committed in the

printing and sale of books, some of which were prohibited and illegal and concerned religion and the state."[36] The Caen printers and booksellers obtained
statutes, as did those in Poitiers in 1634. The printers and booksellers in Angers
had a guild from at least as early as 1648 and maintained close connections with
the university in their town, holding their meetings in university rooms.[37] By
the end of Louis XIII's reign, printers and booksellers in Toulouse, Rennes, and
Bordeaux had statutes granted by the king and registered by their parlements
and, early in the reign of Louis XIV, the trend continued: the Metz printers
and booksellers had guild statutes dating at least from 1656.[38] The Montpellier
printers and booksellers formed a guild in 1665 and those in Châlons in 1650.[39]
From the early seventeenth century on, guild membership had become an important facet of the identity of a large number of provincial printers.

Ever attentive to their glorious beginnings, printers drafted statutes generally aimed at reviving a once-noble art that had slipped into a state of disorder.[40] The Bordeaux statutes declared that King Henry IV had been informed
by the Bordeaux masters that abuses were rampant in the printing and selling
of books in the town in recent years and that many were "full of odious and
evil things." The king wanted all books and printing to be sold by masters
so that, if anything were found in the books that ran counter to his government or offended the honor and reputation of his subjects, those at fault could
be punished. The jurats approved the statutes on 30 April 1608, and they were
confirmed by letters patent in November 1609, registered by the Bordeaux
Parlement on 15 February 1610.[41] The preamble to the Paris statutes of 1618
stated that printing had deteriorated since its early days of glory because of recent war and political strife. The rules were not being obeyed, and such license
brought disorder. Now was the time for a new beginning to reform and revive
the laws of previous kings. In 1623 in Rennes Louis XIII confirmed the "good
laws" of his predecessors and approved the statutes drawn up by the printers
and booksellers to combat abuses, including the sale of prohibited books and
books concerning religion and the state. Printers' and booksellers' guild statutes, like those of other trades, all decried rampant disorder and abuse and suggested that strengthening corporate control would remedy this.

All these different statutes set out a number of claims and rules. The special
status of printers was confirmed: in university towns such as Paris and Bordeaux, it was clearly stated that printers, booksellers, and binders were part of
the *corps de l'Université,* completely distinct and separate from other artisans, and
beneficiaries of all the rights, freedoms, and prerogatives that this affiliation

entailed. Even where no university existed or printers claimed no connection to it, statutes clearly asserted that booksellers, printers, and binders were distinct from other artisans and were to benefit from the privileges that previous kings had granted them. The Bordeaux guild walked in town processions on religious and other holidays just behind the university faculty and ahead of all the other guilds.[42] The monopoly on the book and printing trades explicitly denied outsiders and members of related trades, authors, or private individuals the right to sell or print books.

The statutes addressed quality control as well as labor and administrative matters. Printing was to be accurate, the types good, and the paper of high quality. Permissions to print were to be obtained. The statutes outlined the policing duties of guild wardens and their deputies, specifying that they should make inspection tours to check for forbidden books, keep registers, and inspect imported books. Journeymen's jobs were to be protected by restricting the number of apprentices masters were allowed to hire. The procedures for electing guild officers were described and the number of guild officers and the length of their tenure specified. In Bordeaux, the twenty-one booksellers and two printers agreed to meet once a year in the Jacobin convent on 8 May, the feast day of St. John at the Latin Gate, patron saint of booksellers, to elect two guild wardens who would handle the guild's finances. In the earliest statutes we find the idea that loose controls over recruitment were responsible for an excessive number of printers: for example, those of Toulouse, Paris, and Rennes stipulated that wardens were to admit one bookseller, one printer, and one binder to the guild each year. This was supposed to prevent abuses, disorder, and the confusion caused by large numbers of scandalous and defamatory books printed by unidentified printers. This idea is also evident in the Rennes statutes.[43] Like other guilds, the early seventeenth-century printers presented a picture of disorder to obtain royal and parlementary support for statutes regulating printer recruitment.

There was no easy consensus in provincial towns about the privileges that printer and bookseller guilds should enjoy. A barrister and local chronicler in Bordeaux, Jean Darnal, approved of guild organization, claiming that it improved the choice of books for the literate in the town.[44] But in some towns, the printers' guilds ran into opposition from the parlements and universities and were forced to modify their statutes to accommodate the members of these institutions. In Rennes, there had been difficulties persuading the Parlement to accept certain statutes and privileges in 1623. The royal council accorded the

Rennes bookmen the same favor enjoyed by Paris printers and consequently, by letters patent, ordered the Parlement of Brittany to register the statutes. The Parlement resisted some of these. New letters patent issued on 7 March 1624 condemned the Parlement for its unwillingness to register the guild statutes, forcing it to do so on 17 April 1624, but with modifications: the Parlement was quite happy to forbid non-Catholic books and those against the king's service, but would not agree to the requirement of four years' apprenticeship for printers and the five-year requirement for booksellers who were not sons of masters. Nor would it agree that a printer who took up the book or print-ing business without having completed an apprenticeship in Rennes should suffer forfeiture of his printing equipment and corporal punishment.[45] In Toulouse, the guild obtained letters patent outlining their statutes in 1620, but the university wanted changes, and the Parlement would not register them without the university's modifications—in this case, loosening the restrictions on the number of presses that printers were required to possess and allowing peddlers to work as long as they identified themselves to the guild warden.[46] Broadly speaking, the universities and the parlements resisted guildsmen's efforts to monopolize the book and printing trades, fearing—unlike the Bordeaux chronicler—that there would be fewer titles and higher prices if the guilds were too exclusive. The parlements, moreover, sympathized with the interests of guild outsiders, such as peddlers. Disagreements among interested parties prevented statutes from being accepted in the larger printing centers of Troyes, Rouen, and Lyon.

Despite these struggles, the guild identity of printers and booksellers became important for many printers, but its centrality to their lives was not as great as most historians of print suggest, because it was only one of the multiple iden-tities they assumed. Local governments often struggled to force the guilds to behave and think like other guilds, but the printing and bookselling guilds always thought of themselves as different—as part of the liberal arts, part of the university, and consequently outside the influence of the local authorities. In many instances printers claimed that their municipal governments had no authority over them and made exaggerated claims about the ineptness and corruption of these bodies and—in that particularly damning way that only printers could manage—they accused local authorities of being illiterate and unable to identify forbidden books. They certainly balked at the duties and fiscal commitments that local authorities sought and turned to Versailles for support in resisting them.

Sometimes the guild identity was paramount, but sometimes it collided with printers' connections with the university; at times, obligations to noble patrons or bishops ate away at printers' corporate identity. Business interests similarly tested the bonds of corporate identity because the booksellers and printers often sought different objectives in matters of quotas and copyrights. Other affiliations, whether religious or intellectual, also shaped printers' self-fashioning, but the main point here is that French provincial printers in early modern France could and did call upon and use at least these four identities to advance their interests. We shall see in the next sections of this book that the increased attention of the growing central government in France intersected with the interests of these printers, influencing and altering them so as ultimately to create a fifth identity—that of loyal officers of the king—which printers added to those of university men, clients, businessmen, and guildsmen. This identity took a long time to develop, achieving its final form only in the eighteenth century, but the story begins in the sixteenth. Three important developments in the sixteenth and early seventeenth centuries drew the royal government into provincial printers' affairs. The first was the religious strife that followed the introduction of Calvinism into France in the 1530s; the second was labor strife in the printing houses in Lyon; the third was conflict over copyright protection.

Religious Conflicts

In the early years of the Reformation Calvinism spread quickly through France, encouraging some printers to set up in provincial towns either to meet the new demand[47] or to compensate for the shortages of imported books provoked by the religious wars that developed. The Reformation also inspired an enormous Catholic publishing response that was to last for the next two centuries. In order to offset the influence of Calvin, Catholic apologists wrote many devotional works, all of which required printing in large quantities. In their desire to promote the publication of Catholic Counter-Reformation literature, kings granted copyrights (*privilèges*), which helped cement relations between monarchs and printers.

The regulation of printing became an important part of the campaign for control. The Affair of the Placards—the simultaneous publication, on 17 October 1534, of broadsheets against the Catholic Eucharist in Paris and other

French towns—constituted a turning point in the persecution of Protestant-
ism in France by firmly linking heresy and sedition in the minds of royal officials. At least twelve men were arrested and convicted in this affair, and nine
were burned at the stake. Henceforth, printers were increasingly persecuted.
The celebrated Lyonnais scholar-printer Étienne Dolet was sentenced by the
Parlement of Paris to be burned at the stake for blasphemy, sedition, and the
selling of banned books. A man of fiery and volatile personality who had been
arrested previously for trading in banned books, Dolet was hanged as a re-
peat offender and then burned. Dolet, not a Calvinist but a classically trained
scholar and an accomplished humanist, was one of those scholar-printers of
the era who participated in the cosmopolitan republic of letters created by
the advent of print.[48] His persecution underlines how the Reformation made
governments focus on shielding the faithful from corrupting influences.

As early as 1521, the Parlement of Paris required that no book be published
without the approval of the faculty of theology. It also banned all Lutheran
books and ordered them confiscated. After 1540, various new laws were drawn
up to outlaw heretical printing. In 1542 the Parlement of Paris issued an ordinance "against the new and heretical doctrines," including Calvinism. In 1545
the Parlement of Paris issued a catalogue of censored books. Royal edicts,
such as that of 11 December 1547, forbade the impression or sale of all books
concerning the scriptures, whether printed in Geneva, Germany, or elsewhere.
In 1551, the Edict of Chateaubriand forbade the importing of any books from
Geneva and other heretical places and systematized and reinforced earlier ordinances governing printing and bookselling. It also banned the sale of forbidden
books and required all translations of biblical and patristic texts, along with
all books written in the previous forty years, to be approved by the Sorbonne.
The Parlement of Paris could grant copyrights only for books approved by
the Sorbonne. Furthermore, all printed works were required to display the
name of the printer, the author's name, and the date of publication. Twice a
year in Paris, and three times a year in Lyon, the shops of all booksellers were
to be inspected, and each bookshop was to have a list of all books for sale
on the premises and a copy of the catalogue of censored books. Royal authorities, while alarmed by the Protestant use of the presses, were even more dis-
tressed by the ways in which the Catholic League—a loose coalition of nobles,
urban notables, and magistrates allied with the Guise family to ensure that
the king of France remained a Roman Catholic—used printing to advance its
critique of the French monarchy and took over the principal publishing towns

of Paris, Lyon, Troyes, Toulouse, Rouen, Orléans, Poitiers, Le Mans, Nantes, Reims, and Bourges.

Book burning—a classical and medieval method of destroying evil books and one that Martin Luther himself carried out—became a powerful symbolic means to contain corruption. At least as early as 1523, the authorities ordered heretical books to be burned. Major book burnings, such as that in Paris in 1562 when cartloads of books were burned, could take days. Not only did the authorities fear heretical books and bookmen, but so did the people; the trials, executions, and officially sanctioned book burnings pale in comparison with the popular fury directed against heretical printers and their books. Both Catholic and Protestant religious rioters targeted "infectious books" and undertook to burn them in their efforts to purify the religious. The crowds took the law into their own hands and attacked the printers and booksellers themselves, as, for example, in 1561 in Aurillac and Carcassonne, and in 1562 in Paris and Sens. During the St. Bartholomew's Day massacres in 1572 in a number of towns, including Paris, Orléans, Lyon, and Rouen, booksellers and printers constituted a relatively high percentage of victims, and there were other cases of Protestant printers massacred by Catholic mobs.[49] In 1567, after Lyon was retaken by Catholic forces, celebrations were accompanied by the burning of enormous numbers of heretical books along the banks of the Rhône.

Heretical books were targets, but it would be a mistake to regard printers as activists in the religious wars. Some, such as Barthélémy Berton in La Rochelle and his successors, certainly were committed Protestants. Some printers remained on the side of the king. Still other printers, however, remained neutral and worked for both sides. In the 1560s, Jean de Minières in Angoulême was printing for both Protestants and Catholics; only later did he become an exclusively Protestant printer. In Lyon, the Protestant printers in the mid-sixteenth century seem to have been rather prudent and, in general, were not bothered by the authorities. The absence there of a parlement and a faculty of theology made things easier, and royal laws, notably the 1551 Edict of Chateaubriand ordering close inspection of printers, were not enforced by the *sénéchaussée* court of Lyon. When the king ordered that all books be examined and approved by the governor or his lieutenant before being published, Lyon's powerful booksellers' association deemed that this rule should not apply to its members, and it went to the sénéchaussée to obtain an exemption. The cathedral chapter complained in 1557 of pernicious, scandalous, and heretical books printed in the town, but it seems that the Lyonnais printers were careful when publishing Protestant works and remained rather independent until Protestant forces took control of the town in 1562.[50] Between 1562 and 1565, Protestant printing flourished. When Catholic forces regained control of the town, the relatively tolerant era of book trade expansion and of erudite scholar-printers (1530–65) came to an end. Publications intended for Catholic clergy and for the Counter-Reformation came to take a central place in Lyon's publishing. The Protestant Jean II de Tournes left Lyon for Geneva in 1585, and the career of Benoît Rigaud, who specialized in cheap books, pamphlets, and royal edicts, began to take off. After 1565 Protestant printers suffered raids and imprisonment, but their persecution should not be overstated. In Lyon, as elsewhere, printers adapted to the changed regime.

While the religious controversies focused attention on the dangerous potential of print, on its propaganda value, and on the printers, early modern leaders did not place printers at the center of the struggle to repress heresy. Royal authorities were much more concerned with the printers' patrons or with the authors of subversive and heretical texts who were the true targets of royal attention. In correspondence among churchmen about the St. Bartholomew's Day massacre in Paris, for example, the printers and booksellers who were mentioned as victims were not even named and, at best, were referred to as clients of patrons or employees of authors.[51] This was true later in the early seventeenth century as well, during a period of political instability that encompassed the minority of Louis XIII and the regency of Marie de Medici following Henri IV's assassination in 1610. The power struggles, principally between Marie and her advisors and the prince de Condé, produced large numbers of pamphlets—the vast majority for the government.[52] Some provincial printers, like Simon Millanges in Bordeaux and Martin Le Mesgissier in Rouen, aligned themselves with the government. Others, such as Jean Janon, a Protestant printer in Sedan, aligned himself completely with the opposition but worked anonymously. Still others, such as Jullieron in Lyon, printed for both sides. It is worth noting the attitude of the duc d'Épernon in 1615 when he engaged in a discussion with the president of the Parlement of Paris about scandalous publications: he regarded the authors, not the printers, to be the legitimate targets of the police, believing that printers were not especially culpable because they were only looking to earn a living. This attitude could also explain the generally lenient treatment of printers in the courts. Judges could order draconian penalties, but, while the Châtelet court would impose them on occasion, they were almost always reduced on appeal to the Parlement of Paris. Only later did governments place printers at the center of their efforts to ensure religious orthodoxy.

Labor Strife

While the place of pamphlets in religious and political quarrels began bringing printers into the orbit of the royal government in the sixteenth century, so too did labor strife in Paris and Lyon. In both towns, workers organized to resist exploitation by the master printers and particularly to defend older customs that the master printers sought to abolish. In the 1530s the masters tried to reduce labor costs by employing more of the cheaper labor provided by apprentice printers and to discontinue paying for their workers' food. As both these initiatives represented deterioration in the workers' status and standard of living, and were especially hard on them because of inflation, printing workers fought back.[53] In Lyon the workers wanted to keep their traditional entitlement to food and were determined to continue a practice whereby they took time off as relief from their long hours of working. Printing workers belonged to a company called the Gripharins, whose traditions and rituals encouraged solidarity and loyalty and helped preserve the higher status printing workers enjoyed among other artisans. Through the Gripharins, the printing workers organized unprecedented resistance to the masters' attempts to exploit them and, in the spring of 1539, the conflicts resulted in a three-month strike in most of the printing houses in Lyon. Lyon's sénéchaussée court attempted to sort out the dispute, but failed. The masters appealed to the king, describing the glorious history of the art of printing in Lyon, equaled nowhere in Christendom. They further claimed that Lyon was where the most beautiful books and the greatest diversity of titles were to be found and where clients, both French and foreign, found good prices. Alas, labor difficulties, according to the appeal, were ruining things. The king's council soon ruled against most of the workers' demands and supported only their continued entitlement to meals. This led to such disorder that the sénéchaussée court sought further support by having the matter referred to the Privy Council, where the ruling was ratified on 21 August 1539 by Royal Letters issued from Villers-Cotterêts. In the years immediately following the 1539 decrees, labor unrest continued and a further edict was issued on 28 December 1541, which was confirmed on 11

September 1544. Some decades of relative peace followed, perhaps encouraged by a sense of shared interests when many masters and workers together went over to the Protestant cause. But in 1570, the printing workers in Lyon went on strike again. The conflict ended in another victory for the masters and was the context of a major piece of royal legislation governing printing in France, the May 1571 Edict of Gaillon. This edict favored the masters even more than in 1541; they no longer had to provide food for their workers, and journeymen were to be given a fixed daily wage. Worse for the workers, masters were allowed to take as many apprentices as they wanted. This ruling sparked protests, which led to a supplementary law of 10 September 1572 limiting the number of apprentices to two and softening the rules slightly. But the Edict of Gaillon also limited entry to the trade: thenceforth, no printer was to set up a printing business unless he had performed an apprenticeship and been certified capable by two booksellers and two printers. Royal authorities were also called upon to settle a dispute in Lyon over whether the town's publishers should be allowed to have their printing done in Geneva, where labor was cheaper.[54] Such appeals to the royal government for assistance in settling disputes drew it into the policing of the book trade in Lyon from a very early date.

It was, of course, no accident that Lyon was the provincial town that first attracted royal regulatory attention—and where master printers' and local authorities' calling on the government for assistance first developed into a tradition. Lyon, far more than any other provincial town, had a dynamic publishing industry and a large workforce, and it was located near potentially damaging Genevan competition. Unlike those in any other provincial town in France, masters in Lyon could make a plausible case for royal help on the grounds that a leading publishing center was threatened with decline. Proximity to Paris and the absence of a parlement in the town also enhanced cooperation between Lyon elites and royal officials; both were intent on taming the workers and preserving the profit margins of Lyon publishers. These same factors did not obtain in other provincial towns. The merchant publishers who sustained the printing business in Lyon and who worked behind the scenes to support the master printers in the labor strife were absent in Rouen, Bordeaux, and other towns. Consequently, other provincial towns were not drawn into the orbit of royal control the way Lyon was. Officially, some royal edicts such as the edict of and Gaillon applied to the whole kingdom but, even in Lyon, they were difficult to enforce, and there is little evidence that they were seriously enforced in other provincial towns. While attempts were made to draw royal officials into the world of provincial printing to preserve true religion and end labor strife, the limits on royal influence in the sixteenth century must be stressed; printers in provincial France in this period were far more concerned with the interests of local patrons and especially the bishops, who had true influence over their economic and political fates.

Copyright

In the early seventeenth century, the influence of the royal government on printers in the French provinces remained limited, uneven, and sporadic, but, over the course of Louis XIII's reign, the growing economic rivalry between printers in the provinces and in Paris—often over copyrights for books and newspapers—created an additional force that drew the royal government into the affairs of the provincial printers. Increasing numbers of books and pamphlets were published in the seventeenth century, reflecting, among other things, the growth of publishing in the provinces, especially after the Edict of Nantes brought a measure of peace to many parts of the realm. This growth began to challenge Parisian dominance in publishing, not as seriously as the Parisians claimed, but enough for them to seek government support. Copyright protection was one of their main concerns, particularly against the pirating of their books and newspapers in Lyon and Rouen.[55] The example of newspapers is revealing: in the 1630s, Théophraste Renaudot established the *Gazette* but very early on had to face the fact that printers in provincial towns also wanted to sell the news in it. In some cases provincial printers went to the local authorities and obtained copyrights. The lieutenant of police in Rouen gave a copyright to Claude LeVillain in Rouen similar to the one that Renaudot had obtained. Facing a fight with the Rouen pirates, Renaudot was forced to compromise, and he also struck deals with provincial printers in Bordeaux in 1638, Tours in 1646, and Toulouse in 1673. Generally these men paid Renaudot to obtain a monopoly on the sale of the *Gazette* in their towns for a fixed time. The printer Pierre de Lacourt in Bordeaux got such an authorization in 1638; in 1641, it went to his colleague, Guillaume Millanges. As these monopolies proved lucrative, they were the source of many disputes. In Rouen in the middle of the seventeenth century, for example, the monopoly led to conflict between the printers Jacques Besongne and Jean Viret and their rivals, Antoine Ferrand and Julien Courant. At the beginning of Louis

XIV's reign, the *Gazette* was published in Rouen, Lyon, Bordeaux, Tours, and Avignon by "authorized pirates" and was very profitable.[56]

Copyright protection was even more important when it came to books. It loomed large as an issue when, around 1635, Cardinal Richelieu and Chancellor Séguier began renewing copyrights on books. It had been widely accepted that copyrights on books were awarded to protect a publisher's investment for a period of time and that the books would eventually fall into the public domain and be available to all printers. However, as part of their effort to favor a few loyal printers and to encourage the huge publishing ventures that were part of the Catholic reform movement, royal officials began renewing privileges after they expired.[57] In this way, they also ensured the correctness of texts. Publishers found the government receptive when they began requesting copyright renewals and gradually came to regard copyright as a form of property, a development that spawned numerous disputes in the following centuries. Although the Parlement of Paris resisted granting renewals for a time, it eventually abandoned strenuous opposition.

Lyonnais pirating so enraged the Paris guild officers that they intervened with royal administrators to block approval of draft proposals for Lyon statutes. Both the Paris and Lyon guilds were within the jurisdiction of the Parlement of Paris. It is not easy to tell to what degree the disputes were aggravated by economic turmoil in the Parisian publishing business and how much the Parisians were really hurt by various crises in the trade and the growth of provincial publishing. We do know that the acrimony galvanized the Paris guild and focused its attention on provincial publishing in new ways. The expansion of publishing in the provinces, the issue of copyright, and the rivalry between Paris and provinces became central questions that drew the Paris and provincial printers into the habit of characterizing each other in perjorative terms for the benefit of the royal officials. The Parisians, being closer to the centers of power, were able to achieve considerable success in the copyright conflicts and in propagating a negative vision of provincial printing and printers.

When royal officials began granting renewable copyrights, especially to Paris publishers, they challenged the traditional role played by the parlements in provincial France in this domain. This was especially the case in Rouen, the seat of a parlement and a significant publishing center. From the sixteenth century on, the Parlement of Normandy had played an extensive role in the supervision of printing matters there, granting copyrights for titles from at least 1521. The Paris copyright holders began to challenge the Parlement's jurisdiction over printers when they requested that certain cases be decided in the Privy Council. This had happened earlier, but very exceptionally; in the seventeenth century it became a more regular practice. On 2 April 1632, the Privy Council annulled a decree of the Parlement of Normandy that had granted a Rouennais printer a privilege when a Paris printer had one for the same work. In 1633 it ordered a Rouen printer arrested for printing a work without permission of the king. In 1645 a Rouen printer successfully transferred to the Privy Council a copyright decision of the Parlement of Normandy that favored two of his colleagues in Rouen. The whole issue of continuations of privileges was aired in 1651, when the Privy Council agreed to have a commissioner hear a case initiated by the Rouen guild when an expired copyright had been extended even though the size of the work in question had not been enlarged. In the 1660s several Privy Council cases addressed Parisian and Rouennais monopolies on titles and, from this decade on, the Privy Council became the crucial venue for these disputes.

Well before the reign of Louis XIII, religious, political, labor, and legal strife had drawn the royal government into the world of provincial printers, but during this reign comments by officials and increased regulation of printing revealed a new level of fear of the printed word.[58] Three major decrees governing printers and printing were issued in 1618 and 1626 and in the famous Code Michaud of 1629. These were ambitious efforts to regulate printing: on 9 July 1618 the Parlement of Paris registered letters patent that organized the Paris printers and booksellers into a guild.[59] This law also confirmed previous requirements to have books approved before publication, but it now directed regulation at the printers: "Any printers, book sellers, or binders who may print or cause to be printed defamatory books or pamphlets will be punished as disturbers of the peace, and thereby deprived of all of their privileges and immunities and declared incapable of ever being able to engage in the profession of printer or book dealer."[60] In 1626 Richelieu, obsessed with the threat posed by pamphlet literature, further regulated the printing trades in Paris with a royal edict verified in Parlement that required permission from the king's council before any publication was undertaken. This edict also prescribed the death penalty for infringing the rules by publishing without indicating the name of the printer, by posting a political placard, or by distributing illegal political pamphlets. In 1629 the Parlement of Paris registered the Code Michaud and its clauses on the regulation of printing that were directed at the printers:

The great disorder and inconveniences that we see arising every day from the ease and freedom of publishing, in violation of our [the king's] ordinances and to the great injury of our subjects and the peace and tranquillity of this State, [and tending to the] corruption of morals and the introduction of evil and pernicious ideas, obliges us to provide therefore a more powerful remedy than has ever been undertaken by previous ordinances. . . . We forbid any printer, whether from Paris or any other city of our Realm, . . . to print, and [we forbid] any book merchants or others to sell, any books or writings that do not carry the name of the author and printer, and do not have our [written] permission. . . . Such letters shall not be executed unless a manuscript copy of the book has been presented to our Chancellor or Guard of the Seals, after which they will assign such persons as they see fit according to the subject and material of the book to examine it.[61]

By 1629, legislation targeted not only authors and patrons but the printers, too, as would many future decrees in the seventeenth and eighteenth centuries. These laws suggest a new importance accorded printers as agents and as a means of controlling print. Just why this happened in the early seventeenth century is not, however, very clear.

One can attribute the changes to the pamphlet production of 1614–18 and the heightened sense of the dangers presented by the press or to Richelieu himself, but it is also worth noting that the focus on printers as agents of control came first in Paris and in the years following the organization of the Paris printers into a guild in 1618. Once this was done, the Paris guild immediately began lobbying the government with its version of the challenges facing the world of publishing, one that attributed abuses in printing and bookselling to "outsiders" and to the activities of the incompetent and unworthy. Exaggerating the strengths, talents, and loyalty of guild members, this view denied any of these positive qualities to non-members and ratcheted up the perception of danger as well. This line of argument placed illegitimate and illegal printers at the center of the battle for ideological control. Government officials accepted this message, understood its implications, and aimed regulatory efforts at printers. As subsequent chapters will show, this policy took on a life of its own and had influence well beyond the designs of its early formulators, lasting right up to the French Revolution.

In the seventeenth century the Paris printers' and booksellers' guild, stressing the potential dangers of printing, engaged in just one of many discourses about print that were balanced by a number of other viewpoints. Print was, for some, a noble art that brought men closer to God. It was also a vehicle for royal propaganda; pro-government printing swamped the opposition in 1614–18 and would again do so during the Fronde in 1648–52. Also, there was considerable range in the degree to which government officials feared print. Henri IV rather famously seemed not to have worried about its nefarious effects.[62] Other officials were of like mind. But this viewpoint was not shared by all, and certainly not by Richelieu and Séguier, who gave control of the press a high priority in the wake of political troubles. The reluctance of the Parlement of Paris to uphold brutal sentences for printing offenses handed down by the Châtelet must be noted: it systematically overturned these on appeal. To what extent printers and printing concerned magistrates in the provinces is not clear. Certainly, they were willing to condemn printing that would mislead the people. The consuls in Agen and the Parlement of Bordeaux in 1614, for example, condemned printing that would lead "the people" to believe in "vain imaginings and promises" of some "grandees."[63] They targeted the authors, publishers, printers, booksellers, buyers, and readers and made anyone found guilty liable to corporal punishment and prosecution as disturbers of the peace. This scattershot approach did not especially target printers because everyone involved was held responsible. There is also no evidence that provincial officials arrested printers often or applied draconian penalties against them. A Grenoble printer, Antoine Blanc, was arraigned along with the publisher Jean Nicolas for printing two *libelles,* one he had written himself entitled *Antidote à la France malade* and another entitled *Chemise sanglante d'Henry le grand.*[64] When both pamphlets were seized, Blanc and Nicolas went to prison. But, in the end, a decree of the Chambre de l'Édit du Parlement de Grenoble, dated 30 January 1616, ordered Blanc to recognize his fault and pay a six-livre fine. The pamphlets were burned, but Nicolas was simply acquitted. In 1614 several publishers were arrested for producing opposition pamphlets, but the penalties were slight, and four of the six continued to print for both sides after their arrest.[65] There is no evidence that printers were seen as major culprits in the pamphlet wars. At best they were considered peripheral accomplices. This began to change as the guilds, especially the Paris guild, began propagating with considerable vigor the idea that printers were a potentially dangerous force—

an idea that was later to become very influential but, at the beginning of the seventeenth century, was just one of many ideas about print and printing that had currency.

Early modern minds did not conceptualize censorship the way we do.[66] The issue of heresy was separate from that of reputation and honor, and both were separate from the maintenance of public order. While this may have changed somewhat as a result of the pamphlet wars of 1614–17, only later did the interconnections among various aspects of our modern notion of censorship become obvious and the French state begin to design institutions to impose unity of belief.[67] Without the modern notion of media control, the idea that printers could be agents of ideological control was quite absent. Printers were integrated into networks of clientage, and their role was not perceived as central when the problems of disorder and heresy were addressed. In political conflicts printers printed for both sides, indicating that they did not intimately link their professional and confessional identities. When authorities sought to restrict printing, they tried to control authors and their patrons but did not especially focus their attentions on the printers. Generally, royal officials encouraged and supported the establishment of printing houses in the provinces and did not fear them as they later came to do. Printers were not considered loyal or disloyal in any broad sense. They worked in association with religious orders, universities, and the bishops. The kind of scholar-printer so characteristic of the sixteenth century had not disappeared, but, by the mid-seventeenth century, there were also many others who principally aimed to survive financially, support their businesses, and preserve their privileges and status. In parlementary towns, printers had very strong links to the law courts, which constituted their major clientele and, in many cases, their social milieu. Only later were printers and printing seen as forces that could undermine the state and religion.

Where, then, did the modern notion of media control come from? A number of factors must be considered. The economic argument, offered by Henri-Jean Martin, blamed the development of media control on the crises of the seventeenth century, especially on the troubles in the publishing industry which, at the time of the Fronde, forced the government to turn its attention to the printing industries in Paris and to begin a long process of containing and controlling them.[68] Martin identified a "coincidence of interests" between the king and some large Parisian publishers: the political interests of the king fitted in with the economic interests of the publishers in such a way that both forces worked effectively to reduce printing done by small printers in Paris or provincial printers. Roger Chartier suggests that media control emerged from the expansion of print itself, because pamphlet and periodical publishing began in these years to take their place beside book publishing and affected political culture by involving a wider public and making politics less secret. From the 1630s on, profits from ephemeral printing were significant, and the struggle for profits encouraged political conflict to evolve in new directions. The authorities began to intervene in the bitter rivalries among printers for profits from the *Gazette* and many other forms of ephemeral printing, granting privileges to certain printers in order to ensure their docility. As this happened more and more often, competing printers were forced to take risks to survive financially, exacerbating the illegal book and pamphlet trade. Thus, the early seventeenth century saw the conjunction of periodical printing, economic interests, ideological struggles, and government manipulation of the media.[69]

The following chapters rely heavily on these explanations but offer an additional angle to explain why a number of issues that were so disparate in the sixteenth century became tightly connected in the seventeenth and eighteenth centuries. While other artisans constructed identities around skill,[70] printers— a profession that shared literacy with influential but small minorities in the late Middle Ages[71]—had by the early seventeenth century already moved quickly to enhance their identities as skilled artisans by emphasizing their additional identities as university men, guildsmen, businessmen, and clients of patrons. As printing spread, however, and was seen increasingly as a danger, printers added a fifth identity to their self-fashioning, one that made them resemble licensed officers of the French king: as "pillars of monarchy." It was this identity that printer licensing would make official. It encouraged them to exaggerate the historic roots of their families in the printing business (as the Lallemant family, mentioned at the beginning of this chapter, did). Like all origin stories, this one served a purpose. Faced with the growth of printing and an increasing focus on its dangers, printers found it beneficial to be players in the growth of the royal administration and to tell stories about the many generations of printing in their families and about their loyalty to their kings. Printers in France moved to distance themselves from any association with marginality, irreligion, and sedition and to ensure themselves a place on the respectable side of any symbolic lines that divided insiders and outsiders in French society. They grouped themselves with those who participated in the growth of a regulated and more disciplined society, not with those who threatened it. Consequently, we must pay serious attention to the ways in which the printers themselves lobbied the government and offered arguments that greatly exaggerated the dangers of the press. In this, they were very influential. One consequence of their lobbying was a major policy initiative, begun in 1667, to license all printers in France. As printer licensing became the rule, the connectedness of ideological control, government supervision, and economic success was forever established in the minds of both the authorities and the printers.

2

THE VICISSITUDES OF A ROYAL DECREE

Enforcing the October 1667 Order in Council Regulating Printers in the Provinces

The kind of material that is most subject to censorship is invariably the work of those shops with only one press and which lack regular work.
—*Paris printer, 1647*

In the early 1640s, various proposals were made to Chancellor Séguier to control printing and bookselling in Paris.[1] The first—probably drafted by the major Parisian printer Sébastien Cramoisy—raised the idea of putting all printers in a factory-like arrangement in rooms of the colleges of the University of Paris. Of the 183 known presses in Paris, he said, only 80 had regular work. The rest were confined to printing ephemeral matter: "occasional Acts, speeches, songs or political squibs." Unemployed printers were dangerous because they were tempted to print illegal works. Putting all under close supervision would eliminate the problem. But Cramoisy went on to reject this rather drastic solution as impracticable: it could aggravate labor difficulties and the printers might corrupt the college staff. Also, in the large crowd of printers and workers, it would be easy to get away with printing a work "critical of God, the state or of royal ministers," and rumor and sedition would spread. Instead, Cramoisy suggested closing down all printing houses that had only one press and better enforcement of the guild statutes. He proposed redistributing the eighty-six presses currently located in printing houses that had only one or two presses to twenty-five of the smaller printing houses to make them larger. These twenty-five reasonably sized printing houses could then operate alongside the current twenty-five larger houses, making fifty printing houses in Paris. All should be located on the main streets of the university quarter. The guild officers should refuse admission to new masters and, if new masters were ever to be admitted, they should be required to have three well-equipped presses, prove to the rector of the university that they knew Latin, and pay 150 livres to the guild. Guild wardens should make frequent inspection tours of the fifty printing houses and be permitted to enter and inspect all printing establishments freely.

A second proposal took a different approach and suggested that three royal officials be appointed to police the book trade. These inspectors would work closely with the chancellor, learn all the rules governing printing, keep registers of titles of manuscripts for which authors, printers, or booksellers requested permissions, organize the distribution of manuscripts to censors, pay the censors, and carry out a number of other related duties—among them, ensuring that no unauthorized books circulated in Paris or elsewhere. These officials were to make inspection tours of printing houses to see that nothing illegal was being printed or sold and, in the event that something scandalous or forbidden was found, to have it seized and presented to the chancellor. As compensation for the costs incurred in examining manuscripts, purchasing their offices, and making their inspection tours, the king would give them the right to print almanacs, alphabets, and judicial and financial documents in the realm. In addition, they would receive tax exemptions on paper and a pension paid from the fines and confiscations. To aid them in the execution of their work, eight bailiffs would be appointed from all over France.

These two proposals differ in a number of respects, notably on whether the guild structures should be strengthened in order to better police printing or whether the king should appoint and give privileges to enforcement officers or agents in the profession. Neither idea was implemented in the 1640s. Printer guilds, like others, tried to regulate their numbers and strengthen their control of the trade, but parlements, universities, and other groups and officials resisted these restrictions. In the 1660s, however, this changed; royal officials began to control tightly the recruitment of printers in France. In the years following the Fronde—a civil war that divided France between 1648 and 1652, during which the number of pamphlets critical of the royal minister (called *mazarinades*) exploded—the idea that a clandestine press seriously endangered the monarchy gained currency. Jansenism, a divisive and arguably heretical movement within the French Catholic church, was also gaining influence among the French public during this period.[2] The notion of the press's threat to the monarchy—only one of a range of attitudes to printing in the early modern era[3]—became particularly powerful because it intersected perfectly with the discourse of the printers and booksellers of Paris, who had been saying the same thing for years. In the turmoil of the Fronde, however, they now found royal officials willing to listen. In 1649 circumstances were ripe for the printers to encourage government fears in order to obtain concessions. Some major printers obtained an edict that reiterated several previously granted privileges but also gave them two new rulings they greatly wanted. The first of these was a restriction on their number. The second was the ability to renew copyrights on titles that would normally enter the public domain.[4] This preserved profits for a small number of publishers. These two concessions were of enormous importance because they protected publishers' market share and increased their profits. Previously, the interests of smaller printers, journeymen, provincial printers, and the book-buying public had been protected by parlements and other authorities who were able to limit the power of the printers' and booksellers' guilds. Even in 1649 there was opposition to these concessions to the Parisian publishers; the Parlement of Paris would not agree to allow the printers to renew copyrights.[5] But during the Fronde, the negotiating position of the printers was strong, and they obtained the edict they wanted in December 1649.

To further this agenda, the Parisians did not hesitate to use an *ad baculum* argument that was very similar to the one Cramoisy had used in 1643: small, second-rate, and provincial publishers were dangerous, and unless the government eliminated them they would threaten the state. The Parisian printers claimed that the new restrictions on their number would improve the quality of the books produced in France: better-quality printing on better-quality paper. They would eliminate the shoddy and illicit printing that brought shame on the profession and "grand dommage à notre État." They would help the French publishing industry compete with those of other countries. One lobbyist pointed out the inadequacy of earlier regulations to the changed reality of mid-seventeenth-century publishing: officials who had drafted the earlier 1618 rules, he said, could not be expected to foresee the disorder that had resulted from the spread of printing in the French countryside, nor that provincial printers would pirate Parisian books.[6] In short, high-quality Parisian publishing was the goal, and the 1649 measures would help attain it.

The argument that small, poor printers were dangerous did not really fit the reality in the provinces because, outside Paris, many of the *mazarinades* were printed by established printers. Much, of course, remains unknown about pamphlet production in the provinces during the Fronde, but some information is available. A study of some 203 *mazarinades* known to have been printed in Bordeaux (about half of those known to be circulating) reveals that three main printers shared the publishing of *mazarinades,* and more than 70 percent of them were printed by the official printer for the Parlement of Bordeaux, Jacques Mongiron-Millanges.[7] In 1649, when the town was united behind the Parlement, Mongiron-Millanges printed most of the *mazarinades.* Later, when the prince of Condé was in power, the king's printer Guillaume Lacourt printed many of them, adding to his title that of "imprimeur de Son Altesse," thus becoming Condé's official printer. (Condé was named governor of Guyenne and took over Bordeaux in September 1651, installing a court there.) The established printers and booksellers in Grenoble and Lyon catered to the demands of the towns' elites, sometimes producing and selling *libelles* against Mazarin and at other times printing large quantities of royalist propaganda.[8] The king's printer in Lyon, Jean-Aymé Candy, sent official pieces to the bookseller Nicolas in Grenoble, who had them reprinted. Nicolas had the printer Frémont print pamphlets on the English Revolution, notably a 1,000-copy run of an account of the English king's execution. In Rouen, the printers Jean Viret, David DuPetit Val, and David Ferrand sided with the Parlement and Jullian Courant with the court.[9] Ferrand's shop near the *palais* was a gathering place where the *parlementaires* could read some of the more than fifty *mazarinades* that came off the Rouen presses. Evidence from the provinces that marginal printers were perceived to be dangerous or that subversive printing was done by the sort of lowlife depicted by the Parisian rhetoric is lacking.[10] On the contrary, the *established* printers and booksellers in the major provincial towns printed and sold pamphlets of all sorts.

Such empirical realities did not prevent the Parisians from continuing to exaggerate the dangers of small printers, and their claims were taken more and more seriously as Jansenism spread in France, forcing royal officials to give printers increased attention in the 1650s and 1660s. In the mid–1640s, the first of the Jansenist controversies began after Rome's condemnation of Cornelius Jansen's *Augustinus.* The persecution of Jansenism had clearly begun by the mid-1650s, when the Sorbonne censored and expelled the Jansenist theologian Antoine Arnauld in 1656 and the government forced French clergymen to sign a "formulary" condemning five propositions in *Augustinus.* Blaise Pascal's wildly popular polemical attacks on Jesuit errors, *Provincial Letters,* began circulating in January 1656 and were rapidly condemned. These struggles over doctrine and power were waged both from the pulpit and in books and pamphlets. The government lived daily with the prospect of both the disorder these materials could cause and the threat they posed to Mazarin's grasp on power. All sides in this conflict among churchmen and the laity gave tremendous importance to getting their version of events or ideas into print and refuting, ridiculing, or suppressing their opponents' views. Both sides had close working ties to printers and publishers in Paris. Chroniclers, such as the Jansenist Hermant, recorded how the Jesuits, the Paris priests, and the men of Port Royal all jockeyed for position in this pamphlet war, crowing with pride in the event of successful maneuvers and denouncing vile intrigues when their adversaries scored a point.[11] Large numbers of pamphlets and placards were produced, and the censoring authorities were inescapably torn by competing forces. At issue were matters of doctrine and jurisdiction, and there could be no consensus on who should censor the press: the king, the Sorbonne, the archbishop of Paris, the priests in Paris, the Parlement of Paris, the Assembly of the Clergy, and Rome all claimed censorship powers.

In this environment, the printers had to position themselves to survive; they counted on protection by their patrons. Stories of intrigue and subterfuge pepper the publishing history of both Jansenist and Jesuit publications. In 1653, when the archbishop of Paris was finally persuaded to censure a Jesuit libel, he knew that his printer, Targa, would encounter difficulties when he tried to print the censure and warned him to expect Jesuit influence on the police to result in a raid. Police officers did indeed arrive at Targa's printing house to try to seize the printing order, but Targa, forewarned, was able to keep the printing job hidden, even from the king's officers.[12] Other printers and booksellers had similar relationships with patrons, among them Sébastien Cramoisy, who published for the Jesuits, and Guillaume Desprez, for the Jansenists. Many printers and booksellers who were persecuted in the 1650s were well-known members of the Paris publishing establishment. Those who published the *Provincial Letters* are cases in point.[13] The bookseller Charles Savreux, who had close ties with Port Royal, was arrested, interrogated, and imprisoned in the Châtelet in February 1656, along with his wife and workers. Found in his shop were seven copies of the first of the *Provincial Letters*. The printer Pierre Le Petit, too, was raided. In a typical story of printer commitment and ingenuity he was saved by his wife, who, when she saw the police commissioner arrive, ran upstairs into the printing house, hid the forms under her dress, and slipped out the front door to a friend's place. The printer Denis Langlois was caught by the police commissioner Camuset in the act of printing one of the *Provincial Letters* and Arnaud's *Lettre apologétique*. Caught too was Guillaume Desprez, who had a few pieces by Arnaud removed from his shop. The printer François Preuveray was arrested in October 1658 for publishing the second edition of the *Provincial Letters*. These men, and others like them, were substantial bookmen with patrons and friends to protect them.

The main printers and booksellers of Jansenist texts in the provinces, too, were established printers. Central to the printers' decision making were their relationships with their local bishops, who guided the ways in which books and printing entered religious life in the French provinces in the seventeenth century.[14] Until the reign of Louis XIV, the bishops were frequently the unchallenged patrons of printing and printers in their dioceses; some brought the first permanent printers to their towns to further the Counter-Reformation. In 1661 the bookseller Jean Berthelin in Rouen was operating as an intermediary between the Elzévirs in Amsterdam and the Paris bookseller Frédéric Léonard, who was king's printer and printer for the clergy. A shipment of Jansenist books was discovered and, according to Hermant, sergeants dragged Berthelin out of his shop, not even giving him enough time to put on his coat.[15] Berthelin claimed to know little about the shipment, but he was not deemed credible, and a court officer visited him at his home to inform him that he would be arrested the next day. He had to decide whether he would flee or try to present his case to the Parlement of Rouen. In the end he was able to produce letters from the Elzévirs inculpating Léonard and reducing the pressure on him, but the book was ordered burned and Léonard ordered to appear in court. In 1679 the Rouen printers François Vaultier and Henri-François Viret were printing Jansenist tracts; by one account, the latter avoided arrest because he was protected by friends in the Parlement. These examples were just the tip of a huge iceberg of unorthodox religious printing in Rouen.[16]

The King Makes New Laws

Despite the rhetoric of the Parisian guild (which would have currency for the next century and a half), there is no very good reason to believe that clandestine printing was in the hands of poor, marginal, and unqualified printers. Some most certainly was, but this notion fails to capture the complexities of clandestine printing and the important reality that it was the printers' "insider" status that made them difficult for intendants and Paris guild wardens to police. Nevertheless, when the Paris guild argued that the clandestine trade was in the hands of outsiders who were foreign, poor, and incompetent, the controller-general Jean-Baptiste Colbert and other officials believed them. In 1666 Colbert organized a committee, or council, to reform the workings of the Paris police with a view toward reducing crime and vagrancy and improving cleanliness in the town.[17] In one of the council's first discussions in October 1666, the problem of press supervision was raised. The council interviewed three printers—Cramoisy, Antoine Vitré, and Robert Ballard—who had submitted memoranda in which they argued strenuously that the problem resulted from too many printing houses and too many ignorant and poor printers. Colbert agreed to regulate the casting of type tightly and to ban new men from entering the guild as well as to expel current members who did not meet the requirements.[18] The idea of retrenching and regulating the printing profession is clear in the order in council of 16 December 1666: the text begins with the lament that rules requiring printers to be limited in number and well educated were not respected and that disorder had been the result. Following Colbert's advice, the king ordered the guild warden to present all previous regulations on printing matters and a list of the names of all printers in Paris to specially appointed royal commissioners, who would decide what was to be done. In the meantime, the guild warden and deputies were not to allow anyone to set up printing businesses or to cast new printing types without the express permission of the *prévôt* of Paris or his lieutenants.

This marked the first time that printer recruitment had been restricted by royal order. Negotiations and meetings continued. Surveys and interviews of convicted printers were undertaken and the results presented to the council. Some printers were pardoned by the council; others were expelled from the printing business. In February 1667 Colbert advocated severe measures against printers and type founders. Another member of the council, La Marguerie, *conseiller d'état* responsible for the press, was wary of Colbert's severity but seems to have agreed on the essentials: there were too many printers, which made control difficult, and most printers were ignorant or destitute, so pending new regulations, the guild should be forbidden to accept any more masters. An order in council dated 17 February 1667 purged the Paris printing industry. It noted that although the rules and statutes of the printers in Paris expressly stated that all printers should be fluent in Latin, able to read Greek, and have two presses, the guild wardens had been lax and had admitted too many men. Currently there were eighty-six printers in Paris, most of them incompetent and poor. Worse, some printers were being tolerated who had already been convicted of corruption. To restore the printing industry to its past glory, it would be necessary to enforce all the statutes and rules. The king ordered the lieutenant of police and the crown prosecutor to visit all printing houses and to write a report on each printer, including any convictions the printer might have. When this was done, thirteen printers were expelled from the printing profession, and the authorities ordered their equipment sold. Guild wardens were forbidden to admit unqualified new printers and were to be ready to present their admission register at any time for inspection by the lieutenant of police.[19] These measures dramatically lowered the number of printers in Paris.

Behind the 1666 and 1667 orders was Colbert, who had adopted the guild view that print culture was best policed by controlling entry to the profession. Colbert sought to promote French publishing in international markets and to use printing for cultural and strategic gains in newly acquired territories.[20] At the same time, he was clearly persuaded that financial need forced poor printers to prostitute themselves and to dip into the gutter world of cheap and unsavory publications. Such printers had to be eliminated. Colbert, like others, felt personally threatened by *libelles*. In particular, he wanted to limit access to presses by the supporters of his disgraced and imprisoned rival, Nicolas Fouquet.[21] For these and other reasons, Colbert placed controlling the press high in his priorities. He enjoyed a close, mutually accommodating relationship with the Paris booksellers' and printers' guild and used printer's licenses to favor individuals. In 1679 he instructed the lieutenant of police in Paris, Gabriel-Nicolas de La Reynie, to support Antoine Cellier's request for a printer's license to exercise his trade in Paris. Cellier had converted from Calvinism to Roman Catholicism and Colbert offered him royal patronage. The printer Cramoisy had enough credit with Colbert to ask him in a rather cavalier manner to give one of his sons-in-law a lucrative commission recently created by the king.[22] Colbert had solid connections to the major Parisian printers, and, unsurprisingly, they came to share views on the role of the media in France. His way of controlling the printing industry involved the physical control of the means of printing itself. Colbert did not elaborate on how eliminating poor and incompetent printers would really prevent Jansenist bishops from having their printers print Jansenist tracts—or, for that matter, keep the duc d'Orléans or Fouquet's friends from ordering printing. The larger idea may have been that royal patronage would break older loyalties of printers to opponents of the government, but this was never articulated clearly. It remains unclear whether Colbert was envisioning the comprehensive printer licensing system that came into effect in the eighteenth century or was simply responding in a more immediate way to lobbying from the Paris printers' guild.[23]

In 1665 and again in 1674 orders in council demonstrated the seriousness with which Colbert took this issue: these orders permitted publishers to renew copyrights and allowed the Parisian guild wardens to order searches anywhere in France.[24] The issue of copyright renewals was not new.[25] In the 1660s Parisian printers initiated much litigation against Lyon and Rouen printers who refused to respect copyrights and copyright renewals granted by the chancery. The Parisians tried to have their cases heard in the royal councils, but provincial printers preferred to have them heard by their local parlements. In 1664, some thirty or so Parisian printers and booksellers joined together to share the legal costs of these cases. The Parisians, who wanted to extend both the length of their monopolies and their number, produced many influential memoranda. They argued for copyright renewal and, over the succeeding decades, began regarding copyrights as forms of property. Royal officials never accepted the idea that copyrights were property but, by continuing to grant renewals and undermining provincial resistance to them, they did contribute to this understanding of copyright. On 27 February 1665 the Privy Council decided a major case between Parisian publishers and a Rouen printer in favor of the Parisians, and in doing so recognized the validity of copyright renewal.[26] Until 1777 many royal decrees took this approach.

The practice of renewing copyrights was not popular in the provincial capitals, and new arguments and special enforcement from outside the towns were needed to make local officials care enough to respect them. On 11 September 1665 the Parisian guild wardens were given the power to inspect and seize books in towns outside Paris. At the request of the guild wardens, these powers were extended on 11 April 1674, with the stated objective of preventing the sale of "forbidden books on matters of state or religion and pirated books."[27] That Parisian publishers could play an active role in policing the provincial book trade was a major departure from previous practice. So was grouping all pirated books, defamatory libels, and unapproved political and religious printing in one category. These three quite different kinds of publishing began to be regularly lumped together and became part of formulaic statements that pervaded discussions of the clandestine trade. The problem of piracy was made to seem a much more serious and dangerous matter than it would have been on its own: by analogy with irreligion and sedition, it threatened public interest and required urgent attention. The private commercial interests of Parisian publishers were thus promoted to an affair of state. The repeated linking of these three kinds of printing, especially by the Parisian publishers when they inveighed against the dangers of the clandestine trade, became a regular feature of official discourse on the media until the French Revolution.

To summarize, royal authorities in France were much more concerned in the 1660s to regulate the domestic book trade in France than ever before. This concern resulted, in part, from the expansion of printing in early modern France. But it also derived from the newly perceived danger of unregulated media after the Fronde and with the rise of Jansenism, and, finally, from the government's determination to revitalize publishing along with many other domestic industries in the face of intense Dutch competition.[28] Articulating these problems for royal officials were the Parisian publishers, who should be credited with more agency in the development of government concern with printing than they have been. They were the economic and lobbying engine behind this new royal interest. The decrees issued between 1665 and 1667 made three important concessions to them: first, ceilings were placed on the number of printers; second, copyrights were renewed; and third, bookselling matters were to be handled by the royal councils. These decrees challenged the local authorities to enforce the book trade in the interest of Parisian publishers, who successfully sold the idea that they were rich, loyal insiders who should have control of publishing to prevent disloyal, poorer, smaller, and provincial printers from undermining religion and the government by engaging—as they naturally would—in the clandestine trade. The publishers, many of whom were close to the centers of power, drafted memoranda and made their view of the book trade that of Colbert and other officials, thus elevating their private commercial interest to an affair of state.

In their rhetoric, the Parisians repeatedly used three arguments: they presented as uncontested the view that poor printers were more likely to engage in the clandestine trade than wealthy ones; they confounded pirated books with prohibited books, presenting them both as threats to political and religious stability; and they described the French provinces as inundated with prohibited and pirated books. As a result of their lobbying, this rhetorical vision of French publishing began to dominate the thinking of government officials and displaced a view that might have been more in keeping with the empirical realities of provincial France. In fact, most of the provincial publishers' output consisted of devotional books and ephemera produced for religious and legal bodies, and many printers were attached to institutions as bishop's printers, king's printers, and parlement printers. Printers worked for the religious and legal elites of provincial towns, and in parlementary towns they had close ties with the judges and other officials in these courts.[29] They were seen as clients of the powerful, not as a dangerous or autonomous force in themselves. Similarly, what came to be characterized after the 1660s as pernicious pirating activity in Rouen and Lyon simply represented a wider public domain in books and an unenforceable national copyright policy. Provincial printers become targets of royal control because the rhetoric of Parisian printers gradually imposed a simplified vision of provincial printing on royal officials.

While the Parisians lobbied officials in Versailles, a second important group began to demand regulation: certain provincial printers began to see the advantages of quotas and to advocate—like their Parisian counterparts—the idea that the provincial printing corps should comprise a small number of reliable printers and that the poor and incompetent should be ousted from the profession lest they cut into their market share, lower the social status of the profession, and dip regularly into the trade in dangerous, prohibited editions. These printers encouraged the implementation of another decree of the 1660s regulating the French press. This one, dated 6 October 1667, was directed at the provinces.

Ban on Printer Recruitment in the Provinces—6 October 1667

On 6 October 1667, ten months after the ban on admission of printers to the Paris printers' and booksellers' guild, a royal order in council banned all new printers in the French provinces. Accompanying the ban were orders reiterating censorship requirements and directions to officers in the *bailliage* and *sénéchaussée* courts to conduct an elaborate inquiry into printing and bookselling in the whole realm. The inquiry would provide Chancellor Séguier with the number, names, and equipment of all printing and bookselling personnel. Guild officers who breached the ban were threatened with expulsion from their profession; aspiring printers who defied it were to have their presses confiscated and to forfeit the possibility of ever becoming master printers.[30]

Few historians mention this order in council (hereafter "the 1667 ban" or "the 1667 order") at all. Those who do claim that royal authorities did not enforce it, suggesting that it should be classified as one of the Bourbon monarchy's many futile efforts at censorship.[31] The archives of the Privy Council show clearly that it issued orders in council settling conflicts that arose over the execution of this decree.[32] The remainder of this chapter will show that certain provincial printers welcomed the 1667 order and sought its implementation and, in doing so, invited royal officials into the process of provincial printer appointment. Unwittingly or not, these provincial printers combined forces with the Parisian publishers who promoted royal regulation of printers in the provinces as part of their program to reduce competition and pirating. These two separate forces—Parisian printers and their provincial counterparts—increasingly compelled aspiring provincial printers to petition royal authorities for authorizations granting them dispensations from the ban. Over time, these "printer's licenses" were required for all printers in France. As the first in what would become a series of decrees that radically transformed the process by which printers obtained authorization to run their businesses, the 1667 order in council has an important place in the history of state-media relations in France.

To show how the 1667 order in council came to be respected in provincial towns, let us consider two detailed case studies, one from the town of Châlons-sur-Marne and the other from Laon.

Châlons-sur-Marne

In mid-seventeenth-century Châlons-sur-Marne, a small town about 150 kilometers east of Paris where printers had worked from early in the sixteenth century, two families competed for printing business.[33] The Seneuze family possessed the rights to diocesan printing, having been chosen by Bishop Félix Vialart de Herse in 1660; in the same year, the family obtained the rights to the king's printing.[34] Bishop Vialart recognized that Hugues Seneuze was a Catholic, a man of integrity, experience, and morals who had always faithfully performed good work in the past. In contrast to the Seneuze family, the members of the Bouchard family were comparative newcomers in Châlons, brought there from Toul by the Jesuits who ran the local college. Booksellers at first, by 1659 they were printers who competed with the Seneuze family for diocesan printing. A rivalry between the two families was played out in the local presidial court as each side tried to convict the other for infringement of rules or copyrights.

Jacques Seneuze took the initiative in trying to implement the 1667 order, first by citing it to strengthen his case against Jean Bouchard, whom he accused of pirating. Presumably, at this stage Seneuze saw the strictures against pirating as relevant and he used them, along with two previous rulings, to justify raids of Bouchard's premises. In 1670 Seneuze and a crowd of local officials—including the lieutenant of police, the crown prosecutor, a clerk, and two bailiffs—raided Bouchard's shop and discovered pirated editions of religious titles and a copy of *Relation extraordinaire du 11ième octobre 1669,* the work that Seneuze had accused Bouchard of printing.[35] Because Bouchard was a well-established printer in Châlons, there was no thought of closing him down, but Seneuze readily used the clause in the 1667 order that banned all newcomers when a third printer, named Nicolas Denoux, tried to set up business in the already contested world of Châlons printing.[36] Denoux was one of Seneuze's former workers. Denoux established a bookselling business in Châlons in 1677 and, by November 1678, had purchased presses in Sedan and begun printing. Seneuze appealed to the local presidial court to enforce the 1667 ban but found the members of this court uncooperative and "in Denoux's camp." The magistrates in the presidial court decided in Denoux's favor on 2 May 1679, having accepted his argument that the two professions, printing and bookselling, went together and consequently it did not make sense to accept him as a bookseller yet refuse him printing rights. The local judges ordered Seneuze to pay costs, conceding that in the future, as a result of the 1667 ban, no one else could set up as a printer in Châlons without the king's permission.

Seneuze was unwilling to let this situation stand; these judges had failed to carry out the king's will, and he was entitled to appeal their decision. Where it would have been traditional to appeal such a decision to the Parlement of Paris, he appealed to the chancellor about the failings of the local judges and asked to have the case heard by the royal council rather than the Parlement of Paris. Seneuze requested that the case be transferred to royal officials in Versailles because Denoux had ignored the recent royal decrees—which, he argued, were well known in Châlons—and had set up a printing house without royal authorization. In 1679 he obtained an order from the Privy Council that required each side to present its case before Armand Thomas Hüe de Miromesnil, the intendant of Champagne, who was to draw up a report for the king's council.[37] Denoux, too, appealed to the chancellor with his story—

described by Seneuze as full of lies—in which he complained that Seneuze's motives were pure jealousy and fear of competition. Seneuze's real worry, claimed Denoux, was that he would not be able to continue to overcharge for his printing the way he had in the past. Denoux claimed that he was fully qualified to be a printer, as he had completed five years of apprenticeship and then perfected his skills in Paris. The inhabitants of Châlons, he claimed, agreed; all the local officials who "knew about his abilities and the public utility that would result, solicited his installation." According to Denoux, both he and Seneuze had equal rights to print because they were both "established by the consent of the people."

To persuade members of the royal council, Seneuze produced a printed legal brief outlining his strenuous opposition to Denoux and to the notion that Denoux be allowed to print with the simple "consent of the people." He acted vigorously because he had learned that yet another potential competitor, Nicolas David, a haberdasher, had purchased printing equipment and planned to print in Châlons—and he wanted him stopped, too. In his brief, Seneuze made a number of arguments to persuade royal officials to quash the decision of the presidial court of Châlons. His principal argument was that after the 1667 order, judges in Châlons no longer had the power to allow Denoux to set up as a bookseller in 1677 and to set up a printing house eighteen months later; the king's permission had not been obtained. Denoux and the judges in Châlons could not claim ignorance, because the 1667 order in council was public, and the judges knew of it because it was mentioned in a report on an inspection tour of a printing house in Châlons in 1670 made by the lieutenant of police and the crown prosecutor. Furthermore, it was registered by Châlons' town clerk on 14 June 1677. Consequently, the authorities should not have allowed the establishment of a printing house after that date. Seneuze further pointed out that in other jurisdictions, the 1667 order in council was being enforced: the Parlement of Metz had forbidden the son of a printer in Metz to open a business without previously obtaining the king's permission. This had been the Parlement's ruling even though neither the bailliage court nor the Parlement there had registered the order in council.[38] In Soissons, the judges had seized equipment and forced the printer Claude Rennesson, who had been working for almost two years without the king's permission, to leave town. In Sedan, the 1667 order was enforced against the printer Pierre Jannon, who was the son of a master. In Vendôme, a case in which the parties had been disputing a printer appointment had been transferred from the local judges to the royal council, and the council refused to let the new printer set up business.[39] After demonstrating that the 1667 ban was being implemented elsewhere in the realm, Seneuze then appealed to the royal council to compel respect for royal decrees. How could the royal council, he asked provocatively, allow the presidial court in Châlons to ignore royal orders and thereby claim greater authority than the parlements?

Both sides of this dispute claimed that the local legal community supported Denoux, but the local bishop, Félix Vialart, continued to protect Seneuze.[40] While the intendant was sorting out this dispute, the bishop reaffirmed his patronage and obtained letters patent granting Seneuze many copyrights to diocesan printing for the next twenty years. Vialart's successor, Louis-Antoine de Noailles (1680–95), continued this relationship, choosing Jacques Seneuze as his printer on 4 June 1681 and, in November of that year, granting both Jacques and his son the rights to diocesan printing for the next thirty years.[41] These two Jansenist bishops supported the Seneuze family and, in 1695, when Noailles was promoted archbishop of Paris (where he would be at the center of the controversy about the bull *Unigenitus*), his even more Jansenist brother, who succeeded him in Châlons, continued to support Seneuze. The intendant, Miromesnil, sided against Seneuze.[42] On 2 August 1680 an order of the Privy Council decided the matter by stating that, although the law was on Seneuze's side, the king would make an exception and allow Denoux to continue as a printer. Denoux was allowed to work as a printer despite and without prejudice to the 1667 ban.

Seneuze lost his case, but his actions meant that royal council decrees began to determine who could become a printer in Châlons. All three Châlons printers developed connections in Paris and Versailles and used them to strengthen their identities as loyal subjects of the king. Seneuze's rivals, too, tried to seek justice from the king's councils and accused Seneuze of piracy, a charge from which he was exonerated by order in council.[43] Châlons' printing matters came before the Privy Council again in 1684 when it upheld seizures of pirated psalters and other devotional works displaying the bishop's arms. An order in council decided that Seneuze alone was the bishop's printer and the only one to have the right to print these.[44] In 1690 Seneuze succeeded in obtaining an order in council that annulled a seizure of his prayer books (a seizure performed at a Paris bookseller's request).[45]

Printers denounced each other and exaggerated the nefarious effects of clandestine printing in order to obtain royal intervention. Although Bouchard had once been arrested in 1691 for printing a *libelle,* in 1699 he was working with the police to combat the clandestine trade. He wrote to the Paris commissioner of police, Nicolas Delamare, to report an invasion of Dutch books traveling through Châlons to Paris to the great detriment of the interests of Parisian publishers and the king. Bouchard and Delamare had met and enjoyed a collaborative relationship; Bouchard had even drafted a memorandum proposing methods to improve book inspection at the customs.[46] Presumably, Bouchard thought it wise to show the Parisian publishers and the police that he could be useful. All three—Bouchard, the police, and the Parisians—had an interest in denouncing the clandestine trade in Châlons.

By early in the eighteenth century, we can see in Châlons a number of features that would characterize provincial printing for the rest of the century. Printers regularly engaged in conflicts over licenses and over the rights to administrative and diocesan printing, and they sought the intervention of the royal council to resolve these. After 1700 such conflicts were handled by the Bureau de la librairie, a bureau of the royal council.[47] The disputes continued unabated: between 1700 and 1704, Bouchard, Seneuze, and Denoux appealed to the royal council on many occasions over rights to licenses and to the king's printing.[48] Denoux tried to argue that he should be able to do at least some of the king's printing despite the fact that the others claimed a monopoly on it. In one submission, he offered five arguments: first, if deprived of this work, he would have nothing else to print, because the younger Seneuze was the municipal printer, and Bouchard, the printer for the college. Second, the prohibition would be contrary to public utility: intendant Miromesnil had said in 1680 that it was in the public interest to have two or three printers in Châlons and no monopoly. Third, the prohibition ran against "natural liberty" and the king's own service, neither of which the king would ever undermine. Fourth, it was absurd to claim that the intendants and tax officials could not choose whom they thought best to print in the service of the king. Fifth, Denoux claimed that in Paris many different printers printed official documents. This affair took over a year to decide; each side mobilized its supporters to appeal to Versailles.[49]

In these conflicts, Denoux wanted to have the business of the Seneuze sons, Edme and Pierre, closed down because they had failed to obtain printer's licenses. This was a desperate move that destroyed any remaining shreds of solidarity among the three printers after many years of acrid disputes, and it killed off any chance of their using the 1667 order selectively against newcomers.

Whether sons of printers required printing licenses was not an issue the Châlons printers wanted the royal council to decide for them. It was no oversight that Seneuze had failed to apply for licenses for his own sons—the very licenses he was so insistent that everyone else get. All three printers knew that there would be problems if the principle of licensing was extended too far and allowed to challenge their sons' claims to positions. The Châlons printers had, in fact, made a secret agreement not to apply the 1667 licensing requirement to their sons. They drew up a pact on 28 October 1699 in which they agreed to execute the 1667 ban on new printing establishments but not to use it against Jacques Seneuze's two sons. They wanted, as did many other printers at this time, to let their sons replace them quietly without recourse to the royal council. In the Denoux fight for administrative printing, however, this secret deal was revealed—and fell apart. Henceforward, all printers—sons of printers included—had to apply for licenses, as did Jacques Seneuze's son at his father's retirement in 1703. Later that year Denoux alerted the royal council to other printers in Châlons who did not have licenses. On 3 March 1704 an order in council licensed two of these and ordered others closed down.[50]

The Bureau de la librairie became the place where decisions about Châlons printing matters were made: between 1699 and 1704, at least thirteen orders in council from the Privy Council dealt with Châlons printers. This process whereby jurisdiction was transferred from local authorities to Versailles—begun in the 1670s and complete by 1704—occurred at the behest of the printers, especially Seneuze. Noteworthy, however, is the messiness of its implementation. Denoux had local authorities on his side who had helped him obtain printing rights in 1680 and who directed official printing orders his way. The law could be manipulated to suit the desire of printers to treat printing licenses like offices that they could transmit to their sons. To keep outsiders out but not deny their own children was an ever-present goal of the printers and, as later chapters will show, royal authorities often honored this wish, but never in principle. The Châlons printers had found an informal way to achieve that goal but, in the end, their litigious relations destroyed it. Their quarrels also may have interfered with an active trade in Jansenist books. Châlons, like other towns in Champagne, was on the route to Holland and carried on a considerable trade in Jansenist and other illegal books.[51] In September 1691, the chancellor wrote to the lieutenant of police in Châlons, requesting that he continue to prosecute Denoux for "commerce de mauvais livres" and to keep him posted on all developments.[52] Chancellor Pontchartrain pursued this trade relentlessly and ordered a major police campaign in 1699 that implicated all the major booksellers in Champagne. Such crackdowns reflect the determination of an administrator like Pontchartrain, but their success has to be seen in the context of two decades of intense communication between the Châlons printers and the royal authorities, especially the chancellor's office. Considerable gains could be made by printers who cooperated with royal authorities by denouncing their competitors. This context made a police campaign easier to undertake and certainly gave it a much greater chance of success than it would have had before 1667. Not all printers were equally vulnerable, though. Unlike Denoux and Bouchard, Seneuze was never arrested for the sale of Jansenist books. His close relationship with the future Cardinal de Noailles, who enjoyed considerable influence, likely helped protect him from persecution.

Laon

In another town, Laon, the introduction of the 1667 order in council seriously disrupted the book trade in the early eighteenth century. Like Châlons, Laon was located on overland routes between the Netherlands and Paris, and booksellers there, like others in Picardy, Champagne, and Lorraine, were active importers of pirated and prohibited Dutch books, which they forwarded to Paris. The town was also a market for Jansenist books from Paris, as Jansenism was strong in several dioceses east and northeast of the capital.[53] Not surprisingly, in 1703 the Laon printer Agrand Rennesson was a client of its Jansenist bishop, Clermont de Chaste de Roussillon.[54] In October 1703, Paris guild officials complained to royal officials that they had been informed that a woman named Audinot, who had a record of selling forbidden and pirated books, had set up a business in Laon. They sent an investigator to Laon: the Parisian bookseller Desclassan, armed with a royal decree and power of attorney to search and examine all bookshops and printing houses for illegal books. Accompanied by a bailiff, Desclassan arrived in Laon, but he found the local authorities singularly uncooperative.[55] Audinot was selling books in a shop she shared with her grocer brother-in-law, but local officers only stalled and would not help with the investigation. Desclassan and the bailiff could achieve nothing when they went with the local officials to inspect the suspect's shop. When they tried to begin the work, the local officials just stood around joking with Audinot. When they attempted to write a report on Audinot's books, the brother-in-law pushed them out of the shop and forced them to make their notes in their hotel room.

Up to this point, the story seems to be a typical case of local resistance to royal officials and Parisian publishers. But, by the early eighteenth century, there was in Laon a royally licensed printer named François-César Caton, who also wanted to close Audinot down.[56] He had little loyalty to the local residents. True, Caton was a native of Laon who had completed an apprenticeship in nearby Soissons, but he encountered opposition from local magistrates when he tried to return home to set up as a printer. The magistrates of Laon, who got along so well with Audinot, had blocked Caton on the pretext that a royal order in council of 1700 had reiterated the 1667 ban on any new printers in France.[57] Undismayed, Caton obtained the support of Claude-Joseph Sanson, the intendant of Soissons, and obtained a license in 1703. No one in Laon seemed happy with Caton's appointment. Lamy d'Andigny, the lieutenant of police, demanded a huge sum to swear him in, something Caton complained about to the chancellor. In 1704, when a member of the Audinot group applied for a printer's license, Caton opposed the license in a letter to the chancellor, and he drew attention to the Audinot group's record in the clandestine trade. Most important, Caton's appointment did not suit the Jansenist bishop, who launched a virulent attack on him in 1709. Apparently, the old printer whom Caton was to replace (Rennesson) had continued in the business until his death in 1708. The bishop supported his widow and nephew in their efforts to continue the business, claiming that Caton had neither the competence nor the equipment needed to be the printer in Laon.[58] Caton tried to defend himself by writing to the chancellor, claiming that there was only one printer position in Laon and that he was its rightful holder. Both sides in the conflict produced requests, memoranda, and inventories. Each marshalled support.

In this context, the resistance of Laon's inhabitants to royal officials and Parisian publishers was weaker than it had been in similar instances in the 1670s and 1680s. Not only was there an outright struggle between two local camps for the printer position, but each also denounced the other to the chancellor for clandestine printing. More important, Caton worked on the side of the Parisian guild and royal authorities: after the effort to close Audinot down failed miserably in 1703, the Parisian publisher Desprez received letters from a printer in Laon (undoubtedly Caton) informing him that Audinot's house was full of pirated and prohibited editions, that she sold nothing else, and that she was well protected. The Audinot clan was untouchable because, at the first sign of trouble from the Parisians, the crown prosecutor in Laon informed a member of the clan, who sent a man to travel through the night to warn the others, including the bookseller Godart in Reims (the brother of Audinot's brother-in-law and partner in Laon). In 1709 the Paris guild gave Caton power of attorney to seize any pirated editions found in Laon. A tremendous power struggle ensued between Caton, aided by his Parisian allies, and the bookselling and official world of Châlons, which was clearly buying and selling Jansenist books. Caton raided Audinot's shop and the local authorities raided Caton's shop, both turning up infractions of the rules. Caton was accused of printing a libellous pamphlet, but he complained of having been tricked into print-ing it. The bishop and his camp accused Caton of being incompetent and ill equipped. The orders in council consistently supported Caton by quashing all the moves the local authorities took against him. Caton's libel conviction cost him only a 100-livre fine, but the lieutenant of police (most certainly with great relish) posted the conviction on Caton's door when he was in the coun-tryside and proceeded to seize his property because the fine was not paid immediately. Caton took this humiliation and mistreatment to Versailles for redress and obtained orders in council in his favor.

The story suggests that the authority of the chancellor and of the royal council over printing nominations was considerable, but it had a limit. A printer in a town like Laon needed diocesan printing and without it could not survive financially. Ultimately, Caton could not keep up the costs of his shop and was forced to cede his rights to the widow Rennesson for 2,000 livres. The widow applied on behalf of her nephew for the only printer posi-tion in Laon. In return, Caton was allowed to take the place of a recently deceased printer in the nearby town of St. Quentin, much to the dismay of a candidate there. The royal licensing policy helped Caton, whose loyalties were to the Parisian guild and royal authorities, both of which protected him from ferocious local opposition. The absence of local support is unusual, however. In most towns, printers who obtained licenses fit in with the local society. What this extreme example shows is that printers could now find support in Paris and in Versailles—in this case, to an incredible extent. What is very typ-ical here, though, is the context for almost all accusations of illegal printing made against individuals: some sort of recruitment struggle underlay most of them, and the accusations were a means of eliminating a competitor. Finally, the limits of royal and Parisian influence are clear. It is difficult to overestimate the influence of bishops over printers in provincial France.

Lyon

In the large printing center of Lyon, where there were thirty-five printers in 1670, the reaction to the 1667 ban was conditioned by a tradition of royal intervention in the affairs of local printers.[59] In 1674 the printer Jean Bruyset appealed directly to the chancellor to obtain a license when the Lyon guild denied him entry on the grounds of the 1667 legislation. He got a license, which made him, as far as can be determined, the first royally licensed printer in Lyon.[60] Licensing subsequently became a regular practice among Lyon printers, because three forces encouraged respect for the order in council there: first, the printing workers thought that it would open access to masterships; second, the established master printers wanted to use it to exclude outsiders; and third, the Parisian publishers wanted the order in council enforced to reduce the size of the Lyon printing community, thereby diminishing competition and pirating.

When two Lyon masters were admitted to the guild in defiance of the 1667 ban, the journeymen complained to the chancellor in 1680.[61] That the journeymen would demand respect for the 1667 order in council may at first seem self-defeating, given that journeymen wanted more, not less, access to masterships. Their position, however, must be seen in the context of the government's role in labor struggles in the printing industry in Lyon. The journeymen wanted access to openings in the guild and thought that this could be achieved by implementing the 1667 order; a major decision in the 1650s by the Parlement of Paris had shown that the royal government supported journeymen's interests better than their local sénéchaussée court, which tended to side with their employers. Since the sixteenth century, the Lyon workers had been organized and, in the seventeenth century, despite various rulings that attempted to suppress these rights, they continued to meet and lobby for their interests.[62] While lobbying in the mid-1650s for shorter hours, the exclusion of foreign workers, and better pay, the journeymen tried to benefit from a parlementary decree obtained by the Paris workers on 7 September 1650. The Lyon guild officers complained in 1653 to the sénéchaussée court that journeymen were ruining the masters because they were attending assemblies and working only when they felt like it. When the sénéchaussée court sided with the masters, the journeymen's representatives appealed this decision to the Parlement of Paris. On 14 August 1655, a parlementary decree favored the journeymen, at least in part, because it forbade the masters from hiring more than two apprentices (i.e., using unqualified labor) and required that the guild warden keep a register of apprenticeships. The masters reacted violently to the news of the decision—so much so that the workers managed to get the Parlement to investigate the masters' conduct. The workers wanted the masters punished (for insulting the court and for threatening and mistreating workers) and ordered to obey the Parlement on pain of fines and imprisonment. Of course, for their part, the masters complained that they were being ruined by endless cabals, assemblies, worker arrogance, and greed: the Lyon workers had, they said, more liberty than their employers and, against all fairness and custom, were organized and trying to regulate the masters. In 1656 representatives of the workers went to a notary to lodge a protest that the guild officers were failing to enforce the decree of 14 August 1655.

This history explains why the Lyon workers sought to have royal authorities regulate them. Lyon journeymen used the 1667 ban as a means of preventing the masters from getting approval for a set of statutes drawn up in 1675 that allowed the masters to control recruitment into the guild tightly. They argued that the statutes were completely at odds with the 1667 ban and would ruin the workers and their families, because an article in them stipulated that a master printer could choose a journeyman to replace him at his death or resignation. The 1675 statutes were approved by the *prévôt* of Lyon—subject, however, to the endorsement of the king's council. But the masters, they alleged, had carefully avoided letting their proposal go before the king's council for approval because they knew that it was not consonant with royal policy. As the local sénéchaussée court was in collusion with the employers, the masters were continuing to admit members, but whenever the journeymen requested admission to masterships, the guild cited the 1667 order to block them.[63] Consequently, the journeymen claimed, they were forced to turn to the king for justice. At this point in their presentation they let their argument slip into a discussion about merit, which was more familiar territory for them. To their frequent displeasure, ignorant men were regularly being admitted as apprentices, and now these same ignorant apprentices were setting up printing houses and becoming masters when widows chose them over more capable workers with many years' experience. Here the argument slipped even further away from the 1667 order to the age-old grievance that widows' new husbands were able to run shops when trained journeymen were not. The Lyon journeymen believed that the 1667 order in council would help them in these struggles.

The journeymen wanted the 1667 ban enforced and all the printers who had set up since 1667 forced to close down. They wanted the penalties in the order in council applied to the offending guild officials, stripping them of their masterships and confiscating the printing equipment of the interlopers, who would forever be denied masterships. In addition, the journeymen wanted the masters forbidden from contravening royal decrees by drawing up statutes that contradicted them. The chancellor sent the grievances of the journeymen to François Dugué, the intendant of Lyon, for his opinion. The journeymen of Lyon clearly attached their hopes to an order in council that was never intended to allay their grievances. Nevertheless, because of their intervention, the Lyon masters were prevented from using the 1667 ban in the selective manner they had hoped. A Privy Council order in council dated November 1681 rejected the notion that journeymen could act as a collectivity and thus began by deny- ing their request.[64] Nevertheless, the substance of the request was considered and, on Dugué's advice, a order in council reaffirmed the 1667 ban and re- stricted the masters to one apprentice at a time. The journeymen, in their col- lective name, had this order presented to the guild officers.[65]

The Lyon masters had reasons of their own to look favorably on the 1667 order because they believed they could implement it in their own interests to exclude candidates they did not want. Such a candidate was Bruyset, men- tioned above. Another was Claude Carteron, a son of a Lyon printing family, who complained to the chancellor in 1690 that the Lyon guild would not admit him because of the 1667 order. He made an eloquent case for himself in his petition: the son of one of the oldest and most experienced printers in town, he had trained in Paris and learned everything needed to carry on the profession, and his father had left him equipment. The 1667 ban, he claimed, was a false pretext for the guild officials to use, because they had allowed a number of admissions since that year. The king's intent, he stated, was to reduce the excessive number of printers, not to destroy a profession that had con- tributed so much to the town, to the administration of justice, and to France's international trade. Printing, which had flourished in Lyon for three centu- ries, would die out if this law were applied universally. The public interest and that of French commerce required that the profession of printing in Lyon con- tinue in the hands of men capable of reestablishing France's previous glory in this art abroad; it was impossible that the king meant to exclude a printer like him. The Privy Council issued a preliminary order requiring Carteron to make his case before the intendant Pierre de Bérulle, who was to listen to both the would-be printer and the guild officers and give his opinion in a report.[66] Bérulle was persuaded of Carteron's abilities and recommended that the license be granted.[67] In 1693 the Lyon guild cited the 1667 ban in its effort to block another Lyon printer, Claude Martin, who wanted to replace his mother. Like Bruyset and Carteron (and presumably others), Martin appealed to the chancellor, who again asked the intendant to provide an opinion.[68] The Lyon printers then began regularly applying for royal licenses: seven licenses were granted in the first decade of the eighteenth century, after which no printer set up without one.[69] Intending to use the 1667 ban against outsiders, the Lyon guild members eagerly enforced it, only to find that the licensing requirement came to apply to their own sons as well.

The Paris printers, fearing competition from Lyon, also pressured royal authorities to enforce the 1667 ban. As we have seen, the Parisians developed a clear policy of lobbying officials in Versailles to regulate provincial printing so as to protect their copyrights and reduce the disorder and danger of unregulated printing in Lyon. They wanted the number of printers there reduced and, like the Lyon journeymen (but for opposite reasons), they thought the 1667 ban would help them prevent the government from approving the proposed statutes that would allow the Lyon masters to supervise their own recruitment. While the journeymen objected to the clause that allowed a master to choose a journeyman to replace him on retirement, the Parisian publishers did not accept the clause that permitted the Lyonnais to admit new masters whenever someone died or retired. They said that this was quite inconsistent with the 1667 ban and lobbied successfully against any further approvals of the Lyonnais statutes, either by the king or the Parlement of Paris. If the Parisians had to accept strict limits on their numbers, how could it possibly be fair to allow the Lyonnais to continue to admit new members? In patronizing tones, they offered to assist the Lyonnais in drawing up future statutes consistent with the 1667 order. (Indeed, the Parisians did eventually advise royal officials on the content of future Lyon statute proposals.)[70]

Thus, three relatively organized groups lobbied to get the 1667 order implemented in Lyon, each adapting and interpreting it to conform to their own economic interests and agendas. All three saw potential benefits from royal intervention. The journeymen's efforts may have forced more consistent admission practices but, on the whole, they gravely misjudged the potential of the 1667 order to help them become printers. It did nothing to open up positions for the workers. Rather—as the rest of this book will show—it served to close off entry into the trade. The journeymen's dream that royal officials would help them was not to be realized, but both the Parisians and certain families in the Lyon printing elite did reap benefits from the ban.

Parlementary Towns

In the parlementary towns, the 1667 order must be understood in the context of the relationship between the towns' parlements and printers.[71] Until the reign of Louis XIV, the provincial parlements granted publishing permits to local printers for their books; they also served as the courts of appeal for guild matters decided in the local courts. Some of the most important guild matters regulated by the parlements were the rules for apprenticeship and for the reception of masters. For example, in 1597 the Parlement of Brittany settled disputes over whether the printers' and booksellers' monopoly denied haberdashers the right to sell books: the *prévôt* had decided in favor of the printers, and the haberdashers' appeal to the Parlement failed. Over the course of Louis XIV's reign, however, the parlements lost jurisdiction over permissions and copyrights for books as the king took over censorship and copyright jurisdiction by requiring that authors and printers obtain royal permits for publications longer than two pages. The 1667 order is one of many designed to effect this transfer of power over the media from parlements to royal councils, but, by banning printer appointments, it also interfered with the parlement's role as court of appeal for disputes on guild admissions. Once a royal licensing policy was introduced in 1667, printer licensing cases and matters concerning printer discipline began to be transferred to the royal councils for adjudication. Orders from these councils not only appointed printers but also punished the wayward ones; they suspended printers, fined them, and expelled them from the trade. Eventually, while jurisdiction over labor conflicts remained with them, the parlements only very exceptionally judged cases involving printers.

Some parlements were slow to relinquish their jurisdiction. Rouen was an old printing center, with fifty-four printers in 1666. The guild there and the Parlement of Normandy simply ignored the 1667 order. Conflicts about printer recruitment went to the bailliage court, and appeals to the Parlement. Rather than use the ban as a means of blocking entry to outsiders, the Rouennais— through a kind of corporate solidarity—continued to handle recruitment and labor disputes using traditional venues.[72] They also ignored later decrees fixing and limiting the number of printers in 1700, 1701, and 1704. The failure to apply these orders was noticed by royal officials in 1706, but, as we will see in chapter 5, it was only in 1709 that the royal council orders were carried out. In Bordeaux, too, where there had been a guild since 1608, the 1667 order was ignored for a few decades, possibly because two of the forces that promoted its enforcement in Lyon—the Parisians and the labor force—had little interest or ability in this relatively small and distant publishing center.[73] In Toulouse, the Parlement clung to jurisdiction over printer recruitment until a bookseller complained and demanded the enforcement of the 1667 order, thus drawing royal officials into determining printer appointments there. In 1687 Pierre Calas, a bookseller in Toulouse, appealed to royal authorities to order the guild warden Dominique Camuset to implement the 1667 ban. Camuset had been allowing the Parlement to admit printers to the profession and to ignore a municipal ordinance of the *juges mages,* whose job it was to enforce the 1667 order in council.[74] Calas was angry because the printer Dordet, who had no capacity in Latin or Greek, was being admitted. The Privy Council issued a order in council in Calas' favor, and the guild warden and Dordet were ordered to pay costs. Consequently, in Toulouse the Privy Council orders of 1667 and 1683 were incorporated into an ordinance of the *juges mages* that was confirmed by the Privy Council in 1689. The Parlement of Toulouse continued to protect its printers into the eighteenth century in a variety of ways, but lost jurisdiction over their licensing.

In Rennes, the guild officials saw no immediate need to implement the 1667 order in council and, in blatant defiance of the ban, they went on admitting printers they wanted to the guild. For example, two printers were sworn in by the lieutenant of police in 1668. Shortly after this, however, guild officials did not hesitate to use the 1667 ban to try to exclude two other printers they did not want. These printers—Mathieu Hovius, a native of Amsterdam, and Pierre Garnier, the son of a local printer—both attempted to enter the Rennes printing guild against the opposition of guild officials, and they appealed the guild's refusals to the local presidial court.[75] The presidial court granted Garnier's appeal, accepting that he was already established before 1667 and thus immune from the ban. Hovius lost his case in the presidial court and appealed to the Parlement. Faced with these decisions, the guild officers requested that both cases be moved to the Privy Council, where they hoped to obtain orders in council requiring that the 1667 ban be respected. A Privy Council order summoned Hovius to appear and forbade the parties to take the conflict to the Parlement of Rennes until ordered otherwise. On 24 March 1671, a Privy Council order in council sent the guild's appeal of Garnier's presidial sentence before the Parlement of Rennes and, in the meantime, forbade Garnier from running a shop until the Parlement had judged whether he had been a printer before the 1667 order. In the end the Parlement retained jurisdiction of these two very early cases (1670, 1671), but they were the last ones it handled. After that, all cases concerning the admission of printers were decided by royal orders in council. In a long struggle between 1696 and 1709, the Rennes guild appealed to the chancellor to close down the business of a certain René Morin; the guild claimed that Morin was more suited to make iron hooks than to be a printer. The Parlement decided in Morin's favor, but the Privy Council refused to respect the Parlement's decree and banned Morin completely from bookselling and printing. Scenarios such as this became typical. The chancellor removed all printer-related cases from the lower courts and parlements and retained final jurisdiction over them.

Despite their loss of jurisdiction over printer recruitment, the parlements continued to play an important role in the administration of the provinces, and it is important not to underestimate their considerable influence on the world of printers. In an effort to make the laws of the land known to the king's subjects, the parlements ordered large amounts of printing. Indeed, one of the arguments made for encouraging the spread of printing in the provinces was that printers were needed for this purpose. Parlements ordered that decrees of all sorts be published and that collections of laws be made. In this way they worked with the king to further the enforcement of royal law in the kingdom. They registered royal nominations to the position of king's printer and appointed their own official printers. Increasingly, the barristers pleading before the parlements ordered legal briefs printed and were thus major clients of printers in their towns. A closer look at the place of the Parlement of Bordeaux in the lives of that town's printers provides an idea of some of the connections. After the revolt in Bordeaux in 1675, the Parlement of Bordeaux was exiled—first in 1675 to Condom, then in 1676 to Marmande, and finally to La Réole in May 1678. It was only permitted to return to Bordeaux in September 1690. The Bordeaux printers followed the Parlement into this exile. Jean Séjourné installed his son Pierre in La Réole between 1678 and 1690, and Claude Labottière, too, moved to La Réole during that time.[76] In a census of printer activity in 1701, a number of printers described the central place of the Parlement in their business. The printer Pierre Abegou described his business as printing parlementary decrees, edicts, and declarations of the king. Antoine Calamy declared that he printed only for "le palais" and that he and Pierre Séjourné both printed legal briefs and decrees. Almost all Bordeaux printers printed factums. At times of struggle between the parlements and royal officials, the loyalties of these printers could be tested, and difficult decisions were made about printing royal decrees before they were registered by the parlements and about printing parlementary decrees or *remonstrances*. Most of the time, however, parlementary printing provided a stable income for provincial printers. The relationship between the world of the courts and that of the printers was close in parlementary towns, undoubtedly influencing issues of printer recruitment in a variety of ways. But by the eighteenth century, parlementary influence on printer appointments was only informal.

Other Towns

In both small and larger non-parlementary towns, the 1667 ban drew the royal council into matters of printer recruitment. This did not happen everywhere; for example, the ban was completely unknown in Limoges until the eighteenth century. Yet it is striking how frequently and how rapidly printers in several towns sought to use it. The very first known effort occurred in 1669 in the smaller town of Vendôme.[77] In Caen the guild was quick to see the utility of the 1667 ban and tried to use it to block a Protestant printer from setting up in 1670. Here, relations between Protestant and Catholics played into the dispute: the Caen printers wanted the Parlement's authorization of a Protestant printer annulled.[78] In several other towns, printers appealed to Versailles to implement the order in council to block newcomers. In 1670 René Meverel, an established printer in Alençon, tried to block two competitors who had recently set up businesses (one of whom, Jean Malassis, had obtained permission to print from the lieutenant of police in 1668). On 22 July of the same year, the royal council summoned the two competitors before it.[79] In Amiens, the first printer to request a license was Guislain Lebel, who presented his qualifications to the royal council in 1669 because he had been made aware of the 1667 ban. Within two years he was appointed king's printer there.[80] In Troyes, when two printers attempted to use the 1667 ban to close off entry to the trade, they rekindled old rivalries that had sabotaged earlier efforts to draw up guild statutes.[81] In Chartres, a printer named Marin Machefort tried to succeed a printer who had died in 1691, but Machefort's former employer invoked the 1667 ban and forced the lieutenant of police in Chartres to order Machefort to apply to the royal council, where he was delayed from presenting his (many) qualifications until 1694. He did not get a license until 5 July 1700.[82]

In these disputes—both in the parlementary towns and in the smaller towns—opponents often tried to accuse each other of unworthiness. One means of doing this was to denounce each other for engaging in the clandestine book trade. In its opposition to the printer Hovius, the Rennes guild tried to make as much as it could of the fact that Hovius had been a Calvinist and had a record of engaging in the clandestine trade. Rennes printers apparently perceived this Dutch printer as a threat, but they were unsuccessful in expelling him from the business: Hovius eventually began printing for the Parlement and followed it to Vannes during its exile there from 1678 to 1690. His descendants became a major force in Breton printing and bookselling, with branches in Rennes, Saint-Malo, Dol, and La Flèche in nearby Maine. His great-grandson was expelled from the trade in the Maupeou years but returned in glory when Louis XVI took the throne. What is important here is that Hovius had his books seized and was convicted of printing irreligious works in the context of a late seventeenth-century struggle over a printer appointment. This was no coincidence; rather, it is one of the earliest manifestations of a pattern of events that would become typical. Not all, of course, but probably most of the intra-professional denunciations of clandestine book trade activity were embedded in printer licensing struggles, a phenomenon that became a permanent feature of state-media relations.[83]

The 1667 ban was the first in a series of decrees that developed into a full-fledged policy whereby the king licensed all provincial printers in France. This development came early to some towns—notably Lyon, and certainly much later to Rouen, where the Parlement retained a role well into the eighteenth century. Beginning with this order in council, jurisdiction over applications for licenses to print in the provinces was gradually removed from the printers' and booksellers' guilds, the bailliage and sénéchaussée courts, and the parlements; such matters were decided by the royal officials, whose decisions took the form of orders of the Privy Council. Certain printers actively intervened to see that the policy was implemented and so did some Parisian publishers, who promoted regulation in the provinces in order to better protect their copyrights. In the largest provincial printing center, Lyon, the misguided lobbying of journeymen printers who thought that royal intervention would help them become masters enhanced enforcement. The success of the policy depended on the role played by groups who saw distinct benefits to be gained by furthering the extension of royal authority in the provinces.

The economic agendas of these groups intersected with religious and political conflicts over Jansenism and Calvinism that helped shape the evolution of policy. Printers voiced considerable unhappiness with competition, piracy, incompetence, and disorder in the printing trade, and their arguments about skill, economic advance, and political and religious control became intertwined. They described a disordered world that was as damaging to the government as it was to them. The Parisian lobby and provincial printers such as Seneuze made royal officials believe that provincial printing needed more and more regulation. The idea that printer recruitment should be tightly and directly controlled gained even greater currency when Louis XIV revoked the Edict of Nantes in 1685. Printers sustained this belief with a continuous message from their towns linking lax recruitment with the spread of sedition and heresy. Royal officials received many accounts of widespread engagement in the clandestine trade, of unworthy or incompetent printers, and of the dangers printers represented to the state, morality, and religion. In 1688 the Bordeaux guild, for example, used just this kind of fear-mongering to obtain statutes limiting their number to twelve, claiming, among other things, that the disorder in the trade encouraged former Protestants in their old errors. Many historians have accepted this notion as true and believe that, until royal rules were implemented, printers and printing were in a state of disorder.[84] But it is important not to listen too closely to a selective set of printers' voices in these matters, of which the loudest was the Parisian publishers' lobby. The vision of disorder created a kind of crisis mentality and affected royal censorship policy because it focused attention on the printers as the object of regulation. What was the case in Paris in the 1660s became, by 1700, the case in the provinces as well. By the eighteenth century, by royal decree, officials were well on their way to confining licit printing to a licensed body of well-known men and women.

There were, however, limits to regulation. Many printers slipped through the cracks in our documentation and we know little about them. Our sources remain silent on much of what happened, especially on the ways in which residents of the provincial towns sorted out conflicts without recourse to local or parlementary courts or to the royal council. On occasion, we get a glimpse into what was undoubtedly a vast array of informal arrangements that resembled the secret deal made by the printers in Châlons to admit printers' sons quietly, without any bureaucratic procedure at all. The desire of many established printers to make printer positions hereditary, similar to royal offices, conditioned their attitudes toward licensing. Informal arrangements were also made between printers and their fellow townsmen; printers in some towns carried on printing with no other authorization than the passive consent of their clients and town officials. But, as time went on, such printers were increasingly at the mercy of their wider community or possible competitors, knowing that a denunciation for printing without a license could come at any time, thereby bringing an end to their businesses or, at the very least, depriving their sons of a livelihood.

A full-fledged licensing policy may not have been Colbert's initial intention, but over time this was what developed. Between 1667 and 1700, information and misinformation on provincial printers made its way to Versailles as printers appealed printing matters to the chancellor. Whereas the 1667 ban was probably decreed for economic reasons and fits well into the economic policies of the 1660s, over the next thirty years it took on a political character. Official awareness of provincial printers increased, and the message of disorder became louder and more threatening in the context of Jansenism and the revocation of the Edict of Nantes. The economic factors behind the inception of licensing lost their central importance, and royal officials increasingly thought of printer management as a method of ideological control. But to understand the next developments in licensing policy, we must understand the thinking of Pontchartrain, chancellor of France from 1699–1714, who held a far more developed view of ideological control than Colbert had. His role was critical to the next two stages in the licensing policy: the establishment of the Bureau de la librairie (chapter 3) and the purges of the print trade (chapter 4).

3

THE ROYAL COUNCIL TAKES CONTROL

The 1701 Inquiry and the Bureau de la Librairie

L'intention des règlements est de n'avoir pour Imprimeurs que des gens connus, solvables, et retenus continuellement par la crainte de perdre leur état.
—*Lamoignon de Malesherbes,* Mémoires sur la librairie, *1759*

In 1700, Louis XIV was informed of the misuse and abuse of printing presses in the realm, which arose "principally from the large number of booksellers and printers who—without the required abilities—were setting up daily in several towns in the realm and were printing all sorts of books that undermined good order."[1] All possible means were to be utilized to eliminate this pernicious disorder. A royal order in council dated 6 December 1700 reiterated the 1667 ban on new printers and directed intendants and municipal officers to carry out a general census of all printers and booksellers. This census, and the many administrative orders required to license the printers and resolve their disputes, created a huge increase in litigation that overwhelmed the masters of requests and councillors of state in Versailles who handled printer petitions. This chapter addresses the institutional response to this demand. First, it describes the 1700 census of the French world of printers and booksellers. Second, it explores the creation of the Bureau de la librairie, a specialized administrative office established to handle the centralization of book trade matters. Third, it offers an overview of the attitudes toward licensing adopted by a number of chancellors, keepers of the seals, and directors of the book trade, underscoring their active role in licensing.

A key force behind the administrative response was Louis Phélypeaux, comte de Pontchartrain, who was appointed chancellor in 1699 and, for fifteen years, took the task of controlling the book trade very seriously.[2] Under no circumstances, Pontchartrain once told the intendant of Rouen, was commercial advantage to take precedence over ideological policing.[3] Pontchartrain appointed his nephew, Jean-Paul abbé Bignon—a young scholar at the center of intellectual life in Paris in the last decades of Louis XIV's reign—as director of book trade matters. This uncle-nephew partnership was one of several between chancellors or keepers of the seals and close relatives that came to characterize the top echelon of royal censorship bureaucracy in the eighteenth century. Despite appointing his nephew to handle many matters, Pontchartrain himself remained very involved in censorship. The two men worked to establish royal control of prior censorship and take it away from the parlements and the church; they demanded that publishers obtain royal permissions—not just local or episcopal ones—before publishing titles; they stepped up repression of the clandestine trade, especially in Rouen and Champagne, both deemed to be conduits for imported Dutch books. In 1710 Pontchartrain and Bignon reduced the number of frontier towns that could legally import shipments of books from abroad. As part of this larger effort to enforce ideological control, both men vigorously pursued and extended the early licensing initiatives of the late seventeenth century.[4] To this end, they had a comprehensive census of all printers in France completed and watched carefully as their subordinates set up procedures to take direct control of printer appointments. In 1704 they established ceilings on the number of printers in every town in France, forcibly reducing the number in some towns.

The 1700 Census: "Le Temps de la Recherche des Incapables"

In the late seventeenth century, royal officials sought information on provincial printers and a number of general surveys were ordered, but none seems to have been taken very seriously. The printers in Rouen, for example, refused to provide printers' names or other relevant information. Some intendants had more pressing concerns and surveys of printers simply did not get done. The 1700 survey was quite a different matter. Persuaded that the provincial book trade was in crisis, Pontchartrain and Bignon ordered a nationwide survey of all printers and printing equipment in France—one they intended to see done.[5]

The royal order went out to the newly empowered arms of monarchical control—the intendants and lieutenants of police—and to the local judges to fill out detailed questionnaires on all printers in France and to include in them their names, numbers, biographies, printing equipment, the titles they printed, and the nature of guild organization if it existed in their towns.

 This process of information gathering was carefully designed to prevent the nonchalance and foot-dragging that had characterized earlier surveys. We can see how this was exemplified by following the stages of its implementation in Bordeaux. On 14 February 1701, the intendant Yves-Marie De la Bourdonnaye ordered the execution of the census in Guyenne, and the local authority in Bordeaux, the jurats—who had purchased the office of lieutenant of police in the town—appointed one of their number, the barrister Raymond Mathieu de Lauvergnat, to execute the decree. Accompanied by a municipal attorney and a police clerk, Lauvergnat visited all the printing houses in the town of Bordeaux and wrote detailed reports describing how, on entering each establishment on the main floor, they climbed up into the rooms that held the printing equipment, where they examined types and presses, taking down the number and names of workers and recording what was being printed.[6] The reports on each of the thirty-one printing and bookselling establishments in Bordeaux were sent to the intendant, who forwarded them to Pontchartrain in the spring of 1701. Intendants like La Bourdonnaye—who, until the survey, had been totally unaware of the existence of printing presses in Périgueux—would, after 1701, never again be as ill-informed about the printers in their *généralités*.[7] The 1700 census was just the first in a number of similar surveys ordered by chancellors and keepers of the seals in the eighteenth century to stay abreast of printing in the realm.[8]

 The census provided considerable information, allowing both royal officials and later historians to characterize provincial printers and printing at the turn of the century. There were 360 printing houses in the provinces and 51 in Paris.[9] Many provincial printers engaged in other activities alongside their printing: some worked as tax officials, customs clerks, or directors of post offices, and others as general merchants of cloth, hardware, haberdashery, or even groceries. Most book publishing was limited to the larger centers, such as Lyon, Strasbourg, Toulouse, Caen, and Rouen; elsewhere, printers printed administrative, judicial, or religious material, schoolbooks, or chapbooks (*bibliothèque bleue*), most of it printed ephemera or small books.[10] In intendancies and seats of law courts, there were vast quantities of administrative and judicial printing. With few exceptions, religious titles dominated the provincial publishing world. Books of Hours and catechisms were to be found everywhere in provincial France. Gazettes and local versions of Parisian newspapers were also produced.

Officials in Versailles also learned about individual printers in the provinces, their training in Paris and other towns, and ongoing antagonisms aggravated by the census.[11] Some printers applauded the idea of the census, but others were not at all happy with the way their families and businesses were represented to officials in Versailles. In Toulouse in 1701 Élizabeth Henault, the widow Boudé, commended the undertaking as an admirable attempt to improve professional standards, describing this period in the history of her profession as "the time when we sought out the incompetent." This was, however, a spin that camouflages a major struggle among printing families vying with each other over who could present the most unassailable claim to the profession. Rival printers in Toulouse, the Colomiés family, had a completely different take on the exercise: the guild deputy Antoine Colomiés and his brother Louis-Guillaume decried the corruption and fraud that they saw at work when the survey was done. Antoine Colomiés criticized the reports submitted to the local authorities, the *juges mages,* for containing erroneous information and falsified credentials. The decree licensing his rival, the widow Boudé, was, he said, "monstrous," and many printers were guilty of fraud and quite incompetent, some being so poor that they borrowed presses to mislead the investigators. According to Boudé, the Calomiés faction was busy undermining the purpose of the census with a number of illegal maneuvers, including secret meetings and elections. The Boudé and Colomiés families had—if we measure by the number of presses and journeymen they claimed—the largest printing houses in Toulouse.[12] In such circumstances, no printers wanted their rivals elected guild officers, so the widow Boudé and her friends wrote to Pontchartrain to ask what venue should be used to get illegal guild elections quashed. Should they go before the *juges ordinaires,* before His Majesty, before the intendant, or before special commissioners named in Toulouse to handle printing affairs? The Boudé family sought central government intervention, appealing to Pontchartrain for help in consolidating their victory on the local level. In 1703, when the widow Boudé wanted her associate Jacques Loyau licensed despite the guild's opposition (on the grounds that he had done his apprenticeship in Paris and not Toulouse), the royal council agreed.[13] Inevitably, in Toulouse and elsewhere, the census results reflected the outcome of power struggles.

While it is impossible to decipher much of the antagonism that the census engendered or to assess the levels of collusion between local police and the printers, it appears that, at the very least, the printers in two towns—Bordeaux and Rouen—were able to manipulate the situation in their favor and keep their families in the trade. In Bordeaux, just a month before the census was conducted, the local government, the jurats, cooperated with some major printing families and allowed five printers to be sworn in on the condition that they not run businesses until they were twenty years of age. The timing could hardly have been a coincidence.[14] Bordeaux printers who were included in the survey were pleased with their insider status and with later legislation that safeguarded that status against a number of challenges. In Rouen, too, there was collusion between the printers and the local authorities.[15] The guild was made up of a large number of smaller and medium-sized enterprises and dominated by a closed group of families of fairly similar circumstances, described by their historian as a "démocratie patriarcale." In their resistance to royal intervention, it helped them greatly that the census was handled by the lieutenant of police, Pierre de Boisguilbert, who colluded to present results to Versailles that would take care of as many of them as possible. Boisguilbert was prepared to swear in a large number of masters, many of them young children, and to conceal this in the census report. A whole world of invisible printers and workers was hidden from officials in Versailles. Still, even working with the artificially low figures, officials in Versailles thought that there were too many printers and booksellers in Rouen. Pontchartrain wrote to Boisguilbert in December 1701 saying that he should not allow a new printing house to be established for that reason. Their excessive numbers made printers poor and more willing to break the rules. Far from increasing the number, Boisguilbert should be trying to reduce it.

Royal Councils and the Bureau de la Librairie

The census data was sent to the chancellor and the masters of requests and councillors of state who worked in the Bureau de la librairie, one of several *bureaux* where the work of royal government was done in the reigns of Louis XIV, XV, and XVI.[16] There were two parts to the Bureau de la librairie. The first was the *bureau gracieux;* the second, the *bureau contentieux.* The bureau gracieux is well known to historians as the office that granted permissions to publish books and, as such, was the central arm of prior censorship in old-regime France. The chancellor and the bureau gracieux had been granting these permissions from at least 1672.[17] From around 1700, the chancellor or keeper of the seals rather informally designated a close collaborator—often a relative—to head up a team of royal censors to supervise the approval of manuscripts.[18] The title of this individual varied: in the early years, he was called *inspecteur général de la librairie* or *chef du bureau de la librairie* and, after 1750, the title was director of the book trade (*directeur de la librairie*). The most famous of the directors of the book trade was Chrétien-Guillaume de Lamoignon de Malesherbes.

The other office, more judicial in character, handled issues of printer licensing and the regulation of printer discipline. This was the *bureau pour les affaires de chancellerie et librairie,* or *conseil de chancellerie,* or *bureau contentieux.*[19] Until the 1690s, different masters of request and councillors of state handled printer's licenses and other book trade matters. In 1692 Pontchartrain's predecessor, Chancellor Boucherat, appointed Bignon to sort out all difficulties between Paris and Lyon printers.[20] On 31 July 1699, he instructed two masters of requests to specialize in chancellery affairs concerning violations of decrees and rules, a move that the newly appointed Pontchartrain took further by appointing two masters of requests to handle book trade matters. The number of book trade decrees increased dramatically in 1703, as is shown in table 1; most concerned requests from provincial printers seeking printing licenses, but others decided pirating and other policing matters. To deal with the onslaught of requests, a decree in August 1703 streamlined the process and relieved the pressure on its resources. But the flow of cases continued, and several masters of request were appointed to handle them.[21] In June 1708 the masters of requests assigned to chancellery affairs and those looking after book trade affairs were grouped together to form the bureau contentieux (hereafter bureau or bureau contentieux) under the presidency of abbé Bignon. Thus, 1708 began a new era when a specific bureau was designated to decide book trade matters and hear appeals from the regular courts.[22] The creation of specialized bureaux to handle book trade affairs was in line with administrative trends generally in Louis XIV's reign. The bureau contentieux continued under the regency of Philippe d'Orléans; even though Chancellor Voisin abandoned it in 1715, it was reestablished the same year. Between 1720 and 1789, usually functioning under the name of conseil de chancellerie, the bureau contentieux handled matters relating to the licensing and policing of printers.

The bureau contentieux was made up of two councillors of state and four to six masters of requests, all chosen by the chancellor or keeper of the seals and nominated by order in council. The longest-serving councillor of state became its president. Between 1724 and 1743, the comte d'Argenson presided. He was followed by two sons of Chancellor D'Aguesseau. Until 1740 several masters of requests were temporarily assigned to the bureau contentieux, but afterwards a few became specialized in book trade affairs, with much of the work being handled by Maboul, Dufour de Villeneuve, D'Aguesseau, and Bertier de Sauvigny. These men and their superiors, the chancellors or keepers of the seals, signed the decrees issuing from the work of the bureau contentieux.[23]

Some directors of the bureau gracieux—among them abbé Bignon, D'Argenson, and Le Camus de Néville—belonged to the bureau contentieux and shared in its labors, but many did not.[24] Malesherbes, the great liberal influence of the mid-eighteenth century, was not a member of the bureau contentieux.[25] The decrees of the bureau contentieux were issued as orders of the Privy Council (*arrêts du Conseil Privé*) or of the Council of Dispatches (*arrêts du Conseil des Dépêches*), but most problems handled by the bureau were not discussed at these higher-level councils. After examining their cases, the councillors of state and the masters of request usually met with the chancellor or

Table 1   Number of Privy Council orders on book trade matters, 1701–1780

	All	Licensing
1701	14	
1702	17	
1703	76	
1704	65	
1705	53	
1706	46	
1707	34	
1709–14	187	155
1719–24	250	203
1739–44	185	172
1755–60	123	114
1776–80	80	75

SOURCES: BN FF 22131 (1701–7), AN V⁶ (1709–80).

NOTE: The Privy Council orders between 1709–80 do not include copyright matters. The decline in numbers of orders at the end of the regime does not reflect a decline in the number of licenses. In the early years, there were often several orders issued for one license—often an *arrêt préparatoire* and then an *arrêt définitif.* At the end of the regime, the bundles include only the final licenses granted to successful candidates.

keeper of the seals, who listened to opinions and then simply made decisions. In fact, there is evidence that the chancellor or keeper of the seals met solely with the president of the bureau to be informed of bureau discussions.[26] Some affairs were not even discussed at the level of the bureau; in straightforward matters, the president simply had a *rapporteur* draft a decree to be sent to the chancellor or keeper of the seals for signing. In 1760 Malesherbes wrote that the bureau was not like other tribunals but was rather a consulting group for the chancellor, who had the deciding vote and could draw up decrees in his *cabinet* on his own authority on information provided him.[27] The bureau contentieux was thus a council in the chancellor's service.

This bureau contentieux was central to the policing of printers in France in the eighteenth century. It handled all the requests for printer's licenses in the realm: no printer could legally work in France without a license from it. When there were several applicants for the limited number of positions, the bureau chose among them. Malesherbes did not like the way printer appointments were mixed in with the mainly judicial matters decided by the bureau contentieux, because he thought that printer appointments were administrative in character and would be more meaningfully grouped with other administrative matters handled by the bureau gracieux, such as permissions to publish titles (and would therefore be under his purview as director). Not only would this have made more sense to him, but he also thought that it would increase his ability to command respect from printers.[28] He regretted that he had no say in printer appointments.

Chancellors or keepers of the seals made the decisions to choose and discipline printers. Pontchartrain, Fleuriau D'Armenonville, Chauvelin, D'Aguesseau, Lamoignon, Maupeou, and Miromesnil were all intimately acquainted with matters of printer appointment and printer discipline. They relied, of course, on the work of the book trade directors, especially when Bignon and Antoine Gabriel de Sartine (who was also the lieutenant of police in Paris) had that position, but much of the correspondence with the intendants was signed by the chancellors and the keepers of the seals as they attended to controversies over printer licensing and other matters of discipline. Historians' accounts of censorship and book trade regulation tend to give pride of place to the directors of the book trade, and especially to Malesherbes. This makes some sense when the principal issue was the approval process that titles underwent, but it should not disguise how closely involved the chancellors and keepers of the seals often remained in other book trade matters.

Table 2 lists several of the members of the bureau contentieux who advised
chancellors and keepers of the seals. Some of these men knew a great deal about
printer licensing. Barillon de Morangis (grandson of Chancellor Boucherat)
and Louis Maboul and his son were experts in matters of copyright, printer
licensing, and printer discipline, settling many disputes among printers and
generally regulating the profession. Not only did they decide who obtained
printer's licenses, but they also ordered penalties—fines, suspensions, and can-
cellations of licenses—when printers violated censorship regulations. After the
establishment of the bureau, only in rare instances did printers accused of censorship offenses go before the regular courts in France. The bureau also settled
cases where ownership of copyright was in dispute, and it settled controversies within guilds, on occasion replacing guild officials. Some bureau members
later became intendants and carried this experience into their future work,
which included responsibility for printers and booksellers in their *généralités.*
Such was the case with Urbain Guillaume de Lamoignon de Courson, who
later became the intendant of Guyenne and, shortly after his appointment
there, received a warm letter from abbé Bignon referring to their previous
work together on book trade matters in the bureau.[29]

While some book trade decisions continued to be issued as orders of the
Conseil des Dépêches, the vast majority of those licensing printers were issued
as Privy Council orders, a development that reflects the increasing bureaucra-
tization of eighteenth-century government.[30] These decisions of the bureau—
issued as Privy Council orders—constituted the essential regulation of printers
in eighteenth-century France and played a more substantial role than the
better-known *déclarations du roi* and edicts. Declarations and edicts had more
legal force than the orders in council because they were registered by the parlements, but there were relatively few of these: the two best known are the
declarations of 1728 and 1757, rulings often cited by historians because of the
draconian penalties they imposed for printing offenses. The rules governing
the Paris guild were issued as an edict in 1686, and those for Lyon were made
into a declaration in 1695. In general, however, parlementary agreement was
difficult to obtain on printing matters. For example, royal officials worked for
years but failed to fulfill Pontchartrain's plan of producing a general code for
the book trade that would be approved by the Parlement of Paris and issued
as a declaration. After both Pontchartrain and D'Aguesseau tried and failed,
Joseph Jean-Baptiste Fleuriau d'Armenonville gave up hope of obtaining parlementary approval and simply issued the 1723 rules in the form of an order of

Table 2 Some members of the Bureau de la librairie involved in printer licensing

Chancellors or keepers of the seals	Years	Some of the masters of request and councillors of state who signed printer's licenses
Louis Boucherat	1685–99	Bignon
Louis Phélypeaux, comte de Pontchartrain	1699–1714	Bignon, Maboul, Lamoignon de Courson, Turgot, De Fenoil, Doujat, Machault, Bosc du Bouchet, Laugeois d'Imbercourt, Barillon de Morangis, Chauvelin, Le Goux de la Berchère
Daniel-François de Voisin	1715	De Machault
Henri-François D'Aguesseau	1717	De Machault, Maboul, Le Goux de la Berchère, Le Pelletier de la Houssaye, Barillon de Morangis
Voyer de Paulmy d'Argenson	1718–20	Maboul, De Bernage, Barillon de Morangis
Henri-François D'Aguesseau	1720–22	Maboul, Barillon de Morangis, Le Pelletier de Signy, Le Pelletier de la Houssaye, Angran, Le Guerchoys, Le Gras, De Harlay
Fleuriau D'Armenonville	1722–1727	Maboul, Barillon de Morangis, Angran, D'Argouges de Ranes, De Harlay, Le Pelletier de Beaupré, Lefèvre de Caumartin
Germain-Louis Chauvelin	1727–37	Rouillé, Voyer d'Argenson, D'Aguesseau
Henri-François D'Aguesseau	1737–50	Maboul, Voyer d'Argenson, D'Aguesseau
Guillaume de Lamoignon de Blancmesnil	1750–63	Machault, Maboul, D'Aguesseau, Dufour de Villeneuve, Taboureau des Reaux, Feydeau
René-Charles de Maupeou (père)	1763–68	Bertier de Sauvigny, Thiroux de Crosne, D'Aguesseau, D'Agay
René-Nicolas de Maupeou (fils)	1768–74	Bertier de Sauvigny
Armand Hüe de Miromesnil[a]	1774–87	Bertier de Sauvigny, Le Camus de Néville, Laurent de Villedeuil
Chrétien-François de Lamoignon de Basville	1787–88	Vidaud de la Tour
Charles-Louis François de Barentin	1788–89	Poitevin de Maissemy

NOTE: This chart is drawn from a sample of several hundred licenses in AN V⁶ 782–1145, December 1700–July 1789, and makes no claim to be comprehensive.

ᵃ In the 1780s Miromesnil signed the licenses with Le Camus de Néville (1776–84) and Laurent de Villedeuil (1784–85). Other members of the bureau signed orders deciding matters such as copyrights and printing house closures. Charles Sartine, for example, signed a decree closing down a printer in Bourg-Saint-Andéol (AN V⁶ 1133, 7 May 1787).

the Conseil des Dépêches.[31] Malesherbes regretted the absence of a declaration governing the book trade that would give more force to the law and permit the use of the regular judicial system to prosecute printers.[32] Instead, the control of printers was increasingly an administrative matter, in the hands of the chancellor or keeper of the seals. The absence of wider approval did, at times, weaken enforcement. Many years after a royal order in council in 1744 extended the 1723 Code for Paris to the entire realm, the intendant in Bordeaux reported that those who tried to enforce its clauses about inspecting imported books would have less difficulty if this simple order in council could have been issued as letters patent.[33]

Printers usually applied to the bureau for licenses for one of two reasons: to have their right to be a printer sanctioned by the king so that it could not be challenged, or, as was virtually always the case after 1704, to obtain a license on the death or resignation of another printer.[34] Printers hired lawyers and petitioned the chancellor or keeper of the seals for the licenses, listing their qualifications and their claims to the position. The chancellor or keeper of the seals passed on the dossiers to the bureau, where the masters of requests and councillors of state examined them. Until the mid-eighteenth century, the bureau tended to issue a preparatory order calling on the printer to present his qualifications locally, usually to the lieutenant general of police in the presence of the guild officers, if there was a guild in his town. In the late eighteenth century, the preparatory decrees were abandoned; the chancellor or keeper of the seals simply wrote a letter asking the guild and local authorities to examine applicants. The lieutenant of police furnished a report on the number of printers currently working in the town, which he sent to the chancellor or keeper of the seals, often via the intendant. Given this information, the masters of requests and councillors of state chose the printer and issued a license (*arrêt définitif*) or else an order specifically denying the request. The process could flounder, stall, or die at any stage; in some cases, several preparatory orders in council were issued for one position. When the decision was made to license a printer, the decree was signed by the chancellor or keeper of the seals and sent to the local intendant, who forwarded it to the candidate. Once in possession of the order in council, the candidate could be sworn in. As we will see in the next chapter, the problem of too many candidates and not enough positions emerged clearly after 21 July 1704, when the king fixed the number of printers allowed in every town in France. All interested candidates were ordered to present their titles locally, and these concurrences of multiple applicants came to be called competitions, or *concours*—a term redolent of the printers' university identity, and one that was used more and more frequently over the course of the eighteenth century.

A few descriptions of the procedure required to obtain printer's licenses exist in contemporary documents. The keeper of the seals, Chauvelin, provided an outline of the process in 1732.

> To be admitted a printer in a town, there must first be a vacant place and this place cannot exceed the ceiling placed on the number of printers for each town by a decree in 1704 to this effect. The candidate must have the required qualities as outlined in Title 6 of the 1723 rules. When these conditions are met, the candidate presents his request to the bureau de chancellerie, where he will be given a preparatory decree which will send him before the local judge of police to show proof of his titles and abilities. If the local *juge de police* makes a proper report and offers a favorable opinion then the candidate is given a licence (*arrêt définitif*) and put in possession of the vacant place.[35]

One of the six decrees that reformed book trade regulation in August 1777 (under Miromesnil and Le Camus de Néville) clearly outlined the application procedures for would-be printers. It began by reiterating a traditional list of requirements for a printer's license: four years as an apprentice and three years as a journeyman (with sons of masters exempted from these first two requirements); the attainment of twenty years of age; and a certificate of knowledge of Latin and ability to read Greek from the rector of the university or, if there was no university in the town, from the principal of the local *collège*. The decree then stated that it was important that printers and booksellers have sufficient capacity and experience; therefore, the king wanted the sons of masters, along with other candidates, to submit to examinations lasting at least three hours in the guildhall. The guild wardens wrote a report of the performance and provided the candidate with a copy, which he sent—along with his baptismal certificate, a certificate of Roman Catholicism, a certificate of completed apprenticeship, and references from masters for whom he had worked—to the chancellor or keeper of the seals. If the candidate received the license, he was later sworn in by the lieutenant of police. Another 1777 description of the licensing procedures or *concours* can be found in *Manuel de l'auteur et du libraire:*

if the ministry receives several requests for the same printing house, it orders a competition (*concours*) which is done in the presence of the lieutenant general of police in the town where there is a printing house vacant. This officer distributes to each competitor the same page of manuscript, which the competitors compose, print, and give to the lieutenant general of police, who produces a report for the keeper of the seals, who picks the most capable of the competitors. This application is then sent to M. Bertier, master of requests, and the reporter in charge of disputed book trade matters, who prepares and sends a license. . . . The requests of the others are declared void and sent back to the barristers who signed them.[36]

By the reign of Louis XVI, the bureaucratic procedures were standardized and well known to all concerned, and some administrators—Maupeou, Le Camus de Néville, and Miromesnil—wanted to extend them to booksellers as well as printers, a development that was partly achieved when one of the August 1777 decrees required all booksellers to apply to Versailles for licenses. Throughout the last decade of the *ancien régime,* booksellers as well as printers applied for Privy Council orders to authorize their businesses.[37]

The growing bureaucracy governing the book trade cost money, and the government sought to pay for it by increasing the fees the printers paid for licenses.[38] The fee schedule outlined in a supplement to the August 1777 decrees set standardized admission fees for the whole realm. Until then there had been a wide range in fees required to become a master printer.[39] In 1723 they were set for Paris at 1,500 livres for printer-booksellers (1,000 for booksellers) and 900 for printers' sons (600 for booksellers' sons), but not until 1744 were these rates applied to the provinces, and even then they were often not collected. The 1,500-livre fee was seen by some in Languedoc as too high, and litigation followed an attempt made by some guild officers to charge it. In Angers in the mid-eighteenth century, printer candidates who were not sons of printers paid 500 livres. In Toulouse, sons of master printers saw their fees increase to 600 livres after March 1744. In Bordeaux in 1750 it appears that no entrance fee was levied, most printers at the time being sons of printers, but by 1764 the sons and sons-in-law of masters were (at least theoretically) to pay 900 livres, and outsiders, 1,500 livres. The 1777 reforms standardized these fees, and part of the money was ordered to go to the keeper of the seals to pay for the costs of administering the book trade.[40] The costs of admission thus went up significantly, and even sons of masters began paying substantial sums.

Chancellors and Keepers of the Seals

Over the course of the eighteenth century, manpower and money were found to carry out the administrative control of printers envisioned by Pontchartrain and Bignon in the last years of Louis XIV's reign. Pontchartrain took Jean-Baptiste Colbert's licensing initiatives to new heights by fixing the numbers of printers for all provincial towns in 1704, an objective that required, as we will see in chapter 4, purging unwanted provincial printers. Everything we know about Pontchartrain suggests that he believed it was both necessary and possible to establish political control of printers in both Paris and the provinces. Unlike Colbert, who allowed economic considerations to soften his determination to control printers, Pontchartrain let little moderate his zeal. Pontchartrain's successors shared his views: the chancellors or keepers of the seals appointed after him all took a very serious interest in book trade matters. All accepted the idea that printers had to be licensed, and all were involved in choosing provincial printers. The following pages piece together the views of some of these men—Fleuriau D'Armenonville, D'Aguesseau, Chauvelin, Lamoignon, Maupeou, and Miromesnil—drawn largely from their correspondence with intendants and local authorities on matters of printer regulation and media control.

The need to police printers preoccupied Fleuriau D'Armenonville, keeper of the seals from 1722 to 1727. He was responsible for getting a long series of regulations—often referred to as the Code de la librairie—into law in order to govern Parisian printers and booksellers. A section of this Code, entitled "Fixation des imprimeurs à Paris et dans les villes du royaume," was devoted to setting the number of printers in Paris at thirty-six and requiring that all printers be licensed. The text of this decree claimed that the king had been informed that the art of printing—which "merited special attention because of its relationship to public order, religion, and the king's service"—was "in decline and degenerating into harmful liberty because of the weakness and greed of men who exercised the printing profession and failed to respect the rules." The concern surfaced regularly in his correspondence with Claude Boucher, the intendant of Bordeaux: he was deeply concerned about the illegal book trade there and shocked to discover in 1722 that the customs officials were not allowing the Bordeaux guild officers to inspect imported books. He made his displeasure known to the intendant and, because of the extreme disorder in the town, he appointed one of the first provincial book trade inspectors there in 1723. D'Armenonville ordered the printers and booksellers in Bordeaux and Rouen to draw up new statutes because the book trade in both towns had fallen into disarray, and he asked intendant Boucher and abbé Despujols, the newly appointed inspector of the book trade in Bordeaux, to give this task high priority because it was an important matter for law, order, and public peace. D'Armenonville wanted to know not only the names of the printers and booksellers in Bordeaux but also their ability and character, so that he could exclude those who were suspected of printing or selling "wicked books." Intendant Boucher sent a draft decree outlining new rules for the Bordeaux guild to D'Armenonville, who revised and then issued it on 1 June 1723.[41]

Between 1727 and 1737 book trade matters were the responsibility of the keeper of the seals, Germain-Louis Chauvelin.[42] In the bureau, Chauvelin was aided by the comte d'Argenson, and both men directed their attention to the licensing of printers. In a memorandum in 1732 dedicated to reviving the book trade in France and regaining this trade from the Dutch and the English, Chauvelin criticized what he described as the shackles (*entraves*) on the French book trade, but he did not deviate from his predecessors' desire to reduce the number of printers in France. In fact, he proposed further reductions in their number, especially in Paris.[43] The first reason Chauvelin gave for this was that a small corps of comfortably-off printers would have too much to lose if it printed forbidden books: "There will be much less fear that they will print forbidden books because they will all be sufficiently occupied or because they will fear risking an established fortune for seemingly mediocre profits which would tempt only needy printers."[44] A reduction in number—especially by the elimination of ill-equipped printers and widows—would bring several advantages, including more prosperity, less pirating, high-quality editions, and better treatment of clients.

For over a decade in the mid-eighteenth century, from 1737 to 1750, Chancellor Henri-François D'Aguesseau[45]—a man Voltaire accused of wanting to prevent the nation from thinking—directed printer licensing and policing and worked hard to create a small and loyal printing corps. In 1737 he ordered a census of printers and, in 1739, further reduced the number of provincial printers. He extended the Parisian regulations of 1723 to the rest of the realm in

1744.[46] In both these moves he was, no doubt, responding to the pressure from the Parisian and provincial guilds: the Bordeaux guild, for example, took the opportunity of the 1737 census to complain of "abuses" occurring in the book trade in their town, particularly of unqualified printers who had nothing to lose and so dared to print all sorts of evil books.[47] The preamble of the 1739 decree stated that the king had been informed that some printers, for lack of work, had been led to produce pirated and prohibited works, and that the 1704 printer quotas were not being respected because local officials were overstepping their authority and authorizing printers to run businesses. The widows who were continuing to work were keeping the printer numbers too high as well. To end these abuses, which "went against royal authority and the public good," the king ordered further regulation of printers: new, lower, quotas were fixed in 1739, the rules that required printers to petition for licenses were reiterated, and local police officers were forbidden to authorize anyone to become a printer. When a printer died leaving a widow, his position was not to be filled until the widow died or resigned. D'Aguesseau did reduce the number of printers in France—but he also caused difficulties by extending the 1723 Code de la librairie, written for Paris, to the rest of the realm in 1744. Many of the Code's rules were not suited to provincial publishing.

D'Aguesseau had to sort out the problems that the conflicting fiscal and political agendas of the French state created for printers.[48] Most of the time, the printers had little trouble maintaining competing identities as artisans, office holders, and university members, but some of the contradictions in their lives came rather dramatically to light in February 1746, when an edict ordered the sale of offices or inspectorships to raise money for the War of the Austrian Succession. Purchasers of the offices were automatically accorded guild membership. The printers and booksellers, like other guilds, would have had to accept new members or agree to buy up these offices themselves in order to keep out unwanted newcomers. But printer numbers were fixed, and printers needed licenses to operate businesses, so how would this work? For the Bordeaux guild, which balked at the idea of paying some 2,400 livres for the offices, the solution was an easy one: they claimed that they were exempt. However, while they stalled, two individuals went ahead and purchased the offices, thus provoking a confrontation on the matter. D'Aguesseau tried to sort out the contradictory policies and found himself deluged with memoranda from both sides: the purchasers of inspectorships, who began working as printers and booksellers, and the guild officers, who regarded these men as completely unacceptable.

D'Aguesseau seems to have thought that bookseller (but not printer) offices could be sold, but he was wary and warned that assurances had to be obtained of the good character and conduct of the recipients before the offices could be sold. As there were already a number of rather shady booksellers in Bordeaux, it was important to prevent the entry of more dubious men into the trade. D'Aguesseau proposed that the guild reimburse the purchasers of the printer offices for the sums they had paid. However, one of the new printers, named Nicolas Phillippot, conducted a major campaign to keep his post, arguing that he was a man of honor and probity, the son-in-law of a Bordeaux master and the sole supporter of his wife's family. He went to Paris for eight months to lobby and was able to obtain support for his cause from a number of important people. The guild spared no cost in opposing Phillippot and, in 1747, it managed to obtain an order from intendant Louis-Urbain Aubert, marquis de Tourny, to close Phillippot down. But Phillippot had by this point convinced some officials that he should stay and, in 1748, Maboul (a member of the bureau contentieux) wrote to Tourny on his behalf. Maboul noted that almost all of the other printers' guilds had bought these offices back, but the Bordeaux guild was both refusing to do this and refusing to allow Phillippot to work. D'Aguesseau, he reported, was worried about this injustice and also concerned that, if Phillippot were simply to be reimbursed for the office, he would still not be able to earn a living. Following Maboul's recommendation to mix rigor with charity in this situation, Tourny granted Phillippot the first vacant position in Bordeaux in which the successor was not a widow or a son, and in the meantime he ordered the guild to let Phillippot work in peace for the rest of his life. When the guild refused to cooperate with the intendant on this, Maboul suggested that Phillippot be given a bookseller position. Maboul, Tourny, and D'Aguesseau struggled with this problem and, at one point, a ruse was contemplated: Phillippot could make a request to appeal the intendant's order to close him down, and the intendant would then suspend the execution of the closure order pending the outcome of an appeal. Phillippot could then work while waiting for the appeal to be heard, and that could be deliberately delayed for a very long time. If the guild pressured the intendant to decide the appeal, he would continue to stall, claiming not to have had the time to study the case or that he had express orders from the chancellor not to decide the affair. Phillippot continued to have difficulties but remained in the printing business. Confusion surrounding a fiscal measure, in fact, gave him an entry into the printing business that it is hard to imagine he would have obtained otherwise. It most certainly would never have happened without the support of D'Aguesseau.

Had the Bordeaux guild members been able to make a case against Phillip-pot for clandestine trading, they could have damaged his support in D'Agues-seau's department, a tactic that they used successfully against another unwanted outsider with Paris connections, Jacques Merlin.[49] Many factors affected D'Aguesseau's support for a given printer, and we know nothing about most of them, but Merlin's story suggests how political reliability could come into play. D'Aguesseau was drawn into a protracted struggle between the Bordeaux guild and Merlin, the brother of a Parisian publisher who tried to set up in Bordeaux. Merlin, a native of Toulouse who had apprenticed there, began his quest to be admitted as a bookseller in Bordeaux in 1728 but encountered stiff resistance from the guild, which claimed that he was only a bookbinder. In 1732 he married a Bordeaux bookseller's daughter and tried again, this time traveling to Paris to get support at Court. The Bordeaux guild informed D'Aguesseau that this unqualified journeyman binder could not be considered for admittance to their guild for lack of skill. In any event, they added, there were too many booksellers in their town, forcing some to sell wicked books. They wanted to reserve places for their children, whom they sent to *collèges* and who were, by implication, not ignorant like Merlin. At D'Aguesseau's request, Boucher, then the intendant of Guyenne, investigated this affair. He inter-viewed Merlin and discovered that he could not read a passage in the Bible in Latin, so he asked D'Aguesseau to forbid the local police to admit Merlin. The guild officials, however, still fearing that Merlin would get around the rules, hired a lawyer, who obtained an audience with d'Argenson and requested a decree officially denying Merlin the right to be a bookseller in Bordeaux. In 1743 Merlin appealed again to D'Aguesseau, who wrote to the intendant. But Boucher, by this time, had softened his stance and suggested some mercy for Merlin: D'Aguesseau could—just this once and by *grâce*—allow Merlin to work as a bookseller in the town. This opinion prevailed, and in January 1744 the jurats swore Merlin in. The guild refused to accept his 200-livre admission fee and appealed to the Parlement of Bordeaux, but lost. They then asked to have the affair transferred to the Privy Council, which quashed the parlementary decree in July 1746. In the meantime, however, guild officials, who had never accepted Merlin, raided his premises and seized Protestant and Jansenist books. On this news, D'Aguesseau granted Tourny (Boucher's successor as intendant) complete authority to try the case. Merlin fled, but Tourny convicted him and sentenced him *in absentia* to fines, the stocks, banishment from the province of Guyenne for six years, and expulsion from the book trade. In November, a Privy Council order declared Merlin's admission as a bookseller by the jurats to be worthless. The two cases—the criminal prosecution handled by intendant Tourny, and the licensing suit handled by the chancellor and settled by Privy Council order—brought an end to Jacques Merlin's aspirations in 1748. They illustrate nicely how the battle against the clandestine trade relied heavily on self-serving policing and denunciations from competitors sent directly to Paris or Versailles. While the incentive to condemn illicit books was no doubt spawned by a genuine fear of immorality and sedition, strategic considerations—fostered by the licensing policy—also played a role.

Guillaume de Lamoignon de Blancmesnil was no less vigilant when he was chancellor (1750–63) and supervised the book trade with his son Chrétien-Guillaume de Lamoignon de Malesherbes.[50] Malesherbes has earned celebrity for his liberal treatment of Enlightenment authors in this critical decade, but his generous attitude did not extend to loosening the printer licensing policy. Although he was not involved in the licensing decisions, Malesherbes subjected the policy to characteristically thoughtful examination and offered his views on the criteria used to select printers. Three factors were to be considered: ability, wealth, and, most important, personal qualities. Wealth mattered because prosperous printers would only very rarely risk their fortunes in the clandestine trade; the loss of the authorization to print would be a heavy penalty for such men to pay. But, he argued, the personal qualities of the candidates were the most important to consider, and here he meant something like loyalty and intelligence. It would be unjust, in his view, to eliminate a candidate for being too poor. For Malesherbes, while the king always favored sons of outgoing printers, and it would be wrong to do otherwise, they did not succeed "by right." The requirement of a license served as an element of control on sons who were unreliable.[51] Malesherbes also advised against the practice of allowing widows automatic succession to their husbands' positions, because this meant that there was no control over them; he wanted the qualifications of widows assessed as well.

Malesherbes examined the arguments for further reducing the number of printer's licenses. From the point of view of commerce, he said, he was against quotas and reductions. The printing business should be left free because it was too difficult to decide on the optimal number of printers and because the positions did not always go to the right people. However, from the point of view of police and administration, Malesherbes believed that two arguments for reducing the number of printers deserved serious attention. The first was Chauvelin's: those with ample work were less tempted by illegal trade. Malesherbes disagreed with this line of reasoning because it was difficult for the government to determine the right number of printers for any given region or to make estimates for the future, and this ability was necessary if the purpose was to ensure that all printers were gainfully employed with authorized printing. Also, since printers could have as many presses and workers as they wanted, and very large printing houses were allowed to exist, the ceilings placed on printer numbers did not necessarily ensure that the printing in a region would be shared in such a way as to eliminate poor printers. Malesherbes was more influenced by the second argument for reduction: the greater ease with which a small number of printers could be supervised. He therefore supported quotas, but for different reasons than those proposed by Chauvelin. Malesherbes wanted concentrations of printers in specified areas of the realm that could be effectively policed. This meant allowing more printers in large centers and fewer or none in the smaller towns. Rather than thirty-six printers in Paris and one in Senlis, he said, it would be better to have forty in Paris, because it was as easy to police forty in Paris as thirty-six. In Senlis, on the other hand, no one could be expected to pay much attention to printing: one could not ask for vigilance and severity from local judges who had nothing to gain or fear from the royal government and who were more interested in getting along with their fellow townsmen. Only in towns with intendants could the policing of printers be effective. Local authorities, he claimed, had neither the general perspective on printing matters that came from direct contact with the ministry nor the authority to act that the intendants possessed. Malesherbes cited the example of a printer in Auxerre who sold large numbers of Jansenist works. When the bishop who had been protecting him died, the printer panicked and confessed his illegal activity to the authorities. Malesherbes wished that the law would let him abolish the license in Auxerre and permit the man to set up as the thirty-seventh printer in Paris; the printer would be delighted with such a turn of events, and he would be easy to control. Malesherbes was not willing, however, in the 1750s, to propose a radical reform of the system, and he finished the discussion rather weakly by arguing that the state should take whatever opportunity arose—with the bankruptcy of a printer, for example—to remove printers from small towns, even if it provoked the ire of local protectors and bishops.

Later in his memorandum, Malesherbes anticipated the objection that he was unduly worried about printers in small towns when most of the wicked books and fraud were in Paris, Lyon, and especially Rouen. He replied that, as measures were implemented in Paris, the *fraudeurs* would try to flee to the provinces and, consequently, the lack of policing in the provinces would become a more serious problem. Malesherbes thus subjected printer licensing to serious assessment, and his reasons for reducing the number of printers differed from those of earlier administrators. He seemed to have been saying that if the policing powers of the state were stronger, then there would be no need to fix printer numbers. While he believed the Parisian guild's rhetoric about a countryside inundated with illegal books, he distanced himself from parts of their traditional position: he did not offer quality-control arguments to justify the printer quotas, nor did he seem confident that a certain level of wealth would assure printers' adherence to the rules. Furthermore, he rejected the hoary myth put about by the printer lobby that there had been a golden era in the past when the book trade was well regulated and had prospered. He knew that it had not been well regulated in the past and that better methods of control and increased police supervision were needed.

Malesherbes believed in printer licensing, but it would not have mattered greatly if he had not because licensing was handled by his father, Chancellor Lamoignon, and members of the bureau contentieux. His influence on printer appointments can only have been indirect. The men who made these decisions—Lamoignon, assisted by Machault, Maboul, and D'Aguesseau, the masters of requests—had no qualms about printer licensing or the need to thin out the ranks of provincial printers. In 1758, Lamoignon conducted yet another printer census and legislated further cuts in their numbers. Writing to the intendants in March 1758, he reported that his sources had informed him that in several cities in the realm there were more printers than allowed by the 1739 ceilings, that some printers were printing without valid licenses, and that some, who had only lifetime positions, were trying to pass on their printing businesses to their children. A census, he claimed, would indicate the special circumstances that might justify temporarily suspending the 1739 quotas or, conversely, identify printers who were not needed and should be closed down.[52] When the census was complete and examined by his men, Lamoignon issued one decree for each *généralité,* reiterating previous legislation on printer ceilings and making additional cuts in printer numbers.[53] In Languedoc, three positions were abolished: those of Carcassonne, Castelnaudary, and Bourg-Saint-Andéol.

Brittany lost two and so did Rouen. In the *généralité* of Lyon, the printer position in the town of Montbrison was suppressed, and cuts were made in the *généralités* of Tours, Dijon, Franche-Comté, Lille, Limoges, and Metz. In some cases, new printer positions were created: Calais, for example, got one, and so did Pamiers.

Lamoignon found solutions to conflicts about printer appointments in the provinces—sometimes by negotiating them, and sometimes by simply imposing them. The 1758 census in Bordeaux brought to his attention the informal arrangements by which his predecessor had managed to allow the printer Phillippot to continue in business despite the guild's opposition. Unhappy with the irregularity, but sensitive to Phillippot's situation, he promised to give him the first vacant position in Bordeaux to which no son or son-in-law made a claim. When Phillippot requested a bookseller position directly from him because the guild was so hostile, Lamoignon backed him unreservedly: no one was to oppose Phillippot's desire to be a bookseller, and he should be treated as a son of a master printer. Lamoignon intervened in printer appointments in other provincial towns, too. In Toulouse he protected a printer from guild hostility.[54] In 1752, when two printers claimed the single printer position allowed in Saint-Malo, Lamoignon denied the mayor's proposal to license them both but avoided choosing between the two, declaring that the printing position of the first printer who died would be extinguished.[55] In Rennes, the 1739 decree reduced the number of printers to four, causing a major struggle for a position among the three sons of Gilles-Joseph Vatar.[56]

Possibly influenced by his son's views on printers in small towns, Lamoignon insisted on closing the only printing house in Sarlat, a small diocesan town in the Dordogne.[57] Malesherbes was very worried about unsupervised printers in small towns, and Sarlat was just this sort of town.[58] When Lamoignon took over the duties of chancellor, he entered into what was already an ongoing struggle over whether a printer should be allowed in Sarlat. Decrees of 1704 and 1739 had denied Sarlat a printer place, and Lamoignon used his influence to see that no printer would be allowed there. The story of Sarlat's quest to procure a printer position against royal opposition is rather long and detailed, but it illustrates Lamoignon's determination. A printer from Agen named Jean-Jacques Coulembet had set up business in Sarlat in 1692 as printers were proliferating in provincial France, generally working as clients of bishops, colleges, courts, or administrators. Unfortunately for Coulembet, the 1704 quotas eliminated the printing position in Sarlat, although officials did allow him to continue in the trade to the end of his life. At the time of the 1737 census, he was still there, working for the tax collectors and for the clergy. Following orders in 1743 from the intendant, the subdelegate investigated and found the aging printer doing a little official printing and printing pastoral instructions for the bishop. The subdelegate saw no harm in letting him continue and offered to check on him from time to time. Then, in 1745, the bishop in Sarlat, Denis Alexandre Le Blanc (1721–47), decided that Coulembet was too old and revoked his title as bishop's printer, giving it to Jean-Baptiste Ferrand, who had formerly worked for Coulembet and had bought presses in Toulouse. Coulembet denounced the bishop's decision in a letter to intendant Tourny, contending that the bishop had contravened a royal decree that gave Coulombet the exclusive right to print in Sarlat until he died. He had clearly been entertaining plans to ignore the 1704 decree and to pass on his business to his nephew, Charles Planton d'Issart, a printer in Agen. When he applied for a printer's license for his nephew, his request was denied. The bishop continued to support Ferrand, as did others, including the subdelegate Jully, who wrote that Coulembet had grown so old and crochety that he could not keep any workers and had even chased Ferrand from his printing house. Much better, argued Jully, to allow Ferrand to print, as he was a young, responsible, and intelligent man whose work was needed by the diocese and the tax collectors. But Tourny refused to have any printer at all in Sarlat. Lamoignon was drawn into this dispute when he learned that a printer named Robin had apparently taken over Ferrand's struggle to survive as a printer in Sarlat. He sent orders to intendant Tourny to have Robin's presses seized immediately because the 1739 decree allowed no printer there. The presses were taken to the town hall in Sarlat and locked away, and Robin was given three months to sell them to licensed printers. This was a very "sad event," Jully reported to Tourny, because Sarlat needed a printer for the bishop, tax collectors, and occasionally for the subdelegate. The 1739 ruling had, in his view, strangely denied a printer to Sarlat when there had been a printer there for many years and it was very inconvenient to send printing orders to Bordeaux. Lamoignon was adamant, however: reestablishing a printer in the town by infringing on the 1739 decree was out of the question, and he asked the intendant to see that no printer set up in Sarlat under any pretext whatsoever. If Robin was qualified as a bookseller, he could make a living selling books in Sarlat.

Between 1763 and 1774, René-Charles de Maupeou and his son René-Nicolas de Maupeou were in charge of printer licensing.[59] Both were assisted by Sartine, director of the book trade from 1763 to 1774 (before being appointed navy secretary).[60] All three men cared deeply about printing in the provinces. In 1764 the elder Maupeou ordered a census of all printers and booksellers in France, an undertaking that had, by then, become almost standard practice when a new chancellor or keeper of the seals was appointed.[61] As he explained to reluctant officials in Strasbourg, these survey results were necessary for the "execution of his general plan." Four years later, in 1768, he ordered yet another census of all printers, explaining in customary formulaic terms that the king had been informed of a considerable trade in the provinces in books against religion, morality, and the tranquillity of the state. Before producing more rules, Maupeou thought it best to first place ceilings on the number of booksellers in every town in the realm. These were to be set in proportion to the needs of the inhabitants and to the size of the book export industry in a given town. Bookselling was to be placed in the hands of licensed men who sold no other merchandise than books and were under the immediate juris-diction of the chancellor or keeper of the seals. Those convicted of selling dangerous books were to be expelled from the trade.[62] In September 1768 he was impatient for the Bordeaux survey results he needed to design his reform proposals for the book trade, a project described as close to the king's heart (*fort à coeur*) and an important means of ending the abuses in the book trade. In 1772 the younger Maupeou ordered yet another census of printers. This time he wanted a list of every book being printed and the nature of the print-ing authorization granted, something he thought local officials were failing to provide. One can detect an element of frustration on the part of the subdele-gates in the smaller towns in Guyenne who, tired of writing detailed reports on printers, began resubmitting information collected in a previous census.

Both the elder and younger Maupeou were drawn into a number of dis-putes in provincial towns over the granting of printer's licenses. In the 1760s the elder Maupeou handled a highly disputed contest among three candidates for a position that became available in Bordeaux on the sudden death of Pierre Brun, the head of a large business that handled a major part of the town's administrative printing. Pierre Phillippot took the opportunity to make a case for himself based on merit, family entitlement, and Lamoignon's promise of the first position available where there was no son or son-in-law making a claim. To try to make a son-in-law claim, the Brun family rapidly married their daughter Eleanor—who was in fact running the business—to Michel Racle, a member of a medical family from Mont-de-Marsan. A third candidate, Paul

Lavignac, was a son-in-law of a printer and had the technical expertise, but withdrew early from the competition. Maupeou had to make the difficult choice between Racle and Phillippot. On the one hand, he was influenced by the intendant, who looked favorably upon Racle because of the Brun family's stature in Bordeaux along with the size of its business and its long history of doing administrative and religious printing. To deny Racle the position was to deny the daughter her patrimony. Nevertheless, Maupeou decided to respect Lamoignon's promise, and he gave the position to Phillippot. The intendant then went about finding ways to keep Racle's business alive.[63]

Maupeou the elder took printer licensing seriously. In 1764, he inquired into what seemed to him a suspicious arrangement whereby Jean-Florent Baour had moved from Pamiers to Toulouse by trading places with Jean-Pierre Faye. Was there some secret motive behind the deal? The subdelegate allayed his fears, explaining that Faye had had difficulties in Toulouse, undoubtedly connected to the guild's hostility, when he tried to move there from Brives.[64] In 1766 he gave the master of requests, Bertier de Sauvigny, the task of communicating to Miromesnil and his protégé, Jacques-Joseph Le Boullenger in Rouen, that the latter's request to be exempted from the licensing formalities was being denied; it was important that printers' sons fear being excluded from the printing business and not regard themselves as automatically entitled to their fathers' licenses.[65] In 1770, when a printer from Dax tried to obtain a printer's license for Bordeaux, Maupeou the younger had to settle the dispute that arose between the guild and the jurats over the appointment. The jurats in Bordeaux complained that there was a shortage of printing capacity there because two printers, Simon Lacourt and Phillippot, were holding two positions each and that two of the remaining printers were not well equipped. Long delays, monopolies, and high prices were the result. The guild, of course, moved quickly to make the typical representations that there were too many printers and that the clandestine trade was always tempting in such situations. Maupeou the younger initially agreed that a competition (*concours*) should be held, but the printers were persuasive and, in 1772, he reduced the number of printers in Bordeaux from ten to eight.[66] Maupeou added an extra printer position in Nîmes because the town was to be the seat of a *cour supérieure,* part of his controversial reforms of the judicial system in the years 1771 to 1774.[67] Like their predecessors, both Maupeous sought to impose order on the book and printing trades in the realm and regarded printer licensing and supervision as essential to their success.

Armand Thomas Hüe de Miromesnil was appointed keeper of the seals by Maurepas in 1774, at the beginning of the reign of Louis XVI, and retained the position until 1787.[68] Prior to this appointment, he had been a master of requests and then first president of the Parlement of Rouen, a position that included responsibility for the book trade in Normandy.[69] Later, when he became keeper of the seals, his Norman origins and his close contact with the Rouen printers influenced his approach to the book trade. Miromesnil never accepted the notion that pirated and prohibited books presented similar threats to public order, and he was very suspicious of Parisian versions of book trade regulation that tended to highlight decisions favoring the Parisian lobby and to glorify the administrators responsible for them. The Parisians wanted to say, for example, that the celebrated abbé Bignon favored copyright renewals, but Miromesnil revised this version of legal history, claiming that Bignon actually wanted to allow more liberty in the book trade and that it was Maboul (and not Bignon) who had favored the Parisians' claims on copyrights, forcing provincial publishers into illegality.[70] Miromesnil named another Norman, Le Camus de Néville, as his director of the book trade from 1776 to 1784. Unlike Malesherbes, Le Camus de Néville was a member of both the bureau gracieux and the bureau contentieux and consequently supervised printer licensing as well as all other aspects of book trade regulation.[71]

Miromesnil's previous experience in Rouen almost certainly conditioned his thinking on book trade issues when he became keeper of the seals and undertook reform of the book trade in 1777, a move well known for the serious opposition it incurred from the Paris guild because it limited the Parisians' ability to renew their copyrights.[72] Miromesnil and Le Camus de Néville withstood tremendous opposition from the Paris guild when they carried out this reform. Miromesnil was unhesitating in his support of printer quotas and licensing. In 1775, just after he became keeper of the seals, he ordered what was to be the last printer and bookseller census in the *ancien régime*. Between 1775 and 1787, he decided many disputes over printer appointments in the provinces and generally believed in holding competitions to award them.[73] He wrote in 1775 to Saint-Priest, the intendant of Toulouse: "I believe that it is important to maintain the *loi des concours* for printer places."[74] On a number of occasions he struggled to weigh family and competence claims when determining appointments. In 1784 he annulled a competition for a printer place in Béziers because it had not been sufficiently publicized and because the intendant had indicated that he feared favoritism toward the son of a bookseller in Nîmes.[75]

In some cases Miromesnil did forego competitions.[76] In general, he made decisions in close cooperation with the intendants (or, in the case of Rouen, with the first president of the Parlement of Rouen) and asserted administrative control over printer appointments.

Between 1777 and 1783 he was drawn into several struggles in Bordeaux among the jurats, the guild, and the intendant over the handling of competitions. Against resistance from the jurats in 1777, he sought to protect the right of Jean-Baptiste Séjourné to replace his mother.[77] In 1783, his irritation with the Bordeaux guild is clear; he ordered it to stop stalling and proceed with a competition for the vacant position that arose because of the death of Marie Dubois, the widow Calamy. Eight candidates had applied to him. When he sent the candidates' dossiers to the intendant he made it clear that one candidate, Alexis Levieux, was to be included even though the guild officers would object because he was not a local man. He instructed the guild officers to write a report on the examination in which they could make any comments they wished, but they were not allowed to exclude anyone. Miromesnil made it explicit that the choice was his: "It is I alone who decides after taking into consideration their observations on merit and capacity." When the guild officers tried to stall, the intendant, Nicolas Dupré de Saint Maur, and Miromesnil forced them to go ahead with the examinations. Dupré was not at all happy with their report and informed Miromesnil that the guild had deliberately favored candidates who had neither the talent nor the means to mount serious printing businesses.[78] Dupré suggested that, while it would be costly, a more impartial assessment could be done in Paris. It could in fact be combined with the competition for the next printer vacancy, which had just occurred at the death of the printer Jean Chappuis. Miromesnil decided, however, to give the license to the son of the widow Calamy but to be more vigilant in the upcoming Chappuis competition; he ordered the documents, examinations, and other materials for all eight candidates to be sent to him and, after reading the damning report sent from the intendant, Miromesnil balked at all of these candidates, annulled the competition by an order in council of the Conseil des Dépêches, and in 1785 appointed his own protégé, a printer in Nîmes named Pierre Beaume who had previously obtained royal favor to set up there. Miromesnil exempted Beaume from all formalities required for admission to the Bordeaux printers' and booksellers' guild.[79]

The issue of printers in small towns reemerged in these years, with the existence of printers in Bergerac and Sarlat causing much anxiety. In 1775 Pierre

Dalvy, the printer in Périgueux, denounced a certain Jean-Baptiste Puynesge for having a press in Bergerac when no printer was allowed there. Adhering to the orthodoxy that a printer could not make a living in such a town and would consequently be forced to sell pirated and prohibited books, Miromesnil ordered Puynesge's presses seized and sold to another printer.[80] Miromesnil, too, finally decided the century-long dispute over the wisdom of having a printer in Sarlat.[81] In 1772 the son of the printer Robin, whose presses Lamoignon had ordered seized in 1758, was benefiting from the support of the subdelegate and the bishop to print there without a license. The bishop made a major effort to obtain a printer's license for the town in 1775 but, despite pressure from the duc de Mouchy (maréchal de France and lieutenant general of the province of Guyenne), the bishop, the intendant, and the subdelegate, Miromesnil was reluctant to allow Sarlat a printer. The subdelegate, who energetically sought the license, may have unwittingly hurt François Robin's case by admitting that it was impossible to provide guarantees that printers would not engage in the clandestine trade. He added, very reasonably, that these temptations were not restricted to small towns like Sarlat but existed even in the big towns. It took ten more years, a new bishop, and much more lobbying for Miromesnil to finally create a printer's license for Sarlat in September 1785. But to the dismay of the bishop, who thought he should be able to place his protégé in the position, Miromesnil told the intendant to have the Bordeaux police and guild officers run a competition to fill it. In important ways, Miromesnil shared the ideas of most eighteenth-century ministers: because of their power, the media needed to be managed in their own special way.

The unprecedented success of the printer survey in 1700 reflects Pontchartrain's determination to rein in illegal printers and the willingness and ability of intendants and lieutenants of police in the provincial towns to carry it out. The census provided royal officials with vast amounts of information about printers in the French provinces, much of it suggesting that printing there was an unregulated and potentially dangerous force. If there was any hope of making printers into a professional body of licensed and rule-abiding men, much had to change. The reports of illiterate men selling books alongside groceries offered fabulous ammunition for the Parisian guild, which argued that regulation in the provinces was necessary to preserve religion, the king, the state, and morality. The 1700 census results contributed to the growing jurisdiction of the Bureau de la librairie, which allowed the chancellor or keeper of the seals and a number of specialized royal officials in Versailles and Paris to manage the details of printer regulation until the French Revolution.

The Bureau de la librairie must be situated in the larger history of the expansion of government in eighteenth-century France.[82] Through it the monarchy extended its control over books, printing, printers, and booksellers and interfered with the traditional bodies that had been regulating printers in the preceding two centuries: printers' guilds, municipal governments and local courts, bishops and other noble patrons, and, finally, the parlements. Local initiative played an important role in this process. Individual printers and guild officers sought the intervention of the royal councils to settle disputes, thus drawing them into the decisions. As in other activities of the absolute state, much negotiation took place between the guilds, the printers, the patrons, the local police, and royal officials. But, in addition to negotiation, the government did not hesitate to impose its authority directly as it took greater and greater initiative in assuring ideological control. In some of these initiatives, we see efforts to work in conjunction with the parlements; this was attempted on the matter of Parisian printer quotas and D'Aguesseau tried, in 1723, to issue the Code de la librairie as a declaration registered by the Parlement of Paris. Malesherbes, too, wanted book trade legislation that was approved by the parlements. But these efforts failed, and the legislation generally took the form of orders of the Privy Council and the Conseil des Dépêches—both councils that had been used historically to bypass opposition to royal legislation from the parlements and to reduce the parlements' power. In book trade matters of the late seventeenth century—more than in some other matters—the royal councils were willing to change the venue by which disputes were decided and to settle them by royal council decrees. By the reigns of Louis XV and Louis XVI, the Bureau de la librairie had regularized this trend and made the deciding of book trade matters by the royal councils an accepted norm. Chancellors, keepers of the seals, and bureau members believed that they had complete jurisdiction over all book trade matters and—while their power to approve or ban books was challenged on occasion—there was little organized opposition to their authority to set quotas and license and discipline printers. Administrators shared a deeply ingrained understanding that wealthy and secure printers would be less likely than poorer ones to sell forbidden books and that licensing was the way to ensure that printers were wealthy and loyal. Only Malesherbes seems to have questioned this assumption. However, there is no evidence that his reservations had any influence on others.

4

THE PURGES

The Enforcement of Printer Quotas in the Provinces After 1704

[I]l est nécessaire qu'il y ait des Imprimeurs-Libraires pour le bien de son service &
l'utilité du Public. . . . [I]l est dangereux qu'il ne s'en établisse un trop grand nombre, de
crainte que ne trouvant pas assez d'Ouvrages pour pouvoir subsister, ils ne s'appliquent
à des contrefaçons, ou à d'autres impressions contraires au bon ordre.
—*Arrêt du conseil, 21 July 1704*

Pour la gloire de la religion, le soutien des moeurs et l'honneur de la communauté, il
est absolument indispensable de la purger des membres qui en sont l'opprobre.
—*Lyon book trade inspector Bourgelat to Sartine, 24 December 1763*

C'est donc attenter en quelque sorte à l'autorité de Sa Majesté, que d'entreprendre
d'exercer l'Imprimerie sans avoir obtenu l'attache du Prince . . .
—*Mémoire pour Pierre Phillippot . . . contre Michel Racle . . . , c. 1770*

Printer licensing was introduced unevenly into the provincial towns; by 1700,
it was respected in some and unknown in others. As dire reports of abuses
poured into the Bureau de la librairie, officials intensified their efforts to
increase compliance and, in 1704, Pontchartrain decided to take licensing one
step further by setting into law printer quotas for every town in France. Earlier ceilings had limited the number of printers allowed to work in certain
towns: in Toulouse, the number was fixed at 12 in 1622, in Paris at 36 in 1686,
in Bordeaux at 12 in 1688, and in Lyon at 18 in 1695. While confirming these
numbers for the larger towns, the order of 21 July 1704 fixed numbers for *all*

towns in France. Vacancies that arose were to be assessed by officials in Versailles who, if they decided to fill them, ordered competitions. The successful candidates would obtain lifetime positions; on their deaths, these positions would revert to the king to be reissued. Pontchartrain's idea—as we saw in chapter 3—was to permit enough printers for the service of the king and *l'utilité public* but no more, lest they engage in pirating and other illegal printing. The order purged the provincial printing corps by reducing the number of legal printing houses in France between 1701 and 1764 from 411 to 309; in the provinces, this reduced the number of printing houses by about one-third, from 360 to 248.[1] In Lyon, where the 1701 census revealed 30 printing houses, the 1704 order in council allowed only 18. In Rouen, 29 printing houses were ordered reduced to 18. The licensing requirement had already affected the lives of many provincial printers, especially in Lyon, but the quotas were to have far-reaching effects for all printers as well as their families and descendants. The process of reducing the number of printers created much conflict. In some cases, the cuts meant that existing printing houses were closed down, and the pain was felt immediately. More often, surplus printers were permitted to continue working, with the provision that their positions would be abolished when they died or resigned; the next generation, then, felt the effects, as sons could not follow in their fathers' footsteps. The victims were many, both inside and outside the trade. Printing families were fortunate if they could place one child in the printing business, leaving brothers and sisters to search elsewhere for professions. Journeymen, who already had a difficult task obtaining licenses, lost hope; after 1704, the number of towns in France in which a journeyman could obtain a printer's license became very small indeed. The major beneficiaries of quotas were the chosen sons of printers, who henceforth dominated the printers' ranks at the expense of many other candidates.

This chapter provides a detailed look at the implementation of the 1704 ceilings in provincial towns, paying particular attention to the larger printing centers. The bureau issued—in the form of orders of the Privy Council—official lists of the names of printers allowed to print in a number of towns. These lists, dating from 1705 to 1712, effected what I have rather dramatically called the "printer purges" of the late reign of Louis XIV.[2] Two of the most important of these came to Lyon and Rouen in the year 1709.[3] Case studies of the implementation of the 1704 quotas show, first, the importance of local interests that wanted the quotas respected. Second, they reveal the ways in which the positions of printers, and more especially of guild officers, were transformed to take on some of the characteristics of royal offices, encouraging their holders to construct an identity suited to loyal subjects of the king who promoted the interests of Versailles in their localities. Some of these men slipped very far into this role. Finally, they show the role of three arms of the growing bureaucratic state in implementing the purges and printer licensing generally: the lieutenants of police, the intendants, and the book trade inspectors.

Lyon

Although the Lyonnais had been applying quotas on printer numbers for close to a decade before 1704, printers resisted the desired shrinkage. The declaration of 1695 had set the number at eighteen and, although both officials and printers took the idea of quotas seriously, ways were found to circumvent the ceilings. Claude Martin, the son of a Lyon printer—whose widowed mother had sold him the printing business and ceded her printing mastership to him in 1693—struggled for years to obtain a printer's license. Martin had been frustrated more than once by the new licensing rules his generation had to face. Because of the 1667 ban, guild officials had denied him entry into the guild. He then applied to the chancellor, who asked the intendant to decide the matter. When he finally obtained the intendant's support, it was 1695, the year of the declaration that restricted the number of printers in Lyon to eighteen. So, again, no license was awarded. The intendant's favorable opinion meant that he was able to continue to work with no official authorization but, when the 1701 survey revealed many extra printers in Lyon, the obstacles facing him seemed daunting. In 1703, at the death of Jean Goy, Martin again requested a license, saying that he had always acquitted himself in the profession with honor and paid his guild fees. In July, he obtained a preliminary order to present his titles before the lieutenant of police in the presence of the guild officers. On receiving the lieutenant of police's report, the bureau eventually decided in Martin's favor and, in October, a Privy Council order licensed Martin. At the same time, several other Lyon printers requested licenses, making it very difficult to reduce the number of printers in the town.[4]

In 1709, bureau officials made a major effort to enforce the Lyon quotas. The Lyon guild officials initiated the purge by complaining to the chancellor in 1708 that, despite their many efforts, abuses were still rampant in the Lyon book trade and they were counting on the king to put a stop to them.[5] The

1704 ceiling of eighteen was not being respected. Surplus printers, who did not have the necessary qualifications, continued to print and sell books, behaving as if they were masters, receiving apprentices, pirating all sorts of books, and selling defective and immoral ones. In the meantime, a small number of legitimate printers were paying all the taxes. The arguments in this guild complaint were varied and intended to alarm officials on many levels: royal laws were being broken, unqualified workers were printing, defective books were being made, pirating and immorality were rampant, and taxation was unfair. The lieutenant of police was ordered to investigate and take statements from the guild officers and from printers about their "titles" and "capacities." By November 1708, twenty-six printers had provided statements to the lieutenant of police, who reported all this to the bureau, which issued in 1709 an official statement of the status of the printers allowed to print in Lyon.[6] Of the twenty-six claimants, fifteen printers would be licensed immediately. Officials would continue to assess the cases of eight more. The eight printers still under consideration—Claude Martin, Claude Justet, Mathieu Valençol, André Molin, Sébastien Roux, Claude Moulu, César Chappuis, and Benoît Vignieu—were to present their cases for licenses. In 1712 the final word came: only four of the eight would be licensed (along with three others—Jean Baptiste Rolland, Pierre Bailly, and Marcelin Sibert), and the other four were to close down. Royal officials thus stated who could and who could not print in Lyon. Printer regulation had reached new heights.[7]

A look at the eight printers whose cases were put on hold in 1709 provides some sense of how the purge played out in Lyon. These men, whom we can only imagine to have been in a state of panic, brought everything they had to bear in their petitions to the chancellor. The fifty-year-old Mathieu Valençol included an inventory of his mother-in-law's printing equipment, valued at 4,640 livres, and certificates from the guild officials that he ran the mother-in-law's printing house and printed only permitted books. He also included evidence that the guild had promised him the first vacant place and that he was paying the guild fees. In 1707 he had been denied a license but, in subsequent petitions, was clearly at pains to counter the arguments made by other candidates, notably by Rolland and Bailly, and to show that his altercations with the authorities for illicit printing were a thing of the past.[8] Valençol was licensed in 1712 along with Martin, Molin, and Justet. These four were among those who came out of the ordeal with strengthened claims because, once they were licensed, guild officers could no longer close them down. Justet, for example, had encountered interference from guild officers who seized books he was selling in 1710 and was undoubtedly grateful to be protected from such incidents in the future.

On 15 May 1711, the guild officers moved to obtain confirmation that the four others—Sébastien Roux, Claude Moulu, César Chappuis, and Benoît Vignieu—were definitively excluded from the trade. The cases of Moulu, Vignieu, and Chappuis offer sad stories. On 25 January 1712, a Privy Council order closed their printing houses down on pain of a one-thousand-livre fine, confiscation of their equipment, and their being made ineligible for any future vacancies. The order was carried out the following June. The three appealed to the chancellor in December 1712 and, over the next two years, both they and the guild officials submitted many memoranda, each side presenting its version of the facts. Unfortunately, all had convictions for pirating, having been denounced in 1702 by the Lyon bookseller Baritel and by Parisian publishers. Vignieu, in addition, was accused of selling prohibited works.[9] When Moulu, the forty-seven-year-old son of a printer in Lyon, applied in 1710 for the vacancy that occurred on the death of the printer Pierre Thened, he received an order to close instead of a license.[10] Vignieu, at seventy, with a long career as a master behind him, claimed that he had been in the guild, paid dues, was fully equipped, and had even trained several apprentices. How could the guild warden do this to him? Vignieu was probably a man of an earlier era who thought that he could ignore the seemingly unnecessary exercise of applying for a royal license and was shocked to find himself locked out of the trade. He claimed in his submission that, because he could not get justice from the warden and his deputy, he was turning to the king. Countering his petition was Baritel's report that Vignieu's books had been seized by the Parisian publishers Pralard, Emery, and Guérin and their agents; that he had not satisfied the penalties levied against him by a decree of the Parlement of Paris; and that he had continued to print while more worthy men were denied access to the profession. Neither Vignieu nor Moulu was granted a license.

Chappuis was denied a license because he had pirated and printed prohibited books, and there is enough information on him to present a fuller picture of this victim of the new licensing policy. In a petition to the chancellor,[11] Chappuis told his story of decades of persecution by the Lyon and Paris guild officers: after completing his apprenticeship in Lyon in 1665, he married the daughter of a master, who gave him his printing equipment. In 1681 he was admitted to the guild as a master. His problems establishing himself as a printer in Lyon went back to the declaration of April 1695, which fixed the quota of eighteen printers for the town. At the time, the warden and his deputy ordered everyone to present their titles to the lieutenant general of police, but guild officers were reluctant to include Chappuis, who was forced to protest and, on 6 September 1697, the lieutenant of police ordered the guild officers to justify their opposition within a month or accept him as a legitimate member of the guild. The warden failed to do this, so Chappuis became one of the eighteen legitimate printers in Lyon. When the 1708 order required all printers to present their titles, Chappuis had done so, but the new guild officials were against him and wanted him forbidden from printing because of his record as a pirate and illegal printer.

Chappuis had indeed been convicted of pirating on several occasions. While his most immediate problem was that he had been expelled from the printing business by royal order of 16 February 1705, this was far from the first time he had been in trouble with the authorities for illegal printing.[12] In 1693 the Paris guild officers, Denis Thierry and Guillaume Desprez, reported to bureau officials that De Sève, the lieutenant of police in Lyon, had gone to the home of Chappuis and discovered that he was printing the fourth volume of *Essais de Sermons* by abbé de Bretteville, a work for which Thierry had the rights. At the same time he was found printing the second volume of *Cas de Conscience,* for which Desprez had the rights. In their report, the Parisians made it clear that Chappuis was an habitual offender who had been arrested several times and even banished. Apparently, he had been banned from the printing business in 1683, and in 1691 he was implicated when a Parisian publisher, André Pralard, seized fifty-six bundles of pirated and prohibited books.[13] It was said that Louis' minister, François-Michel Le Tellier, marquis de Louvois, had ordered Chappuis imprisoned for six months. Thierry and Desprez claimed that current law already gave them the right to have the lieutenant of police in Lyon seize and sell Chappuis' presses. But, as an extra sign of their submission to the king, they requested an additional and specific royal order for the seizure—a sign, no doubt, that Chappuis had supporters in Lyon who had been protecting him for many years. In 1702 Chappuis was caught printing Rodrigues' *Pratique de la perfection Chrétienne* and was convicted by the lieutenant of police in Lyon.[14] The lieutenant of police fined him 150 livres and ordered his printing house closed for two months, the books pulped, and the fonts used in the pirating sold for the profit of the Lyon hospital. Chappuis appealed this sentence to the presidial court in Lyon, which blocked its execution. However, a Privy Council

order quashed the decision of the presidial, ordered the sentence of the lieutenant of police executed, and forbade the presidial officers to overturn the
lieutenant of police's sentences. After the presidial was denied a role in the
policing of printers, Chappuis was clearly more vulnerable; in October and
November 1704, the Lyon guild officers carried out inspection tours and
reported his lack of cooperation and his many infractions of the rules to the
chancellor.[15] Chappuis would not let them enter the printing house, for example, and had his journeyman use force to keep the door closed until he had
time to break his printing forms and hide his paper. When they did get inside
the printing house, they found a page of the *Mémoires d'Artagnan*. A Privy
Council order on 24 November 1704 demanded an investigation.

Chappuis was again caught in 1704.[16] On 31 December the police officers in
Lyon—acting on information that printers Vignieu, Moulu, and Chappuis were
all pirating—carried out a raid. They found nothing in Vignieu's printing house
but suspected him of having a secret hiding place where he did his pirating;
when they went to Moulu's printing house, his wife misled the police and managed to lock them out for several minutes, allowing incriminating evidence to
be removed. When they went to Chappuis' room in an attic, his children and
a journeyman refused to provide a key, so a locksmith had to be brought in to
open the door. Wet pages of two books for which Chappuis had no copyright
were found: *Le Practicien français* and *Catéchisme du concile*. Along with his pirating, Chappuis also contravened an order of 6 October 1704 that required printing houses to have only one door to the outside and be locked only by a latch,
thus allowing free access by officials during inspection tours. A Privy Council
order declared Chappuis' printing and bookselling rights forfeited and his
presses to be confiscated and sold, with the profits given to the Lyon hospital.
His journeymen were never to become masters or work as journeymen again.

Remarkably undaunted, Chappuis responded to this with yet another appeal
to the chancellor, in which he made five arguments.[17] First, he was not present
when the lieutenant of police drew up his report about what was happening in
his printing house, so he could not verify it. Second, he had a large family that
he could barely support. Third, the pages of *Le Practicien français* were not found
in his printing house but rather in the attic, and it was his journeyman who
had undertaken the job. Fourth, the printing equipment that was seized was
not his property either, as it belonged to his children as heirs of their mother,
Anne Channot, who had provided it in her dowry. Fifth, it was, after all, a small
infraction to be printing one page of *Le Practicien français:* the original privilege

had expired, and the work had nothing to do with politics or religion. Chappuis claimed that he had always been a man of honor and probity and appealed to the king for clemency. Chancellor Pontchartrain denied the appeal. Two years later, the Paris bookseller Nicolas Pépie sent a request to the chancellor claiming that, despite Chappuis' expulsion from the printing business, he and his son-in-law, Jean Veron, were still pirating books daily, and he wanted the police officers in Lyon to carry out an inspection tour. It must have come to no one's surprise that Chappuis and Veron, who were indeed discovered to be pirating the work, put up a fight.[18] Chappuis was ill-placed to make a good case for himself at the time of the purge in 1709. Even after his expulsion in 1712, he did not give up. At seventy years of age and in poor health, this final petition could be little more than an appeal to pity: he was sending his son to court to plead for him, "to throw himself at the feet of council members asking for mercy and justice."[19]

In 1714 a Privy Council order denied Moulu, Vignieu, and Chappuis their appeals.[20] Vignieu and Moulu could apply for positions if the number of printers in Lyon went below the official ceiling of eighteen, but, as Vignieu was over seventy years of age, this was not encouraging. Chappuis, on the other hand, was given no hope either for himself or for his family. His career spanned a period of momentous change in state-media relations in France. As a young man, Chappuis could have expected that by apprenticing and marrying a printer's daughter he would become a printer, but the introduction of quotas and licensing meant that he was forced to struggle, and, for much of his career, to rely on informal tolerance by the authorities. He could also have expected to print books for which copyrights had expired or simply to get away with pirating, but this was much more difficult after the Parisians began sending their men to Lyon to force the authorities to raid and prosecute printers without royal permissions and copyrights. Finally, he could have expected the presidial court to judge his actions, but in the course of his career the lieutenant of police was given power to supervise the book trade, and appeals henceforth went to the chancellor and the Bureau de la librairie. Chappuis was among the few people in this archival record who tried to draw attention to the fact that there was a difference between subversive printing and pirating, because only the first was a threat to the public. This argument was generally drowned out by the many pleas that coupled pirated and prohibited works into one corrosive force. After the purge, the rules for printer recruitment in the new regime in Lyon were much less contested.

Rouen

In 1709 the Privy Council also issued a order naming the printers allowed to
operate in Rouen.[21] Although Pontchartrain had demanded it in 1701, there
had really been no royal intrusion into printer appointments in Rouen until
this point. Before 1709 no Rouen printers had applied for royal licenses (as
required by legislation in 1667, 1674, 1700, and 1704). Nor did they make
much effort to get permissions and copyrights from the royal council, virtually
ignoring the legislation that required them; they obtained only three royal
copyrights between 1664 and 1672 and only eleven between 1672 and 1687, far
fewer than those granted to the Lyon printers in these years. Only in the last
two decades of the seventeenth century did the Rouennais, according to their
historian, "finally begin to have dealings with the chancellery" and obtain
royal copyrights for the books they published.[22] The Rouen purge began with
the preamble to an order of 21 June 1706, which stated that the king had
noticed that in Rouen the orders requiring printer's licenses and fixing the
quota of printers at eighteen were not enforced; far too many ill-equipped
booksellers and printers were still pirating and printing all sorts of books contrary to religion, the state, and morality. The classic sequence of arguments
was presented in this preamble. An excessive number of printers undermined
respect for royal permissions and copyrights and, in turn, produced low-quality
publications and pirating. Because of this, works against religion, the state, and
morality were proliferating. The order of 1706 demanded respect for the quotas in Rouen, forbade the guild officers to admit new printers, and required all
printers to present their titles to the intendant, Lamoignon de Courson, who
was told to inspect all the printing houses and to submit a detailed report.

Unlike the order in council for Lyon, the one dealing with Rouen, dated
18 March 1709, did not ban anyone from the printing trades. However, it gave
full authorization to only three printers (Laurent Maury, Jacques Dumesnil,
and Jean-Baptiste Machuel) and permitted two widows to work as long as
they were widows. It allowed the remaining twenty-two printers to work only
by the mercy of the king and on the condition that they obeyed the rules and
showed proof within three months that they were properly equipped to do so.
Otherwise, the intendant was to close them down. The order indicated that the
king would no longer tolerate an older practice in Rouen whereby children of
printers and booksellers would enjoy the title of printer and even guild membership while not actually running printing houses. No new printers would be

licensed until the number was reduced to eighteen and, under the supervision of the intendant, new statutes for the Rouen guild were to be drawn up immediately. All this was to be done to maintain "good policing and proper order" in the Rouen guild.

The guild officers in Rouen protested the quotas to the intendant, who tried to find a compromise. The Rouen guild warden and deputy made a direct plea for their "family" vision of the printing trade: they argued that the Rouen guild was already restricting admissions to the sons of masters, since it was the only town in the realm that had not trained apprentices for over a century. They wanted the quota raised and wanted their sons to be able to set up, as they had before 1700, without having to obtain expensive licenses in an era of hard times for the book trade. In general, the guild viewed licenses as possessions, which sons should be able to inherit. Even though their view fitted poorly with the general direction of book trade reform, the intendant, Lamoignon de Courson, tried to negotiate a compromise that would maintain printer licensing and reduce the number of printers in Rouen but still be acceptable to the guild. He suggested forbidding apprenticeships, restricting licenses to sons of printers, and filling each vacancy with the oldest son capable of carrying on the profession. All sons could not be licensed, but perhaps the two positions of king's printer could be regarded as separate from the quota of eighteen, which would allow twenty positions in Rouen. In 1714 the intendant rejected the guild complaint that licenses were too expensive and tried to stress that the larger purpose of licensing must be kept in view: because of the importance of printing to the state, the royal council must supervise entry into the profession. Surplus sons of master printers (eighteen or nineteen) could be accommodated by being allowed to sell books. The intendant provided information on a number of pending requests for printer's licenses and on how the twenty-seven printers identified in 1709 had gradually been whittled down by five, even though a new printer (Jean-Baptiste Besongne) had been licensed in 1713.

Overall, the intendant's report was quite measured and devoid of the fear of subversion that characterized much official discourse. He described his dilemma over whether to allow fifteen-year-old Claude Jorre to carry on the family business after his father had been deprived of the right to print and imprisoned in the Bastille for illegal printing. The son—exempted from the age requirement and admitted as a master in 1701, before licensing had been enforced in Rouen—was described as knowledgeable beyond his years and well brought up. By the old rules, he was entitled to a license, despite his age, as long as he set up a proper printing house. The family needed someone to run the business but, given the reasons for his father's expulsion and current imprisonment in the Bastille and his young age, the intendant was wary. Would young Jorre have more self-control and circumspection than the father? He suggested waiting for as long as the chancellor deemed appropriate before licensing him. While, at first glance, one might think that the young son of a printer in the Bastille would be an obvious choice for exclusion, the intendant—despite licensing and concerns for ideological control—took the family's claim seriously and weighed it carefully. The intendant's fear of clandestine printing seems moderate at best. He did not seem unduly concerned about the fact that, in 1714, the Rouen guild had not yet moved to draw up statutes as it had been ordered to do in 1709, reporting that this was not being pursued with much enthusiasm. He suggested that royal officials give them another extension of three months.

Caen

The Caen purge began when royal officials, on being informed that the printing trades there were rife with abuse, issued a Privy Council order in 1709 giving the printers and booksellers one week to present their qualifications.[23] The Caen guild used the opportunity to strengthen its grip on the book trade and to sideline the Parlement of Normandy from the business of appointing printers in the town. The 1709 order reopened disputes that had been seething beneath the surface in the Caen book world: the Parlement had been protecting a number of printers and booksellers from expulsions ordered by the lieutenant of police at the guild's request.

Until the 1709 order, an uneasy compromise had been in place in the long-standing dispute between the Caen guild and Jacques Houel, who was running a printing house by virtue of a parlementary decree. Unfortunately for Houel, this situation did not survive the scrutiny of Versailles officials when the printer Antoine Jouanne drew their attention to it in his petition for a license. Houel appealed to the chancellor to let him print and to forbid guild officials from troubling him. In October 1711, the Privy Council quashed the Parlement's decree allowing Houel to be a printer. Nevertheless it allowed Houel, by special favor, to be a bookseller on the condition that he give up being a haberdasher as well. Supporting Houel in this struggle were a number of local authorities, including the rector and professors at the University of Caen, the mayor, the lieutenant of police, the town aldermen, and the crown attorney in Caen, who claimed that Houel had been printing with honor and integrity for fifteen years. Houel was probably overconfident in this support, because he kept his printing business. In March 1712 the guild, in its final request to close him down, reported to royal officials that it had raided his printing house and seized his equipment. The guild wanted Houel to pay 500 livres in damages, pay an additional 120 livres in costs, and sell his equipment for the profit of the guild. A Privy Council order reiterated the prohibition on Houel's printing but allowed the equipment returned to him to sell for his own profit within three months. A similar order ousted another bookseller in Caen, Jean Le Baron, who had also enjoyed parlementary support. The Caen purge strengthened the guild's hand and allowed it to overcome local support for the men it wanted to exclude.

Rennes

Throughout the first decade of the eighteenth century, Rennes printers and booksellers struggled to use the licensing system to stop the Parlement of Brittany from interfering with their attempts to limit competition. Their efforts bore fruit between 1709 and 1713, when a realignment of power brought about an order of the Privy Council that dramatically quashed a parlementary decree that had authorized the printer René Morin to print despite guild opposition—and, in effect, ordered the Rennes purge.[24] Five established printers in Rennes (François Gaisne, Pierre Le Saint, Jean-Baptiste Hovius, Sébastien Durand, and Nicolas Audran) welcomed the denial of parlementary influence in printer nominations and moved to further their advantage by requesting Privy Council orders to help them enforce licensing and quotas. An investigation in 1709 had shown that nine printers were running printing houses in Rennes, far more than the permitted four. In 1713, a list of authorized printers produced in Versailles named the eight who could continue: Gilles Le Barbier, Claude Denis, Audran, Gaisne, Le Saint, Hovius, Durand, and Pierre-André Garnier.

Morin, who had been ousted from the printing trade, was not happy about printer licensing, and neither were two Rennes printing families—Vatar and

Garnier—who found themselves in trouble. Jean Hébert, who was expelled in the purge, was in fact running the printing house of the Vatar family until their young son came of age. Hébert's authorization came from the Parlement of Brittany, which allowed him to work as king's printer in Rennes while Guillaume Vatar (b. 1696) grew to adulthood.[25] Members of the Vatar family were king's printers and benefited from all the lucrative printing contracts that this entailed, and it is likely that the five masters who requested the purge were targeting this arrangement. With the purge, the Vatar family seemed vulnerable despite its status and connections, because it was no longer possible for a boy to hold the title of printer.[26] In the end, however, the links between the Parlement and the family were strong enough to maintain the family's position until the young Guillaume Vatar obtained a license in 1719.

While the Vatar family was (at least temporarily) made uneasy about licensing and quotas, so too was another major printing and bookselling family. On 31 December 1708, Pierre-André Garnier, the rich son and grandson of Rennes printers, obtained a preparatory order to apply for a printer position and made a strong case for himself, based on guild support and on the Rennes statutes that said that sons of masters were to be received at their first request. The lieutenant of police claimed that Garnier's large printing house and his fortune were useful to the public because he, unlike other masters, could undertake large publications. Nevertheless, because the quota of four printers had been reached, Garnier's petition was rejected in a Privy Council order on 28 January 1709. The following May he was allowed to become a bookseller, but for a printer's license, he had to wait for an opening—which did not come until 1713. Although the Rennes guild received the 1704 quotas positively, and the 1713 purge brought undeniable benefits, there was a price to pay: members could no longer claim automatic entry into the profession for their sons and, in a general sense, their autonomy was weakened.

Bordeaux

By attempting to obtain licenses in Bordeaux for two of his sons, Claude Labottière brought on the Bordeaux purge, an order dated 20 February 1713 that named all the printers allowed to continue printing in the town. The order listed only one of his sons and omitted the newly appointed king's printer, Charles Lacourt, who blamed this on unjustified animosity toward

him. Lacourt was forced to go before the jurats and then the bureau to get special authorization to be a printer and, like Vatar in Rennes, succeeded. After
these critical events in 1713, all printers in Bordeaux petitioned the royal government for licenses.[27]

Two other printers in Bordeaux—Pierre Albespy and Antoine Furt—were
hit by the purge, which reopened an ongoing dispute in the town about
whether the printers who worked in the privileged area of Saint-André were
included in Bordeaux's quota of twelve printers. The Sauvetat de Saint-André
was under the jurisdiction of the cathedral chapter of Saint-André and independent of the civil, political, and criminal authorities in Bordeaux. The chapter
insisted on its right to permit printers, along with other artisans, to work there
and resisted all the efforts of the Bordeaux guild officers to require guild membership. The dispute went to the intendant and to Pontchartrain, who decided
in favor of the guild, denying licenses to the Saint-André printers in the 1713
purge. The order did not, however, bring about any resolution of the conflict
because, as the guild officers Simon Lacourt and Jean-Baptiste Vialanes informed abbé Bignon in May 1713, Labottière had kept the 1713 purge order
secret, still hoping, presumably, to obtain a license for his second son. Consequently, the printers in the Sauvetat were continuing to print, and Lacourt and
Vialanes presented a frightening picture of their unregulated activities: the
chapter members were bringing in books by the cartload, and the customs officials were handing over shipments without inspection. Now that the War of
the Spanish Succession (1702–14) had ended, there would be a veritable plague
of books from Holland.

The guild vision was, of course, contested by members of the chapter.
Pontchartrain commissioned intendant Lamoignon de Courson to carry out
an inquiry, which he did in 1714. The jurats opposed the existence of printers
in the Sauvetat because they were out of the range of their police. So too did
the guild officials, who claimed that although it was permissible for members
of the mechanical arts to work in the Sauvetat as unregulated tailors, carpen-
ters, shoemakers, and the like, there should never be unregulated surgeons,
jewelers, wigmakers, or members of the *arts libéraux*. The warden of the chapter defended his right to govern the Sauvetat, claiming that it was not an issue
of privilege but rather a matter of "natural liberty and common law" that
the chapter accept the artisans it wished. The two printers who worked in the
Sauvetat contributed their view that there was no problem at all with their
capacity or their morals and that the guild officers were only pursuing them

out of jealousy because they wanted high reception fees. They also pointed out that they had paid wartime taxes. In the end, the intendant wrote a report favoring the guild and the jurats and rejecting the claims of the chapter and the two printers. The chapter could permit other artisans to work in the Sauvetat, but printers were in a class apart, regulated by special laws. It would be impossible to enforce the 1704 ceilings and also allow these printers to continue in the Sauvetat. About a year later, a Privy Council order fixed the number of printers in Bordeaux at twelve and ordered that no more were to be allowed, not even in the Sauvetat, on penalty of a 3,000-livre fine. Albespy and Furt could, nevertheless, work elsewhere in Bordeaux for the remainder of their lives or obtain licenses to set up in other towns.[28] Here the letter of the law was tempered by mercy.

Grenoble

When it looked as if he might be the victim of a purge in his town, the printer for the Parlement of Grenoble, Gaspard Giroud, presented a strenuous defense to the chancellor. In 1708, when the guild tried to use the 1704 ceiling of four printers for Grenoble to deny him a printer's license, Giroud responded aggressively.[29] While it was true that his father was only a bookseller, his claim to a printer's license was not, he said, based on his father's rights but on his own titles and capacities. And as for the matter of the quota, he asked rhetorically, who did the local masters think they were, telling the king, the royal councils, and the chancellor how many printers should be allowed in Grenoble? The king was aware of the numbers when he issued Giroud a preparatory order in 1708, directing him to present his titles to the lieutenant of police, so what right had they to intervene? It was not the place of the Grenoble guild to decide the number of printers that it suited the bureau and the chancellor to appoint. Giroud also criticized the lieutenant of police for overstepping his jurisdiction by allowing the printers' objections to delay his license: a printer's license was not a matter of ordinary jurisdiction, and a lieutenant of police should merely relay information and not play the role of judge. Giroud was able to turn the guild rhetoric back on itself to suggest that he—and not the guild—was the loyal servant of the king. Undoubtedly supported by the legal community in Grenoble, he obtained his license despite opposition from both the guild and the lieutenant of police.

Other Towns

In other towns, similar purges took place. We have information on those in Toulouse, La Rochelle, Limoges, Orléans, and Quimper.[30] Certain patterns are clear: following the 1704 imposition of ceilings, the guilds tended to write to the chancellor to draw attention to surplus printers and the dangerous disorder in their towns. In La Rochelle, for example, the masters referred to the obvious danger presented by an ex-Protestant who was selling books. Such a man would surely have no idea how to protect the subjects of the king from subversion. Here and elsewhere, printers' descriptions of unreliable, lowly outsiders (and often women) who were populating the trade grew out of more specific agendas, the one in La Rochelle being the ousting of a competitor, François Courson, who was actually a competent printer authorized by the lieutenant of police.[31] In Quimper, the 1704 quota quickly came into play when Jean Périer asked the *sénéchal* court to enforce it, notably by prohibiting a certain Jean-Baptiste Duchesne from printing. In 1707, when the bailiff there communicated the order to close his printing house or face the confiscation of his merchandise and printing equipment, Duchesne threatened to crack open the heads of Périer and his wife if they dared to try to enforce the order. Not surprisingly, Duchesne refused to sign the document.[32] Despite this inauspicious beginning, licensing became a reality in Quimper and elsewhere. Printers and booksellers made frequent recourse to the Bureau de la librairie to try to obtain orders to shore up their own positions and weaken those of their competitors. Printer licensing focused hostilities everywhere: it provided ways of undermining enemies and encouraged printers to present a vision of disorder around them.

Guild Wardens

The purges in the last decade of Louis XIV's reign would not have been possible had not some members of the profession cooperated actively with royal officials and the Parisian publishers, undermining local solidarity and local efforts to ignore orders.[33] Certain Lyon guild members developed close ties with Paris publishers and royal officials: the Lyon bookseller Baritel denounced the many failings of the Lyonnais bookmen, their engagement in the clandestine trade, and their lack of respect for the king's orders to royal officials, using the Parisian bookseller Guérin as his intermediary to forward letters.[34] Baritel described the dangers of the clandestine trade: evil books were dangerous because they were against the state, eroded the people's loyalty, softened religious belief, and undermined the good morals and modesty of the young.[35] A more balanced source of information was the Anisson family, major publishers in Lyon in the seventeenth and eighteenth centuries. The Anisson brothers knew how to benefit from the growth of royal government; the more famous, Jean Anisson, a "créature" of royal ministers late in Louis XIV's reign, obtained in 1691 the lucrative and prestigious position of director of the Imprimerie Royale and moved from Lyon to Paris.[36] His brother Jacques remained in Lyon and was guild warden in 1700 when Pontchartrain wrote to the lieutenant of police, Louis Dugas, to complain of the disorder in the Lyon book trade. Pontchartrain commended Anisson's actions as guild warden, writing that he was a "very good subject" in whom Dugas could have complete confidence and whom he must use to reestablish proper order.[37] Guild wardens like Anisson were charged with combating the clandestine trade, and for this reason royal officials (often prompted by Parisian guild officials) intervened heavily in provincial guild elections in the eighteenth century to be certain that the right men were "elected."[38]

Guild wardens worked with varying degrees of commitment as they adopted identities as agents of Versailles. Some in the early eighteenth century were general promoters of the licensing policy. In two provincial towns—Nantes and Dijon—the guild wardens dramatically joined forces with the Versailles officials and eagerly adopted their new identities as government agents: their stories merit detailed recounting. The guild wardens in Nantes from the 1680s to 1718 were members of the Maréchal family, who worked closely with officials in Versailles. The older of these two brothers, Sébastien, worked relentlessly to implement the 1667 order that banned printer appointments unless authorized by the king.[39] In 1707, Jacques Maréchal was taking his police duties as guild warden seriously and seizing Jansenist publications. His activities prompted a Privy Council order closing down a printing house for six months and levying fines. In July of that year, when Maréchal requested that he, too, be given additional powers that had been awarded the guild wardens in Lyon, he presented a frightening picture of the uncontrolled movement of books through the town of Nantes. He described one inspection tour in which the printer Joseph Heuqueville refused to let Maréchal's men enter because his workers needed time to dismantle the frames. Only when threatened with force did the workers open the door, and there was a great scramble to tear up proofs and stuff them in their pockets or otherwise conceal the evidence. To avoid this in the future, Maréchal wanted printers and booksellers to be required to open their premises to the guild officials. Maréchal also wanted to tighten up the inspection of books imported into France through the port of Nantes. His duty as warden was to examine all shipments of books addressed to the residents of the town but, in addition, he wanted to inspect all shipments passing through the port of Nantes on their way to other towns in the region. In these efforts he was unable to obtain the support of the local lieutenant of police and consequently corresponded directly about the matter with royal officials in Versailles. In letters to abbé Bignon and others, he referred to previous correspondence in which he had informed them that a large number of book shipments had entered France through the port of Nantes. Maréchal complained that he encountered interference from local officials: the lieutenant of police had released a shipment of books for delivery to Rennes without his approval. Maréchal told Versailles officials that, in these circumstances and to satisfy their orders, he was sending his reports on the contents of imported shipments directly to them. Maréchal's sense of duty was applauded by the lieutenant of police in Paris, d'Argenson, who criticized the actions of his counterpart in Nantes and informed Maréchal that he was entirely within his rights to insist on inspecting the book shipments.[40] Maréchal and d'Argenson seemed to have worked well together and influenced each other. In 1710 Maréchal confiscated books that he claimed infringed one of his own copyrights. In 1717 he was able to obtain bookselling licenses for one of his own workers as well as for a relative of his wife, and, in the same year, an order confirming his monopoly on all royal printing. Although the bureau did not always decide in his favor, he was certainly the motivating force that ensured that printing affairs in Nantes would be decided by the bureau and the royal councils.[41]

In 1717 Maréchal was at the height of his power. His reign ended the following year, however, when he was accused of printing *libelles* himself and of passing them on to hawkers so that he could then seize them. An inspection of his premises was ordered and a large number of pamphlets seized, all of which "threatened the tranquillity of the state and the honor and security of the government." Maréchal was apparently caught in the act of ripping up and burning so many pamphlets that the neighbors complained of the smoke. Following this, his monopoly on the king's printing was successfully challenged, and he was ignobly ousted from the guild wardenship and barred from serving in that position again.

Maréchal and others like him in other towns moved to sidestep local control, which they viewed as too complaisant, and appealed printing matters directly to the royal council. Many of these matters concerned the repression of the clandestine trade, but embedded in these was the implementation of printer licensing. The guild wardens were in no sense disinterested administrators and certainly were not regarded as such. Maréchal did not have to be fair or disinterested (or actually loyal to the king) to be the force that transferred the handling of licensing, copyright, and censorship matters from local jurisdictions in Nantes to Versailles.

Maréchal's counterpart in Dijon, the guild warden Jean Ressayre, was the force behind a purge there in 1707. He had his work cut out for him, however, because Dijon was a parlement town, and the Parlement was reluctant to step aside while Ressayre tried to consolidate his power by working with officials in Versailles.[42] The son of a notary in Cahors, Ressayre arrived in Dijon in 1668. He married into the printing business and, by 1701, had the largest printing house, boasting both the Jesuits and the government as clients. He became king's printer in 1689, the first deputy of the guild, and then guild warden for about six years, ending in 1712. In January 1707, he reported many infringements of book trade rules in Dijon to the chancellor and complained that local magistrates were not enforcing royal orders in matters of the book trade. Over Ressayre's objections, the town authorities had permitted a barrister, a dancing teacher, a tailor, some saleswomen, a town drummer, a haberdasher, and many others outside the profession to print and sell books. These incompetents were involved in the clandestine book trade and sold all sorts of books that were an insult to religion and morality, something that was especially easy in a town near Geneva. The lamentable tolerance of this state of affairs, claimed Ressayre, showed a lack of respect for the king's orders.

Ressayre's picture of chaos and danger formed the background against which he inserted his main complaint—that Jean-Bertrand Auger had purchased a widow printer's equipment and set up business as a printer in Dijon without obtaining a license. The municipal authorities in Dijon authorized Ressayre to seize Auger's equipment in July 1706, but Auger successfully appealed to the Parlement of Dijon, which ordered Ressayre to return it. Ressayre then asked that the affair be transferred to the Privy Council, where the parlementary decree could be quashed. He did so on several different grounds, some of them based on Auger's infringement of guild statutes (no apprenticeship, no talent) and others on Auger's contravention of royal legislation. In all of this, Ressayre deliberately associated Auger with unreliable elements: women, the illiterate, and the lowly.

Before the Privy Council decided, the Parlement issued a further decree in favor of Auger, holding Ressayre and his deputy personally responsible for the costs of the raid. Ressayre objected to being charged with these costs, which, it seems, he did not pay, and consequently the bailiffs seized some of his furniture. The costs of the raid, he claimed, should be considered part of a guild warden's official functions, because he and the deputy were acting in the public interest. Ressayre claimed that Auger was trying to break him financially so that he could not continue in his quest to have the parlementary decree quashed, but that was wrong, because he was only doing his duty as outlined in the 1667 order, registered by the bailliage of Dijon on 2 June 1677. Ressayre also criticized one of Auger's submissions as a defamatory libel and a tissue of lies directed unfairly against him when he was only enforcing guild statutes and royal orders. The Parlement seemed to be authorizing all the insults that Auger was spreading about him in his *libelles,* and this lack of respect for guild officials contravened the statutes, because bookmen in Dijon were supposed to respect and obey their guild officers, not insult them. Auger, who could barely read (as Ressayre never tired of stating), did not merit indulgence for his offenses.

Ressayre traveled to Paris in March 1707 to make his case, and his trip was followed in April by a Privy Council order in his favor quashing the parlementary decree that had permitted Auger to print. In addition, it forbade six individuals from selling books and ordered Ressayre to close them down; it also empowered Ressayre and his deputy to make inspection tours of all printing houses and to inspect all books imported into Dijon. In August of the same year, Ressayre went further. Although the legislation did not require booksellers to obtain royal orders, Ressayre took advantage of the powers granted him in the April order and seized a load of books belonging to the bookseller Antoine Migneret, prompting the latter to apply to the chancellor for authorization to sell books in Dijon.

These developments led to the first full-scale competition for a printer's position in Dijon. Four candidates submitted dossiers and at least one presented a printed legal brief (*factum*) in his support.[43] Auger applied; so did the sons of masters Leonard Grangier and Claude Antoine Michard. Antoine Fay, who had done an apprenticeship in Dijon but was currently working as a journeyman in Paris, entered the competition as well and produced a printed legal brief that stressed his technical expertise and knowledge of Latin and Greek and asserted that he was one of the best journeymen in Paris, where he had worked for the large firms of Léonard, Coignard, and Langlois. Even Ressayre acknowledged his abilities. Fay claimed that his competitors lacked talent, presses, or money to set up business and that the whole conflict over who was to obtain the position could be ended on the spot if all three candidates were given a page of Greek to compose. Fay's ability and Paris connections permitted him, rather than the local candidates, to get the license, and he went on to become a formidable competitor for printing business in Dijon. His career could not have happened without the intervention of the Bureau de la librairie in Dijon's printing affairs. Between 1707 and 1714 the Privy Council issued no fewer than fourteen orders governing printing matters in Dijon, a development made possible in the initial stages by co-opting the loyalty of the rich and established Ressayre.

Lieutenants of Police, Intendants, and Book Trade Inspectors

Notwithstanding their ability to carry out less public and even quite secret agendas about which we know little, a number of provincial printers made very plausible cases for themselves as loyal officers of their king. Other groups were also instrumental in enforcing the printer quotas in provincial France: the lieutenants of police and the intendants, who were later aided by inspectors of the book trade.[44] In the first years of licensing, royal officials thought that the policing of the book trade would be handled by the newly appointed *lieutenants généraux* of police. The model here was Paris, where the holders of the position of lieutenant of police were strong, influential figures. However, although the institution of lieutenant of police was successful in Paris, such was not always the case in the provincial towns. The lieutenants of police or the local officials and governments that purchased these offices (jurats in Bordeaux, *consulate* or *prévôt des marchands* in Lyon, the *juges mages* in Toulouse, *prévôt* in Nantes, *maire et echevins* in Dijon) carried out surveys and wrote many reports for use by the bureau on the qualifications of individual candidates. Nevertheless, they struggled to assert their competence against other local courts that also claimed jurisdiction over printers.[45] For example, the *sénéchal* (and *siège présidial*) court in Lyon lost jurisdiction over printers by 1702, when a Privy Council order quashed the sentence of the presidial court against César Chappuis for a pirating offense and forbade the court from intervening in the future.[46]

A year later, on 19 March 1703, André Laurent saw his effort to apply for a printer's license before the officers of the sénéchaussée of Lyon unceremoniously quashed by an order of the Privy Council, which declared this procedure void (*nulle*) and ordered Laurent to present his titles and capacities to the lieutenant of police.[47] In Toulouse there were a number of disputes over who had authority over printers and booksellers. The *juges mages* owned the title of lieutenant of police and successfully wrested jurisdiction away from the Capitouls.[48] Early in the eighteenth century, the lieutenants of police consolidated their power to varying degrees over the book trade but generally did not establish the level of control that the lieutenants of police had in Paris.

In the years 1719–24, the lieutenants of police were involved in most of the applications for licenses, producing assessments of candidates' qualifications and of printer needs in their towns for officials of the bureau. Some of these assessments still exist. One written by the lieutenant of police in Chartres in 1721 shows painstaking and meticulous application. Clearly, he was working hard to find a solution to suit everyone when faced with two candidates—Nicolas Besnard and Jacques Roux—for one vacancy. He reported that because of André Nicoloso's resignation, there was currently only one printer in Chartres (Claude Peigne), two widows (widow Tiger and widow Cottereau), a bookseller (François Fetil), and Fetil's mother. Only the widow Tiger had a journeyman working for her, and Peigne, with no journeymen, really did very little. The printing house of the widow Cottereau should not really count in the quota because the woman was so poor that for twenty years she had had neither presses, characters, nor journeymen. With all this in mind, in the matter of the competition between Besnard and Roux for a printing license in Chartres, there was reason to prefer Besnard, because he had all the titles and capacities required and was from the town of Chartres. Nevertheless, if Roux married the widow Tiger, then the number of printers would not increase, and officials could give a license to Roux as well.[49] In the same year the lieutenant of police in Rouen was facing a similar problem with a printer vacancy there. In making his recommendation, he reasoned as follows: Pierre Dumesnil should be chosen over Georges Machuel because he had exercised the art of printing for more than twenty years and because his ancestors had printed for a very long time with spotless records. In addition, in the 1709 purge, Dumesnil's father's entitlement was recognized as stronger than those of others, as he was licensed *comme ancien* and not *par grâce*. With several children, the Dumesnil son would have much to complain of were he forced to sell his father's printing equipment and ruin his family by being reduced to a simple worker.[50] Lieu-tenants of police were often accused by printers, intendants, and subdelegates of indifference to issues of media control, but their role in licensing in the early eighteenth century belies this often biased message.

In their dealings with Versailles, the lieutenants of police sometimes sup-ported the printers in their towns, but when they did not they provided for the historical record an alternative voice that often contradicted the stridency of the printers' guilds.[51] In 1691 the lieutenant of police in Vitry-le-François was criticized for being too lenient with the printers and not enforcing regu-lations; he was told that, while the king was persuaded of his zeal, if some con-sideration for booksellers or their families reduced his rigor, the king would be very angry. Later the lieutenant of police in Rennes worked to restrain the power of the guild, sending assessments to royal officials that undermined the guild's often self-serving descriptions of the Rennes book world. In one instance, the Rennes guild protested a Privy Council order of 14 May 1708 that permitted Nicolas Devaux, a bookseller from Paris, to set up business in their town. The guild claimed that there were too many masters and that Devaux had not done his apprenticeship in Rennes. The lieutenant of police refuted this objection by saying that the residents of Rennes were suffering because the two widows selling books there could not supply the needs of men of letters and of the legal community. Consequently, there was every reason to admit Devaux to the trade.[52] In 1708, the lieutenant of police in Lisieux defended the claims of an outsider for a printer's license because of the poor qualifications of the local printer, who, he said, knew no Latin or Greek.[53] In Rouen, the lieutenant of police recommended in 1720 that Jean-Baptiste Machuel's son Laurent be allowed, by special favor, to take over his father's license before the father was ready to retire.[54] In Nantes, the lieutenant of police would not support the purge and the guild warden, Maréchal, had to go over his head. Various outsiders and claimants could often get a more sym-pathetic hearing by the lieutenants of police, who often refused to close them down when appealed to by the licensed printers and guilds. In Bordeaux, the jurats defended the outside candidate Paul Cailler-Gobain in 1710 and in 1770 took Michel Racle's side against guild opposition when he applied for a license. Gobain's argument was that the lieutenant of police had jurisdiction over printer licensing, not the intendant, who was more responsive to the guild and the bureau. In Le Mans, in the 1720s, the lieutenant of police decided to ignore the quotas but had his decision quashed by a Privy Council order and was

charged the costs.[55] The lieutenants of police, then, undermined and con-
strained the pretensions of established printers on some occasions, reflecting
their wider communities' desire for more printing options.

By midcentury, the lieutenants of police faced challenges to their jurisdiction over printers and booksellers from intendants and inspectors of the
book trade. Because the lieutenants of police were local men who sought compromises, they came under criticism not only from the printers but also from
the intendants and book trade inspectors, who increasingly took control of
printer licensing in the eighteenth century. As the intendants established their
power and as inspectors of the book trade were appointed, the lieutenants of
police found themselves described as as wildly incompetent, an assessment that
pervades the archives of the bureau and the intendants' correspondence. The
printers encouraged this notion and communicated it to the intendants, who,
no doubt, uncritically accepted it because it allowed them to expand their
own jurisdiction over the local police. One report from Bordeaux, for example, said that the jurats could not read. It is difficult to evaluate much of this
criticism but it should certainly not be taken at face value. Broadly speaking,
the lieutenants of police played an important role in early printer licensing,
supervising the purges and some of the first competitions. In some cases they
acted as a force to contain the printers and their excessive zeal for quotas and
licensing. Over time, however, their role was eclipsed by the growing influence
of the intendants and subdelegates, who seem to have been more willing to
work with the printers to enforce licensing and quotas, and later by the book
trade inspectors.

Printers, in general, preferred to be under the jurisdiction of the intendants.
In Vannes, the Galles family appealed a *sentence* of the lieutenant of police in
1761 to the chancellor because it allowed a paper merchant and binder to sell
books. In 1759 workers mistakenly delivered a shipment of paper and books
intended for Lamoré to the Galles brothers' shop. The Galles brothers had his
premises raided, but the lieutenant of police declared the book seizure invalid.
In their submission, the Galles brothers specifically demanded that this matter,
and all matters pertaining to the book trade, be handled by the subdelegate in
Vannes and the intendant of Brittany and that any appeals be sent directly to the
royal councils. They were upset that the town council had deliberated on the
benefits and disadvantages of establishing a second printer in Vannes, and they
wanted the subdelegate to strike the deliberation from the registers because
it contained harmful innovations. In their attempt to close down Lamoré, the

Galles brothers faced considerable opposition from those who wanted a second bookseller: the town council, officials in the sénéchaussée, and the navy
commissary of the marine all thought that Lamoré's presence in Vannes kept
the price of books down.[56] In Rouen, the printers in 1772 were adamant about
preferring the jurisdiction of the intendant over that of lieutenant of police
and told Maupeou that the intendant was a cheaper, less lenient, and less corrupt authority.[57]

Printers also tended to claim that they themselves made better, more responsible, and more loyal representatives of the state's true interests than the
local police. In 1765, in response to Antoine Gabriel de Sartine's query about
book inspection in smaller towns, several printers eagerly used the occasion to
urge more regulation of the book trade.[58] They presented themselves as allied
with the monarch against the many forces of ignorance and malice that threatened them both. Jean Besse in Narbonne, a properly licensed printer since
March 1744, came from a old printing family that had enjoyed the local archbishop's protection for more than a century. He complained of the lax supervision of the local magistrates; the municipal judges and the lieutenant of
police in Narbonne were to supervise the book trade, but they changed office
every year. Many came from merchant families or more lowly professions and
could not, therefore, judge books. For a time their negligence was compensated
for by the old subdelegate, who struggled hard against unauthorized booksellers, but now he had gone and his replacement was not doing his job. The
abuses that were being tolerated were hurting his business. Besse was upset
by a number of things. One of his old workers, who had never completed
an apprenticeship, was being allowed to run a bookselling business and had
obtained a parlementary decree for this purpose. Besse complained about this
through the archbishop to the chancellor, but in the meantime, the archbishop
had been elevated to Reims, and nothing was done. Second, peddlers were
selling pirated editions and eating into his profits. Third, an "étranger" from
the Auvergne named Roussel—a print seller—had for the past six months
been publicly selling pirated books and suspect and forbidden ones. Besse got
nowhere when he complained locally about this. He had invested much in his
business, and he questioned Sartine: Was not it very sad indeed that he was
being ruined by disreputable and unauthorized men? All this facilitated the
sale of pirated editions from the papal enclave of Avignon, and because the
common people cared only for cheap books, this business was profitable for
interlopers; they sold low-quality books at low prices and did not pay any of

the fees and taxes paid by good subjects like him. "You and your *confrères de Paris* are my only hope," he wailed.

By the late eighteenth century, in most of France, the intendants had prime responsibility for printer licensing, but the role of other officials was significant. That of the lieutenants of police was not entirely eclipsed: when the inspector of the book trade in Lyon, Bourgelat, was appointed in 1759, the printer Jean-Marie Bruyset inquired whether he would be responsible to the *consulat,* who collectively held the position of lieutenant of police. Or, he asked, would he be accountable to the intendant?[59] In Rouen, the intendants were in charge of the book trade at the end of Louis XIV's reign but did not maintain jurisdiction, which returned to the first president of the Parlement of Normandy, who acted as the link between Versailles and the Rouen printers and booksellers for most of the eighteenth century.[60] The subdelegates played an important role in collecting information on printers and passing it on the intendants or the bureau. Finally, many of the intendants began to be assisted by local inspectors of the book trade—a new layer of bureaucratic officialdom—that had begun to appear during the reign of Louis XV.[61] These men worked directly under the chancellor or keeper of the seals in the larger towns to supervise the activities of the printing and bookselling guilds, to inspect imported books, and to make regular inspection tours of bookshops and printing houses. The first was appointed in Bordeaux in 1723 and, by 1737, there were twenty-seven inspectors in provincial cities. The institution died away in midcentury but was revived by Malesherbes and later reinforced under Maupeou and Miromesnil. The four inspectors we know the most about—Claude Bourgelat in Lyon, Charles Villeneuve in Toulouse, Jean Cortot in Dijon, and Charles Havas in Rouen—handled the *concours* of printer positions, alerted the chancellor of the keeper of the seals to vacancies, reported on whether a new printer should be appointed, and furnished information on candidates' strengths and weaknessess.

The intendants and the officials in the bureau were from similar backgrounds and tended to think alike about licensing and quotas. Many intendants learned about book trade issues in Versailles when they were masters of requests before obtaining their positions. In 1714 abbé Bignon and intendant Lamoignon de Courson in Bordeaux had a close relationship, having worked together in Versailles on book trade regulation before the war. Bignon began a letter to Courson in January 1714 by saying "Did I not tell you, *mon cher monsieur,* that peace would put us back in touch over book trade matters." When Bignon advocated seizing the widow Labottière's shipment of books from

Holland, he reminded Courson of his past views:"you have not forgotten your old maxims on pirating and you have seen that, on many occasions, the entire shipment is confiscated when pirated books were found, even if most of the books are legal." Bignon went on to lament how little attention was being given to book trade rules, which, he thought, could not be implemented with too much rigor. Nevertheless, in the Labottière case, if Courson believed in the widow's good faith, he could let her off lightly.[62] Bignon allowed Courson room to maneuver (despite the severe official punishment ordered by Pont-chartrain) and to take credit for any indulgence he subsequently offered. What really mattered was that an example was made. The shared vision of printers, intendants, and bureau officials eased cooperation between the three groups and gave them a singularity of purpose that was not available to the lieutenants of police, who had to respond to the needs of the wider urban community and for whom licensing and quotas were difficult issues with dire consequences for local families, book buyers, and printing clients.

The 1704 order cannot be grouped among the many futile efforts to con-trol the press that historians have condemned as brutal, unenforceable, or mis-guided. Nor can its implementation be understood if the cooperation of the industry is not recognized. In research on the nature of the early modern state, it has become commonplace to demonstrate that royal officials negotiated their relationships with nobles and towns.[63] As the licensing system was messily implemented, provincial printers became one of the groups with whom royal officials negotiated. Licensing was one of a myriad of special arrangements whereby printers, lieutenants of police, and intendants worked out deals to make regulation not only palatable but mutually beneficial as well. There were both winners and losers; certain printing families benefited greatly, increas-ing their wealth and influence, while others lost out. By the early eighteenth century, the institutional structures of the state were strong enough to make the survey of 1700 a success and to implement quotas in many towns. The intendants and their subdelegates increased institutional regulation of printing and bookselling later in the century. In an era when virtually no one believed in freedom of the press, printers reacted to and encouraged these developments in ways that were similar to those of other corporate groups. The printers' embrace of government intervention has not been well understood by many historians of the book trade. A rather naive faith in printers' commitment to lib-eral principles has confused some earlier historians of printing. The Bordeaux guild's emphasis on the dangers of unregulated printing, for example, has been described as very perplexing: a "zèle assez étrange chez les gens qui par état auraient dû être plus favorable à la diffusion des lumières."[64] This same idea pervades a recent work that presents printer quotas in the mid-eighteenth century as the handiwork of an enlightened administration, not the desire of the industry itself.[65] Why did those who sought licensing regard it as beneficial? Quotas brought obvious economic advantages to the survivors, but printers had many additional angles on licensing as well. One way to find out how printers thought is to look at what they said about their licenses and how they made sense of them. The following chapter presents the arguments they made in their petitions for licenses made to the royal council.

5

The objective of the 1667 order banning all new printers was to raise the level of education and training of French printers, permitting them to produce high-quality books rivaling those of other European countries, especially the Netherlands. By 1704 this line of thinking had undergone considerable development: well-trained, well-educated, and wealthy printers would be loyal to the king, whereas marginal men were a threat. How did this happen? The early orders in council simply banned newcomers and required that printers obtain authorization before setting up business. However, as printers began to seek the requisite approval from Versailles, they employed the legal training and rhetorical skills of lawyers to produce petitions justifying their professional existence to the authorities. In them they defined relevant criteria, made the arguments they considered legitimate and persuasive, and generally constructed the image of the competent and loyal printer that they thought the king should be seeking. As they summarized printers' arguments and provided acceptances, refusals, or comments, royal officials entered into this dialogue, further contributing to developing ideas about good printers. The arguments in the petitions studied here were the product of a cross-fertilizing, three-way exchange of ideas between printers, the lawyers who put these ideas to paper, and the royal officials who reacted to them.

The early orders in council that brought in successive degrees of licensing (1667, 1700, 1704) provided no guidance about the criteria required for royal authorization. Consequently, the first printers to apply drew upon their own ingenuity and experience and came up with a wide range of criteria.[1] Some printers used economic arguments in their petitions. One very early and very simple economic argument made by a perplexed candidate was that licenses needed to be granted because, if they were not, then neither printers nor the book trade could thrive. Other economic arguments included more complex statements of the importance of the domestic and foreign printing trades and the need to keep book prices down. A group of printers in Limoges said that unless they were given licenses, they would not be able to pay taxes. Some thought that they needed proof of activity in their trade; others referred to the important printing that they were doing for bishops, intendants, and the courts. Their reputations, or that of their fathers, as men of honor and integrity were underscored by some. Two candidates offered statements of their political views: Nicolas Denoux in Châlons stated that he had set up business by the "consent of the people," and several in Limoges stated that they were established "on the strength of public liberty." One offered to redouble his wishes for the king's health and prosperity if he were to be given a license. Evidence of earlier royal favor bestowed on their families was thought helpful, as were appeals to sympathy, which stressed how their families would be ruined if they did not receive licenses. The diversity of these arguments reflects an equal diversity in the circumstances and political sophistication of provincial printers in the seventeenth century.

Many of the first petitioners for licenses employed a range of arguments as they struggled to defend their livelihoods when challenged by those wanting to enforce the 1667 ban. We can reconstruct those made in 1669 by Claude Grinet when Sebastien Hyp, the printer in Vendôme, invoked the 1667 ban to close him down. Grinet pointed out that he was a very competent printer and had married the local printer's widow. Grinet and his father had both been admitted as master printers in Rouen and he had apprenticed in Paris to the well-known printer Coignard. Through his wife he had inherited printing equipment and books. He possessed a royal copyright to print *Le Chretien intérieur* and provided favorable testimony regarding the edition he published. He was careful to convey that he was someone who obeyed laws, defending himself against a charge of pirating and noting that he had given the required copies of his book to the king and chancellor. In addition, he made an economic argument, claiming that prices would be lower if the single printer in Vendôme had some competition, an opinion shared by several principal residents of the town.[2]

Grinet and others drew some of their ideas from printers' and booksellers' guild statutes of the seventeenth century. The principal of these—Paris, 1618 and 1686; Bordeaux, 1608 and 1688; Toulouse, 1620, 1673, and 1687; Reims,

1623; Rennes, 1624 and 1678; Lyon, 1675 and 1695[3]—outlined recruitment rules. The Bordeaux printers in 1608, for example, were to be good men who knew how to carry out their profession properly. Those in Paris were to behave well and faithfully carry out their art. Generally there were three main components to the entrance requirements: completion of apprenticeship, a tour of duty as a journeyman, and the payment of fees. Typically, further provisions exempted sons of masters from these requirements, admitting them at their first request, and granted printing rights to widows. These regulations offered a convenient and broad template to petitioners, and the printers used it regardless of whether their own towns had guilds. Entrance requirements were standardized in 1744 when a major piece of legislation governing the book trade for Paris—the 1723 Code de la librairie—was applied to the whole realm.[4] The Code was a negotiated agreement that took many years to produce and was very influential, even though its framers could not get it approved by the Parlement of Paris. In the 1723 Code, masters had to have the required abilities and be fluent in Latin, able to read Greek, twenty years of age, and of good "life and morals." By specifying that the abilities of sons and sons-in-law were to be scrutinized and that quotas were to be respected and licenses obtained, the Code ended some of the confusion in the late seventeenth-century statutes where, in one clause, the sons and sons-in-law of printers were to be admitted masters "at their first request" and, in another clause, a quota was specified. The Code kept alive a guild discourse on printer and bookseller receptions.[5]

Long before the standardization of 1723, printers began making arguments in their petitions. They included family entitlement claims, competence claims, and other sorts of arguments that had been made by the guilds for decades. With licensing and quotas, limits on these notions had to be set, but just where the limits were was unclear to the hundreds of printers drafting petitions for licenses and to the officials handling them. Many of them believed that printers should be recruited from printing families. But this view did not go uncontested: applicants for licenses who were not from printing families wanted to be eligible and favored merit, patronage, or other considerations in the criteria they recommended. Through the continuing interchange and communication between the printers and royal authorities, the characteristics of good printers were identified, adopted, refined, reinforced, or abandoned. This ongoing negotiation was central to state-media relations in the eighteenth century and gradually expanded the technical criteria that Colbert had in mind in 1667 to include loyalty to the king and ideological suitability.

What follows is an attempt to interpret the argumentation in the petitions that printers submitted to the government between 1669 and 1781. Six main categories of arguments can be identified: merit arguments, family arguments, property arguments, economic and legal arguments, appeals to sympathy, and character arguments. All were made by individual printers and their lawyers who dealt directly with officials in the Bureau de la librairie. Printers also developed the concept of a "good printer" by describing its opposite, the "bad printer," in the counterarguments in petitions targeting unacceptable candidates. Some of the silences in the official argumentation, too, will be examined: a number of considerations that played a role in the choice of a printer never formally entered the official discourse, presumably because they were not deemed appropriate arguments. The most important of these was patronage. As the features of modern bureaucracy emerged in early modern France, patronage continued to play a role, but it was not the accepted and public role of earlier times. Analysis of the positive and negative characteristics of printers—as well as the silences in the documentation—suggests an emerging, limited but recognizable consensus about the qualities of an ideal printer.

Merit Arguments

Many applicants for licenses believed—like the Toulouse widow who referred to the purges as "the time when we sought out the incompetent"—that the intention of the 1667 ban and the later ceilings was to ensure that printers had the necessary technical qualifications to produce high-quality printing.[6] Consequently, in their petitions, they emphasized what could be called their acquired skills.[7] They cited their experience as apprentices and journeymen as well as their abilities in French, Latin, and Greek and in typesetting and correcting. Apprenticeship and language aptitude were at the core of merit arguments and the principal evidence of skill. A completed apprenticeship signified the transmission of not only the technical skills of composing and correcting text but also of the values and the thinking of a master printer. An apprentice in Soissons in 1719 referred to his knowledge and probity, both of which he had acquired from his master.[8] Printers also pointed to their education in local *collèges* and universities, many saying that they had completed their "humanities" and sometimes even more advanced levels. Some, especially in Toulouse, made claims to hold law degrees, legal training being especially useful for the large quantities of legal printing done. A candidate in Dijon claimed to be a professor of rhetoric.[9] All attempted to convey that they were fluent in Latin and could read Greek, a stipulation written into guild statutes after 1686 and reiterated in all legislation on printer recruitment. Many arguments against outsiders mounted by the officers of the printers' guilds hinged on the aspiring printer's ignorance of Latin. Knowing Latin was more than being able to read, write, and correct the language; it was evidence that someone came from a good family, above the ranks of other artisans. A few petitions mentioned other languages. A candidate in Quimper, for example, knew the Breton that he would need in the diocese there; a candidate in Metz was fluent in the German necessary in this frontier town; and one in Aix, having apprenticed in Carpentras, knew Hebrew.[10]

Proving ownership of printing equipment was another way of demonstrating merit. Printing equipment was expensive, and many petitioners wanted to convince officials that they indeed intended to run serious printing houses and did not regard the license as simply an office or a status symbol. Here they were heeding the many complaints in the seventeenth century that masters and their sons hoarded positions but never actually ran businesses. Officials were serious about enforcing the rules and issued orders demanding that printers be properly equipped or face losing their licenses. Consequently, in their applications, printers made a point of mentioning that they had presses and fonts and often explained how they had come to own them: Antoine Alibert had purchased his in 1712 from a retiring printer in Besançon, and Jean-Baptiste Morgan of Amiens produced a copy of his marriage contract, showing that his father-in-law had given him two printing presses, his shop, and his stocks of schoolbooks as the dowry.[11] When in 1714 Henri-Charles Huguier in Troyes applied for a license, he referred to the wonderful printing equipment of the widow he had married and said that it was one of the best printing houses in town, furnished with three presses and all the type necessary.[12]

Some candidates used what might be called "time-served" arguments. In 1703 in Lyon, Claude Martin claimed that he was the longest-serving journeyman in the town, and Thenet said that his name headed the list in the journeymen's register. In 1719 another Lyon printer, Antoine Chize, claimed that his name had been on the guild register since 1703 and it was his turn to be admitted. These time-served arguments were prevalent in Lyon, where the town's long history of conflict over guild membership conditioned thinking.[13] In Nantes, the journeyman Pierre Douette used a time-served argument

(among others) in 1719 to try to compete with an opponent who was a master's son. In doing so he made one of the last full-fledged defenses of the view
that journeymen should be given access to the profession. He began by saying
that a master in Nantes had resigned in his favor and the guild had accepted
him. He had done his humanities and philosophy year at the local Oratorian
collège. He had completed an apprenticeship, had worked for a number of masters, and had already been admitted to the guild as a bookseller. Unfortunately
for him, just as he was about to get his license, Antoine Queros, a master's
son, petitioned for the place. Douette then tried to argue that Queros could
not do this at this stage because there was no longer a vacancy: the outgoing
occupant (Joseph Heuqueville) had resigned in his (Douette's) favor. Furthermore, Queros' claim was weak, because he was the son of a master who had
died in 1709 and whose place had already been filled. There were, Douette
maintained, limits on the entitlement of sons, and he offered an interpretation
of the parlementary decree of 3 March 1704 that had been issued for the Paris
guild: sons and sons-in-law should be given preference only for the vacancies
left by their fathers or fathers-in-law and only if they were capable. As for
other vacancies, he said, booksellers, apprentices, and sons of (other) masters
could all compete for them, and licenses should be granted on the basis of
seniority; if the names of several applicants were entered into the guild register on the same day, then preference should go first to sons, then to sons-in-
law, and then to booksellers' sons and their sons-in-law. In short, sons had rights
to their own fathers' licenses but, to fill other vacancies, they needed to be at
the top of the waiting list. For Douette this meant that he, and not Queros,
should get the vacancy in Nantes: he was older, he was a bookseller, and he had
even been a guild officer. Queros was young, not yet admitted to the guild
even as a bookseller, had little talent, and was not really keen to be a printer
(or was, at least, not upset when his mother planned to sell the printing equipment). Furthermore, Queros refused to be examined for his competence in
Latin. Douette then bravely moved ahead in his petition to deal with the unfortunate fact that, when Queros made his claim, the Nantes guild had met and
voted that sons of masters had preference over apprentices. Douette responded
to this by denying their right to have done so because the printers in Nantes,
lacking their own statutes, used those of the Paris guild of 1686, which did not
give preference to sons unless it was for the father's place. The Nantes printers
could not break the law in favor of their own children. If sons of masters were
to be given preference for all the vacancies, then why would apprentices sign

on? They only did so in the hope of becoming masters. The sophistication of this journeyman's argument is worth noting; there was much more here than a time-served argument because much more was needed. He interpreted the licensing rules and the 1704 decree of the Parlement of Paris as possibly favoring the interests of journeymen like himself. This was a fond illusion in 1719. A year later, Douette lost his license to Queros.

The time-served arguments made by journeymen disappeared over the course of the eighteenth century. By the end of the century, it was not their place in the queue but their technical ability that journeymen stressed if they had no family claim. One such candidate in 1775 was Jean Nicole from Lisieux, who had done an apprenticeship in Rouen but was applying for a printer position in Bayeux. His argument was based entirely on technical expertise: he had worked in Rouen, Paris, and Brest and, when in Brest, directed the printing of *Les signaux d'évolution de l'escadre du roy commandée en 1772 par le sieur d'Orvilliers, chef d'escadre,* which had received great praise. He had worked with the well-known Parisian firm Didot and he had been directing the printing house of the widow Briand in Bayeux. Now that she had resigned, he wanted a license to take over from her.[14]

Merit arguments were insufficient on their own, but members of printing families increasingly needed them to broaden the repertoire of arguments they used to compete for the restricted number of printer's licenses. In 1719, Jean Regnault, a printer's son in Blois, found his claim to a license challenged by Etienne Charles, a trained journeyman who began his petition with the statement that he had been in the printing business for thirty years, had completed an apprenticeship, and had worked in Paris and elsewhere in the realm. He had worked for some prestigious Paris printers, such as Coignard, Valleyre, and Thiboust, all of whom attested to his ability. Having reached a certain age, he wanted to set up his own business and had been asked by several prominent residents to set up in Blois because the only printer there had just died. Charles stated further that Regnault had previously chosen to enter the church, had never worked in printing, and consequently lacked the ability necessary to exercise the profession to the satisfaction of the public. Regnault did have family and education in his favor: he had studied philosophy, then law, and then theology before entering the church. But after his father died, he applied for a license, perhaps on the insistence of his family. He admitted his uncertainty about the profession for which Providence destined him. He went to Paris to further his claim, which he knew would require some serious lobbying.

He argued that it was common practice to prefer the sons of deceased printers who had fully equipped establishments over outsiders. Regnault not only
wanted the license for Blois, but he also argued that the printer quota should
be kept at one for the town. It would not be fair, he claimed, to allow a second
printer to set up and provide competition, because his printing business had
to support several people, and his father had invested heavily in the business.
Regnault's family may have become nervous about his chances because they
married his sister to a trained printer, Joseph Masson, to whom Regnault
ceded his claim. In his petition, Charles faced the hard fact that at least someone connected with the Regnault family would probably win, so he went on
to say that if the royal council decided in favor of the son of the family, then
he wanted a second position created in Blois; the town was big, an episcopal
see with a *chambre de comptes,* presidial court, other courts, and a college. He
ended his request by expressing the hope that the king would pay attention to
his age, his long experience in the trade, and the public interest, which required
that the profession be filled by capable persons.[15] Fortunately for him, a second
printer's license was created for Blois.

Family Arguments

The claim to be the son of a printer could trump almost any other argument,
but the pressures of licensing pushed printers' sons to make additional arguments. In the seventeenth century, before the introduction of quotas, a son was
automatically entitled to be a printer, but new ceilings meant that not all sons
could become printers. Sons claimed to have been raised in the trade and
taught the skills and values of a good printer by their fathers. There was no
better preparation than working in the trade during early youth. Sons' rights
were sometimes recognized by journeymen who, on occasion, explicitly stated
that they did not wish to obtain positions they considered to be destined for
sons. Under pressure, the printer Antoine Chize in Lyon claimed that he was
not only the son of a printer but also a grandson of master printers in Lyon,
with several relatives currently in the profession.[16] He had his father's printing
equipment, and the guild officers and the lieutenant of police stated that he had
the required qualities. Nevertheless, his request for a license failed. In 1724 he
applied again, stating that he should be exempt from orders closing unlicensed
printers down because he was a son, son-in-law, and grandson of printers. In

the later petition, he decided to elaborate on the dedication of his father and grandfather by describing them as men who were eager to serve the public and the state. He said that he was the last of the unlicensed printers in Lyon and only able to continue because he enjoyed the favor of the guild, which recognized his abilities and the investment his ancestors had made in the printing business. Chize then appealed for sympathy, saying that his printing equipment was his only property, that he had paid out all the inheritance claims he owed to his brothers and sisters, and that he now had responsibility for his own large family. The guild officers themselves had asked the municipal authorities to allow him to continue in Lyon. If this printing house were split up and sold, it would be a loss to the town, because of the special Greek and Hebrew characters he possessed. Chize went on to say that there were several elderly masters in Lyon, and it would not be long before there was a vacancy. His printing house offered all that was beautiful and interesting in the art, being especially good in Greek and Hebrew printing. He got his license in 1724 but only did so by moving well beyond the claim that he was the son of a printer.

Printer licensing, then, changed the nature of family entitlement from a right to a favor. Some certainly continued making rights arguments for a while: in 1710 the printer Claude Muguet in Verdun claimed that the right of a son of a master was a birthright.[17] Jean Delacourt, in a 1720 petition from Bordeaux, used the term *grâce,* but he meant something closer to a right when he claimed that a license was a favor that the king did not refuse to sons who chose to embrace the profession of their fathers.[18] Increasingly, printers' sons employed a rather formulaic statement in their petitions about having chosen printing as children and having been trained all their lives in the techniques and values of master printers. Although not the son of a printer himself, an applicant in Soissons in 1719 thought that the preference for sons was based precisely on this, and he tried to appropriate the heredity argument in such a way that he could use it himself: he had had such a good master that his training was as good as any son's, his master having taught him both knowledge and probity in the same way a father would inspire a son.[19] Etienne Michard, the son of a printer in Dijon, was too young to take his father's place but later competed with a journeyman for a license for Châtillon-sur-Seine and made a case for sons over journeymen. This preference was written into the statutes, he pointed out; moreover, he was the son and grandson of a printer in a capital city who had prepared himself for the profession for twelve years, and the Dijon masters attested to his ability. He had studied at the Jesuit college in Dijon, where he had learned Latin and Greek and then worked with his father for nine years. He should thus have preference over simple journeymen, a preference that was in no way unusual and should not surprise or distress his competitors because it existed in all merchants' and artisans' guilds and must be respected because it was founded on principle, reason, and equity.[20] (For the purposes of this petition, Michard was willing to call upon a wider artisanal identity because it worked in his favor, but such a move was very rare in the petitions.)

Some family claims were founded on the fact that the printing business had been in the family for many generations and, in a few cases, a candidate was the descendant of the first printers to set up printing in the town; such men were entitled to the king's favor. Other petitioners praised the talent and reputation of their ancestors in the printing business. Jacques Lefevre in Troyes wrote that he was the son and grandson of printers who went back almost two centuries and were all men of honor and probity.[21] In Toulouse in 1711, François-Sebastien Hénault made a particularly strong case about the talent of his ancestors: he was from a very old printing family whose ancestors had distinguished themselves so well in the art of printing that Louis XIII had chosen one of them in 1618 to direct the printing house of the Louvre. Another had invented fonts that were highly esteemed. His grandfather, who had printed in Toulouse, was greatly admired and exercised the profession with honor.[22] Nicolas Caranoue in Toulouse in 1722 cited his ancestry as well. He was the son of a major bookseller and municipal officer who had made the book trade flourish in Toulouse, providing the public with editions of royal laws and all sorts of useful and beautiful books.[23]

Two other types of family arguments include those made by printers' sons-in-law and the new husbands of printers' widows. Both claimed preference for vacancies in order to allow printing families to continue to run their printing houses. In the seventeenth century, sons-in-law were generally given preference similar to that of sons, but as the licensing system was implemented, the claims of sons-in-law were increasingly regarded as weaker than the claims of sons and, at the end of the century, sons-in-law were required to pay higher fees than sons. In a world of tough competition for licenses the claims of sons-in-law were challenged; their training, too, came under scrutiny, forcing them to bolster their family claims with arguments about their competence. In a major controversy over the licensing of the printer Michel Racle in Bordeaux in the 1760s (see below), the whole notion of giving preference to sons-in-law was examined and found wanting.

Despite the increasingly competitive atmosphere surrounding printer recruitment, the right of a widow to continue after her husband's death remained absolute.[24] By law and custom dating at least from the early seventeenth century, printers' widows were entitled to continue their husbands' businesses, and there is abundant evidence that many widows ran printing businesses in the eighteenth century.[25] Statutes of early printing guilds, later statutes drawn up at the government's insistence, and the 1723 Code all said essentially the same thing about widows in the printing trades: if they did not remarry, they could continue their husbands' businesses and see to completion current apprenticeships, but they could not take on new apprentices.[26]

Very little was said about widows in official discussions of licensing and quotas; with few exceptions, neither officials nor printers showed an interest in acknowledging the presence of widow printers or in examining the issue of widow entitlement. There was a remarkably narrow range in the arguments offered by the widows. If their claims were challenged or they wanted special favor, widows tended to claim that they were young, had large families and no other profession, and would be reduced to poverty if not allowed to continue printing. Some, like the La Rochelle widow in 1708, argued on the basis of ownership: she wanted to sell her rights.[27] One strain of argument made by male printers was that widows did not count in the larger scheme of things, an assumption evident in attempts to leave them out of official counts or in the frequent claim that there was "only a widow" holding a printer position. Master printers and officials may have been silent on the subject of widows because their presence was at odds with printers' cherished identity as semi-official bulwarks against sedition. Printers promoted the licensing policy by endlessly repeating that the public interest required trained, honorable, licensed printers to maintain standards and propriety in a realm inundated with pirated, seditious, and irreligious books. Competence and loyalty were at the heart of the arguments favoring licensing, and it was difficult to include widows, whose education was informal and talents untested. Widows could not easily be portrayed as protectors of religion, the state, and good morals and therefore were made as invisible as possible, but they were allowed to work because printers, like other artisans, needed to assure their families' livelihoods in the event of an untimely death. Men had to be competent, loyal, and knowledgeable about Latin and Greek, but they did not hold their positions by any "right." Widows, though, could run printing houses entirely by a "right" that the king recognized over and over again.

Property Arguments

The early eighteenth-century petitions reveal that printers thought in terms of property rights, but there were real limitations on this line of thinking and it did not develop over the course of the century. One printer in Rouen tried to clarify the relationship between buying the mastership and obtaining a license by treating the license from the Privy Council as a ratification of the transfer that had previously taken place before notaries.[28] Generally, property rights were downplayed in the petitions.[29] The printer Jean-Baptiste Guérin in Vesoul mentioned that he signed a contract in 1705 whereby he sold all his printing rights and equipment to the printer Tonnet.[30] The property language is clearer in notarial documents than in the petitions to the king, presumably because the printers felt less pressure to conform to the notion that printer positions were royal favors. In the early eighteenth century, printers started resigning their printer positions before notaries in formal legal transfers to which candidates could refer when they petitioned for licenses. The language in the widow Labottière's official transfer is similar to that used to sell a house.[31] Even in the notarial documents, however, printers acknowledged that they needed the approval of royal officials. The printer Joseph Heuqueville in Nantes went to the notaries in 1719 to transfer his printer rights to Pierre Douette at the pleasure of the keeper of the seals.[32] Over time, and especially in the last decade of the regime, the tendency was for resignations of printers' rights to be made "into the hands of the king." Few printers at the end of the *ancien regime* could have believed that they owned printing licenses like other forms of property.

Character Arguments

By the reign of Louis XVI, character arguments had joined merit arguments to bolster family claims. The Paris statutes of 1686 and the 1723 Code specified that journeymen candidates for masterships needed to provide proof that they were Roman Catholic and proof of their good morals. This requirement seems to have incited printers to offer a variety of arguments to demonstrate that they were of good character, a practice that became more common over the century. The simplest and most usual was to prove one's Roman Catholicism. Other claims were intended to suggest that the candidate was a good worker.

Some testimonials to the regularity of morals took the form of references to regular work habits or suggestions that the candidates were loyal subjects, men of honor and integrity. In 1703 the printer Jean-Claude Bogillot in Besançon referred to himself as a man of probity and, a year later, Jacques Maréchal in Nantes claimed that his father was a man of honor and probity. That same year, Etienne Leclerc in Limoges claimed to have exercised the profession honorably. For some, the honorable applicant was a law-abiding one. In 1704 a petition by Brice Antoine in Metz claimed that his father had always conformed to the laws governing printing and bookselling with honor and probity, to the satisfaction of his superiors and the public. He added that he currently held the position of king's printer and, to obtain it, had been questioned by members of the Parlement of Metz on his "birth, life, morals, conversation, Roman Catholicism and his loyalty to the king's service."[33]

These petitions suggest that good character was learned in the family. When applying for his son in 1719, Jean-Baptiste Machuel, an elderly printer in Rouen, wrote that he was seventy-two years old, that he had been in the business for more than fifty years, and that there had never been a complaint against his conduct or his integrity and he had raised his family "in the same probity." In 1723 the printer Guillaume Virot in Lyon made the claim that he had always behaved as an honest man, there had never been complaints about him, and his printing house always met with public approbation.[34] Jacques Lefevre of Troyes was certainly trying to convey that he would obey the king's laws in 1705 when he wrote that he had always lived honorably without ever having been convicted on any complaint; he had always lived with the probity that the profession demanded.[35] The printer Pierre Dumesnil in Caen stated in 1704 that he was complying with the licensing requirement because he was a guild officer and should set an example to the others of perfect obedience. Furthermore, he offered his twenty-eight-year term as an elected guild officer as proof of his capacity and attachment to his profession. In 1712 in Vesoul, a printer accused of including forged documents in an application was moved to outrage and demanded exemplary punishment for the lie because he was a printer, and it was important for printers to be free from any stain on their reputations, particularly in the matter of reliability.[36] The Tours printer François Vauquer claimed that he was beyond reproach in conduct and morals.[37] One father in Rodez, petitioning for his son, described his ability to retain the esteem of both the patriots in town and his superiors.[38] A printer had to be a man who would print honest, accurate versions of texts and respect royal laws. Loyalty, integrity, accuracy, faithfulness, and moral strength were all linked.

Both secular officials and churchmen provided candidates for printing licenses with many testimonials of moral uprightness. The lieutenant of police in Dijon confirmed that Antoine-Marie Defay had been in printing from childhood, ran the printing house of his father, and was irreproachable.[39] The lieutenant of police in Laon attested to the good conduct of the applicant Courtois, who had been directing a printing house there for twelve years without reproach.[40] Derrieu's integrity while working as a bookseller in Brest was mentioned in his application for a printer place in Quimper, as was that of his intended father-in-law, whom he was applying to replace.[41] A *juge mage* in Toulouse certified that Desclassan had managed the printing house of his cousin with honor and distinction for the five years preceding his application.[42] Churchmen also provided testimonials of moral uprightness and competence.[43] Canons of the local chapter in Saint Brieuc vouched for Louis-Jean Pudhomme's morals and his ability in 1778.[44] The bishop of Laon wrote in favor of Courtois, and a canon there testified that Courtois printed the most difficult and most abstract works for the diocese.[45] The testimonies of prominent men in the town were indispensable in the campaign to obtain a printer's license.

Although family, talent, and character arguments dominated the petitions, a variety of other arguments also surfaced. Some printers argued that they were natives of their towns and should be given preference over outsiders. Such printers referred to the town as their *patrie*. But while there was agreement that *étrangers* had weaker claims, the category itself was contested: in the 1720s Joseph Moreau and Jacques Merlin, both applicants for bookseller positions in Bordeaux, found themselves accused of being foreigners because they were from Chinon and Paris. They refuted the charge by pointing out that foreigners were from outside the French realm.[46] Some argued that they, or members of their families, were official printers of a parlement, the king, an intendant, or a municipality. Several reported that they paid guild dues or attended guild meetings, and Pierre-André Garnier in Rennes chose to include that he had been selected as militia captain in Rennes.[47] One line of argument that became less popular over time was the appeal to sympathy. Several printers, including Nicolas Phillippot in Bordeaux in the 1740s, pleaded for the king's mercy, referring to their large families who would suffer if they were not given licenses. How could they feed, clothe, and educate their children? Guilds and competitors feared the effectiveness of such appeals and took pains to counter them, often correcting exaggerated versions of misery and suffering offered by the petitioners.[48] By the end of the century such appeals were infrequent.

Policy Arguments

The petitions offer many different legal interpretations of the printer licensing laws. For example, some questioned whether the quotas applied to printers who were admitted before 1667, before 1700, or before the date at which a local court or parlement registered the royal orders. The printer Bonaventure Lebrun, whose family had a long history in the Rouen book trade, argued that he should be exempt because his father was admitted to the local guild in 1666, before royal orders began setting the numbers.[49] Another said that the decrees and bans had not been registered or published in his town and consequently did not apply there. Some said that the restrictions applied only to outsiders. Printers cited precedents and presented many arguments about men in the same circumstances in other towns who had been granted favorable decisions. The printer Pierre Douette in Nantes in 1719 raised the issue of the legal status of an order in council requiring a candidate to present his credentials. He claimed that when a candidate had obtained an order in council, no one else could contend for the position; he clearly did not anticipate the practice that became the norm later in the century, when such preparatory orders in council were used to open competitions for positions. All sorts of arguments were made about the extent to which sons could claim preference. Did a printer's son's preference extend beyond the vacancy caused by his father's or mother's death or resignation? Could one not argue that being the son of a guild member was what counted, and thus that booksellers' sons could have preference too? In 1710 Claude Muguet, a bookseller in Verdun and a member of an old printing family in Lyon, offered a wider definition of the category of printer's son, saying that the right of a son was a birthright. Consequently, what mattered was one's situation at the time of birth, not when petitioning. When he was born, his father was a printer-bookseller, and it should not matter to his status that, after his birth, when the licensing requirement was introduced in Lyon, his father had been denied one.[50]

In their petitions, printers offered many arguments about whether the 1704 quotas were appropriate for the towns. Predictably, many offered versions of the guild claim that tight quotas helped preserve order, but petitioners also invoked consumers' interests and debated the proper definition of the public interest. In 1714 the printer in Salins claimed that there was a conflict between the *bien public* and the *bien particulier:* because the public interest was always more important than the private one, two printers, and not just one, were needed in Salins.[51] Others challenged the ceilings set for their towns by claiming that more printers were needed, often asserting that printing was in high demand because the town was the seat of a bishopric or a judicial center. While the guilds and the established printers tended to underplay the demand for printing in their towns and stressed the need to reduce the numbers of printers further, still others asserted that, on the contrary, the local printers could not meet the demand and judicial officers and churchmen were forced to go to neighboring towns to have their printing done. Claude Muguet in Verdun in 1710 argued that a second printer should be permitted to set up business: it was not only convenient but also necessary for government service and public utility, because Verdun had a bailliage court, a presidial court, many clergymen, and a college. Printing prices needed to fall because even the bishop was being forced to go out of town to get decent printing prices for his printing orders.[52] The argument that prices would be lower with more printers was echoed in many petitions from other towns.[53] In 1723, Joseph Sirot in Dijon claimed that the four licensed printers would not be able to meet the needs of the new university in town. It was public knowledge, he claimed, that, because the licensed printers were unable to provide the printed legal briefs as promptly as the courts needed them, trials were being delayed.[54] In putting these arguments in their petitions, printers were representing the desires of many in the judicial world who wanted printing done inexpensively and quickly, especially at times when the courts or estates were in session. In 1738, for example, regional officials in Aix wrote to the keeper of the seals describing how four years earlier, the Estates had requested raising the quota in Aix from two to four, which the intendant had supported. Royal ministers Germain-Louis Chauvelin and Louis Phélypeaux, comte de Saint-Florentin, had refused, fearing *libelles* and prohibited books. The officials went so far as to suggest that, if the 1704 quotas needed to be respected, Aix could take two of the positions allotted for the commercial town of Marseille, which did not need them.[55] In a full and detailed petition from 1774, Pierre Beaume provided a new angle, making the case for a second printer in Nîmes on the grounds that it could be "abusif" if the same printer printed the factums for two opposing sides in a legal dispute.[56]

Lieutenants of police, intendants, and subdelegates tried to assess the validity of these claims on behalf of the chancellor or keeper of the seals.[57] Given general downward pressures on printer numbers and the many printers who favored the trend, the ceilings on printer numbers were rarely raised, but when they were, it was a noteworthy event.

Printers tried to link arguments convincingly.[58] Technical merit and morality went together in an honorable printer: apprenticeship or training in one's father's printing house equipped a printer with both the skill and the values necessary to carry on the profession. High-quality, accurate printing was the work of well-educated and properly trained men who would not be tempted to engage in the clandestine trade; the possibility that a properly trained printer might lack good character or that the son of a good family might be incompetent or disloyal was not entertained. Family and merit became increasingly intertwined in printers' claims, no doubt because printers, like other educated men and women in the eighteenth century, adopted an increasingly environmentalist view of talent and training.[59] The more men and women were seen as products of their environment, the easier it was to combine family and merit arguments. A family tradition in the profession grew in importance—and eventually a family argument became a form of merit argument in itself.[60] Family and property, too, were linked. Members of good families were propertied and never needed to dip into clandestine trading to support themselves.

While there was some range in the arguments made about what constituted a good printer, there was remarkable consistency in the descriptions in the petitions of unacceptable intruders into the profession. Generally, these were poor, uneducated men, often involved in some manual trade.[61] In the minds of petitioners, if the interlopers were women or had any Protestant connections, very little further argument was needed. The consistent message was that marginal people could not be allowed to have printing presses; presses must be in the hands of men educated enough to know what they were printing and wealthy enough to stay out of the clandestine trade. Artisans, binders, tooth pullers, women, members of Jansenist religious orders, or Protestants must all be denied access to presses. From the early days of licensing, the unacceptable printer did not respect royal law: for example, in 1669 the printer Sebastien Hyp attacked his competitor for a position in Vendôme by saying that he had been caught pirating a book and had printed without the permission of his superiors. The unacceptable printer was untrained and lacked the education, skills, and values of printers.

The Racle Controversy in Bordeaux

The arguments summarized in printer's licenses give us a glimpse of what printers were saying, but they are really only the tip of the iceberg. A major controversy over the appointment of a printer in Bordeaux—when the guild tried to have the son-in-law of an established printing family denied a license—provides insight into the more fully developed counterarguments that were made. Very rapidly after the death of her brother in 1766, Eleanor Brun, who ran the largest printing business in town, married Michel Racle, the son of a medical family from Mont-de-Marsan. The guild tore into Racle's claim to a license with a vituperative printed legal brief that outlined why sons-in-law were given preference for licenses and why Racle was entirely unacceptable. Printed legal briefs such as this were designed to make the printers' cases to members of the royal council and to influence public figures who could help them.[62] In January 1770 the Bordeaux guild officers begged the chancellor to have Racle closed down, arguing that he was not a trained printer and denigrating his medical training as much as possible by calling him a tooth puller: "For four years now a tooth puller named Racle—bored with his trade—has taken it into his head to change it. Unfortunately for the printers, it is their profession that appeals to him most and he appears to want preferential treatment so as to enter it."[63] They regarded Racle as an outsider, refusing his claim to son-in-law status because he had never been trained, having married into the family only after the father-in-law's death:

> Mr. Racle pointlessly bases his claim on being the son-in-law of a printer but this qualification does not apply to someone who married the daughter [of a printer] long after her father's death. Part of the reason preferential treatment is given to a son-in-law is because it is presumed that there was a close affinity contracted [with the father-in-law] which put him in a position to receive regularly and attentively lessons in the Art of printing; but Sieur Racle has never had a close association with a living printer.[64]

He had not gone through the stages to become a master, had never been a student, had never been a worker, and had no special talents. This raised an insurmountable barrier to becoming a printer in Bordeaux. The guild officers asserted that Socrates, who knew many things, was proud of having had no teacher, but Racle was no Socrates. Racle's technical incompetence was so pronounced, they charged, that during the examination he had taken seven hours to set a page that should have taken one hour, and made 119 errors.

In a rather desperate effort to present Racle as a danger to public order, the Bordeaux guild officers impugned his character: he had no respect for the law, given that he had broken it by running the widow Séjourné's printing house. For a printer to break the law was a much more serious offense than for other artisans, because printer statutes were different from those of other guilds, whose only purpose was to further guild members' interests. Rules governing printers were for the public good, and if some brazen printer were permitted to break the rules and avoid government inspection, how could the spread of poison in society be prevented? Since the early days of printing, policing had been important, because printed works were the depositories of the thought of educated men—but never was it as important as in the current century, when "everyone was reading and thinking and could dip into a brochure to set up a new system of ideas or keep alive an old one." This was a time, they went on, when serious conversations were all about the variety of works men and women were reading. An attentive administration prevented ranters from troubling the minds of men and leading them astray, and likewise should offer the same protection from the disorder caused by the vast number of evil writings. Books, which were a vehicle for the national spirit, had the greatest ability to alter morals, and the government could not do too much to monitor their potential danger. Even if Racle could manage to be a bookseller (and that was debatable), the knowledge required to be a printer was far greater, because a printer was the intermediary between the genius who created and the merchant who sold. Printers helped authors influence men's minds. The guild's use of both *ad baculum* and slippery-slope arguments here was truly impressive.

In his favor, Racle made a public service argument—that he was needed because his large printing house printed for the intendant and the *bureau des finances*—but the guild countered this, too. There was hardly a printing house in existence, the guild officers pointed out, that did not do administrative printing or work for a bishop or the courts. There was nothing special about Racle in this regard. Furthermore, could the certificates attesting to the excellent quality of his work really be trusted? Racle may have begged people to give them to him, and they could be as invalid as his medical credentials. The guild then turned to another of Racle's arguments—that he had a wonderfully equipped printing house and that the town needed him because the other printers in Bordeaux were not up to the job. This, the guild responded, was no argument at all; while it was true that Racle had a large printing house, there was no good reason to leave it in bad hands. The notion that the Bordeaux printers actually needed such an incompetent was preposterous. There were sons and sons-in-law who wanted and deserved the license because they had been working for years and had even been directing printing houses in Bordeaux. Some were married with children, and others were waiting to obtain licenses "so as to bind their interests with those of their country and state." The guildsmen then returned to the public order argument, claiming that they wanted no responsibility for what might happen if Racle were given a license. After all, the decision was not in the hands of the Bordeaux printers. If Racle failed they should certainly not be blamed.

Lies and Silences

Rhetoric has its limits as a historical source, and that found in petitions of printers and guild wardens is no exception. Often the rhetorical creations bore little resemblance to the actual lives of the printers who were the targets of attack. Many unacceptable outsiders were not at all the lowly types depicted in the discourse. Several men disparagingly described as mere bookbinders were successful booksellers. The dancer in Dijon became an established printer and guild warden; the dancing was apparently a reference to the activities of one of his parents. Racle, the tooth puller of Bordeaux, was a member of a prestigious medical family in Mont-de-Marsan (his wedding was attended by the first president of the Bordeaux Parlement). Racle was an administrative printer who worked mainly for the intendant's office, and the argument that he posed a danger truly stretched the truth. Perhaps it was for this very reason that the guild officers had to pull out all the stops in their legal briefs and play to the larger audience with every rhetorical excess imaginable.

Behind the scenes, a variety of factors played a role in printer appointments. We get only glimpses here and there of how the process worked, but we know that certain patron-client relationships had a role.[65] While patronage was influential, it was less acceptable to mention it openly in the late eighteenth century. Jansenism is never mentioned, but the increasing rarity of Jansenist bishops may have entailed the collapse of networks of support that printers enjoyed and might explain why some printers ran into opposition. In Nantes, the raid on the printer Jacques Maréchal's shop and the discovery of illegal printing that led to his disgrace in 1718 was preceded by the replacement in 1717 of Gilles de Beauvau de Rivau, a bishop of Gallican sympathies, with the more zealous anti-Jansenist La Vergne de Tressan. It is also possible that the Jansenism of the bishop of Laon played a role in his resistance to the royally appointed François-César Caton. Later in the eighteenth century, Malesherbes described how vulnerable the printer in Auxerre became when the Jansenist bishop who had protected him died.[66] The silence about these issues in the petitions was just part of a number of major silences in official dialogue on printer licensing, such as the possibility that there might be competent women printers or that the sons of good families who were well trained in the art might engage in the clandestine trade. Royal officials agreed on a number of rules that governed what should be allowed into the official record and what had to be suppressed: family, training, and character were at the center of the acceptable clauses. Printers, their lawyers, and royal officials forced this mold on a very mixed range of real motives, beliefs, and circumstances.

Conclusion

In their petitions for licenses, printers produced a dense matting of intertwining arguments based on family, property, training, loyalty, and sympathy. If there were voices suggesting the value of a free press, this matting was certainly thick enough to smother them. Family right, technical competence, and good character were central to the thinking of both petitioners and officials. Over time, the nature of the family entitlement claim changed somewhat; it was increasingly founded on a lifetime of training in technical and moral matters.[67] The contradiction between merit and family seemed to fade as the lifelong training in a printing family was transformed into a merit argument easily used to counter the claims of technically trained journeymen and others who might compete for the ever-shrinking number of printer positions. By Louis XVI's reign, the ideas of lifelong training and moral formation had become something like ideological suitability. The union of family and merit arguments meant that the state could assert its authority over printers in the realm and, at the same time, continue to patronize the major printing families. When printer licensing was first introduced, many printers encountered hardships as the state reduced their number, but the conflict between officials and the major printing families eventually disappeared because the king chose more or less the right printers to license. In the long run, licensing only infrequently alienated the large printing families and generally did not undermine them. Consequently, the idea that the king chose the printers, and that printer positions were favors and not rights, progressed remarkably unimpeded. The family-rights thinking that was evident in Lyon, for example, in the seventeenth century and was threatened by the licensing policy came in through the back door by the end of the regime: the entitlement of sons was really strengthened, in the end, as it took on a more environmentalist character and was thought to be rooted in family training. While property and patronage considerations did not disappear, one might say that they slipped underground or out of the official record. Even as some *philosophes* were separating family from merit, then, the printers and their allies were tying the concepts even more closely together.

6

Five Case Studies in the Reign of Louis XVI

. . . la conduite que l'on doit tenir avec eux doit être melée de douceur et de
fermeté; Protection, graces de toute espèce pour les bons, punition sans remission
pour les mauvais . . .
—*Chauvelin,* Mémoire, *1732*

In August 1788 the Lyon publisher Jean-Marie Bruyset sent a letter to the
director of the book trade in France asking him to transfer his printer's license
to his second son. He began his letter:

> I have the honor of sending you the unconditional resignation of my
> title and my place of printer in this town [Lyon] which I have exercised
> since 1744, without ever incurring even the slightest reproach from the
> administration, a long and sustained period in this difficult and delicate
> profession. . . . I have a high enough view of myself to think that I merit
> letters of *noblesse* or at least admission to the Order of Saint Michel . . .
> such a reward from the sovereign can only excite emulation and help
> maintain public order, which is no small objective in a commerce such
> as the book trade . . .[1]

Bruyset went on to describe how he had obtained copyrights for certain
dictionaries and, when the Parisian publishers complained, Malesherbes, the
director of the book trade, had defended him in the royal council. His views
on the book trade were well known, he claimed. In recognition for making

printing flourish in Lyon, he had received letters from the royal ministers Louis Phélypeaux, comte de Saint-Florentin, and Henri-Léonard-Jean-Baptiste Bertin, both expressing the king's satisfaction with his work. Bruyset attached copies of these letters and also included a third letter, dated 1777, showing that the director of the book trade, Le Camus de Néville, had chosen him to be the printer for the royal lottery in Lyon. After offering the respects of a humble servant and signing the letter, Bruyset added a brief postscript in his own hand asking that the director of the book trade have the keeper of the seals send orders to the guild officers in Lyon to examine the qualifications of his second son, Pierre-Marie Bruyset.

In this letter Bruyset demonstrated several complementary and competing identities that printers in eighteenth-century France regularly adopted in their lives. What is noteworthy, though, is that he only mentioned the guild identity at the end, and in a postscript. Usually printers gave pride of place to their guilds—venerable institutions of corporate privilege that allowed them to flourish. So too have many historians.[2] This guild identity, which has left important archival traces, had been very useful in ensuring printers a high position in the hierarchies of their towns. In town processions, printers walked behind the university, visually communicating to their fellow townsmen and -women their superiority to other artisans. They lobbied the government through their guilds; the guilds were a powerful force in the development of licensing, one of the main voices demanding regulation and protection from the state. When provincial printers wanted to counter the influence of the Parisian publishers, their guild officers spoke for them—very ineffectively in the early part of the century, but with more success in 1777, when some of the guilds (in Rouen, in Toulouse, in Nîmes) lobbied together for copyright reform. Printers' guilds collectively resisted infringements of privileges, sales of bookseller's licenses, new inspection rules, and taxes on paper. Under Louis XVI the guild's role in policing was not diminished by the appointment of book trade inspectors, because the energies of both sets of officials—those of the guild and of the state—were deemed critically necessary to enforce book trade regulations. While they were not autonomous bodies by any means, printers' and booksellers' guilds, like other corporate bodies in *ancien regime* France, demonstrated considerable flexibility and adapted to the rise of absolutism. Guilds were the unquestioned public face of printers and booksellers in 1789.

However, the licensing policy and the establishment of the Bureau de la librairie also brought printers opportunities to deal individually with the state and offered them a direct voice to add to the corporate statements of their guild officers. Eighteenth-century printers had additional lines of communication with Versailles, something few of their ancestors enjoyed. This undermined corporate solidarity to some extent, but it strengthened the ties between certain printing families and royal officials and allowed them to negotiate a shared understanding about printers' place in society. By the last decade of the regime, certain provincial printing families were so well known to authorities and so well connected that officials began to exempt them from the competitions for printer's licenses, which earlier chancellors and keepers of the seals, such as Louis Phélypeaux, comte de Pontchartrain, Henri-François D'Aguesseau, and Guillaume Lamoignon de Blancmesnil, had demanded. When administrators received a request from a son of a long-standing printing family to replace his father, they were less concerned than in earlier years to preserve the fiction of a competition by ordering a group of candidates to go through the motions of applying. In 1788, for example, the director of the book trade, Charles Poitevin, baron de Maissemy, wrote to the Dijon guild stating that, while he conceded that the rules required that all printing vacancies must be put up for competition, "in order to assure the merit of the one who obtains it ... [nevertheless] ... the keeper of the seals [Lamoignon], having judged that when a printing house has been in a family as honorable as this one for a long time, and when the claimants are family members in a position to run it [the printing business] well, we can dispense with this formality." They could, he said, respect the elder Causse's wish to pass his license to his son, Pierre, as long as the son submitted to an examination.[3] In the period 1780–1789 competitions were increasingly deemed unnecessary for sons of the major printing families.[4]

It was in this context that Versailles officials began to receive a few—a very few—female applicants for licenses. The women obtained licenses in their own names as a way of assuring the licenses stayed in the family, an objective that royal officials understood. In 1778 officials replied favorably to Aimé Delaroche's request that his daughter Rose be given a license in Lyon and, in 1783, to the proposal to license Madelaine-Félicité Malassis, the daughter of Marie-Madelaine-Elizabeth Dumesnil and Jean Malassis, the only printers in Evreux.[5] Madame Dumesnil had been running the printing house there for many years and wanted the license for her only child, a daughter whom she had trained in the printing business. Her daughter's health was too delicate for her to marry, but, unless the young woman was granted a license, she would lose her profession on the death of her mother. Armand-Thomas Hüe de Miromesnil, and Le Camus de Néville accepted the argument and granted the woman a license.[6] In 1786 the wife of Jacques-Jean-Louis-Guillaume Besongne, a member of a family that had been in the printing business for generations, was given her husband's license, one of the ten allowed to the town of Rouen. Besongne claimed that his wife was in a perfect position to run his printing house, and he was resigning in her favor for reasons of humanity and justice.[7] The grant of a printer position "in perpetuity" to the Lallemant family in Rouen in 1775 underlines the increasing tendency of the government to favor established families overtly.[8] The state had appropriated a guild or university idea when it implemented printer competitions in the reign of Louis XIV, largely to purge the printing corps of what were perceived to be the many unnecessary and unreliable printers in the country. Over time the competitions were adapted and molded to accommodate established and well-known printing families who increasingly thought of printing licenses as family possessions.

Five of these printing families—Bruyset and Delaroche in Lyon, Vatar in Rennes, Mossy in Marseilles, and Lallemant in Rouen—developed major publishing enterprises in cooperation with officials in Versailles. To understand their success, we must move beyond their local guild identity. These men were large individual operators with strategies, agendas, and direct connections with government that dwarfed the importance of their corporate identity in their lives. We must also move beyond an understanding of the early modern media that places the printers in some way outside the state and try to examine printers' understanding of the eighteenth-century state and their role within it.[9] Especially important here were their patrons and their lobbying. This chapter will explore interactions between provincial printers and state officials, drawing attention to the communication circuits printers established with highly placed administrators that belie older ideas about state-society dichotomies in eighteenth-century France.[10]

Jean-Marie Bruyset in Lyon

The Bruyset dynasty in Lyon used the publishing business to rise to spectacular influence and power. In 1674, Jean Bruyset, the founder of a printing and bookselling dynasty that lasted until the French Revolution, was the first Lyon printer to obtain a license.[11] In 1700 he was elected deputy to the guild warden

Jacques Anisson. By 1731 his sons were running one of the largest printing houses in town.[12] His grandson, Jean-Marie Bruyset, began a truly remarkable career in 1744 when he was admitted as bookseller to the Lyon guild the year after he married the daughter of a Marseille *négociant*.[13] In 1758, he obtained a second printer's license for the family, and his application reveals that he enjoyed considerable support from local notables: the *prévôt des marchands;* Cardinal de Tencin, the archbishop of Lyon; the intendant of Lyon; and François de la Rochefoucauld, marquis de Rochebaron, the commandant of the town of Lyon.[14] Jean-Marie Bruyset became a member of the Academy and was a freemason and major promoter of the Enlightenment in Lyon. He was a huge publisher and bookseller of religious books and also of editions of works by the major *philosophes,* including Montesquieu, Rousseau, Helvétius, and Voltaire, and has been called "a committed agent of civilizing cosmopolitanism."[15] To spread enlightenment and also to raise his family to power and prestige, Bruyset developed many connections in Lyon, Versailles, and Paris.

Bruyset bulked large in the affairs of the Lyon printers' and booksellers' guild. He was elected guild officer and lobbied for the Lyon guild interests in Paris: as deputy warden, for example, he worked on the Lyon guild's bid for changes to the 1723 rules, which Parisian publishers called the Code de la librairie, to make them more suitable to Lyon and smaller towns in general when they were applied to the whole realm in 1744.[16] In 1754 Bruyset protested, along with other Lyon guild officials, against the grossly unfair advantages the Parisians had over the Lyonnais. He particularly objected to the raids made in Lyon by Parisian publishers and the ease with which the Parisians renewed their copyrights after their original terms expired.[17] Later in the century, Bruyset, along with his guild, supported the major reforms of the book trade in 1777.

But while he may have been a conscientious and effective guild member, Bruyset had many direct connections in Paris and Versailles, which permitted him to lobby royal officials quite independently of his guild. One connection was Jacques Anisson-Duperron, the director of the royal printing house, who regularly advised royal officials on a wide range of printing matters. Thus Anisson consulted with Bruyset in 1755, asking him to assess the effect on Lyon of proposed new legislation banning *colporteurs* from selling books. Bruyset replied in considerable detail, explaining the utility of peddlers in distributing books in the provinces, and he tried to undermine the Paris publisher David's efforts to repress this activity.[18] He and his son opposed the laws of

June 1783 that required all imported books to pass through Paris.[19] Although the guild warden, Jean-André Périsse Du Luc, sent a guild submission to Versailles, the Bruyset family did its own independent lobbying, first of foreign minister Charles Gravier, comte de Vergennes, and then of the keeper of the seals, Armand Thomas Hüe de Miromesnil, and controller-general Charles-Alexandre Calonne. In their memo they underscored the importance of the provinces in the realm generally and of provincial printers and booksellers specifically. A capital, they argued, should not get the government's exclusive attention. Capitals swallowed up men and wealth as much as they produced enlightenment and riches. The provinces that fed the capitals in so many ways were the limbs of society, and "the head would perish quickly if separated from the body." Intellectuals and enlightened men in the capital came from the provinces, so it was necessary to encourage the early germination of talent in provincial towns, where men received their early education before leaving for the metropole.[20]

In many instances Bruyset's interests conflicted with those of his guild. It was not his guild identity he was assuming when he worked hard along with Malesherbes and the intendant to smooth the way for the appointment of a book trade inspector in Lyon in 1758. The printers' and booksellers' guild protested against the creation of this new position, as did the municipal government, the consulate.[21] Close ties between Bruyset and the new inspector, Claude Bourgelat, worried the guild and the consulate, who feared that Bruyset would get special treatment and be allowed to print what he wanted. Bourgelat took offense at the suggestion that he and the intendant would authorize Bruyset to print works against the government, religion, and good morals. Nevertheless, he felt uneasy about his close relationship with Bruyset and claimed that he took great pains to show that he was impartial, even to the point of being excessively severe with him. We do not know how much collusion there was between the two men, who saw themselves as brothers in the cause of the *philosophes* and fellow *encyclopédistes*. It was not enough to prevent Bourgelat from following up on orders to raid Bruyset's business in February 1760 in search of an unauthorized edition of works by Frederick II.[22] Following this, Bruyset contacted Joseph d'Hémery, the book trade inspector in Paris, to get a clear description of the authority and responsibilities of the new book trade inspector in Lyon.[23] It is hard to interpret Bruyset's and Bourgelat's accounts because of their posturing for the benefit of the local authorities, local printers and booksellers, and officials in Versailles. The charge of favoritism toward Bruyset was not misplaced: Bruyset was able to discuss his edition of *Émile* with Bourgelat in advance and could count on Bourgelat to defend him when it came under fire. When fellow guild members accused Bruyset of denouncing the printer Jean-Baptiste Reguilliat to Bourgelat in 1762 for undertaking an edition of the *Social Contract,* they may have been right: five years later, when Reguilliat was expelled from the printing business for clandestine publishing, Bruyset reported to d'Hémery on how little the man was affected by the punishment. According to Bruyset, Reguilliat seemed unembarrassed that his expulsion had been announced by the town criers, was making lots of money from the forced sale of his stock, and had plans to continue with a front man.[24] What is clear is that Bruyset was seen by his colleagues as a kind of government man. When describing Bruyset's extensive trade with Italy, Germany, and Holland in a report to Sartine in 1763, Bourgelat claimed that Jean-Marie Bruyset was one of the printers in town deserving of ministerial protection.[25]

Bruyset had valuable friends in Malesherbes (whom he met), Bourgelat, d'Hémery, and Henri-Léonard-Jean-Baptiste Bertin, who was the intendant in Lyon from 1754–57, lieutenant of police in Paris in 1757, and, in 1763, controller-general of finances.[26] But even men of this stature could not protect him against competitors who could call on assistance from even higher levels in society. In the spring of 1761 the Parisian publisher Jean-Baptiste Garnier and his wife, who was specially protected by the queen, obtained authorization for a raid on the Lyonnais printers and booksellers. Bourgelat, intendant Jean-Baptiste-François de la Michodière, and Malesherbes were given prior warning but did not dare warn Bruyset. Madame Garnier arrived in town and insisted on carrying out the raid against Bruyset immediately, presenting Bourgelat with her petition to the queen and a package of orders from de la Michodière and Malesherbes. With Bourgelat in tow, Madame Garnier requested that the lieutenant of police, De Seyne, employ the mounted police in guarding all the doors of the shops and houses during the raid. De Seyne provided one bailiff and seven or eight men who proceeded to Bruyset's printing house, storehouses, and home to discover a few copies of *Traité de la confiance en Dieu* by De Soissons and four copies of the *Traité des Dispenses* by Collet, which Madame Garnier ordered seized. Bruyset was furious; Bourgelat reported that he behaved like an *enragé,* howling with indignation about the undeserved damage to his reputation. Bruyset protested Madame Garnier's presence at the raid and was adamant in refusing her and the police access to his account books without a special royal decree. Maybe inspector Bourgelat had the right to carry out a raid, but certainly not, he insisted, in the presence of interested parties. Even when he was informed of the interest taken by the sacred person of the queen, Bruyset stood firm and, in the end, Madame Garnier was asked to remain behind while Bourgelat continued the raid. Bourgelat found nothing to add to those books already found, except a further copy of the *Traité de la confiance en Dieu.*[27] After, Bruyset inundated Versailles with his letters: he wrote to Malesherbes saying he was sure that Malesherbes could not have approved of such treatment because it was against the laws of the realm to allow interested parties to attend book seizures and to examine account books, something allowed only in bankruptcy cases. Because of the scandal and the commotion he wanted to press for damages, but when Bourgelat informed him that Malesherbes disapproved of this course of action, he desisted, saying he wanted to maintain good relations with Malesherbes and hoped that his obedience would merit him further patronage. Nevertheless, he demanded the return of the seized books, arguing that the copyright that Madame Garnier was trying to enforce had expired.

Bruyset cared deeply about his reputation, particularly at this time, because he had plans to become king's printer in Lyon and to take over the lucrative business of printing royal laws (then held by the printer Pierre Valfray). In the summer of 1761 he saw his chance to act, having been secretly informed that the crown attorney in the Parlement of Paris was unhappy with Valfray for refusing to produce poster versions of recent parlementary decrees.[28] Bruyset's informant advised that this might be a wonderful opportunity to ask Malesherbes for the position of king's printer, but he also warned him to be careful to test the waters (*tâter le terrein*) before making any moves.[29] Within days, however, Bruyset was sending money and detailed instructions to a friend who was in a good position to take the pulse of the Bureau de la librairie, asking him to help oust Valfray from his post as king's printer or, at least, to transfer royal printing work in Lyon to Bruyset in the short term, with a view to securing the official position later on.[30] Bruyset insisted that his friend must move quickly "to put his irons in the fire."

Suspicion and duplicity pervaded the enterprise. Bruyset's informant demanded anonymity and was counting on Bruyset to burn his letter. Bruyset queried his motives and wondered whether the real reason he had sent him inside information was to help out another Lyon printer, Geoffroy Regnault, who had been caught infringing on Valfray's printing monopoly. If Bruyset drew attention to Valfray's delays in getting official printing done, this would help exculpate Regnault. Whatever the informant's motive, there is no doubt about Bruyset's duplicity in his dealings with his own guild; in order to copy out the terms of Valfray's appointment from the guild records, he needed to fabricate a plausible story, and he pretended that he was investigating judicial printing for the general interest of all members of the guild. This was completely untrue, and his contempt for the gullibility of his fellow guild members—who were clearly pawns in his plan—is palpable.

Bruyset's letter says much about the nature of the job of king's printer. While he feared there might be a cost, he was told there was not; the letters patent made it clear that a king's printer position was at the king's disposal and without charge.[31] The king's printer position in Lyon had passed from the Barbier family to the current holder, Valfray, in 1742. Bruyset instructed his friend to check the registers of the Paris Parlement for the letters patent issued in June 1741 granting Valfray the position; it would look suspicious, he claimed, if he were to try to do this in Lyon. If necessary, the friend was to hire a talented writer to pen a formal request for the position, and he was to avoid those writers who could not make a compelling argument. The formal request was to stress that Valfray had no children, was rich, spent all his time on his country property at two to three leagues from Lyon, and only came to town for three days in January, April, July, and October to settle accounts. Consequently, the heavy responsibility for publicizing the king's business was left to a mere printing house director. Service was slow and printing not as accurate as it should be. Bruyset further directed that the formal request should close with the following sentence: "Given the certificates provided by Jean-Marie Bruyset when he was admitted as a master printer by Bertin (then the intendant), by Cardinal de Tencin, the archbishop, by the Marquis de Rochebaron, commandant and the *prévôt des marchands,* the king appoints Jean-Marie Bruyset as Pierre Valfray's successor and can take up his duties immediately."[32] Bruyset stressed that it was important that the letters patent specify that he *alone* was to have the rights to virtually all official printing in Lyon. While he understood that the monopoly on government printing was typically less extensive and often did not include customs printing and other tax printing, he nevertheless wanted it all because this was what Valfray held. Under no illusion that Valfray would accept this lying down, Bruyset instructed his contact to do all he could to obtain the help of a number of persons quickly. He was confident of the support of Bertin, the controller-general of finances, and of Bourgelat, the book

trade inspector. He also knew, however, that he could not count on the intendant, who was fond of Valfray.

Bruyset had further ideas for his friend to propose to the chancellery. These
included transforming king's printer positions into venal offices.[33] Considering
the French state's well-known need for money, he suggested making an offer
to Bertin for all the king's printer positions, which would be subsequently sold
to those who would exploit them. Bruyset had a financial backer in mind and
told his friend that he could have whatever role in the enterprise he wanted,
specifying, however, as a reward for having the idea, that Bruyset himself
should get the Lyon king's printer office for free. Bruyset claimed that he had
friends in the controller-general's office and the controller-general himself was
favorably disposed toward him. The sum needed, he thought, would be 30,000
to 40,000 livres. Bruyset counselled his friend to proceed with great secrecy
because he did not want to be the victim of his own idea. Even if the general
plan to create offices did not go forward, he intended to do everything he
could to make the Lyon king's printer position an office if he obtained it. He
could then pass it on to one of his children and keep it in his family. To do
this, he hoped to take advantage of the good will of Bertin, who, for the sum
of 10,000 livres, would create the office but, even better, give him a receipt for
21,200 livres so that he could have higher annual interest payments (*gages*).
Recognizing that this bit of corruption might be regarded as a charge on the
state and an obstacle to his request, he was ready to abandon the *gages* and pay
a lower price for the office (only 4,000 or 6,000 livres) but still expected a
receipt for an inflated sum of 12,000 livres. Bruyset was not a man to think
small, worry about honesty, or miss an opportunity.

Bruyset's lobbying was partially successful. In 1762 he obtained authorization from Saint-Florentin to succeed Valfray as king's printer at the time of
Valfray's death or resignation. However, since the king was happy with Valfray's
work, this authorization was to be kept secret. Two years later, in 1764, Bruyset
also obtained an official certificate (*brevet*) as king's printer from Bertin as a
reward from the king for his many years of zealous and faithful service to the
Lyonnais. This arrangement, too, was secret and was only to be revealed when
Valfray resigned or died. In 1766, when he heard that Valfray had sold his printing rights and business to the Lyon printer Aimé Delaroche, Bruyset sprang
into action. In a letter to d'Hémery, he reported that, as soon as he heard this
news, his first instinct was to rush to Paris to solicit the documents granting
him the position of king's printer, but friends advised him to wait until the

Valfray resignation was accepted; if Valfray realized that he could not pass on the king's printer position to Delaroche, he could withdraw the resignation and all would be lost. Bruyset was eager for information about what to do to be in the right position when Valfray's resignation became irrevocable. On 7 July 1766, he asked d'Hémery to find out whether the resignation had been accepted and whether he should go to Paris. Bertin had given him hope, he wrote to d'Hémery, and while he could count on some people, he worried that he had no ties with La Barborie, who was handling the affair in the Bureau de la librairie, and he knew no one close to Vice-Chancellor René-Charles de Maupeou.[34] Bruyset leaned heavily on d'Hémery to help him with La Barborie and generally to seek out people in the vice-chancellor's office who could help. He also asked him to obtain a copy of Valfray's resignation and to hire a barrister to represent him to oppose Delaroche's bid for the position.[35] By 22 July 1766, Bruyset had become quite agitated, having heard from neither d'Hémery nor La Barborie. He needed to know, he wrote, whether he should be in Paris, whether the decision would be made by Bertin or the vice-chancellor, and whether Valfray knew of his claim yet. No time must be wasted, because Valfray had a brother and friends in Paris who could work quickly to oppose Bruyset once they knew he was making a claim. The wait was killing him: "I am in boiling oil waiting."[36] On 13 August, still without news from d'Hémery, he wrote again reiterating his confidence and entreating him to register immediate opposition to the Delaroche appointment because he had heard that the affair would be decided in the *grande chancellerie* by a *secrétaire du Roi*. Through the help of the intendant, Bruyset had received a copy of Valfray's resignation.

What Bruyset did not seem to realize until 10 August was that the archbishop of Lyon, Antoine de Malvin de Montazet, had written to the vice-chancellor and to Bertin supporting Delaroche for the position of king's printer.[37] Bruyset rushed to inform d'Hémery that his sources had provided further details of the Valfray plan to sell his business, his license, and his king's printer position to five people for forty thousand livres: Delaroche and his wife; his printing house director, Jean-Louis Marteau; and the latter's wife and father-in-law. Their plan was for Marteau to apply to get the printing license and then to run the Valfray printing business collectively, with Delaroche taking the king's printer rights.[38] With the news that Marteau was applying for a printer's license, Bruyset asked d'Hémery to obtain two copies of the Privy Council order that would start the licensing process for Marteau. This would prove that Valfray's resignation had been accepted. Once accepted, it would be irrevocable, and Bruyset could go public with Saint-Florentin's authorization and secure the king's printer position for himself. By 15 August Bruyset was more at ease because he had a clearer idea about the procedure for appointing a king's printer and had heard from La Barborie, who was ready to proceed with the drafting of his provisions as king's printer as soon as Bruyset sent him the Valfray resignation. Alas for Bruyset, procedures did not go smoothly: someone informed Valfray of Bruyset's claim, and Valfray moved quickly to oppose its registration by the Lyon Cour des monnaies, by the Lyon police, and by the Lyon guild. Hearing this, Bruyset ordered his opposition to Delaroche's provisions as king's printer be recorded locally and asked d'Hémery to block any registration of Delaroche's appointment in the Parlement and chancellor's office. Some hope remained in mid-August when Bruyset finally received a letter from d'Hémery, dated 11 August, reporting on his efforts to obtain supporters close to the vice-chancellor and requesting money. On 22 August, d'Hémery was again trying to reduce Bruyset's anxiety, but by late September Bruyset found himself writing a sober letter to d'Hémery thanking him for all his work, even though their enterprise had failed. Bruyset knew that he had been outmaneuvered. Things might have been different had he been able to obtain proof that the Valfray resignation had occurred. But Delaroche's supporters had been able to retrieve the resignation in time, allowing Valfray to keep his position as king's printer. What this fiasco did mean, though, was that Valfray—now aware that Bruyset had been promised the next king's printer position and that he could not negotiate an attractive deal with a successor—was not about to resign any time soon. Hoping to outlive Bruyset and subcontracting the king's printer work to Delaroche, he hung onto both his license and his king's printer provisions until he died, almost twenty years later.

On Valfray's death in the 1780s, the debate reopened.[39] What sort of arrangement could be made? Valfray's widow wanted to resign, but, if she did, she had to contend with Bruyset's cherished letter from Saint-Florentin granting him the king's printer position. There was much to argue about. Could Bruyset's son reap the benefits of Saint-Florentin's letter to become king's printer in Lyon? What should be done about Delaroche, who had paid the Valfray estate ten thousand livres and argued that he should be able to continue subcontracting from the widow? How extensive was the monopoly on official printing? Was, for example, the printing for the customs office included? Could there be two king's printers? The dispute put Bruyset up against some powerful forces in

Lyon, notably the archbishop and the Millanois family, into which Delaroche's widowed daughter had married.[40] Bruyset, however, had the support of Vergennes and of Antoine Jean Terray, the intendant of Lyon.[41] Many memoranda were produced and sent to officials in the Bureau de la librairie and elsewhere. In the end, Vergennes and Terray accepted an arrangement whereby Bruyset would pay the widow Valfray ten thousand livres and Bruyset's son would be king's printer in certain years, alternating with Delaroche and his son-in-law, Charles-François Millanois. Delaroche wanted the deal to extend to his grandson, but Vergennes expressed his worry in a letter in 1785 to Terray that this might give the impression that king's printer positions were hereditary, a notion he adamantly opposed. If Delaroche did not accept these terms, then Vergennes, who by this point was losing patience, would, he said, give the entire position to Bruyset. On 10 August 1785, Vergennes reported to Terray that he had received Delaroche's acceptance of the terms.

The Bruyset family was a dominant force in Lyon publishing until the French Revolution. In 1777, when a royal lottery was set up in Lyon, Bruyset became its printer; he established good relations with De la Tourette, Bourgelat's successor as book trade inspector in Lyon, and with the director of the book trade, Le Camus de Néville, who had supported him for the lottery position. He and his sons got a special exemption from new requirements in 1783 that provincial booksellers route imported books from Geneva through Paris for inspection.[42] When Bruyset resigned in August 1788, he described his wonderful career since 1744 in the letter quoted at the beginning of this chapter.[43] True to form, he mentioned that he had enjoyed the support of Malesherbes and Saint-Florentin and that he had never been in trouble with the ministry. With characteristic bluster, he claimed to have carried out such a delicate job so well for so long that he merited admission to the *noblesse,* or at least to the order of Saint-Michel. The inspector, the director of the book trade, and the keeper of the seals all concurred with his self-appraisal, readily agreeing to grant his second son a printing license. The chancellor ordered the guild to examine Pierre-Marie Bruyset's qualifications, specifying that there would be no competition for this opening. Pierre-Marie had his license by 13 October 1788. Bruyset's sons were planning careers like that of their father, who was in many ways a successful Enlightenment publisher, one who helped the cause of Versailles ministers in Lyon just as they helped him. But the sons were soon to find themselves in a radically different world than the one their father had mastered. Only the elder son was to succeed, even becoming a book trade inspector under Napoleon[44]—but his younger brother's career came to an abrupt end when his newly minted license failed to protect him from the guillotine in the fall of 1793.

Aimé Delaroche in Lyon

Like Jean-Marie Bruyset, Aimé Delaroche was a very successful printer; he is well known to historians of the press as the man who brought the local periodical press to Lyon and who was confident that a "just the facts" form of journalism was possible and desirable.[45] Like Bruyset, he was a committed agent of the Enlightenment in Lyon, writing in 1765 about the wonderful ways in which literature enlightened all branches of human knowledge. Also like Bruyset, Delaroche occasionally played a role in guild politics, and his power base went well beyond this. Delaroche's supporters were closer to home than were Bruyset's, and they represented the more traditional powers in Lyon politics: the archbishop, the *prévôt des marchands,* the Millanois family. While Bruyset's self-justifications placed great emphasis on the services he had provided the king and the high rank of his patrons, Delaroche put the accent on family entitlement, on local alliances, and even on the blood in his veins: he wrote in 1784, "I am related by blood to honorable and distinguished families in the *bonne bourgeoisie* and by marriage (*mes alliances*) to other highly esteemed families in town." Delaroche began his long career as a printer in 1736, and he represented the fourth generation of printers in his family. He obtained many titles: printer for the archbishop and the clergy, printer for the duc de Villeroy, governor of Lyon, and printer for the Academy, for the Society of Agriculture, of the colleges, and of the bureaux de l'Hôtel Dieu and l'Hôpital général de la Charité. In 1749 he acquired Valfray's book stocks for 125,000 livres.[46] His business was substantial. In 1763 Bourgelat reported that Delaroche had the biggest printing operation in Lyon: eleven presses, of which seven or eight were in use. In the *Almanach de Lyon,* which he published, he bragged that he had the best printing house in the country after that of the Louvre, and later had between twenty-four and thirty-two employees working on the *Affiches de Lyon* and the *Almanach de Lyon.* From 1766, he subcontracted government printing from Valfray, who had the monopoly on king's printing in Lyon. In 1769 he obtained the title of king's printer in Dombes from Bertin and was installed in that office by the Parlement of Dombes in 1770. These last two positions were little more than titles, because he did not move from Lyon and there was little printing needed in Dombes after its Parlement was abolished in 1771. Nevertheless, he sported them proudly in the struggles with Bruyset in the 1780s, arguing that they strengthened his case to become king's printer in Lyon.[47]

Although we have no evidence that his relations with the Lyon inspectors Bourgelat and La Tourette were especially close or amicable, the Bureau de la librairie and administrators in Versailles facilitated Delaroche's career. When a brochure he printed was seized in Paris, Bourgelat intervened with Malesherbes to show that the permission indeed had been obtained. In the early 1760s, at Bourgelat's request, Malesherbes protected Delaroche's edition of the archbishop of Lyon's *Instruction pastorale* by forbidding the Parisians from publishing it. Officials were helpful on other occasions too: Delaroche benefited from royal favor that awarded his daughter Rose-Françoise possibly the first license granted to a printer's daughter in the realm. A few years later, in 1783, when Rose-Françoise died, Delaroche sought as a further special favor to transfer the license to his son-in-law, Charles-François Millanois, so that his young grandsons could eventually hold it when they were old enough. The matter was important because, at the time of her death, his daughter shared property with her husband estimated at 96,216 livres, including a large business in ecclesiastical books.[48] At this point Delaroche was almost seventy, but he nevertheless launched into periodicals, publishing the *Journal de Lyon* in 1784 and *Le Courrier de Lyon* in 1789. Delaroche described himself to royal officials as a man who had exercised the art and science of printing with distinction for forty-eight years and had never been in trouble with the authorities. Because he preferred the hard work of his profession to the quick fortune attainable by pirating books, he scrupulously avoided any printing that could harm his art.

While officials in Versailles often helped Delaroche, they could also cause him considerable grief, and it is clear—at least from the documents available—that he believed that the increasing bureaucratic control of the book trade had significantly frustrated his career and interfered with his plans. In 1762, Bourgelat complained to Malesherbes that Delaroche did not respect the procedures for obtaining permission to publish a work, describing him as "a printer who was not well versed in the duty of respect."[49] In 1776 Delaroche was not happy with the Bureau de la librairie's decision to deny him the right to publish the *Ordo divini officii recitandi,* an ecclesiastical calendar that he had been publishing regularly ever since taking over Valfray's business in 1750. Val-fray and his ancestors had always printed this work by permission of the *juge de police* but, by the 1770s, the priests of the maison Saint-Magloire were claim-ing the rights and had them transferred to the Parisian publisher Lottin.[50] In this protest, Delaroche bolstered his usual arguments about family entitlement and need with an impassioned plea against monopoly: he argued that free competition brought low prices and favored the consumer and the family. Delaroche was a licensed printer who subcontracted king's printer work and benefited enormously from monopolies, but there is no sign in the adminis-trative documents we have that he ever saw himself as privileged. Quite the contrary, he presented himself not as a beneficiary of the increased presence of royal bureaucracy in the provincial book trade, but rather as its victim.

The source of much of his resentment was the rise of the upstart Bruyset, whom he decried as an ambitious man who deceived powerful and influen-tial people. How painful it was to accept that officials in Versailles supported Bruyset. How could Delaroche have known that this individual would let his ambition upset all the rules? Even though the fair-minded minister responsible for Lyon saw the rightness of Delaroche's case, he could do nothing to reduce his sense of powerlessness as Bruyset's son was presented to the comte de Ver-gennes by the *prévôt des marchands,* whose secretary was Bruyset's nephew.[51] Bruyset's grand style upset Delaroche, who expressed moral outrage at the cov-etous and vain upstart who planned to deprive Delaroche's orphaned grand-children of a business that had been in the family for four generations and to which they were entitled. As a result of Bruyset's intrigues, these grandchildren were practically at the door of the poorhouse. Delaroche claimed that Bruyset had "the satisfaction that the ambitious enjoy when they succeed," but he and such people should know where to stop and not try to deprive orphans of their entitlements.[52] Bruyset's greed was without limits: when Delaroche's son-in-law died, Bruyset tried to move in to take over printing for the municipality, but the consulate, Delaroche noted, did not go along, remaining faithful to his two young grandsons. Delaroche was also furious that Bruyset had gone to the governor, the duc de Villeroy, to obtain the position of governor's printer, but he was able to report that Villeroy fortunately remembered that he had granted this position to the grandsons. As he denounced the way in which Bruyset worked behind the scenes, Delaroche believed that he had public opinion on his side and that people were saying quite publicly that Bruyset had been wrong to have used secrecy to obtain the king's printer position.

Delaroche was so confident in his connections and the reputation of his family that he proposed the creation of two positions of king's printer in Lyon—one for him and one for Bruyset. Bruyset opposed such a plan, because this would mean, in effect, that Delaroche could keep much of the government printing. The right to official printing would mean little if Delaroche secured all the contracts and orders. To bring official printing into his printing house, Bruyset needed to be the only king's printer in Lyon. In 1785, to persuade Vergennes, each man offered arguments to bolster his agenda. Delaroche claimed that there were six king's printers in Paris, which helped keep the prices of printed decrees down. Bruyset countered this argument by saying that the king's printer positions in the provinces were quite different from those in Paris, where the royal printing house existed for royal legislation and the title of king's printer was really just an honorific. In the provinces, the king's printers actually did the printing for the king and intendant. Vergennes rejected the idea of having two king's printers in Lyon; like Bruyset, he thought the Paris analogy was flawed because of the difference in the size of the two towns. Lyon did not need two king's printers, and it was important to keep the number of these positions to a minimum so that they would be highly sought after. A clinching argument for Vergennes—and one that made persuading him a hard job for Delaroche—was that those who secured positions of king's printer should not be allowed to think that they could pass them on to whom they pleased.

Unlike Bruyset, Delaroche moved into the expanding world of newspapers, which took up much of his attention in the decade before the Revolution.[53] He adapted quickly to the Revolution and became a major newspaper publisher who printed papers in which he did not hesitate to publicize his own moderate, conservative ideas about peace and order. In 1784 he began to publish the *Journal de Lyon,* which, in 1788, provided considerable political coverage and supported calling the Estates General. The editors invited Louis XVI to Lyon in 1789 and applauded Honoré Gabriel Riquetti, comte de Mirabeau's proposal of an English-style constitution. In 1789 Delaroche launched the *Courrier de Lyon ou résumé général des révolutions,* published almost daily. The editors described the purpose of this paper: "to develop the principles of politics and government, the science of legislation, moral precepts, the elements of commerce, the arts and the secrets of agriculture." They also sought to encourage everyone to work together for the common good and to publish accounts of praiseworthy actions, hoping to turn readers away from actions that broke the laws or upset morality or public order. In its extensive coverage of the work of the National Assembly, the journal was moderate, praising property, liberty, and the king and trying to present both sides of issues. Delaroche argued in one edition that the king should retain the veto over decisions made by the National Assembly, and the editors presented the opposite view as well. By February 1791, when the *Courrier de Lyon* and the *Journal de Lyon* joined together to became *Journal de Lyon et de Rhône-et-Loire,* Delaroche's only role was that of printer. Shortly afterwards he found it too dangerous to stay in Lyon, abandoned his printing house, and left town. The radicalization of the Revolution brought his quite amazing career to an end by sending him into hiding and killing one of the cherished grandsons whose welfare had been the object of his campaign against Bruyset for more than a quarter of a century.

In Bruyset and Delaroche we have the stories of two successful late eighteenth-century provincial printers with different relationships to the state. Both came from old Lyon printing families and both focused on assuring their heirs' succession to privileged positions. Both were moving into the nobility.[54] Bruyset relied more on royal officials and ministers and seems to have known how to capitalize on the growth of centralized government better than Delaroche, who relied more on Lyon families and on the archbishop. The rules the two men followed were different. To become king's printer, Delaroche thought that he should negotiate an arrangement with Valfray, the local notable and current holder of the position. He may well have been right when he claimed that public opinion in Lyon was on his side, judging that he should have the position for reasons of blood and family. By the end of the eighteenth century, however, the rules had changed, and Delaroche—at least in his official letters—seems to have only incompletely understood this. He believed that Bruyset was breaking the traditional rules to get the king's printer position and had done so by secretly dealing directly with Versailles officials. For Bruyset, because royal ministers gave out the positions in return for service, loyalty, and merit, the royal officials in the Bureau de la librairie and protectors in Versailles mattered. Over his long career, Delaroche too began to appeal directly to Versailles, notably to obtain copyrights and permissions for the different books and newspapers he published; in matters of printer licensing, however, he systematically made family arguments, often mixing appeals to family and blood with appeals to pity. In the 1780s these arguments did not persuade Vergennes, who resisted anything that smacked of hereditary claims to printing positions. So, in 1784, Bruyset won the king's printer position in

Lyon in alternating years with Delaroche, a rather powerful symbol that alternative ways of looking at printers and the state were alive and well in the last years of the regime.

Still, before the Revolution, the archbishop of Lyon remained Delaroche's protector: in 1787 Bruyset complained that he had received no printing commissions from the new Provincial Assembly because the archbishop headed this body and gave all of its printing work to his protégé. The old ways had triumphed, if only for the moment. The simplicity of 1749, when he made arrangements with Valfray to take over his business, must have seemed far away to Delaroche. Since then he had suffered from Bruyset's secret appeal to Versailles, which had not only hurt him but also shown that he needed protectors beyond the archbishop. Delaroche had also seen the abolition of the Parlement of Dombes and had spent sixteen years waiting to see what the future held for him, knowing that if Valfray's death preceded Bruyset's, his subcontracted business of government printing would come to an end. In 1749 it would have been unimaginable for his daughter to receive a printer's license, but here he benefited from royal licensing. In 1749 he could not have anticipated the rise of the provincial newspaper press nor the Revolution that would make his complaints about Bruyset pale into insignificance. At almost eighty years of age, his life had not gone as he had hoped, but despite his frustration and carping, he had profited richly from a system of printer protection that had greatly intensified over his lifetime.

Mossy in Marseille

Jean Mossy, a very successful late eighteenth-century printer in Marseille, went so far as to criticize the whole idea of corporate organization and to attack his guild for small-mindedness and laziness. While there is no sign that Delaroche or Bruyset criticized the institution of guilds, Mossy quite consciously placed himself outside the guild mentality, which he regarded as outdated and corrupt.[55] In June 1789, at the age of seventy, he asked the newly appointed keeper of the seals, Charles-Louis François de Paule de Barentin, to grant printing licenses to his two sons, requesting an exemption from the rules that would have restricted the family to one license. He argued that he was a major printer, bookseller, and publisher; his family had built up a large printing business in Marseille despite opposition from the printers' and booksellers' guild, which had tried to deny Mossy's father a license and for which he understandably had little use.

Mossy provided an account of his family history in his application. The great Colbert himself thought that there should be six printers in Marseille, but when his father had sought a license, there were only three printers, and the guild informed the intendant that there was no room for another.[56] The three Marseille printers had no vision and simply stuck to retail sales, which kept the book trade in Marseille very limited and very closed. No one had the ability to imagine the possibilities of growth. Marseille's bookmen failed to realize the great opportunity provided by the city's situation on the Mediterranean, not far from Spain, from Italy, or from the Levant, with access to all trading nations and almost all the lands on earth. As a result the book trade languished. Even when they saw the Dutch and Swiss move some thousands of bundles of books through the Marseille guildhall from Paris, Lyon, Bordeaux, Geneva, and the principal towns of Europe, they still remained blind to the possibilities. Mossy's father eventually overcame guild opposition, obtaining a fourth printer position from the government on the grounds that the population of the town had increased and a taste for letters had spread. He went on to achieve splendid success, undertaking major speculative adventures, opening a direct trade with Portugal, Spain, Italy, and the colonies, and printing useful and important works, among them the respected *Dictionnaire italien et français,* other dictionaries, books on maritime insurance, a local natural history, and the *Almanach historique de Marseille.* When he had started up, there had been only eight workers and two bookbinders in Marseille. Now, he alone had forty workers, and his colleagues had more workers and more business as well, all because of his ventures in publishing and bookselling. Unlike his uninspired colleagues, he did not regard business success as a zero-sum affair and did not share their desire to keep the number of printers down. Consequently, he requested that both his sons be licensed. The family was already running two printing houses in Marseille—their own and one they leased from the widow Sibié. Mossy had supporters write to the chancellor about his flawless reputation, his honesty, and his scrupulousness.

Jean Mossy might have added other details to this request: that he was king's printer and the printer for the navy and that he printed the *Affiches de Marseille* (1760–80) and later the *Journal de Provence* (1780–89).[57] He would, of course, not mention that he engaged in the clandestine trade and had written to suppliers in Switzerland in 1782 and 1783 about his efforts to evade controls, his false letters, his worries about spies, and about a recent raid in Lyon.[58] Mossy was a large and successful entrepreneur for whom guild organization had little importance. He wanted to convey to the administration that the only people who counted for him were the officials in the Bureau de la librairie; if he meant what he said here, he felt little but contempt for his guild identity. In 1789, as events transpired, Mossy's second son did not need a license to set up a printing business. The two Mossy brothers ran printing houses during the Revolution, printing pamphlets and newspapers, including Mirabeau's *Courrier de Provence* at a run of 10,000.[59] Auguste Mossy, who was both a barrister and a printer, was a fervent republican and mayor of Marseille from 1795 to 1805.

Vatar in Rennes

The Vatar family was an old and substantial printing dynasty in Brittany that dated back at least to the 1640s, when Jean Vatar established a press in Rennes across from the Parlement that operated until the French Revolution.[60] Jean Vatar became king's printer and printer for the Parlement in 1673 and followed the Parlement in its exile to Vannes after its revolt in 1675. Until the Revolution, the many members of this large family who worked as printers, booksellers, and in the judiciary were a significant force in and beyond Brittany, in Rennes, Nantes, Vannes, Lyon, and Paris. Members of the Vatar family had large bookselling businesses as well as printing houses and introduced the periodical press to Nantes as early as 1754 and later, in 1784, to Rennes.[61] In the reign of Louis XVI, Vatar family members had a near monopoly on official printing positions in Rennes and Nantes, often experiencing uneasy relationships with their guilds, the town authorities, and the intendants and other royal officials.

While many factors contributed to their complex relationships with royal authorities in the eighteenth century, printer licensing certainly played a role in shaping these. In the next chapter we will see how, during the Brittany Affair, Nicolas-Paul Vatar in Rennes lost his license for printing for the Parlement but regained it as a hero after Louis XVI took the throne. This struggle to hold a license was, however, just one of several struggles that had been framing this family's relationship with the royal government since the advent of printer licensing in Rennes in 1709. In 1718 Julien Vatar was granted a license against the wishes of the Rennes guild, referring in his application to the guild's *animosités, calomnies, la chicane et la haine,* criticisms echoed by many of his successors.[62] In 1758 the Nantes guild officers challenged the Vatar license there and designated the widow Vatar as supernumerary, meaning that at her death her license would be extinguished.[63] This designation was passed on to the subdelegate to the intendant to the royal council and became law on 12 May 1759, but it did not stand for long. The widow Vatar protested vigorously and used all her influence to have the royal council rescind its own order: her strong family claims and the fact that she had ten children made her the wrong person to target. She went to Paris to lobby to transfer the supernumerary status to another widow in Nantes, and her letters to the intendant in Rennes allow us to trace her activity. By 30 June 1759 she got an order in council opening up the issue and sent it to the intendant, asking him to put together the paperwork. By 18 July she was impatient for results and complained to the intendant that officials in Nantes were not furnishing the required documentation; moreover, her lengthy stay in Paris was hurting her business. She wanted the intendant to give a deadline to his subdelegate in Nantes, who was suspiciously inactive; the subdelegate was closely connected to the widow Vatar's opponents, who had every interest in prolonging her absence.[64] In August, she was still in Paris, writing to counsel the intendant on the language he was to put in his report to the royal council and the chancellor, urging speed; he needed to get his report in soon so that she could get back to work. Finally, in September she wrote that, if her efforts to preserve the printing license for her children did not get results soon, she would have to return to Nantes and would have spent three months in Paris for nothing. If the intendant could take care of this matter at his first convenience, she would be most grateful for this favor and pray for him. By 8 October 1759 she had won her case, and an order in council transferred the supernumerary status to the widow Maréchal, leaving the widow Vatar with a license she could pass on to her children.[65]

The widow Vatar knew well what losing a printing license could cost, because the Rennes branch of her family had been torn apart just two years earlier by conflict that involved her brothers-in-law and her cousins over which members of the family could keep licenses. In 1739 the quota for printers in Rennes was set at four, but there were still five printers when Gilles-Joseph died in 1757 with ten children. Three sons laid claim to his large business printing for the Breton Estates. At the same time, other Rennes printing families (those of Julien Vatar and Nicolas Garnier) were waiting to transfer licenses to the next generation.[66] In fact, the death of Gilles-Joseph upset a situation in which all license transfers in Rennes were in a holding pattern because of the quota. Chancellor Lamoignon insisted that it was urgent that the number be reduced to four and engaged the intendant and the subdelegate to find the best way to do this.[67] Because of the size of the Vatar printing houses, Lamoignon decided that they should be allowed to continue, but, for this to happen, he extinguished the license of a more modest printing family: the printer Nicolas Audran's license would disappear at his or his widow's death, despite his position as guild warden. The Vatar family was to pay compensation to the Audran family and to buy their printing equipment and stocks.

Once this decision was made, further conflicts arose among Gilles-Joseph's three sons, who all wanted the license. One son, Jacques-Jean, sieur de La Mabilais, was a successful bookseller, a doctor of law at the University of Paris, and a barrister in the Parlement of Paris. The two others—Jacques-Julien and Nicolas-Paul—were working as printers, the latter having recently returned from America. The intendant, the subdelegate, members of the Bureau de la librairie, and Lamoignon struggled with the problem. The intendant initially favored the second son, Jacques-Julien, but when Lamoignon proposed an arrangement whereby he and his brother would jointly run the printing house, Jacques-Julien refused to accept it. Consequently, Lamoignon gave the license to Nicolas-Paul, who was to pay eight thousand livres to his co-heirs so that, in Lamoignon's words, royal favor could fall upon the whole family. After he received eight credit notes worth one thousand livres for each of the Vatar brothers and sisters, Lamoignon ordered the guild to admit Nicolas-Paul Vatar as a printer.[68] This created significant acrimony in the family and beyond. Audran—quite understandably upset at the obliteration of his family's claim—refused to fulfil his duty as guild warden to register Nicolas-Paul's license, provoking the fury of both Nicolas-Paul and Lamoignon. Nicolas-Paul took his frustration to the intendant, forcing a visit on the unhappy man, who was ill in bed, coughing up blood.[69] Nicolas-Paul's disappointed brothers were forced to accept the decision, but this was not easy: Jacques-Jean sold his bookselling business and bought the office of *conseiller du roi* in January 1764. Jacques-Julien at first ignored his brother's license and continued printing until a royal order ousted him from the printing business late in 1759, forcing him to go to Paris and then to Lyon, where he married the daughter of the Delaroche dynasty.[70] We do not know if he commiserated in Lyon with his father-in-law, Aimé Delaroche, about the increasing interference in their lives of a growing book trade bureaucracy, but we can speculate about the broad national perspective on political life that he and his family members must have shared in the reign of Louis XVI. The striking image of the Rennes guild warden being asked to register a decree declaring his own license extinguished speaks volumes about the limits of their guild identity in interpreting these printers' lives.

Members of the Vatar family had powerful patrons. The intendant and subdelegate in Rennes were deeply concerned about the Audran family, drawing attention to the high price the family was paying and noting Audran's reproachless record as well as his fidelity to his art in his work as guild warden, but the best they could do was to persuade Lamoignon to allow Audran a lifetime position. In 1777 Jeanne Le Saulnier, the young widow of François-Pierre Vatar, king's printer in Rennes, requested special permission to keep the business—something widows were not allowed to do—when she married her husband's close friend Bruté de Remur, a barrister and *directeur des domaines du Roi* in Rennes. Miromesnil agreed to this arrangement, which had at its heart the protection of her young son's claim on the printing license.[71] The power of the Vatar family in Brittany was founded on their connections with the Parlement and the Estates. Family members in these conflicts called upon highly placed supporters, and there are unmistakable signs in the archival record of the sense of entitlement buttressed by these connections. Nicolas-Paul Vatar, for example, preferred to deal directly with Lamoignon and not the intendant. That he would barge into the intendant's sickroom, seemingly oblivious to his illness, to get him to act so that the printing for the Breton Estates could begin is a sign of his confidence. Similarly, the correspondence from the widow Vatar with the intendant reveals an impatient woman telling her intendant to lean on his subdelegate and get some action. In 1786 a Vatar daughter in Rennes wrote to Miromesnil to quash guild opposition to her bookselling business. Was the daughter, granddaughter, and great-granddaughter of Rennes printers to starve to death in the back of her closed-up shop while all sorts of *gens— intrus dans cet état dangereux*—were allowed to sell books publicly?[72]

Lallemant in Rouen

In 1775 the printer Richard Lallemant withdrew from the Rouen printers' and booksellers' guild because membership in it was inconsistent with the noble status he had achieved. Throughout the eighteenth century the Lallemant family had been an influential and long-serving printing dynasty in Rouen, running a major business in religious and classical books.[73] Early in the century, the royal government counted on the Lallemant family to represent its interests in Rouen by making Richard Lallemant guild warden during the purge of 1709 and keeping him in that position for several years. In 1753, when Nicolas Lallemant—who was also an alderman in Rouen—wanted the position of king's printer, the intendant wrote a powerful recommendation in which he described him as "the son and grandson of printers commendable in their art" who "brings to his talent and experience in his profession, a gentleness of manner and of character that comes from both an excellent nature and a good upbringing."[74]

Nicolas' son Richard had a close and cooperative relationship with Miromesnil during the latter's tenure as first president of the Parlement of Rouen from 1757 to 1774, when he was in charge of book trade regulation. On very familiar terms with Miromesnil, Lallemant turned to him for help of all sorts: to deal with labor difficulties, for example, or to obtain copyrights for books. On occasion he provoked criticism from Joseph d'Hémery, who saw Miromesnil's favoritism as undermining the rights of Parisian publishers. In 1764 the Lallemant printing house, with five presses and twelve workers, was the biggest operation in Rouen. According to Miromesnil, it published classics and printed works with official approval, and Lallemant enjoyed an excellent reputation. In 1766, when Lallemant heard from Paris that orders had been issued to raid his business along with two others in Rouen, he asked Miromesnil to use his influence with the lieutenant of police in Paris, Antoine Gabriel de Sartine, to stop the plan. Since Miromesnil knew him, could he not find a way to spare him this disgrace? The dishonor would damage him, his house, and his brother, abbé Lallemant, an author who had just been awarded a pension from the king. Miromesnil wrote a strong letter to Sartine in which he described the printer's many very fine qualities, saying that he was rich and consequently would not break the law. Lallemant, he wrote, was a consular judge, a member of the chamber of commerce, an alderman whose wisdom was well known and a man "distingué par son mérite et ses vertus." As if this were not enough, Miromesnil went on to describe his illustrious family, which had been in the printing business for many generations: abbé Lallemant was a distinguished author of a translation of the *Fables de Phèdre,* and another brother was a highly regarded crown attorney in Rouen's financial court.[75] Miromesnil sent Lallemant a copy of his letter to Sartine, adding a personal note in which he asked him to have the abbé Lallemant use Miromesnil's name to obtain an interview with Sartine. He ended the letter by furnishing information about the health of his wife.

The ties between Lallemant and Miromesnil endured after 1774, when Miromesnil became keeper of the seals, responsible for book trade matters for the whole realm. Le Camus de Néville was criticized for unduly favoring a Rouen printer—almost certainly Lallemant—by giving him the information six months early that the government was going to legitimize existing pirated editions in the provinces as part of its program to reform the rules governing copyright in 1777.[76] In 1775 Lallemant received the noble title of *écuyer*, and the family was given a hereditary printer privilege in perpetuity. The male descendants of the Lallemant family were to enjoy this privilege, which would not harm the rights and prerogatives of their noble status. The decree reinforced the fiction that the Lallemant family had brought printing to Rouen from Germany.

Patronage and Bureaucracy

The connections between royal officials and these five provincial printers—Bruyset, Delaroche, Mossy, Vatar, and Lallemant—were clearly mutually supporting. Similar relationships existed between Versailles officials and other provincial printing families such as Beaume in Nîmes and Bordeaux, David in Aix, Pijon in Toulouse, and Machuel and Oursel in Rouen. Major provincial publishers sought and obtained special attention from royal officials to their economic concerns, often obtaining exemptions from guild restrictions and inconvenient laws. Whenever they wrote in search of favor, they stressed their families' long service and loyalty to the king. They had much in common: they wanted king's printer positions, they tended to be appointed guild wardens, they had close relations with intendants and book trade inspectors, and several had descendants who entered the nobility. Although there were some important differences among them, as a group they were mediating agents between the royal government and their provincial communities. They policed printed production in the realm, publicized royal laws informing the judiciary of the royal will, and were clients of ministers.

Important to these men were relationships with local notables, intendants, officials in the Bureau de la librairie, and royal ministers. The support of the intendants or their subdelegates was critical to obtaining a printer's license or a king's printer position—or protection if a printer needed lenient treatment in the event that he or she were caught engaging in the clandestine trade. When he wanted the king's printer position, Bruyset benefited from the support of the intendant, as did Lallemant in Rouen. The printer Félix Faulcon in Poitiers wrote to his son Félix in 1776 that he was indebted to the intendant for his position of king's printer: "I owe a large debt to the Comte de Blossac, our intendant, who has done much to help me in this affair. He is a magistrate to whom we should be loyal. The respect and kindness that he has shown our family require it."[77] Failure to cultivate the intendant's support could cost a printer dearly. In Bordeaux, in 1783, the Labottière brothers lost their privilege for the *Annonces et Affiches de Bordeaux* two years before its expiration because the intendant wanted to transfer it to another.[78] Beyond the intendant, other connections were necessary, especially people in the chancellor's office or in the Bureau de la librairie. Bruyset asked d'Hémery to cultivate men in the Bureau de la librairie close to Maupeou. The Faulcon family in Poitiers called upon their friend Boucherot du Fey, first secretary of the keeper of the seals, in 1783 to help fight off a contender for the position of king's printer there.[79] Chancellors and keepers of the seals, such as Lamoignon and Miromesnil, and directors of the book trade, such as Malesherbes and Le Camus de Néville, all had their protégés. So too did high officials in the administration outside the chancellor's office.

Leaning on the men in the royal administration were noble patrons who expected older notions of patronage to operate and whose pressure sometimes could not be ignored. The duc de Mouchy, the lieutenant of the duc de Richelieu, governor of Guyenne, intervened in favor of the Labottière brothers in 1777 when they were in trouble for printing the remonstrances of the Cour des aides, and he and his wife supported the candidacy of the printer Jean-Claude Pinard, who was a printing director in the Labottière printing house.[80] In 1784, the noble secretary of the intendant of Bordeaux, D'Estavayé de Taberly, was said to have tried to favor the printer Levieux in a competition by using his influence with the intendant, Nicolas Dupré de St. Maur.[81] Bishops continued to try to control the appointment of printers. As we have seen, the bishop of Sarlat protected a printer in his town, and so did others: in May 1788 the bishop of Oléron, for example, wrote to Lamoignon, the keeper of the seals, requesting the reinstatement of the printer Vignancourt in Pau, whose license had been suspended.[82] A number of aristocratic women wrote in favor of candidates to intendants and other administrators: the duchesse de Duras was interested in Jean-Baptiste Garde,[83] and Madame Duroy and her cousin Madame Letellier wrote letters to the secretary of the intendant in Bordeaux to support the candidate Pallandre in 1772.[84] In 1753 the princesse de Conti protected Lefebvre, a bookseller in Versailles, and wanted him licensed for Paris. Her wishes were communicated to the lieutenant of police, Nicolas-René Berryer, by the wife of Aligre, the first president of the Parlement of Paris, who also intervened on behalf of the Dijon bookseller François Desvente, imprisoned in the Bastille for unauthorized book sales.[85] Noble patronage certainly continued to influence the choice of printers, but it was not as direct as it had once been and was mitigated by what the printers called "the administration." The officials in the Bureau de la librairie politely informed Madame de Lafayette, who had recommended Vincent Capon for a printer position in La Rochelle, that there was to be a competition for the printer's license there, and they hoped that her candidate would win.[86] Similarly, when the bishop of Sarlat protested that he had never imagined that it would not be his prerogative to choose the printer in his diocese, he was told that a competition would have to be held.

Printers' Views

Some administrators held the guilds in contempt, but what did the printers think about the wearing away of corporate identity and whatever power their guilds might hold? Heavily reliant as we are on administrative documentation, it is difficult to get past the posturing of these men and women to discover what the printers actually thought about these developments and whether they resented the imposition of administrative control. Private correspondence, such as Faulcon's fulsome praise of the intendant in Poitiers in a letter to his son, can be revealing, but it is rarely available. Chroniclers like Hardy in Paris and Bernadau in Bordeaux offer some insight, but Hardy's views reflect the position of the Parisian guild, and Bernadau seems to have despised the Bordeaux printers (along with many other people). The archives of the Neuchâtel printing house, the Société typographique de Neuchâtel, hold a large number of letters from French printers and booksellers about importing pirated or prohibited books into France, but this documentation—where printers can be found to praise Swiss freedom and to decry the inconvenience of import rules—also has its biases, because the foreign import trade is the main subject, and commercial interests dominate.[87]

Given the pressure to flaunt their identities as loyal and obedient servants of the state and to put the accent on acceptance and conformity in all their dealings with the administration, the instances of resistance that we do find may well be the tip of a rather large iceberg of resentment and hostility. In Louis XVI's reign, the Toulouse guild met regularly to discuss their affairs, which included their chapel and their purchase of a house to serve as a guildhall. Most of their meetings, however, were devoted to registering the many royal decrees sent to the guild by the Bureau de la librairie and the many letters from the directors of the book trade—Le Camus de Néville, Laurent de Villedeuil, Vidaud de la Tour, and Poitevin de Maissemy. Much in their registers suggests dutiful obedience to royal officials, but there are also signs of underlying resistance.[88] Some guild members balked when the keeper of the seals ordered the admission of a bookseller they did not want. There was clear unhappiness at putting a significant portion of reception fees in a special account (to be forwarded to the Bureau de la librairie in Versailles) and at the loss of their ability to choose their guild officers. Inspection fees also met with resistance, and the book trade inspector's activities prompted some members to try to appeal over his head to the keeper of the seals. Royal officials would accept no criticism of inspectors, and the intendant ordered the entry critical of the inspector to be struck from the guild register. Not only in Toulouse but elsewhere, too, there was resistance to the inspectors. In 1778, the Marseille bookseller Allemend insulted the inspector Pierre Durand and behaved so badly toward him that he was suspended. In 1784, the inspector in Caen was having trouble imposing his authority. The king's printer, Gilles Le Roy, refused to have book shipments inspected at the guildhall and, when pressed by the inspector, behaved disgracefully. Officials deemed Le Roy's behavior particularly offensive because, as king's printer, he should have exemplified submission to the rules and respect for his superiors. Le Roy's shipment was confiscated and he was fined. His presses were dismantled, and he was suspended from the printing and bookselling business.

The Nancy guild split apart over its relationship to the Bureau de la librairie, and many of its members went into virtual revolt against the imposition of administrative control.[89] In 1778 its warden was suspended for insulting the book trade inspector Chassel. A guild member initiated legal action against Chassel in the Parlement of Lorraine to resolve a dispute over fees, but this was blocked by a royal decree of 1785, which ordered that more respect be given to the inspector and specifically prohibited booksellers and printers from suing inspectors. In 1788 guild members were in trouble again because of their mistreatment of their inspector. They would not accept orders from Miromesnil, the keeper of the seals, who outlined the procedures to be followed for guild elections and their supervision by the inspector. More generally, they rejected the central control that the very existence of an inspector represented. In secret deliberations they decided not to recognize certain orders, claiming that the keeper of the seals should deal with them directly and not leave the task to a subordinate. They refused to submit their accounts in the form required, claiming that it was too expensive. Nor would they pay the inspector, despite a blanket order to all guilds from Miromesnil to that effect; they wanted a direct order from him in his capacity as keeper of the seals for each payment. Who was the director of the book trade, anyway? What title did he have that allowed him to give them orders? Letters signed by him were just scribbled by clerks who got signatures on whatever they wanted. A guild member who disagreed with the rebels suffered insults and abuse.

This discourse intersected with anti-ministerial discourse in the parlements in the late 1780s and the arguments being made by many of the printers' relatives in the judiciary. While criticism was focused on the inspectors, it went beyond this when the guilds presented themselves as guardians of legitimate laws against the innovations of intrusive ministry officials. When the directors began insisting on a two-stage election procedure to select guild officers, the guilds complained that this was against the law as laid down in the decree of August 1777. They did not want to select three names to be sent to the chancellor who would then, on the advice of the inspectors, select the warden and deputies. The Nancy guild resolved not to recognize any ministerial orders that contravened royal decrees and claimed to have the right to debate orders from Paris. In the eyes of their inspector, these printers were ridiculously pompous, elevating themselves to the level of magistrates of the highest rank. In April 1789 Barentin instructed Poitevin de Maissemy to warn the Toulouse guild of his "surprise" when he heard that they had deliberated about registering a decree nullifying guild elections in Nancy. The whole guild needed to know that such a deliberation was strange, unacceptable, and contrary to the respect due to royal decrees. They had wanted to add their own clause with the registration, but Maissemy threatened to remove their guild officers if they did this: the keeper of the seals was counting on them to give up this idea, he wrote, and to no longer deliberate over registering matters not proposed to them.[90] The guild backed down and simply registered the decree in question. Some guilds, then, adopted the political discourse of the parlements to confront directly the results of a century of change in royal regulation of the book trade. Licensing was not at issue. Nor was the necessity of policing. Rather, the objects of criticism were taxes, fees, inspectors, intrusive ministry officials, and, at the limit, the very legitimacy of the Bureau de la librairie, which denied them direct communication with their rightful leaders.

Despite their varied circumstances, many provincial printers in different towns cooperated to further agendas they shared. One of the results of administrative growth was that printers in general had extensive connections beyond the towns in which they lived, giving them a nascent national perspective that undermined provincial particularity. Provincial printers had extensive connections and familiarity with Paris, of course, even before the eighteenth century. They bought huge numbers of books from Paris publishers and many provincial printers trained in Paris, often in the big printing houses. Many traveled to Paris on business trips.[91] Many had relatives in Paris: the Anisson family in Lyon, the Labottière and Lacourt families in Bordeaux, the Vatar family in Rennes, Louis-Nicolas Frantin in Dijon, and the Périsse family in Lyon, to name just a few.[92] The licensing system encouraged ties between provincial towns as several families, finding themselves unable to place second sons in the printing business in their own towns, managed to place them in other provincial towns: Vatar (Rennes, Nantes, Lyon), Hovius (Saint-Malo and Rennes), Labottière (Bordeaux and Bayonne), Brun (Bordeaux and Nantes), and Robert (Castre and Toulouse). Furthermore, the struggles with the Parisian publishers over copyright drew provincial printers together in collective action to some extent: the Rouen, Toulouse, and Lyon guilds cooperated in writing a memorandum in 1776 against the practice of renewing copyrights that favored the Parisians.[93] Provincial guilds sought information from each other when attempting to protect privileges and exemptions or to define the role of the king's printer. In the seventeenth century, printers began to build their cases for Versailles officials by citing as precedents Bureau de la librairie decisions made for other towns, a practice that was very common by the late eighteenth century. Provincial printers also played a major role in importing, selling, and reprinting news from Paris and elsewhere. Printers printed and sometimes edited the *Affiches* that spread throughout the provinces, offering local journalism to French provincial towns.[94] They promoted ideas of the Enlightenment, awareness of local, national, and international news, commercial values, consumerism, and possibly even notions of equality.[95] They were not able to discuss politics directly but, nonetheless, offered information on some of the major issues of the day—judicial reform, the slave trade, municipal reform, and royal finances. The *Affiches* in Toulouse was especially audacious in this regard.[96] Historians have long known about the international orientation of the book trade in eighteenth-century France and the far-flung connections of the many printers who carried on large wholesale and retail bookselling businesses. One might speculate that among the three hundred or so printers in France, licensing promoted a more developed national sentiment than was shared by their ancestors.

Conclusion

In 1789, with the calling of the Estates General, men like Bruyset and Delaroche were forced back into the mold of an artisan guild to adopt their corporate identity and draw up a list of their grievances.[97] Like other French men and women, printers and booksellers took the opportunity to look critically at the place of the state in their lives and assess its legitimacy.[98] It was a difficult task. The Bruysets, the Delaroches, the Lallemants, the Vatars, and the Mossys had to try to agree on a number of issues with their fellow guildsmen, many of whom had quite different visions of guild decision making, quite different individual relationships with state officials, and quite different connections to the parlements and other courts that no amount of shared Enlightenment culture could reconcile. Some printers resented the growth of administrative control, but it is unlikely that Beaume, Bruyset, Lallemant, and others agreed with them. As the state and the media evolved between the 1660s and the Revolution, the ideas of both administrators and printers about merit, guild entry, and competitive examinations were manipulated to serve a wide range of agendas. Administrators did not challenge the hold of established families on the printing profession—and indeed, these families saw their influence grow. By the reign of Louis XVI, recruitment had slipped out of guild control.

7

BEHIND THE RHETORIC

The Social Position and Politics of Provincial Printers, 1750–1789

Par arrêts du Conseil d'État Sa Majesté a fixé le nombre des imprimeries dans toutes
les villes du Royaume; le motif de cette fixation a été de prévenir les impressions de ces
Écrits, que la passion enfante et que sème la licence, et procurer par ce moyen à chaque
Titulaire des imprimeries réservées, la faculté de vivre par un travail licite
—*État des imprimeries de la ville de Bordeaux, 1775*

By the late eighteenth century, lobbying was second nature to provincial printers, who had relied on patrons for centuries and, in more recent decades, appealed to officials in the royal administration on a wide range of issues. What
connection was there between the rhetoric in their lobbying and the social
reality it purported to describe—printers' wealth, their families, their work,
and their sense of honor and place in eighteenth-century provincial life? Generally, there were four recurring themes in printer rhetoric. First, the printing
profession had not maintained its economic position and had been in serious
decline from its past days of glory. Second, unqualified outsiders were invading
their profession, lowering both artistic and moral standards. Third, printers
constituted a special class of royal servants—socially superior to other artisans—
who promoted the noble causes of religion and science and had been favored
by kings since the advent of print. Fourth, these responsible and loyal subjects
assisted their monarch in the face of the many forces of ignorance and malice
that threatened them both. This chapter shows that while the rhetoric matched
reality on the matter of printers' elevated social position in their towns, there
was very little substance to the other three claims. In fact, despite their rhetoric,

printers were a relatively rich and closed group who often engaged in the clandestine book trade.

Wealth

The reduction in the number of printers, coupled with the growth in the demand for printing in the eighteenth century, increased printer wealth in provincial France.[1] While variations in wealth existed, licensed printers in the second half of the eighteenth century were comfortably well-off members of the urban bourgeoisie who achieved considerable prosperity from the exploding demand for printed ephemera and—in some cases—from bookselling businesses they ran alongside their printing houses. (See appendix A for a survey of printer wealth drawn mainly from dowries and post-mortem inventories.)

The most complete evidence comes from Bordeaux.[2] Early in the eighteenth century, there were a number of less well-to-do printers in Bordeaux and a few very prosperous ones. The king's printers, Jean Lacourt and Pierre Brun, were wealthy, but they appear to have had several poorer colleagues. Profits in the second half of the century were generally high for everyone who owned a printing house. A study of wealth at the beginnings and ends of several printing careers shows rising prosperity among printers in Bordeaux at the end of the eighteenth century. When Jean-Baptiste Lacornée took over his father's business in 1721, he was worth about 4,500 livres. His wife brought him 7,000 livres as a dowry in 1727. At the end of his career, he owned property worth more than 30,000 livres and had given his niece 15,000 livres in dowry. Simon Lacourt inherited 9,500 livres from his parents in 1777. In the 1780s he gradually built up an estate in Macau and, at his death in 1794, the printing house alone was worth 66,954 livres. His home, country estate, and property should be added to this—and all were separate from his wife's estate in Pissos. Similarly, the printers Michel Racle, Jean-Baptiste Séjourné, and Pierre Albespy, who inherited very modest sums from their families, made comparative fortunes during their careers, all buying country estates. Three of the six late eighteenth-century printers—Simon Lacourt, Michel Racle, and the Labottière brothers—possessed property worth more than 50,000 livres. Two others, Jean-Baptiste Lacornée and Pierre Beaume, were worth close to 50,000 livres, and the widow Calamy's business alone was worth more than 20,000 livres at her death in 1777. With the exception of Pierre-Godefroy Calamy, who did not obtain a printer's license until 1784 and had made a poor marriage to a servant, it can be said that Bordeaux printers all made comfortable fortunes in the last decades of the *ancien régime*.

In Lyon, too, there are signs that printers ran large businesses, and many became wealthy.[3] Of those about whom we have information on their wealth, many were prosperous: Aimé Delaroche,[4] Pierre Valfray,[5] Jean-Marie Bruyset, Jean-Marie Barret,[6] Jacques-Julien Vatar, Jean-Baptiste Delamollière, Michel LeRoy, Charles-François Millanois, Claude-André Faucheux, and Jean-André Périsse Duluc.[7] In 1731, Jean-Marie Bruyset claimed that he made book sales worth 1,000 to 1,200 livres a week and, in 1784, his son provided a dowry of 27,000 livres and received one from his bride of 40,000.[8] Millanois, a member of a powerful clan of Lyon notables who had married into the Delaroche printing family, became a printer and shared with his wife a business worth 96,216 livres in 1783. Millanois Delaroche was the printer for the intendant in 1789 and for the Provincial Assembly in 1790. His lifestyle on the eve of the Revolution is indicated by a list of some of his confiscated belongings: his library, paintings, maps, engravings, statues, and decorative clocks.[9] In the 1780s the Périsse family possessed three country estates as well as their house on the rue Mercière in Lyon. Each of the seven brothers and sisters in the family claimed a substantial inheritance.[10] During the Terror, Périsse Duluc had to defend himself against the charge of being rich. Other Lyon printers could be described as prosperous as well. Claude-André Faucheux made a respectable marriage to the daughter of a jeweller, and her dowry indicates a comfortable lifestyle: 3,500 livres of clothing, jewels, and cash.[11] When Jean-Baptiste Delamollière married in 1781, his bride brought him a 10,000-livre advance on her inheritance.[12] At their deaths in the Terror, both of these men had very large businesses. Henri Declaustre, on his death at midcentury, had a significant estate, and his heirs distributed the sum of 35,800 livres.[13] There were exceptions, but many printers in Lyon were affluent.[14]

In two other major provincial centers—Rouen and Toulouse—there are signs of general prosperity. Of the last two generations of printers in Rouen, eight of the ten families were prosperous: Lallemant, Seyer, Le Boullenger, Machuel, Behourt, Besongne, Oursel, and Dumesnil.[15] While in 1700 there had been twenty-eight printing houses, some poor, by 1760 there were fewer and bigger printing houses: Lallemant (five presses and twelve workers); Seyer, who had taken over the Behourt business (five presses, seventeen workers); Le Boullenger (five presses, eight workers); Machuel (four presses, fourteen workers);

and Laurent Dumesnil (eight workers). We know six of the ten families holding printing licenses at the end of the regime in Toulouse, and all were well
off.[16] The printer and barrister Jean-Henry Guillemette's daughter was married in 1773 with a 12,000-livre dowry and, in 1780, two of his children had
their inheritances increased to 16,252 livres and 15,814 livres, respectively.[17] In
1794, Jean-Florent Baour left his son a fortune evaluated at 37,637 livres, which
included two houses, one in Toulouse and the other in the country.[18] When
the widow of Jean-François Desclassan remarried in 1780, she had a dowry of
22,000 livres.[19] The printer Jean-Joseph Douladoure's nephews, who took over
his business, provided substantial dowries when they married: Jean-François
(16,000 livres) in 1787 and Joseph (25,000 livres) in 1786.[20] Survey information places members of the Robert family and Jean-Baptiste Rayet among the
five largest printers and booksellers in the town in 1767.[21] Robert, who was
a printer, bookseller, and barrister, received a dowry of 12,000 livres when he
married in 1786 and had capital of 140,000 livres in Year III.[22]

Less comprehensive information on the wealth of printers in other provincial towns reveals that in the second half of the eighteenth century, there
were, at the very least, some very wealthy families, and more data would probably suggest that this wealth was shared generally by provincial printers. In
three other parlementary towns—Dijon, Rennes, and Toulouse—printers were
clearly prosperous. In Dijon, Antoine Defay, Arnaud-Jean-Baptiste Augé, and
Louis-Nicolas Frantin became wealthy.[23] The son of a tailor in Gevrey, Defay
became rich as a printer, and his daughter married a *maître de comptes:* an entry
in the *Mercure dijonnais* announced Defay's death at the age of seventy-nine in
1757, describing him as a "riche et fameux imprimeur." Somewhat shakier evidence for Augé's wealth comes from his litigation with the noble barrister
Guillaume Raviot over an edition of *Arrests notable du Parlement de Dijon.* Part
of Raviot's case hinged on Augé's unseemly wealth. Augé had an extremely
profitable business printing for the courts and bragged of belongings worth
50,000 livres and of being able to give 10,000 livres in cash to each of his
daughters. This was quite an achievement, given—we are told—that Augé and
his wife inherited nothing from their parents. Frantin, a member of the Dijon
municipal council in the 1780s, had married in 1775 with a dowry of 71,242
livres. In Rennes, the Vatar family took over printing in the town and possessed
three of the five businesses in Rennes, all of them major.

Similar indications of the wealth of printers can be found in some non-
parlementary towns. According to the subdelegate in Montpellier, the two

printers there in 1764 possessed fortunes of more than 100,000 livres, a result, he implied, of their overcharging the courts and the administration for printing.[24] Pierre Beaume, one of two printers in Nîmes, married the daughter of a *négociant* in 1776 and received a dowry of 8,500 livres, including 1,000 livres of jewellery. His was a big wedding with twenty-three signatures; representing Pierre's mother was an *ancien conseiller en la cour souverain de Nîmes*.[25] In Troyes the printer Jean-Antoine Garnier was reported in 1777 to have property worth more than 100,000 livres.[26] In Marseille, where there were four printing families in 1789—Mossy, Brébion, Sibié, and Favet—the Mossy family was very rich, possessing lands in Châteauneuf, Martigues, Fos, Saint-Mitre, and Arles. The Brébion widow in 1749 had five houses.[27] One cannot help but compare these success stories with that of a poor unfortunate early eighteenth-century printer in Marseille, Jean-Antoine Mallard, who went bankrupt in 1725 because of the plague and the loss of shipments to Havre de Grace and the West Indies. He had not paid rent since 1719.[28] While bankruptcies of booksellers did occur in the late eighteenth century, they were extremely rare among provincial printers.[29] In almost all cases, where we have indications of the wealth of printers in the late eighteenth century, they were comfortably well off, if not rich.

The level of material comfort enjoyed by printers was modest compared to that of many large wholesale merchants or, of course, of the nobility, but it certainly undercuts almost all official descriptions of printers' economic circumstances provided by the guilds and passed on through royal officials to Versailles.[30] In 1775, for example, the survey by the intendant's office of Bordeaux printers included the observation that most of the printers in town were without work. In 1784 the inspector of the book trade in Rouen wrote that it had come to his attention that the book trade had diminished considerably; most printing houses in Rouen were limited to very modest activity. In general, this branch of trade was wasting away, and the booksellers and printers in Rouen could not pay the taxes levied on their guild.[31] Until the end of the regime, the guilds continued to camouflage the fact that several of their members were major operators and many were wealthy. Their reasons are obvious: they wanted to discourage any increase in taxes, any infringement on their privileges, or any measures that might increase the number of printers. As we have seen, the strategy achieved some success. The French provincial media were wealthy local notables, far from being poor. As we shall see, they also played a part in the political and intellectual life of their towns.

The Closed World of Eighteenth-Century Printers

Fears that the printing profession was being invaded by unqualified outsiders were entirely unfounded. An analysis of printer licensing in the French provinces shows that, over the course of the eighteenth century, the printers were drawn to an increasing extent from the closed milieu of printers' families (see table 3). In the period 1719–1724, 68 percent of printers were either sons, sons-in-law, nephews, or widows of printers. In the period 1739–1744 this figure declined slightly to 63 percent, but in the second half of the eighteenth century, it rose to 83 percent for the years 1755–1760 and to 90 percent in the years 1776–1780. A much larger sample for the years 1780–1789 confirms the trend: 78 percent of new recruits were from established printing families. Printers on the eve of the Revolution had generally been raised in the profession or had married the daughters of printing families.[32] More than in other artisanal trades, entry into the printing profession was restricted to family members.

Printers in the major provincial capitals in 1789 were virtually all sons or sons-in-law of printers. The last generation of *ancien régime* printers in Lyon, Rouen, and Dijon were all from printing families: sons, sons-in-law, brothers, or nephews. In Bordeaux and Toulouse, all but one of the printers at the time of the Revolution were sons or sons-in-law of local printers. Of the nineteen

Table 3   Family connections of licensed provincial printers (AN V[6])

	1719–24	1739–44	1755–60	1776–80	1780–89	Total
Licenses	69	77	35	39	80	300
Printers' sons	39	33	27	30	52★	181
Printers' nephews		1	1		4	6
Married into families of printers	7	7	1	2	5	22
Widows	1	8	0	3	1	13
Total family links	47	49	29	35	62	222
% with family links	68	63	83	90	78	74

NOTE: It is assumed that a candidate would mention a family connection in the petition if one existed. The number with family links has been adjusted to prevent printers' sons who married printers' daughters or widows from being counted twice.

★ The "sons" category for 1780–89 includes two brothers, two nephews, and one daughter; one wife is in the widow category. For evidence beyond the petitions that two candidates were nephews: Pierre-Joseph Calmen, who took over from the widow Adibert in Aix in 1787, was her nephew (Billioud, *Le Livre en Provence*, 18); Jean-Baptiste Delamollière was the nephew of Vialon in Lyon when he took over that license in 1781 (*contrat de mariage*, ADR, notary Soupat, 1 February 1758).

nonrelatives of printers who obtained licenses in the last decade of the *ancien régime,* six were licensed for very small towns (Boulogne, Bourg-en-Bresse, Embrun, Dole, Perpignan, and Sélestat), and the circumstances surrounding the appointment of some of the others reveal how difficult it was for outsiders to obtain licenses. Pierre Beaume, who was licensed in Bordeaux in 1784, was a protégé of Miromesnil, who already ran a large printing business in Nîmes and had printed for the new supreme court established there at the time of the Maupeou reforms. As we have seen, Vincent Capon in La Rochelle enjoyed the patronage of Madame de Lafayette.[33] Noel-Etienne Sens was a well-established bookseller in Toulouse, and Pierre Bellegarique was a printing house director for forty-five years.[34] Generally, newcomers became established with outgoing masters and made arrangements to take over their businesses. Although a few men broke into the printing business from time to time, what must be noted is how well-connected they had to be to do this. Printing was concentrated in the hands of an identifiable group of families, especially in the larger towns.

Social Status

L'intérêt public exige donc, où de supprimer les Brevets de Librairie, où de ne les confier qu'à des personnes connues, dont la naissance et les talents puissent s'adapter à l'exercice d'une Profession affiliée à l'université et que nos Rois ont eux-mêmes distingués des arts mécaniques; Profession tient un rang honorable dans le Royaume, et à laquelle des avocats célèbres, des Docteurs en l'Université, n'ont pas dédaigné d'être admis.
—À Monseigneur le vice-chancelier de France, *1767*

Because of the closed nature of their profession, the expansion in the demand for print, and their increased wealth, printing families began to advance socially in the hierarchy of their provincial towns. There had been some spectacular cases of social ascension among printers' families in the sixteenth and seventeenth centuries, but this kind of success occurred more regularly in the eighteenth century. An exploration of the wider milieu in which printers' families lived—their fathers-in-law, uncles, cousins, nieces, and nephews—situates printers among merchant, professional, legal and, in some cases, noble families in their provincial towns.

   In the port town of Bordeaux, of the fifteen printers' fathers-in-law identified in the eighteenth century, seven were merchants and six were professional men: a surgeon, a pharmacist, a doctor, an architect, a barrister, and a bailiff.[35] The final two were a *bourgeois* and a printer. Such alliances placed the town's printers among the merchant, professional, and legal families. The absence of artisans' daughters among printers' wives is noteworthy, as is the almost total absence of marriages between members of printing families: only one took place in the second half of the eighteenth century. Of twenty-five uncles, ten were merchants, seven were in the Church, four in the legal professions, and two in the medical professions. (One of the latter was the rector of the University of Bordeaux.) Related to members of the legal, commercial, and ecclesiastical communities from birth, the family members of the printers' own generation (brothers and brothers-in-law) further consolidated these links: of forty such generational contemporaries identified, eighteen were merchants (most often *négociants*), ten were in the legal professions, five in the Church, and five in the medical professions.[36] At the end of their lives, printers had a number of nephews in the mercantile and legal establishments, and some could even claim a relationship to nobles: of twenty-eight nephews, eleven were merchants (almost all *négociants*), five were in the legal professions, four were nobles, and two held landed property (*propriétaires*). The remaining were a clergyman, an insurance broker, a professor of mathematics, an army officer, a gilder, and a *bourgeois* of Paris.[37]

Three Bordeaux printing families were able to place their progeny in the nobility. The printer Jean Lacourt married the daughter of the surgeon Larré, and in 1755 she passed the printing business on to her nephew Simon because, as she declared in a notarial act, her sons had chosen "another profession." This, we find out elsewhere, was an attempt to enter the nobility by purchasing for her son Nicolas the ennobling office of counsellor in the Parlement of Bordeaux.[38] Nicolas married Marie Gombault, daughter of the noble Marc Antoine de Gombault, and Larré's second son became a military officer. The social ascent of the Lacourt family was spectacular; in general, printers were at least two generations away from nobility. The Labottière and Lacornée families had nephews who entered the nobility, making some printers close relatives of nobles. In the case of the Labottière family, the printer Claude's son, a *négociant,* married into the wealthy Duport family, permitting his granddaughter to marry the noble military officers Buynaud and Barthélémy de la Barrière. Pierre Lacornée's sister married Lamarque, *bourgeois et chirurgien,* and their daughter married the noble Labadie. These printers' children became part of, or placed their children in, the upper strata of Bordeaux society.

Evidence about the careers of printers and their families in provincial towns outside Bordeaux is less complete, but elevated social connections were certainly in evidence. In Toulouse the Pijon family entered the nobility after Jean-Armand-Honoré-Marie-Bernard Pijon became a Capitoul in 1775. Dijon printers Antoine Defay, Louis-Nicolas Frantin, and Jean-Baptiste Capel had *négociants,* barristers, attorneys, and canons among their relatives. Frantin was a member of the elite municipal council in Dijon.[39] In Nantes the king's printers Joseph-Mathurin Vatar and Pierre-Issac Brun, the Angers printer André-Jacques Jahyer, and the Rennes printer Nicolas Audran were each called a "noble homme," a term that indicates an upper bourgeois status.[40] The Lallemant family in Rouen entered the nobility: the printer Richard Lallemant was alderman and mayor in 1785, and his son, Richard Gontran Lallemant, purchased the ennobling office of *chevalier d'honneur au bureau des finances de Rouen.*[41] In Lyon the printers had many links to the nobility. Members of the Anisson family became ennobled; the printer Pierre Valfray was a noble, *échevin,* and seigneur de Salornay, and his brother a *maître de l'hôtel du roi* in Paris.[42] Jean-Marie Bruyset's sister married the noble Colomès, the son of a *conseiller du roi* and *receveur général des finances* in Languedoc, and his daughter married into the noble Buynaud family.[43] Delaroche's daughter married the son of the noble Millanois family.[44] A sister of the printer Charles-François Millanois married the marquis de Regnauld de Bellecize, *commissaire de la noblesse* in Lyon, the last *prévôt des marchands* of Lyon, and commander of the royal fortress of Pierrescize until 1792.[45]

In the earlier stages of this process of social ascension, members of successful printing families typically became wholesale merchants, bought judicial offices—some ennobling and some not—or became barristers. In Poitiers in 1782, Félix Faulcon, the son of a printer, rejected his father's profession and bought an expensive office in the presidial court of Poitiers, claiming that he needed to establish himself and noting in his diary that he felt "almost naked" in society without an office. The son of the Abbeville printer Devérité bought an attorney's office in the local bailliage court before taking over his father's business.[46] As we have seen above, the son of the Jean Lacourt family in Bordeaux became a counsellor in the Parlement of Bordeaux. The printer Albespy became a *receveur des lotteries;* his son was a barrister and one of his sons-in-law was a *secrétaire du parquet des gens du roi au bureau de finances.*[47] Earlier in the century, the son of Jean Ressayre had the position of substitute for the attorney general in the Parlement of Dijon before he obtained his father's printing license.[48]

The son-in-law of the printer Calamy in Bordeaux, Pellusset, was *directeur de la régie des biens et procureur de l'hôtel de ville* and later bought other offices. In Rouen, Jean-Baptiste Machuel inherited from his father-in-law the office of *maître des ports, ponts et passages de Normandie et juges des traites* in Rouen and Guibray and held it until its suppression in 1772.[49] The father of Balthazard Mouret, a printer in Aix, was *secrétaire du parquet et procureur général du parlement de Provence.*[50] Martial Barbou in Limoges was a *greffier en chef de l'élection* and an alderman in Limoges.[51] One son of the Rennes printer Gilles-Joseph Vatar purchased property outside Rennes in 1756 and became sieur de La Mabilais. He was also a doctor of law at the University of Paris and a barrister in the Parlement of Paris and, in 1764, became a *conseiller du roi.*[52] The son of the printer Deliege in Sainte-Ménehould bought the office of *conseiller du roi président en la juridiction des traites-foraines de Saint-Ménehould.*[53] Two brothers of Charles-François Millanois in Lyon, held offices: Joseph-Léonard was *conseiller assesseur du point d'honneur au tribunal des maréchaux de France* and the future member of the Constituent Assembly, while in 1787 Jean-Jacques-François became *conseiller du roi en la sénéchaussée de Lyon.*[54] Early in the eighteenth century in Besançon, Louis Rigoine bought the office of *conseiller du Roy et trésorier receveur et payer des gages des officiers au parlement de Besançon* and became a noble.[55]

The world of provincial printers overlapped considerably with that of the courts. A significant number of printers were barristers. In the seventeenth century a member of the Millanges family in Bordeaux ran into difficulty carrying on the two professions, but this was not a problem for eighteenth-century provincial printers.[56] Many printers had relatives who were barristers: Louis-Nicolas Frantin in Dijon married a barrister's daughter. Jean-Florent Baour in Toulouse had *négociants* and barristers in his family. In Poitiers the printer Jean-Félix Faulcon was a barrister, and his son-in-law who replaced him in 1783 was *licentié es loix.*[57] In Besançon the printer Louis Rigoine's son became a barrister.[58] Jean Albespy, the son of a Bordeaux printer, became a barrister and claimed during the Revolution that he had been born "without fortune and preferred the profession of lawyer to that of (his) ancestors which one knows is not lucrative but was the only profession that suited a citizen who was jealous of his independence and his liberty."

The story of the Albespy family's ascension is an interesting example of the rapid social rise that may have been a little easier in the booming port town of Bordeaux than elsewhere in the realm. In 1744 the printer Pierre Albespy married the daughter of an upwardly mobile merchant family, Dubrocar. This family had moved quickly from farmer to carpenter and had arrived at *bour-geois* status in 1705. We find a Jean Dubrocar at the Jesuit College in 1702. Two years before his own marriage, Pierre married his sister to a barrister. Albespy and Dubrocar were able to buy an estate, and Pierre became a leader in his parish. He later became a collector for the royal lotteries, and his son became a barrister. One son-in-law was a wholesale merchant and the other an office-holder (*secrétaire du parquet des gens du roi au bureau de finance*). Those in attendance at the weddings of these children included notaries, professors, and the high church official Broc, canon of the St. André cathedral. Albespy's barrister son became a local notable. Still, the family was never very rich; the children's dowries were modest and the family estate was sold to provide them. Pierre's son Jean, a barrister, declared at his marriage in 1782 that he had four thousand livres "in silver and in books" in his library. Nonetheless, this was enough to attract a bride with a dowry worth thirty-seven thousand livres.[59] The son of the Poitiers printer Jean-Félix Faulcon became a lawyer before becoming a judge in the presidial court. Both the younger Faulcon and Jean Albespy became politicians in the Revolution, as did the son-in-law of the Bordeaux printer Simon Lacourt and the brother of the Lyon printer Charles-François Millanois, both barristers. Millanois' brother became a judge in the sénéchaussée court in Lyon in 1787 and, as noted above, was later a member of the Constituent Assembly.[60] Through their education and work and that of their cousins, sons, sons-in-law, and other relatives, printers had close links with the legal world of late eighteenth-century France.

Clearly, collective family strategies both for maintaining status and for advancing it were being pursued.[61] Such strategies required sacrifices from individual family members. All ten members of the Périsse family, for example, lived in one house and contributed to the family's promotion in Lyon society. Many members of the printers' families remained celibate. We cannot know the motivations in these often deeply religious families, but a large number of daughters and sons entered the Church: several members of the Bruyset family entered orders, and Jean-Marie's brother and cousin were canons (one in Marseille and the other in Lyon). Felix Faulcon in Poitiers, Pierre Phillippot in Bordeaux, and Declaustre in Toulouse are just a few of the printers who had brothers who were priests; Faulcon's three daughters and Declaustre's sister are some of the women in printers' families who entered convents. Aimé Delaroche in Lyon had occasion to describe the sacrifices made by his daughter, Rose, to keep the license in the family. Since she was an only daughter, she had to marry

a printer and, when her young husband died before obtaining a license, she had
to work hard in the printing house and keep her sights firmly fixed on securing the license for her sons. Rose Delaroche actually obtained the license her-
self—the first in the history of licensing where a daughter (not a widow) of a
licensed printer obtained one. She then remarried. Her father gave his account
of her difficulties a particularly eighteenth-century twist, attributing her death
to overwork and breastfeeding. More typically (and less dramatically), printing
families used their licenses to assure better marriages for their children. A printer
in Tours made this quite explicit when he requested a printer's license for his
thirty-one-year-old son in 1777, claiming that it would guarantee his establishment and would allow him to make an advantageous marriage.[62] Even in
cases where one son was able to climb up the social hierarchy by becoming an
officeholder or a lawyer, efforts were often made to keep the printing license
in the family by passing it to another son, a son-in-law, a nephew, or a cousin.
Because the licenses were a critical component in these families' social ascent,
they relinquished them only at the end of the long process.

   The licensing system held out the possibility of social ascension but also intensified some of the pressures on family relations already felt by the wider sector of the eighteenth-century bourgeoisie.[63] In the Faulcon family in Poitiers,
conflict arose when a son aspired to become a barrister and then a judge rather
than a printer. This had significant repercussions for family members. His
father felt honored to be a printer and, even more, to be a king's printer, and
he tried to convey this to his son. An uncle, a *curé* in Poitiers, along with other
friends and relatives tried hard to persuade the young Faulcon that printing
was an honorable profession. The uncle wrote in 1776 describing the position
of printer in society as one the boy should embrace:

> The profession that your ancestors have carried on with distinction and
> praise, the profession for which your family has destined you for a long
> time—a family that is far more attached to you than you seem to be to
> it—, the profession that your sincere, true, judicious and right-thinking
> friends want you to take up, the profession that prominent leaders (*chefs*)
> in the province and the town expect you to embrace, the profession that
> your father for whom you should be a source of satisfaction and consola-
> tion but who sees with pain and sorrow your disdain and scorn. A father
> so good, so tender, so devoted, does he not deserve, dear nephew, that
> you make some sacrifice for your own sake and for his?[64]

Félix Faulcon's decision to resist this advice provoked anguish in the family, but they adapted—and, more important, found a way to keep the printing license in the family. Félix's sister married François Barbier, who then took over the family printing business and successfully applied for a license, eventually obtaining the position of king's printer. Later in life—before he became a judge and his prospects were not looking good—Félix had second thoughts about his choice. A friend wrote and suggested that he consider rejoining the family printing business. He thought about this, and even acknowledged that his father might be accommodating enough to make the arrangements, but decided that he could not go back on the solemn promise he had given his sister that he would never try to reenter the business. She had agreed to alter her life and to contract a marriage that would keep the printing business in the family, and he was honor-bound to keep his word. Félix Faulcon's views resembled those of the son of the Bordeaux printer Pierre Albespy; both men explained their decisions to choose the law rather than the printing house as the result of a desire to be independent. (They did not admit to a desire for social betterment and, although Faulcon actively denied this, he was not especially convincing.) The Lyon printer Aimé Delaroche described the daughters of his colleague, Pierre Valfray, as "rich enough not to marry printers," perhaps a further indication that the profession served as a springboard into the elites of provincial towns.

Evidence of problems like those faced by the Faulcon family is very rare, but because bureau officials were occasionally involved in settling conflicts arising within families over which son would get the license, some documentation is available. Conflict became public when two brothers applied for one license and an internal family conflict was passed on to Versailles for resolution. This happened in Bordeaux when Raymond and Charles, the sons of Claude Labottière, both applied for his printer's license.[65] In Toulouse, when two brothers in the Desclassan family fought over the position in the 1760s, the bureau chose, taking into consideration the father's views. There was terrible acrimony in the Vatar family over the son who would take the Rennes position in the 1750s. Some families hit on the solution of sending second sons to other towns to set up as printers: Brun in Bordeaux and Vatar in Rennes are two such examples. The Brun son (Isaac) went to Nantes, married a printer's daughter, and set up there.[66] In Rennes, Vatar sons went to Nantes, Paris, and Lyon.[67] A rather general solution to the problem of extra sons, and one used across the realm, was to set them up as booksellers. Some booksellers began requesting bookselling licenses from the bureau in the eighteenth century, undoubtedly to protect themselves and to make their standing official, but the licensing of booksellers did not become a general practice until the 1777 reforms of the book trade. Several members of the Labottière family in Bordeaux ran major bookselling businesses, for example. Family conflicts were undoubtedly endemic but mostly stayed out of the records. The few that we see suggest clearly that the licensing system strained relations between siblings and between parents and their children.

Printers in Political Life

Eighteenth-century printers played an important role in political life in their provincial towns. Several printers or their family members participated in the closed world of urban politics before the Revolution: Pierre Valfray, Jean-André Périsse Duluc, and Claude-François Millanois did so in Lyon. Richard Lallemant in Rouen was a mayor and alderman. Others were aldermen or municipal judges in their towns: Louis-Nicolas Frantin in Dijon, François-Augustin Malassis in Alençon, Félix Faulcon and François Barbier in Poitiers, Pierre Toussaint in Saintes, André-Jacques Jahyer in Angers, Pierre Chalopin in Caen. The Dole printer Pierre-François Tonnet's father-in-law was an alderman, and Raymond Labottière's father-in-law was a judge in Bordeaux. Faulcon's sister married an alderman in Poitiers, one daughter married a municipal judge there, and another cousin was a municipal judge. Yet beyond the official political world, printers' shops were centers of activity in the growing public sphere of late eighteenth-century France, where intellectual, cultural, and political ideas flourished. In 1745 the shop of the Labottière brothers in Bordeaux near the Palais de l'Ombrière, where the Parlement of Bordeaux held its sessions, was described as the meeting place of most of the *nouvellistes,* a spot where many people gathered to learn what was going on when the mail arrived in town.[68] The ten chairs listed in 1754 in the postmortem inventory of Raymond Labottière's shop suggest that it was a reading room even before his sons took over the business and branched into journalism. Men spent time in printing houses and bookshops discussing literature, news, and politics. In some cases, men were ridiculed for unwarranted literary pretensions in the shops and, on occasion, suffered physical violence for their political views. In the bookseller Mathieu Chappuis' shop in 1788, for example, a grocer with royalist sympathies was slapped in the face by an enraged patriot tired of "bavardage ministériel."[69] Both Pierre Phillippot and Antoine Pallandre were denounced in 1791 because of the aristocratic cliques that regularly frequented their shops. Phillippot ran a reading room in the Parlement buildings.[70] The *parlementaires* gathered to discuss legal cases in Vatar's boutique in Rennes; indeed, it was in Vatar's shop that a judge in 1763 became so carried away in one of these discussions that he was forced to recuse himself from a case. The journalist and lawyer Linguet offered a critical account of the politicized atmosphere in the Rennes book-shops: "There are no cafés in this town; the bookshops take their place and are the rendezvous of all the idle people who regularly malign their neighbors and reform the government."[71]

Printers enjoyed regular social contact with the elites in their towns. Many were freemasons. André Faure de Beauregard, who was both a barrister and a printer in Grenoble, worked closely with nobles and *parlementaires* on a project to develop a library there.[72] Many nobles are listed in Raymond Labottière's account books.[73] Printers often had their businesses next door to or inside the buildings of the local parlements, in close proximity to the judicial world in these towns. In Lyon Président Dugas (and presumably many others) spent considerable time in Jean-Marie Bruyset's shop and, in his case, the connections led to further invitations. Dugas wrote in 1731 to a correspondent that he had just had Bruyset and his daughter to dine: "We talked a lot about books, editions and of the book trade. How much would you guess that Bruyset makes from the retail sale of books in a week? Between 1,000 and 1,200 livres, I would never have believed it. He is particularly happy with the Capuchins and he says that there is not another [religious] community who buys more books and pays so well for them."[74] Printing houses were like masonic lodges and academies, places where the urban elites met and discussed affairs.

Printers in the Clandestine Book Trade

Despite their rhetoric, the printers and booksellers of provincial France did not shun the trade in pirated and prohibited editions (see appendix B).[75] Business concerns and personal ties often trumped other identities and drew printers into the clandestine trade. Undoubtedly, the way they had packaged themselves as pillars of monarchy for the last century restrained their involvement in the clandestine trade to some extent, but we will never know by how much: it is impossible to gauge the extent of the trade in illegal books. We do know that when printers and booksellers dealt with this issue, they displayed a cold pragmatism that contradicts the shocked innocence of their corporate comments and has led some historians to argue that printers were economically rather than ideologically motivated.[76] This may have been true, but printers were also members of cliques and networks and drawn into the political struggles of the late eighteenth century.[77] Integrated into the legal milieu of their towns, they had close contact with the principal figures in disputes within the judiciary and between the judiciary and the ministries in the reigns of Louis XV and Louis XVI. In times of political crisis they had to navigate choppy waters indeed. Between the Seven Years' War and the end of Louis XV's reign, these struggles were the main feature of political life in France and they flared up again late in Louis XVI's reign, especially in the years 1787 and 1788.[78] One important aspect of these battles was the attempt by the parlements to make their views public through print.[79] Because they were such important clients, the barristers and judges in parlementary towns had special influence over the local printers. When asked to print pamphlets, controversial decrees, or remonstrances, printers made judgment calls on a daily basis. Provincial printers printed the opinions of both sides for the widening reading public, which was more and more interested in hotly contested constitutional struggles.

To print parlementary remonstrances and pamphlets in favor of the cause of the parlement was technically illegal, despite the widespread criticism of this policy. No less a figure than Chrétien-Guillaume Lamoignon de Malesherbes in his *Remonstrances des Cours des Aides* offered a strong defense of publicity in government, arguing that the advent of writing in recent centuries had allowed a number of administrators surrounding the king to make laws in secret without heeding the representative assemblies that should be ruling France. The administration that resulted was thus arbitrary, repressive, and clandestine. But now printing offered the chance to return to a kind of transparency, because the new art had increased the number of educated men sufficiently to make up an enlightened public that could be reconnected to their sovereign by discussion of public issues in print.[80] Malesherbes' view, outlined before he became a king's minister, however, reflected only one thread of ministerial views on freer expression. Louis XV's minister Etienne-François, duc de Choiseul, may have agreed, but other ministers continued to regard parlementary remonstrances as private communications between the parlements and their king.[81] In 1763 one royal order described parlementary printing of this sort as dangerous because it disseminated "alarm, defiance and discouragement" into the minds of the king's subjects.[82] The legitimacy of public discussion was at the heart of the great ideological debate being played out. Because some thought that the views of the parlements and other bodies should be aired, French provincial printers were drawn into the constitutional struggles.

To examine the relations between French provincial printers and the parlements, we have to revisit the claims historians make that Louis XIV removed jurisdiction over censorship matters from the parlements during his reign.[83] It is important to recognize how influential the parlements remained in their provincial towns. Indeed, parlementary influence over printing may have been increasing under Louis XVI's reign.[84] Parlements were important employers of printers.[85] Printers in parlementary towns had many influential relatives in the judicial world. In Metz the printers' ties with parlement were so close that they sent remonstrances to Maupeou in 1771 to complain of the suppression of the parlement.[86] The parlements provided privileged spaces where their printers could work outside the control of municipal and royal officials, allowing them an independence analogous to that enjoyed by merchants protected by the duc d'Orléans in the Palais Royale.[87] In Grenoble in 1704, François Champ complained that pirated editions of Latin primers were being sold by booksellers inside the very buildings of the Parlement where in 1764 the printer André Giroud had his business.[88] In Montpellier there was a protected bookshop in the buildings of the Cour des aides.[89] Nicolas-Paul Vatar's printing house in Rennes was inside the quarters of the Parlement of Brittany and, in 1771, he argued that he could not be arrested without parlementary permission. In 1767 the Toulouse municipal authorities could not inspect Jean-Baptiste Rayet's printing house, which was located in territory under the Parlement's jurisdiction. Whenever they tried to police Rayet, they faced obstruction from the judges in the Parlement. When queried about this, the *doyen* of the Parlement made it quite clear that the Parlement would brook no challenge to its jurisdiction; indeed, it was impudent to have raised the issue. In justifying his stance he repeated the standard view that rich printers did not print prohibited books and, since Rayet was rich, he would not dare compromise his position in this way. At one point in this discussion, an official suggested that to improve policing in Toulouse, all printers and booksellers should be forced to move into a defined precinct in the town. If printers were more centrally located and in the same part of town as the booksellers, schools, colleges, and universities, it would be easier to inspect them. Most important—and this was no doubt the purpose of the proposal—printers would no longer be near the Parlement of Toulouse, where they took refuge.[90] In 1766 Armand Hüe de Miromesnil, then first president of the Parlement of Normandy, and the intendant Jean-Baptiste-François de la Michodière moved quickly to have Antoine Gabriel de Sartine rescind an order from the secretary of state, Louis Phélypeaux, comte de Saint-Florentin, to raid the shop of the widow Besongne and her son, because it was in a courtyard attached to the Parlement of Normandy and policed by it. Miromesnil explained that these printers had many protectors in the Parlement who would protest if a raid were executed against them.[91]

The ties to the parlements and to the courts were sufficiently strong that many provincial printers printed and sold pamphlets, parlementary decrees, and remonstrances when asked to do so. They thus ran the risk of royal displeasure and paid a price if their parlementary protection broke down. In 1763 André Giroud went to jail for two weeks for printing the remonstrances of the Parlement of Grenoble.[92] In 1764 the Rouen printer Jean-Jacques Besongne and his mother were arrested for printing pamphlets—including *Secret des finances divulgés,* one of the many contributions to the contest between the Parlement of Normandy and the king in that year. Seven years later, in 1771, Besongne printed and sold a range of pro-parlement literature.[93] In 1766, an investigation in Bordeaux revealed that Antoine Labbotière and his brother had bought forty-three copies of a pamphlet in favor of the cause of the parlements entitled *L'esprit des magistrats philosophes.* Later, in 1777, they printed the *Remonstrances des Cour des aides* and found themselves in serious trouble. When a royal council decree ordered Antoine Labottière's presses seized and his printing house closed, the intendant's office came to his aid, as did the duc de Mouchy, maréchal de France and lieutenant general of Guyenne.[94] The parlements and the courts knew how to time the release of controversial printing strategically: in order to prepare the way for their impending *coup* against the king's agent, the Cour des aides in Montauban kept secret a controversial parlementary decree of 10 April 1764 until the end of May, when they quickly posted it before the intendant could stop them.[95] Printers had close ties to the Parlement of Dijon, which ordered large numbers of their remonstrances and pamphlets printed: in a celebrated dispute between the Parlement and the Estates of Burgundy, the printer Louis Hucherot cooperated with the Parlement in January 1762 by printing a pamphlet written by the councillor Joly de Bévy entitled *Parlement outragé.*[96] The *Mercure dijonnais* reported that this pamphlet, a defamatory *libelle* against Jacques Varenne, the *secrétaire des États,* was distributed widely and in large enough numbers to turn the people against him. By one account, the judges had it secretly distributed at night into the courtyards and homes of the Dijonnais. Hucherot was arrested and taken to the Bastille, where he was interrogated. On hearing this, Joly de Bévy came forward to admit authorship, and Hucherot was eventually released. Printers who printed for Varennes, too, got into trouble: the Parlement of Dijon put pressure on the Cour des aides of Paris (which had jurisdiction in Lyon) in 1762 to pursue Louis Buisson, the Lyon printer of his *mémoire* defending the *élus* and the Estates of Burgundy. Buisson was arrested, though if the inspector Bourgelat can be believed, Malesherbes' protection spared him (but only after lengthy interrogation). Printers sometimes claimed to have been forced to print for the courts, which may have been true. Members of a parlement could make life very difficult for printers and booksellers who did not cooperate and, perhaps more important, ensure advantages for printers who printed for them.[97]

Two Case Studies in Brittany in the Reign of Louis XV

As it is difficult to get a close look at the relations between printers and the judges in the courts who embarked on anti-despotism campaigns in the provincial towns, two cases providing insight into these relations during the later years of the reign of Louis XV—the Brittany Affair and the Maupeou years—repay careful examination. The Brittany Affair was a major conflict between the Parlement of Brittany in Rennes and the regional military commander, the duc d'Aiguillon, which reached a point in the summer of 1765 when the magistrates in the Parlement resigned and the government established a new court of supporters and clients.[98] The Breton magistrate Louis-René Caradeuc de La Chalotais, a leader of the former parlement's campaign (the so-called patriot cause), was arrested and put on trial, but when no conviction could be obtained the king sent him into exile. In the following year the Parlement of Paris, joined by other provincial parlements, denounced the illegality of this act. The conflict produced a number of pamphlets, *libelles,* parlement decrees, government decrees that quashed parlementary decrees, remonstrances, and *affiches.* Members of the government attempted to restrict public access to these texts in what one historian has called "the war of the decrees."[99] Louis XV permitted the ministry "triumvirate"—his chancellor René-Nicolas Maupeou, his controller-general abbé Terray, and the duc d'Aiguillon—to cripple parlementary opposition in what has become known as the Maupeou coup, wherein the parlements were reconstituted and recalcitrant magistrates purged. The coup provoked a pamphlet war of unprecedented scale between 1770 and 1774. Ministry officials "took to the streets" to a greater degree than ever before with subsidized pamphlets, and writers favoring the cause of the parlements responded in kind.[100] Two of the printers who chose to print for the parlements in the Breton towns of Saint-Malo and Rennes were Louis-Philippe-Claude Hovius and Nicolas-Paul Vatar.

Saint-Malo

When the Paris edition of La Chalotais' famous *Mémoire,* one of three publicizing his defense, sold out in 1767, Louis-Philippe-Claude Hovius, the only printer in Saint-Malo, undertook a new edition.[101] But the duc d'Aiguillon was informed of this venture early, and Louis XV's minister Saint-Florentin ordered a search of Hovius' premises on the night of 16 April 1767. Eight hundred copies of the *Mémoire* were seized during the search and handed over to the intendant, who had orders to burn them. Hovius and a collaborator were imprisoned in the fortress of Saint-Malo. To try to help her husband, Hovius' wife claimed that he had changed his mind about printing the work and was actually breaking the forms when he was arrested, but officials remained skeptical. On 25 April 1767, a royal council order banned Hovius from the printing trade, forbade him to print or sell books, and fined him two hundred livres. The lieutenant of police in Saint-Malo sealed up his shop.

Hovius enjoyed enormous local support, however, and royal officials found it impossible to keep him out of the printing business. He tried to work as the secret partner of his predecessor Sébastien Delamare, who sought a parlementary decree authorizing him to print. Royal officials reacted vigorously to this plan. Local authorities had informed them in early July 1767 that Hovius and Delamare were regarded as "specially protected by all the republicans in town": if they did not appoint a printer quickly in Saint-Malo, Hovius and Delamare would appeal to the local courts, and "all the republicans in town who were protecting Hovius would move heaven and earth to reinstall him." On 1 December 1767, the government arranged to transfer the Saint-Malo printer's license to Julian Valais, a former worker for Hovius and a client of the duc d'Aiguillon. Valais thus became the official printer for that camp.[102] Valais' life, however, was far from easy: he both denounced illegal printing from the anti-government camp and was himself imprisoned for a brief period.[103] Meanwhile, with his many loyal supporters, Hovius tried to continue printing, but on 24 February 1769 a new decree banned him from the business.[104] The sub-delegate again sealed Hovius' printing house. Efforts were made to have the seals lifted, but Maupeou would not cooperate. He wanted to suspend Hovius for a long time to end the intrigue and force him to recognize the "impossibility of running a business that two royal decrees had [already] forbidden him to run."

Nevertheless, Hovius continued.[105] In 1770 he undertook to produce an edition of the 1768 pamphlet *Procès extraordinairement instruit* and used the services of his Alençon and Caen partners—Jean-Zacharie Malassis and Manoury—to distribute it. The enterprise was denounced to the government as soon as the edition came out. Saint-Florentin heard about it in late April and royal officials worked quickly to suppress the work. On 3 May none other than D'Hémery, the famous Paris inspector of the book trade, made the trip to Caen and had Hovius, Manoury, and Malassis arrested. D'Hémery knew better than to count on the local police in Saint-Malo to catch and hold Hovius, so he made special arrangements to have him imprisoned in Caen.[106] Hovius and two others were sent to the Bastille and not released until October 1771.

After Louis XVI took the throne in 1774 and the parlements returned, Hovius was able to set up as a bookseller in Saint-Malo, where Valais was still the printer. The privilege for *Étrennes Malouines,* a local commercial newspaper, was taken from Valais and returned to the Hovius family. Valais protested this decision at least four times and was able to garner the support of both the intendant and his subdelegate. In this battle he produced and printed a memorandum addressed to the keeper of the seals. Times had changed, however. Miromesnil banned Valais from the printing business in 1775 for defaming Hovius in his memorandum but reinstated him two months later.[107] When Saint-Malo had no printer at all, official printing could not be done: no ordinances, or prices of bread, or tax forms could reach the people. Officials thought of having printing done in nearby Dinan, but this, too, posed problems. In these circumstances, Hovius made a request for a license in which the argument was completely new. He wanted the license as compensation for the suffering he had undergone during the Maupeou years. Having been suspected of publicizing secret information about La Chalotais' trial ("les pièces secrètes d'un procès commencé contre quelques uns des Magistrats du Parlement de Rennes"), he had lost his printer's license, been imprisoned in the Château de Saint-Malo and in the Bastille for several months, and had his types and books taken from him. In addition to all these "calamities," he had been forced to endure the pain of seeing his business pass to Valais, his former journeyman, who had managed to unite both printing houses in Saint-Malo under his direction. Hovius had accumulated debts, as he had been unable to work to support his family. With a license he could work to pay these off and no longer be "the victim of events beyond his control which the king wanted to end." He was granted a lifetime license on 19 May 1776. Throughout the next decade Hovius and his son fought with Valais over the single license in Saint-Malo. In 1785 Hovius' son, Henri-Louis, got a lifetime license in Saint-Malo; in the face of Valais' opposition, however, the authorities rescinded this order and instead gave him a newly authorized position in Dol in 1786.[108]

Rennes

Clearly, the royal government did not lack resources to handle opposition printers. But Hovius' story certainly suggests something about government weakness in the face of the parlements' influence over provincial printers. In Rennes a course of events took place that echoed the one in Saint-Malo. When the pamphlets for and against the Parlement of Brittany, the Breton Estates, and La Chalotais began inundating Brittany in 1766, the intendant and the subdelegates in Rennes began to watch the printers and booksellers closely. From 1765 on, the widow Vatar's shop was under surveillance as a center of patriot activity and a place frequented by La Chalotais.[109] Saint-Florentin received reports from the subdelegates and the intendant that the *Lettre d'un patriote,* a response to two recent ministerial pamphlets, had been written and was about to be printed in Rennes. In 1766 the subdelegate Audouard raided the printing house of Nicolas-Paul Vatar, who printed patriot pamphlets (and has become something of a local hero for Breton historians).[110] In 1769 the last of another multigenerational Rennes printing dynasty, Pierre-François-Marie Garnier, was in trouble for unauthorized printing and had his license suspended for three months, a term that was shortened when his many supporters wrote to Maupeou.[111] In 1770 the subdelegate Audouard was under no illusions about Nicolas-Paul Vatar's loyalties and, as soon as pamphlets denouncing the suppression of the parlements began appearing, Vatar was suspected of publishing *Réponse des États de Bretagne au mémoire du duc d'Aiguillon,* a tract in which the

Breton Estates replied to Linguet's pro-ministerial *Mémoire* in favor of the duc d'Aiguillon. Vatar's shop and house were raided again.[112] This time, we are told, the police ransacked his entire house in search of the pamphlets and even sequestered the belongings of the bishop of Léon, who lodged with him during the sessions of the Breton Estates. They discovered the forms of *Réponse des États,* which Vatar admitted printing on the Estates' orders. In November 1770 he was imprisoned in Mont-Saint-Michel. The royal decree suppressing this title, dated 2 January 1771 and signed by Chancellor Maupeou, indicates royal officials' refusal to condone opposition printing:[113]

> His Majesty had difficulty believing that any of the orders of the [Breton] Estates had a part in producing a tract that bears all the characteristics of *libelles* and clandestine writings with which the enemies of good order and public tranquillity infect the realm during the troubles which have agitated the province.... In effect, the authors of the memorandum . . . [have] blackened the administration by making odious claims with no foundation . . .

The decree went on to deny the constitutional position taken by the Estates and suppressed the memorandum because it attacked royal authority and slandered a person honored by the confidence of the king and his administration.

Two days later, the intendant reported to Saint-Florentin that they had broken Vatar's printing forms. Initially, the subdelegate had warned the intendant that Vatar's printing house was inside the walls enclosing the Parlement, which would insist on its right to control any intrusion into the area. Somehow he persuaded Vatar to move the forms outside the enclosure and then seized and broke them. Vatar went into hiding and his family faced the prospect that he would lose his printing license. On 20 December 1771 Vatar's wife pleaded in his favor in a letter to Maupeou.[114] Their family, she said, was one whom Maupeou—who was well known for his goodness and for helping the unfortunate—had deigned to assist in the past, and now they needed him more than ever before. Madame Vatar's efforts were in vain; on 5 January 1772, Nicolas-Paul Vatar lost his printing license. His equipment and books were ordered sold, and the printer Nicolas Audran—destined until these events to have his printer position suppressed on his death—was raised to the status of one of the four official printers in Rennes, with the right to pass the position on to his son.[115]

After the parlements were reestablished in 1774, Vatar petitioned Miromesnil, the new keeper of the seals, for the return of his license, outlining the injustices he had suffered since 1766 for which he deserved compensation. This request could not easily be granted: Audran was now duly licensed, and he was neither about to give up his license nor happy about accepting another printer in town. Relicensing Vatar would not only hurt his business but also make five printers in Rennes instead of the permitted four. The government solved the problem, for the moment, by issuing a decree on 23 July 1775 that would extinguish the license of the first of the five printers or widows to die without a son or son-in-law to take over.[116] This temporarily made room for Vatar. Meanwhile, the Parlement and the Breton Estates moved to honor their martyr by choosing him as their official printer; the Parlement let him set up his printing equipment, rent free, in the *palais de justice*. Vatar died in 1788 and, in 1789, his cousin was among the patriots in Rennes, along with Audran's son, who had received a printing license in 1784.[117] By the 1760s the Vatar family had profited from the printer licensing policy for at least two generations. Like other provincial printers, they had been dealing directly with royal officials to obtain licenses and king's printer privileges. Nevertheless, the competing ties with the Parlement and the Breton Estates were strong and enduring and, in times of crisis, could trump those with the ministry. In a move to counter these local ties in Rennes in the 1780s, the government installed a book trade inspector and a *chambre syndicale* to supervise the Breton book and printing trades more effectively.

Printers in the Prerevolutionary Crisis of 1788

Conflicts between the government and the parlements were at a high point in 1788 and printers were again under strong pressure to print for opposing sides. After the failure of the Assembly of Notables—an attempt in 1787 by Louis XVI and his controller-general Charles-Alexandre de Calonne to bring together representatives of the French elites to endorse a program of financial and other reforms—the king's new minister, Etienne-Charles de Loménie de Brienne, found that he had to break the power of the parlements in order to resolve the financial crisis. The Edict of 8 May 1788 replaced the parlements with new plenary courts, which would render justice but not play a political role. This coup led to massive protest in many towns and an explosion of pamphlets from both sides—the so-called *campagne de brochures*.[118] During what has been called the Pre-Revolution, both ministry and parlementary proponents tried to ensure that their side of the issue was publicized and their opponents' efforts censored. A huge number of pamphlets were printed anonymously. Some were sold and others distributed free of charge. The Assembly of Notables itself had produced many pamphlets criticizing Calonne, but the ministry and Calonne's team printed even more supporting his program and attacking Jacques Necker, Louis XVI's former and very popular finance minister, who was attempting to make a comeback. As spokesmen for the ministry, finance minister Loménie de Brienne and the keeper of the seals, Chrétien-François de Lamoignon de Basville, produced a stream of pamphlets defending the reforms and generally criticizing the parlements. Writers and printers who worked for the government had to be protected from persecution by the parlements. The journalist Mangourit, for example, recounted afterwards how he enjoyed ministerial protection to have pamphlets such as *Le Pour et le contre, Le Tribun du peuple au peuple,* and *Les Gracques français* printed in Nantes by Augustin-Jean Malassis and sent to Versailles in the carriages of the keeper of the seals and of Antoine-François de Bertrand de Molleville, the intendant of Brittany from May 1784 until December 1788. Anti-ministerial pamphlets opposing the reforms also streamed off the presses. One of the most famous, entitled *La Cour plénière,* mercilessly ridiculed the ministry's reforms. These pamphlets were printed anonymously or with false imprints: Nicolas Bergasse, a major spokesman for the cause of the parlements, printed "at the printing house of liberty" or "under the sign of the Revolution."

As during the Brittany Affair and the Maupeou years, printers in provincial towns had to choose sides—but for a number of reasons, the political climate in the late 1780s differed from that in the early 1770s, and printers were more willing to print parlementary decrees and pamphlets critical of royal policy. The parlements were claiming greater control over printed production than a generation earlier, and they were less accepting of the Bureau de la librairie, which they decried as an instrument of despotism. They could no longer see why they were not the best judges of what was fit to print. In the 1780s the Parlement of Provence authorized the printing of a collection of parlementary decrees entitled *Journal du Palais de Provence,* and in doing so it usurped the role of the Bureau de la librairie in giving out authorizations to print. The keeper of the seals indignantly informed the Parlement that ever since the establishment of censorship, the parlements had not been giving out permissions or privileges to print, and he forced the Parlement to apologize.[119] In a letter in 1788 to the keeper of the seals, the printers and booksellers in Rennes claimed not to be able to follow the rules of the book trade because several parlementary decrees were opposed to them.[120] This assertion of parlementary control was accompanied, rather paradoxically, by the increasing currency given to ideas about the freedom of the press.[121] The success of the virulent publicity campaign against the Maupeou experiment cannot have encouraged loyalty to Lamoignon and Brienne in 1788.[122] The unhappy fate of those judges and others who had demonstrated loyalty to the ministry during the Maupeou years, only to be abandoned when the former parlements were reestablished in 1774, was known to all who cared to look, including the printers. Vatar's status as a hero when the parlements returned triumphant in Rennes in 1774 might have made printers in parlementary towns wary of counting too heavily on the government protection they would need if they were to abandon the cause of the parlements.

Even though we cannot fully elaborate the printers' role in the pamphlet wars of 1788, strong evidence comes from Rouen on how events pressured the provincial printers.[123] The Parlement of Normandy was able to publish its opposition to the May decrees establishing the plenary court; the judges began by meeting between midnight and 5:00 A.M. on the night of 5–6 May to denounce, in advance, the illegality of the decrees they were to be forced to register on 8 May. The attorney general, Godart de Belbeuf, had this denunciation printed and sent to the lower courts. To make sure that the public got the government's version of events, Boullenger, the newly appointed lieutenant general of the grand bailliage, ordered the publication of its version of the 8 May session highlighting the Parlement's submission to the king's orders. He and his men worked hard to prevent the Parlement from meeting again to condemn the forced registration. Along with other government supporters, including members of the aristocratic d'Harcourt family with a long history of representing the king's interests in Normandy, Charles Havas (the inspector of the book trade), and Jacques-Joseph Le Boullenger (warden of the printers' and booksellers' guild), Boullenger worked to contain the influence of the Parlement on public opinion. To his complete dismay, the Parlement did manage to meet on 25 June 1788 to issue an incendiary and amazingly disrespectful decree protesting the May Edicts that was printed immediately. One tactic of the government was to refuse to dignify the Parlement's decrees with royal orders formally quashing them but, instead, to treat them as "clandestine writings deserving to be scorned and forgotten." Nevertheless, it did quash the Rouen Parlement's decree of 25 June 1788, saying that it "represented insubordination of the worst sort" and was "seditious, an assault on royal authority, illegitimate and intended to mislead the people about the king's true intentions." All sorts of printing were being done. The duc d'Harcourt, the governor of the province, wanted to arrest Belbeuf's porter, known as a major supplier of clandestine pamphlets, but ran into difficulty. Havas, as the book trade inspector, saw it as his duty to send many reports to Versailles on the pamphlets circulating.[124] In July the duc d'Harcourt complained of the abundant distribution in Rouen of clandestine works in the current circumstances that were "capable by their nature of getting people worked up and spreading dangerous maxims."[125] The same month, Lamoignon ousted Pontcarré, the first president of the Parlement of Rouen, from his role supervising the book trade in Rouen—thus abruptly ending a long practice, unique to Rouen, where the first president, and not the intendant, supervised printing. This anomaly was deemed no longer appropriate.[126]

The guild warden, Le Boullenger, remained loyal to the government, making regular inspection tours of the printers to keep pro-parlementary printing at bay.[127] According to one undoubtedly exaggerated account, Havas and Le Boullenger and one hundred agents made persistent visits for a month to all the printing houses but found nothing.[128] Le Boullenger, who was from a very old and privileged printing family in Rouen, paid dearly for his zeal after Brienne resigned in August 1788 and the Parlement returned. He, along with Havas and the lieutenant of police, marquis d'Harcourt, were in a most unenviable position.[129] The Parlement prosecuted them for their actions in the summer, forcing them to seek help from Versailles. In the fall of 1788 Le Boullenger was in such total disgrace among his colleagues that the director of the book trade had to work with the first president of the Parlement—now restored to his position in charge of the book trade—to seek some honorable way to remove him as guild warden. Given the loss of his reputation, both agreed that he could not continue.

Patriot hostility toward Le Boullenger was truly without measure. In a pamphlet satire against Lamoignon's plenary courts written up in the form of a play in 1788 and entitled *La Cour plénière: Héroi-tragi-comédie*, a patriot author presented the king's ministers as his anti-heroes.[130] Lamoignon, Maupeou, Breteuil, Brienne, and Lenoir all made appearances and were given dialogue: referring to their *libelle* against the parlements, Jean-Charles-Pierre Lenoir,

Louis XVI's lieutenant of police, laments, "Not a printer in Paris will print it. We were counting on the printers in Rouen. But even they are impertinent and difficult these days. [The Rouen printer] Oursel[131] has been treating our publisher [the lieutenant of police, marquis d'Harcourt] quite badly. . . . But fortunately the lieutenant of police has found us a certain Le Boullenger." The marquis d'Harcourt enters the scene at this point and praises Le Boullenger. Readers were informed in a footnote that Le Boullenger was the private spy of the marquis d'Harcourt, particularly despised because he had betrayed the confidence of several magistrates and barristers who naively trusted him, thinking him a talkative, silly, and stupid person whom they never suspected of secretly supplying information to the police. Readers also learned that Harcourt had bribed Le Boullenger with lavish dinners paid for by Lamoignon, just as he tried to bribe the magistrates in the newly created plenary court. Le Boullenger was so overcome by the honor of being received at the table of a marquis that, if given the chance, he would have put the whole Parlement in jail. Indeed, because of him, a number of worthy magistrates were imprisoned. To further tarnish Le Boullenger's reputation, the pamphleteers hauled out an accusation made regularly by victims of printers' denunciations: while secretly disparaging the others, Le Boullenger was, of course, making a fortune by printing the offending pamphlets himself. The theme of Le Boullenger's betrayal of the Parlement was a subject in other pamphlets, notably in one describing him as "a printer without character, privileged spy, *mari Kornmanné* and an abhorred royalist."[132] Printers who did not cooperate with the parlements had much to fear in the court of public opinion if not in the courts themselves.

Rouen is just one town, but there is evidence that the printers in other provincial towns faced similar difficulties. Many chose to cooperate with their local parlements. In Besançon, the printer Daclin's license was suspended, and the inspector sought advice about how to deal with the "*libelles* relative to the parlements."[133] In Dijon, the guild warden, Louis-Nicolas Frantin, claimed that he had done a tour of all the printing houses, but he must simply have lied when he said that nothing was being printed "concerning government affairs," because shortly afterwards the book trade inspector Jean Cortot announced his resignation and the intendant accused Frantin himself of printing decrees against the government—perhaps a clue to the inspector's departure.[134] In fact, on 4 August 1788, an order was drafted to fire Cortot for taking up the cause of the Parlement *avec trop de chaleur*.[135] In Nancy and Pau, printers had their licenses suspended for printing against the government.[136] In July 1788 the government banned the Rennes printer Nicolas-Xavier Audran—who had benefited from the printer Vatar's disgrace for parlementary printing during the Brittany Affair—from the printing business for printing material for the opposition.[137] In Bordeaux, too, the printers printed for the Parlement; the exile of the Parlement of Bordeaux had the whole legal establishment up in arms. The courts commanded considerable loyalty and there was a torrent of publications in favor of the Parlement. Pierre Bernadau, the local chronicler, wrote in January 1788 that there were too many items for him to keep up, and the local police could not control the flood.[138] The Parlement's printer Pierre Phillippot published pamphlets using a London address and reprinted parts of *L'Esprit des lois* in June 1788. Members of the Cour des aides had their printer, Antoine Labottière, print their remonstrances and, in March 1788, protected him when he printed a protest about the king's reply to their remonstrances. The book trade inspector in Bordeaux, a barrister, seems to have placed loyalty to his colleagues in the legal profession above his obligation to suppress anti-ministerial tracts: when the lawyers printed a pamphlet calling for the return of the Parlement in January 1788, he forbade printers to print anything for or against the work. Support for the parlements and the demand for pamphlets was not limited to parlementary towns.[139] In Nantes, Malassis, though banned from printing anything at all, was selling everything he could both in favor of and against the government.[140]

In Toulouse, there is much evidence that the sales of both imported and locally printed pamphlets were high and that the Parlement vied with the government for control of the media. In April 1788, when the book trade inspector, Villeneuve, wrote to the director of the book trade to ask what to do about the sale of parlementary decrees and remonstrances, he was told to ban them.[141] In May 1788 he suspended a shipment from Bordeaux for Pierre Bellegarique containing *Le Donjon de Vincennes,* one from Paris for the bookseller Sacarreau containing *M. de Calonne,* and one for Jean-Baptiste Brouilhet containing ten collections of parlementary decrees.[142] In July 1788 Villeneuve wrote that sedition was increasing in Toulouse.[143] In September the inspector seized an "assortment of remonstrances" being sold by Brouilhet. Some idea of Bellegarique's printing can be gleaned from the fact that the Parlement rewarded him for his loyalty during the summer by giving him the official position of parlementary printer and ousting their former official printer, Jean-Armand-Honoré-Marie-Bernard Pijon. The new appointment, according to

Villeneuve, would make Bellegarique's fortune. Indeed, a few months later Bellegarique reported that he was benefiting handsomely, because the lawyers and judges were shunning Pijon and another printer in Toulouse who was in even deeper disgrace for having taken the title of official printer for the grand bailliage during the Parlement's exile.[144]

Villeneuve reported on Bellegarique's new good fortune to his superiors in Versailles, who were not at all happy. Villeneuve tried to be reassuring, claiming that Bellegarique would be more circumspect in the future because he henceforth had something to lose. In September Villeneuve reported that his health was bad and asked for a leave.[145] He was not the only book trade inspector to have sudden health problems in the summer of 1788. The Toulouse inspector continued to complain of all sorts of political pamphlets, provided by Bellegarique and others.[146] The Parlement continued its struggle with the Estates of Languedoc into the fall of 1788 and, in late November, *libelles* were being sold in profusion. Their distributor was the Famulus du Palais, a pseudonymous and mysterious character whom the Parlement protected. In January 1789 the inspector wrote of general insurrection against the Estates of Languedoc and asked Versailles whether he should prevent the printing of a memorandum by Louis-Alexandre de Launay, comte d'Antraigues.[147] He himself thought not, reporting on the "widespread cry for freedom of the press," saying that it would be better to wait until spirits were calmer because it was just this sort of persecution against Bellegarique that had made the Parlement decide to appoint him as their printer and place him entirely under their protection.[148]

Conclusion

French provincial printers in the eighteenth century took their rhetorical positioning very seriously, but rhetoric did not necessarily coincide with reality. Printers' assertions of poverty and of a declining standard of living do not withstand examination. The rhetorical dissimulation obscured a complex story: printers had adapted to the growth of absolutism—ultimately becoming some of its major beneficiaries—by managing a number of different identities.[149] When political tensions were low, times were good for the licensed printers of provincial France, who faced little competition in a period of unprecedented expansion of print and saw their children make good marriages and enjoy elevated social standing. Printers were a closed group; they participated in a milieu on the fringes of the elite world in their provincial towns and tried to emulate that world. But their position and ambitions linked them in complex ways to the political world of the late eighteenth century.

The rhetoric of provincial printers and publishers knew no limit when it came to presenting themselves as loyal subjects of the king. In 1789 the Lyon bookseller Los Rios provided his version of the loyalty of the Lyonnais bookmen during the reign of Henry IV. Henri IV had called several Swiss publishers to Lyon to limit the appeal of what remained of the Catholic League and, when the king could not pay his troops, these publishers were so full of zeal for their prince that they sold two houses for sixty thousand *écus* and put the money in the king's coffers without asking for interest. This was a timely story of loyalty in 1789. No doubt some domestic French printers felt this kind of loyalty to the monarch, but many others owed him only strategic loyalty or subservience. The concepts of loyalty and subservience, though, fail to capture the critical issues faced by printers in the constitutional strife between the ministry and the courts and among royal ministers. The issue was loyalty to whom—and how much. Calculated decision making by very well-connected men and women preceded decisions to print or sell political pamphlets about the judicial and financial matters that captivated public attention. Printers balanced their own interests—financial and other—against the interests of their patrons, who could be officials in the parlements, in the Estates, or in government. They struggled to make good judgment calls, to survive and to prosper, and at times undermined the rhetoric that had served them so well in more peaceful times.

One might speculate that the collapse of royal control of the media in 1788 occurred in part because the control mechanisms were designed to fit a rhetorically created world, divided between insiders and outsiders, the moral and the immoral, the loyal and the disloyal—a vision of the printing world that the printers themselves had fostered for over a century. While no doubt much opposition printing came from abroad, was printed by disreputable characters, and attacked religion and the sacred character of the monarch, this model, for the most part, did not fit the realities of the constitutional crises. In these affairs the elites in France themselves were very divided. Members of the judicial world wanted to appeal to public opinion, and even some members of the government thought that they should be able to do so.[150] The inadequacies of the overly simplified vision became clear when, by 1788, parlementary decrees, remonstrances, and political pamphlets were lumped together with *libelles* and irreligious, seditious, and often pornographic literature and treated the same way.[151] Of course, many rejected this association, including the printers themselves, who were socially integrated into the judicial world of provincial France and thought like the lawyers, barristers, and judges who were busy debating the strengths and weaknesses of France's judicial and financial systems.

The idea of loyalty to an absolute monarch may have had limited currency for the printers of provincial France, who bore the king only a grudging and contingent loyalty, exemplified by the idea that if the king would give them the material circumstances to avoid clandestine trade, they would do so. The misunderstanding of the nature of the clandestine trade left agents of book regulation—lieutenants of police, book trade inspectors, intendants, and subdelegates—vulnerable, because when they tried to treat parlementary printing like clandestine literature, they came under heavy criticism from very influential people and lost credibility. When in the crisis of 1788 the divided and only shakily loyal forces of the printing profession were called upon to battle the tremendous influence of the parlements, they broke ranks and failed.

Conclusion

The men and women who ran the increasingly large and prosperous printing houses of provincial France were not among the voices demanding freedom of the press at the time of the French Revolution.[1] Despite the undoubted liberalism of many printers, there were good reasons for their silence on the issue. They had advocated a regulated industry for more than a century, and the relations between printers and the French state were mutually sustaining and complex. Such an established pattern of exaggerating the dangers of a free press could not easily be reversed. This study of the first century of printer licensing underscores the identity that printers adopted as pillars of monarchy and how they used it to lobby the government of early modern France. The Paris booksellers' and printers' guild had begun doing this in the mid-seventeenth century; the provincial guilds and individual printers with privileged access to the heart of government emulated them. Guild officials and individual printers made skillful use of rhetoric and appeals to fear to frame printing issues for the officials in the expanding royal governments of Louis XIV, XV, and XVI. They offered a familiar guild template in which to view their role in the larger context of ideological control: quality controls on their product were necessary and they—as the judges of quality—should be permitted to control recruitment to their profession. Like other artisans, they reiterated the dire consequences to the French state of low-quality products. But printers had an edge on other artisans because the quality of their products included the ideas in the books they printed.[2] Since the advent of print, ideas in books had been seen as potentially dangerous, but only after about 1660 was the notion elaborated (excessively and relentlessly) that dangerous printing would undermine the French state as well as religion and morality and that the government needed to act vigorously to prevent such developments. Their arguments worked too well. The printers overplayed their hand and drew the state so deeply into the regulation of the trade that it curtailed the autonomy and power of the guilds themselves. Royal officials ultimately developed the elaborate apparatus that regulated printers in provincial France that is the subject of this book. For other corporate groups, the fiscal needs of the state were the key force behind royal intervention; for printers, that force was the widespread fear of the subversive·effects of print.

Historians have often exaggerated or discounted the government's efforts to control the media, tending to point either to misguided draconian laws or to the failure to enforce them. If media control is construed in terms of repression, these views are understandable. Yet the larger program of favoring certain publishers to make them, as Bruyset said, the objects of "emulation" was a project that was flexible and more effective—and one that fits well into a considerable body of research on French absolutism that stresses the ways in which the state in early modern France negotiated power with the elites in the realm. This study does not deny the role of repression but intends to move it out of the limelight as the means by which the government attempted to influence the media. It also, I hope, offers reasons to reconsider some broadly held assumptions in most historical works on state-media relations in early modern France. The first is that control of the press was tight and draconian in the first centuries of print, especially in the reign of Louis XIV, but declined in the eighteenth century because of state weakness or liberal ideas. By focusing on printer licensing, we see that control, if anything, was increasing in the eighteenth century, but it was not effective enough to withstand the tremendous influence of important factions in the parlements when they were in conflict with the king's ministers. Second—and more broadly—most studies place printers in opposition to state officials in a struggle to police the printed word, but here we see, on the contrary, that in many ways officials and printers shared a vision of media control, one that printers themselves had a major role in constructing.

Printers saw their identity as loyal subjects of the king as just one of several. While administrative documentation overwhelmingly stresses this identity, it was never completely accepted and far more contested than these documents would suggest. Printers were also astute businessmen who often carried on large bookselling businesses on the side and were clients of bishops and *parlementaires.* In these ways they played a pivotal role in the expansion of print culture and the extension of the public sphere in the eighteenth century: they not only contributed to the spread of religion and the publicizing of laws but also to the spread of the Enlightenment—some of it sanctioned by the royal government, and some of it not. Their role was critical to the development of newspapers and to the dissemination of political ideas. They also contributed to the vitality of a clandestine book trade that has attracted considerable historical attention. Printers would not have seen these activities as undermining the monarchical order or desacralizing the monarchy, although this may have been the net effect. Many historians have offered arguments about how print under-mined monarchy in eighteenth-century France, and this study of provincial printers adds to a well-established line of thinking.[3] However, it also draws attention to the ways in which print was used to strengthen monarchical gov-ernment in eighteenth-century France. Printers certainly thought control was desirable, but so too did many other members of French society, at least until the constitutional crises broke this consensus.[4] This idea should have a more central place in our understanding of state-media relations and should displace a tendency to believe that the media and the people naturally wanted a free press but were denied it by the repressive powers of the state.

Printer licensing gave provincial printers a new intellectual understanding of the state that was not in evidence at the end of the seventeenth century.[5] In the seventeenth and early eighteenth centuries many provincial printers regarded royal decrees as instances of misguided royal collusion with their enemies, usu-ally the Parisian publishers. After being convicted of importing a huge ship-ment of pirated and prohibited books from Amsterdam, the widow Labottière in Bordeaux showed anything but remorse in her irate letter to the director of the book trade in Paris, demanding the books be returned to her. She was quite incapable of seeing royal intervention other than as the product of the unfair influence of her commercial rivals. Provincial printers at the beginning of the eighteenth century could not be convinced that there was any laudable principle—such as ideological control or public interest—at play when their books were seized. Rather, they saw only naked greed and self-interest on the part of competitors, who had somehow managed to co-opt royal officials. They were not wrong; Parisian guild officials did help draft royal decrees on the book trade and served as sources of information on printing matters for government officials.

Gradually, however, the benefits of cooperating with state officials became evident. Once the licensing policy was implemented, provincial printers were in constant communication with royal officials who knew their names and possessed considerable information about them drawn from the numerous sur-veys of printers in the eighteenth century. An increasingly identifiable group of officials—chancellors, intendants, lieutenants of police, officials in the Bureau de la librairie, and inspectors of the book trade—were aware of the interests of provincial printers. These officials listened to their accounts of struggles against outsiders and to their interpretations of ideas about literary property, which differed considerably from those of their Parisian counterparts. It is possible that legislation on book trade matters was viewed with less hostility by the middle of the eighteenth century and that a more favorable conception of state regulation developed among provincial printers, one less synonymous with the interests of the hated Parisian competitors. The 1777 reforms that greatly enlarged the public domain of titles available to provincial printers may have emerged as a by-product of better communication between provincial printers and the government. Loyalty could only have been enhanced by the growing notion that printer masterships were favors granted by the king, not family property. When printers retired, they passed their privilege to print "into the hands of the king" or "into the hands of the chancellor." It was a favor that could be suspended at any time.

One of the side effects of better government and industry communication was that the printers joined other forces for control in French society, such as the Church, and elaborated a fairly uncontested vision of a threatening clandestine book and pamphlet trade, based in the provinces or abroad, that would tempt all printers and booksellers who did not have enough work. The accuracy of this vision will always be difficult to assess. Licensing of provincial printers began in 1667 and the critical developments took place in 1700, when the bureau was established, and in 1704, when quotas were established for all the provincial towns in France. These major initiatives in administrative controls fit poorly with most research on the clandestine book trade, which emphasizes its growth in the mid-eighteenth century and later. Printer lobbying and licensing encouraged by their very nature a crisis mentality when there may not have been much of a crisis at all. The timing of the new laws fits well, however, with recent research on the late reign of Louis XIV, revealing extensive growth in the power of the central government in these years.[6] The establishment of the Bureau de la librairie in 1700 and the setting of quotas on printers in provincial towns in 1704 took place because Louis Phélypeaux, comte de Pontchartrain, and his officials were led to believe that there was an almost permanent crisis in the book trade and that ideological control should take precedence over other concerns. They were completely convinced that the printing profession needed unprecedented state intervention.

This vision of a dangerous clandestine book trade, formulated in the reign of Louis XIV, may have gradually come to fit the social reality of printing and bookselling in the late eighteenth century better, but it also distorted that reality because it could not incorporate the notion that opposition printing was a product of France's own elites working with its own domestic printers.

During contestations between the ministry and the parlements, especially in the prerevolutionary crisis, this was probably the nature of much clandestine printing. Had officials not been so fixated on the notion that clandestine printing was foreign-based or produced by poor, disloyal outsiders, they might have responded differently to the challenges of opposition printing. What might officials have done differently had they more fully understood the nature of provincial printing? The answer is not obvious because the divisions were within the elites of French society and at the very heart of the crisis of the old regime. Still, it is difficult to imagine that the Bourbon monarchs would have tempered their support for the program of cultivating the media in the provincial towns, a program that was well under way by 1715. The governments of the nineteenth century would try to do the same in a new era of mass readership and industrialized production, when the book trade gave an enormous place to educational books and newspapers.[7] But the successors of France's *ancien régime* printers had at their disposal new and powerful competing visions of press freedom born of the principles of 1789. An era in state-media relations in France had come to an end.

Part 1: Dowries in printers' families in the eighteenth century, by town

Name	Relation	Year	Dowries	Source (notary or historian)
			Angers	
Pavie	Bride	1781	6,000 advance	Pasquier and Dauphin, *Imprimeurs,* 194
	Self	1781	4,000	
			Besançon	
Rigoine	Son	early 18c	40,000	Vernus, *La Vie comtoise,* 2, 178
			Bordeaux	
Albespy	Bride	1744	3,000	ADG, notary Lacoste, 29 April 1744
	Self	1744	2,000	
	Son-in-law	1781	4,000	ADG, notary Rauzan, 19 November 1781
	Daughter	1781	2,000 advance	
	Daughter	1782	2,000 advance	ADG, notary Dugarry, 26 January 1782
	Son	1782	4,000	ADG, notary Rauzan, 10 September 1782
	Daughter-in-law	1782	37,000	
Beaume	Daughter	Year VIII	30,811	ADG, notary Collignan, 18 Fructidor Year VIII
	Daughter	Year XII	20,000	ADG, notary Baron, 2 Messidor Year XII
Brun	Daughter	1759	10,000	ADG, notary Séjourné, 9 May 1759
	Son-in-law		60,000	
Calamy	Bride	1764	198[a]	ADG, notary Séjourné, 12 March 1764
Calamy	Daughter	1758	15,600	ADG, notary Séjourné, 20 April 1758
Labottière	Bride	1714	13,000	ADG, notary Commes, 12 August 1714
	Bride	1725	24,554	ADG, notary Déjaneau, 20 December 1725; testament, Notary Rauzan, 16 June 1787
Lacourt	Bride	1759	4,000	ADG, notary Séjourné, 26 April 1759
Lacornée[b]	Bride	1727	7,000	ADG, notary Delisle, 22 June 1727
	Self	1727	3,450	
	Niece	1749	18,000	ADG, notary Bouan, 17 September 1749
	Husband		15,000	
Phillippot	Sister	1766	2,000	ADG, notary Séjourné, 26 March 1766
	Bride	1793	5,000	ADG, notary Séjourné, 11 October 1793
	Self	1793	10,000	

Name	Relation	Year	Dowries	Source (notary or historian)
Racle	Daughter	Year III	113,994	ADG, notary Hazera, 23 Ventose Year III
Racle	Son	Year XII	30,000	ADG, notary Mathieu, 23 Floréal Year XII
Séjourné	Bride	1774	20,000 (approx.)	ADG, notary Séjourné, 30 March 1774 and 21 November 1774
	Self	Year X	10,000	ADG, notary Séjourné, 6 Germinal Year X
	Bride		2,000	

Dijon

Name	Relation	Year	Dowries	Source (notary or historian)
Frantin	Self	1775	71,242	ADCD, notary Menu, 13 February 1775
Defay	Daughter	1769	5,400 advance	ADCD, notary Bouché, 9 April 1769

Dole

Name	Relation	Year	Dowries	Source (notary or historian)
Tonnet	Bride	1748	3,000 advance	Lefebvre-Teillard, *La Population de Dole,* 85

Lille

Name	Relation	Year	Dowries	Source (notary or historian)
Boubers de Corbeville	Bride	1785	12,000 florins	Barbier, *Lumières du nord,* 213
	Self		1,283	
Lalau	Bride	1754	10,000 florins	Barbier, *Lumières du nord,* 347
	Self		19,360 florins	
Péterinck	Bride	1785	4,000 and 8 houses, lands, annuity	Barbier, *Lumières du nord,* 413
	Self		17,500 and 2 buildings	

Limoges

Name	Relation	Year	Dowries	Source (notary or historian)
Barbou	Daughter	1748	36,000	Ducourtieux, *Les Barbou,* 56

Lyon[c]

Name	Relation	Year	Dowries	Source (notary or historian)
Barret	Bride	1764	1,600	ADR, *contrôle des actes,* 29 December 1764
Bruyset	Self	1743	40,000	ADR, notary Soupat, 7 February 1743
	Bride		12,000 advance	
	Sister	1742	50,000	ADR, notary Soupat, 9 December 1742
Vialon	Bride	1749	1,000 advance	ADR, notary Soupat, 13 September 1749
	Self		150	

Name	Relation	Year	Dowries	Source (notary or historian)
Delaroche	Bride	1764	6,000	ADR, *contrôle des actes,* 9 August 1764
Faucheux	Bride	1767	4,000 advance	ADR, notary Faucheux, 27 September 1767
Delamollière[d]	Bride	1781	10,000 advance	ADR, notary Chastelus, 8 September 1781
Bruyset	Bride	1784	40,000	ADR, 58Q9, 18 December 1784
	Self	1784	27,000	
Périsse	Brother	1780	10,000	ADR, notary Perrodon, 1 December 1780
	Bride		1,000 advance	
Le Roy	Bride	1785	60,000	ADR, 58Q9
	Self		60	

Nîmes

Name	Relation	Year	Dowries	Source (notary or historian)
Beaume	Bride	1776	8,500	ADGard, notary Darlac, 6 January 1776

Rouen[e]

Name	Relation	Year	Dowries	Source (notary or historian)
Lallemant	Bride		50,000	Quéniart, *L'Imprimerie,* 234
Machuel	Bride		30,000	ADSM J217
Machuel	Daughter	1718	2,600	Quéniart, *L'Imprimerie,* 233
Dumesnil	Self	1719	8,000	Quéniart, *L'Imprimerie,* 234
Vautier	Bride	1719	6,000	Quéniart, *L'Imprimerie,* 234

Toulouse

Name	Relation	Year	Dowries	Source (notary or historian)
Lecamus	Daughter	1741	10,000	Page "Claude-Gilles," 85
Baour	Self	1743	6,000	Blanc-Rouquette, "Un Imprimeur," 299
Guillemette	Daughter	1773	12,000	ADHG, notary Arnaud, 4 July 1773
Douladoure	Nephew	1786	25,000	ADHG, notary Arnaud, 9 April 1786
	Bride		6,000	
	Nephew	1787	16,000	ADHG, notary Vidal, 17 April 1787
	Bride		10,000	
Desclassan	Widow	1780	22,000	ADHG, notary Arnaud, 17 February 1780
Robert	Bride	1786	12,000	ADHG, *table de contrats de mariage*

NOTE: Dowry amounts are given in livres unless otherwise specified.

[a] The Calamy family considered this a scandalous marriage to a servant.

[b] The printer uncle provided the dowry for his niece.

[c] In Lyon early in the eighteenth century, 3.6 percent of couples had dowries over 10,000 livres, and at end of that century the figure rose to 6.6 percent. Average dowries of master artisans rose from 1,160 to 2,840 livres over the course of the century. See Françoise Bayard, *Lyon sous l'ancien régime* (Paris: Perrin, 1997), 161.

[d] In this case, 6,000 livres of the dowry was in cash and 4,000 in trousseau. Her jewels were estimated at 12,000 livres. She was the daughter of Boutroue, a textile merchant.

[e] In Rouen, most printer dowries were between 2,000 and 3,000 livres, according to Quéniart, but the sample is from early in the eighteenth century and is not restricted to master printers.

Part 2: Inventories, inheritances, sales, and estimates of printers' property, 1750–1810 (in livres)

Name	Year	Business	Stocks	Cash	Accounts receivable	Furniture/ property	Real estate	Total	Liabilities	Source (notary or historian)
Aix										
David	1789							80,000		Éboli, "Les David," 368–69
Arras										
Lemaistre de La Sablonnière	1809			5,732.85		9,302	55,204			Barbier, *Lumières du nord*, 364
Bordeaux										
Labottière, R.	1754	47,509		13,708	13,000	6,929	70,502	15,1648	53,702	*Inventaire après décès*, ADG, notary Loche, 10 October 1754
Labottière brothers	1755	46,680	829		13,000	4,046	32,000	96,555	72,937	*Transaction*, ADG, notary Loche, 14 July 1755
Phillippot	1758	2,251	2,213	719		480		5,663		*Inventaire après décès*, ADG, notary Séjourné, 22 November 1758
Lacornée	1772	6,491	15,000	1,986		3,500		30,166		*Inventaire après décès*, ADG, notary Baron, 13 April 1772
Calamy	1779	20,000								ADG, *contrôle des actes*, QB 206, 29 November 1783
Lacourt	Year II	64,895	2,057			3,467				ADG, Q 923-4. 1 Pluviose Year II

	Year									Source
Labottière brothers	Year III	130,000[a]								*Vente*, ADG, notary Troupenat, 2 Pluviose Year III
Beaume	1800	60,00	36,448		11,631	3,580		125, 189	1,942	*Inventaire après décès*, ADG, notary Collignan, 26 July 1800
Châlons-sur-Marne										
Seneuze	1790	80,000								An v'553
Frantin	1775							98,299		*Contrat de mariage*, ADCD, notary Menu, 13 February 1775
Dijon										
Weins	1777	12,265		1,800	6,685	6,080	Many houses	11,052		Barbier, *Lumières du nord*, 456
Dunkirk										
Danel	1763							105,000 florins		Barbier, *Lumières du nord*, 102–3
Lille										
Boubers de Corbeville	1785	6,854	2,375	1,150	2900	1,987	House	15,267	9,457	Barbier, *Lumières du nord*, 214
Limoges										
Barbou[b]	1750	100,000		50,000		10,000		269,400	468,400	Ducourtieux, *Les Barbou*, 64–65

Lyon

Name	Year	Business	Stocks	Cash	Accounts receivable	Furniture/property	Real estate	Total	Liabilities	Source (notary or historian)
Declaustre	1754	543,173								Dureau, "A' propos de quelques sources lyonnaises," 146
Vialon	1761		18,072							Dureau, "A' propos de quelques sources lyonnaises," 146
Vatar	1777		40,000			8,484		48,484		Chartier, "Livre et éspace," 84–85 (chart)
Vialon	1778		16,800		9,113	2,224		28,217		Chartier, "Livre et éspace," 84–85 (chart)
Delaroche	1784	150,000c								ADR, 1C221
Delaroche Millanois	1783		35,431		51,436	9,349		96,216		Chartier, "Livre et éspace," 84–85 (chart)
Barret	1786		121,054		65,253	1,748		18,8055	154,433	ADR, inventaire, BP 2294, 16 August 1786
Faucheux	Year III		28,571		23,211	64,000		124,782	96,005	Chartier, "Livre et éspace," 84–85 (chart)
Reguilliat	1775		32,100							ADR, 7C9
Delamollière	Year III		276,573			511	90,000	398,566	926,766	Chartier, "Livre et éspace," 84–85 (chart)
Bruyset & Buynand	1807	40,000	557,000		902,474			210,000	810,668	ADR, Série U, 1807

Printer	Year								Source
Nîmes									
Beaume	1800		67,530						*Inventaire après décès*, ADG, notary Collignan, 26 July 1800
Rouen									
Besongne	1753			7,500	6,651				Quéniart, *L'Imprimerie*, 245
Behourt	1759	20,000			4,000	1,812	5,000–10,000	4,000	Quéniart, *L'Imprimerie*, 245
Besongne	1784	65,000			7,812[d]	5,000	32,000	93,600	Quéniart, *L'Imprimerie*, 245
Lallemant[e]	1797	9,175			15,193	4,672	137,550	91,639	Quéniart, *L'Imprimerie*, 245
Toulouse									
Guillemette	1780s							60,000 (est.)[f]	*Accords*, ADHG, notary Arnaud, 1 January and 9 September 1780; *contrat de mariage*, ADHG, notary Arnaud, 4 July 1773
Baour	1794						34,000	37,637	Blanc-Rouquette, "Un Imprimeur toulousain au XVIIIe siècle," 317
Pijon son[g]								24,333	Sentou, *Fortunes et groupes*, 284–85
Hénault	1791							136,000	Page, "Claude-Gilles," 85
Desclassan	1793							20,886	Page, "Claude-Gilles," 85

Name	Year	Business	Stocks	Cash	Accounts receivable	Furniture/property	Real estate	Total	Liabilities	Source (notary or historian)
						Troyes				
Garnier	1777							100,000		1777 *État*, BN FF 21832
						Valenciennes				
Henry	1783						72,900			Barbier, *Lumières du nord*, 317
Henry	1795	14,032								Barbier, *Lumières du nord*, 313
Other indications of wealth										
						Boulogne-sur-mer				
Battut	1781	Will[h]								Barbier, *Lumières du nord*, 198
						Lyon				
Bruyset	1790	Rent paid[i]								Edmonds, *Jacobinism*, 312
						Poitiers				
Faulcon		Son's situation[j]								Doyle, *Venality*, 207; Faulcon, *Correspondance*, 1:8
						Toulon				
Mallard[k]	1789	60,000 loan								Crook, *Toulon in War*, 81

NOTE: The figures given are in livres unless otherwise specified.

a Labottière sold his business for 130,000 livres. Later he sold the same business for 80,000 livres (ADG, notary Darrieux, 18 Ventôse Year III).

b Included for the Barbou family are two offices, *greffier de l'élection* and *trésorier des ponts et chaussées*, evaluated at 39,000 livres.

c The 150,000 figure for Delaroche in 1784 is an estimate of the value of his printing equipment (ADR 1 C 221).

d This figure does not include the huge losses that led to the bankruptcy of the firm.

e Lallemant paid 91,750 in advances to his two daughters, and his wife's property was evaluated at 37,800.

f Guillemette's total is a rough estimate that is surely low. Three children received inheritances of 12,000, 15,814, and 16,212 livres, respectively, and I am assuming that the general heir received at least 16,000 livres, and probably more.

g Printer Bernard Pijon's son was a priest and *docteur en théologie*.

h Battut left 12,000 livres to two brothers, frères des Écoles chrétiennes.

i The younger Jean-Marie Bruyset paid 1,400 livres' rent in 1790, the second highest in the municipality.

j Printer Félix Faulcon gave his son, by one account, a yearly income of 25,000 *livres de rente* and bought an office for him worth 7,000–8,000 livres. He also, since at least 1766, had a country estate.

k In Toulon the printer Jean-Louis Mallard lent 60,000 to the naval authorities to bring to an end a dockyard strike in 1789.

SOME LICENSED PROVINCIAL PRINTERS INVOLVED IN THE ILLEGAL
BOOK TRADE, 1750–89, BY TOWN

Printer	License date	Year of accusation, offense, or condemnation for pirating (P) or clandestine trade (C)	Source
Abbeville			
Deverité	1775	1776 (C)	Lepreux, *Gallia,* vol. 1, p. 147
Alençon			
Malassis	1770	1771 (C)	Lepreux, *Gallia,* vol. 3, pt. 2, pp. 53–55
Amiens			
Godart	1714 (father)	1752 (C/P)	BN FF 22075
Angers			
Pavie	1780	1782 (C)	Pasquier and Dauphin, *Imprimeurs,* 195 BN FF 22070
Billault	1770	1772 (P)	Pasquier and Dauphin, *Imprimeurs,* 92
Auxerre			
Fournier	1742	1771 (C)	Sarazin, "Un 'Chalotiste,'" 44
Avranches			
Le Court	1766	1771 (C)	BN FF 22101
Besançon			
Charmet	1761	1777–85 (C)	Darnton, *Édition,* 225
Daclin	1787	1788 (C)	BN FF 22070 #71
Couché	1754	1762 (C)	BN FF 21832
Bordeaux			
Labottière	1755	1766 (C) 1777 (C)	ADG C 3314 AN E 2538; ADG C 3315
Phillippot	1766	1789 (C)	Bernadau, "Tablettes"
Calamy	1784	1775 (C)	ADG C 3315
Beaume	1786	1788 (C)	BN FF 21869

Printer	License date	Year of accusation, offense, or condemnation for pirating (P) or clandestine trade (C)	Source
Chappuis	1726	1766 (C)	Bib. de l'Arsenal 12295
		1767 (P)	ADG 10B 56

Brest

Malassis	1758	1774 (C)	Lepreux, *Gallia,* vol. 4, pp. 187–88

Caen

LeRoy	1765	1780 (C)	Lepreux, *Gallia,* vol. 3, pt. 2, pp. 388–89
		1785 (P)	BN FF 22075
		1789 (P)	AN V^1 549

Cahors

Richard	(1777)^a	1775 (C)	AN E 2513

Clermont-Ferrand

Delcros		1777 (P)	BN FF 22075 #134
Viallanes	1736	1776–77? (P)	BN FF 21832

Coutances

LeRoy	1762	1768 (C)	BMDijon Ms 1431
		(P)	Lepreux, *Gallia,* vol. 3, pt. 2, pp. 27–28

Dijon

Frantin	1753	1788 (C)	BN FF 21869
Hucherot	1744	1762 (C)	Clément-Janin, *Les Imprimeurs,* 60–62
Capel	1778^b	1776 (C)	Darnton, *Édition,* 33

Douai

Willerval	1776	1778 (C)	AN E 2549 (Schmauch, *Arrêts*)

Grenoble

Giroud	(1777)^a	1763 (C)	Rigogne, *Between State,* 85

Lyon

Reguilliat	1756	1762 (C)	BN FF NA 3344
		1767 (C)	Varry, "Jean-Baptiste Reguilliat"

Printer	License date	Year of accusation, offense, or condemnation for pirating (P) or clandestine trade (C)	Source
Bruyset	1758	1758–59 (C) (2x) 1760 (C) (3x) 1762 (P)	Varry, "Une Famille," 117 Varry, "Une Famille," 118–22 BN FF NA 3344
Cutty	1759	1762–63 (C)	Varry, "De la Bastille à Bellecour," 578–79; BN FF 22128
Faucheux	1765	1752 (C) 1782 (C) 1772–80 (C)	ADR 1 C 252 BN FF 22070 #58 Fortuny, "Les Éditions lyonnaises," 172
Périsse	1766	1776 (P)	Darnton, *Édition*, 53
Buisson	1755	1762 (C) 1777 (P)	Moulé, "Correspondance," 227 BN FF 22070 #53
Regnault	1756	1763 (C) 1773–74 (P) 1772–80 (C)	BN FF 22128 #99 Trénard, "Commerce et culture," 16 Fortuny, "Les Éditions lyonnaises," 172
Barret	1754	1772 (P) (C) 1777 (P)	Varry, "Gens du livre," 303 Darnton, *The Corpus*, 223 Coyecque, *Inventaire*, 2:438
Vialon	1736	1763 (C) 1772–80 (C)	BN FF 22128 #99 Fortuny, "Les Éditions lyonnaises," 172

Marseille

Printer	License date	Year	Source
Mossy	1768	1766 (P) 1773–84 (C)	Billioud, *Le Livre*, 76 Darnton, *Édition*, 54, 228
Sibié		1749–50 (C)	ADR 1C 252

Montargis

Printer	License date	Year	Source
Lequatre	(1777)[a]	1777 (C)	BN FF 22070 #51

Nancy

Printer	License date	Year	Source
Lamort	(1777)[a]	1788 (C)	BN FF 22070 #74
Le Seurre	1768	1778 (C)	AN E 2549 (Schmauch, *Arrêts*)

Nantes

Printer	License date	Year	Source
Malassis	1770	1788 (C)	Darnton, *The Corpus*, 213, 226; Lepreux, *Gallia*, vol. 4, Documenta, pp. 153–54; BN FF 21869

Printer	License date	Year of accusation, offense, or condemnation for pirating (P) or clandestine trade (C)	Source
Vatar	1750	1751 (C)	ADI-et-V C 1462

Orléans

Couret de Villeneuve	1776	1770s (C)	Darnton, *L'Édition,* 137

Pau

Desbarats[c]	(1777)[a]	1765 (C)	BN FF 21832
Daumont	1779	1788 (C)	BN FF 21869
Vignancourt	(1777)[a]	1788 (C)	BN FF 21867

Provins

Michelin	1758	1761 (C)	BN FF 21832; Smith, "Helvétius," 294

Reims

Jeune-homme	1761	1775 (C)	AN E 2519 (Gallet-Guerne, *Arrêts*)

Rennes

Vatar	1758	1771 (C)	BN FF 22070 #22
Audran	1784	1788 (C)	BN FF 21867
Garnier	1758	1769 (C)	Lepreux, *Gallia,* vol. 4, Documenta, pp. 118–19

Rouen

Jacques Ferrand	1752	1759 (P)	BN FF 22078
		1761 (C)	ADSM J 217
		1766 (C)	ADSM J 218
Ferrand	1788	1789 (C)	AN V¹ 551
L. Dumesnil	1752	1759 (C)	ADSM J 218
		1760 (C)	ADSM J 217
J. Dumesnil	1753	1760 (C)	Beaurepaire, *Le Contrôle,* 24–25
Dumesnil		1764 (P)	ADSM J 217
Dumesnil		1766 (C)	ADSM J 218

Printer	License date	Year of accusation, offense, or condemnation for pirating (P) or clandestine trade (C)	Source
Besongne	1757	1764 (C)	Lepreux, *Gallia*, vol. 3, pt. 2, Documenta, p. 363
		1766 (C)	ADSM J 217
		1770 (C)	ADSM J 218
		1771 (C)	BN FF 22070 #15
		1774 (C)	Quéniart, *L'Imprimerie*, 224; Darnton, *Édition*, 93
Viret	1753	1764 (C)	ADSM J 217
Le Boullenger	1752	1759 (P)	BN FF 22078
Lallemant	1754	1761 (P)	ADSM J 217
		1765 (C)	ADSM J 218
		1787 (P)	BN FF 21867
R. Machuel	1715	1753 (C)	Quéniart, *L'Imprimerie*, 220; BN FF 22075
Et. Machuel	1752	1767 (C)	ADSM J 218; Quéniart, *L'Imprimerie*, 186
Boisjouvin	1721	1752 (C/P)	BN FF 22075

Saint-Malo

Valais	1767	1775 (C)	AN E 2519

Saint-Omer

Boubers de Corbeville	1753	1767 (C)	Lepreux, *Gallia*, vol. 1, pp. 103–4

Senlis

Desroques	(1777)[a]	1775 (C)	AN E 2516

Soissons

Waroquier	(1777)[a]	(C)	Darnton, *The Corpus*, 213

Toulouse

Bellegarique	1785	1788 (C)	AN V[1] 549
Sens	1785	1768 (P)	BN FF 22075
		(C)	Darnton, *The Corpus*, 213.
Rayet	(1777)[a]	1777 (C)	AN E 2530 (Schmauch, *Arrêts*)
		1781 (P)	BN FF 22075 #138

Printer	License date	Year of accusation, offense, or condemnation for pirating (P) or clandestine trade (C)	Source
Baour	1764	1772 (C)	Blanc-Rouquette, "Un Imprimeur," 304
Troyes			
Widow Michelin	1743	1758 (C)	Lepreux, *Gallia,* vol. 2, pp. 165–66
Febvre	1769	1772 (C)	Morin, "Les Febvre," 420
Vannes			
Galles	1758	1760	Lepreux, *Gallia,* vol. 4, p. 289

[a] Listed in the 1777 survey; actual date of license unknown.

[b] In 1776 Jean-Baptiste Capel was a bookseller working for his father-in-law, the printer Defay, and got his own license in 1778.

[c] In Pau, Dlle Desbarats and Dugasé were banned from the printing business in 1765 because they were suspected of secretly printing "des remonstrances sur les affaires du parlement de Pau."

Notes

The following abbreviations occur frequently in the notes.

ADCD   Archives départementales du Côte d'Or, Dijon
ADG   Archives départementales de la Gironde, Bordeaux
ADHG   Archives départementales de la Haute Garonne, Toulouse
ADI-et-V   Archives départementales d'Ille-et-Vilaine
ADR   Archives départementales du Rhône, Lyon
ADSM   Archives départementales de la Seine Maritime, Rouen
AMBx   Archives municipales de Bordeaux
AMLyon   Archives municipales de Lyon
AN   Archives nationales de France, Paris
BMBx   Bibliothèque municipale de Bordeaux
BMDijon   Bibliothèque municipale de Dijon
BMToulouse Bibliothèque municipale de Toulouse
BN   Bibliothèque nationale, Paris

Introduction

1. Bibliothèque municipale de Dijon (hereafter BMDijon) MS 745, 26 October 1780, 21 January 1781; Archives nationales (hereafter AN) V^6 1099, 18 December 1780.

2. The group included the lieutenant of police and two barristers in the Parlement of Dijon, who were acting in their capacities of crown attorney, *syndic* of the town, and secretary of the *hôtel de ville* of Dijon. The surrounding towns within the jurisdiction of the *chambre syndicale* of Dijon were Auxerre, Châlons-sur-Saône, Chaumont, Langres, Moulins, and Nevers.

3. The Fay and later Defay family dynasty began printing in Dijon the early eighteenth century, when Antoine Fay made the first attempt to obtain a license in 1704 (AN V^6 797, 14 July 1704). On the Defay family, see Michel-Hilaire Clément-Janin, *Les Imprimeurs et les libraires dans la Côte-d'Or* (1883; repr., Geneva: Slatkine, 1971), 63–66.

4. Le Camus de Néville's decision was relatively simple because Defay was the only applicant. For many printer's licenses, there were several applicants (Bibliothèque nationale [hereafter BN]) FF 21870).

5. Several historians have studied the August 1777 decrees for their reform of copyright rules: Raymond Birn, "The Profits of Ideas: *Privilèges en librairie* in Eighteenth-Century France," *Eighteenth-Century Studies* 4 (1971): 131–68; Robert Dawson, *The French Booktrade and the "Permission Simple" of 1777: Copyright and Public Domain* (Oxford: Voltaire Foundation, 1992); Carla Hesse, *Publishing and Cultural Politics in Revolutionary Paris, 1789–1810* (Berkeley: University of California Press, 1991), 39–45. Jack Censer suggests that the copyright reforms indicated increased control of the press under Vergennes; see *The French Press in the Age of Enlightenment* (London: Routledge, 1994), 183.

6. AN E 402, 6 October 1667.

7. On 21 July 1704 the king fixed the number of printers allowed for every city in France, and printers were ordered to obtain licenses. For a copy of this decree, see Claude-Marin

Saugrain, ed., *Code de la librairie et imprimerie de Paris ou conférence du réglement arrêté au conseil d'état du roi le 28 février 1723 et rendu commun pour tout le royaume, par arrêt du conseil d'état du 24 mars 1744 avec les anciennes ordonnances . . .* (1744; repr., Westmead: Gregg International, 1971), 203.

8. For an overview of publishing in France in this period, the indispensable volumes are Roger Chartier and Henri-Jean Martin, eds., *Histoire de l'édition française,* vol. 1, *Le Livre conquérant: Du moyen age au milieu du XVIIe siècle,* and vol. 2, *Le Livre triomphant, 1660–1830* (Paris: Fayard, 1989, 1990).

9. Among their other works, see Robert Darnton, *The Business of Enlightenment: A Publishing History of the Encyclopédie, 1775–1800* (Cambridge, Mass.: Harvard University Press, 1979); Darnton, *Édition et sédition: L'Univers de la littérature clandestine au XVIIIe siècle* (Paris: Gallimard, 1991); and Elizabeth Eisenstein, *Grub Street Abroad: Aspects of the French Cosmopolitan Press from the Age of Louis XIV to the French Revolution* (Oxford: Clarendon Press, 1992).

10. French provincial printers have been the subject of recent work in the thriving field of *histoire du livre.* Especially notable here are Jean-Dominique Mellot's work on Rouen (*L'Édition rouennaise et ses marchés (vers 1600–vers 1730): Dynamisme provincial et centralisme parisien* [Paris: École des chartes, 1998]); Dominique Varry's many articles on Lyon; Frédéric Barbier, *Lumières du nord: Imprimeurs, libraires et "gens du livre" dans le nord au XVIIIe siècle (1701–1789): Dictionnaire prosopographique* (Geneva: Droz, 2002); and Thierry Rigogne's study of the 1764 survey of printers and booksellers, *Between State and Market: Printing and Bookselling in Eighteenth-Century France* (Oxford: Voltaire Foundation, 2007).

11. J. Michael Hayden, "The Uses of Political Pamphlets: The Example of 1614–15 in France," *Canadian Journal of History* 21 (1986): 143–66; Jeffrey K. Sawyer, *Printed Poison: Pamphlet Propaganda, Faction Politics, and the Public Sphere in Early Seventeenth-Century France* (Berkeley: University of California Press, 1990), 57–60.

12. Henri-Jean Martin, "Un Grand Éditeur parisien au XVIIe siècle: Sébastien Cramoisy," *Gutenberg Jahrbuch* (1957): 186; Christian Jouhaud, "Écriture et action au XVIIe siècle: Sur un corpus de Mazarinades," *Annales E.S.C.* 38 (1983): 45–46; Hubert Carrier, *La Presse de la Fronde (1648–1653): Les Mazarinades: La Conquête de l'opinion* (Geneva: Droz, 1989), 1:139–42.

13. Henri-Jean Martin, *Livre, pouvoirs et société à Paris au XVIIe siècle (1598–1701)* (Geneva: Droz, 1969), 2:570. There is a one-volume English translation by David Gerard, *Print, Power, and People in Seventeenth-Century France* (Metuchen, N.J.: Scarecrow, 1993).

14. Martin, *Livre, pouvoirs,* 2:590–91.

15. This is done in two masterly sections of the second volume of *Livre, pouvoirs,* the first entitled "La Mutation du siècle (1643–1665)," 555–96, and the second, "La Réaction royale (1661–1702)," 662–772.

16. Martin, *Livre, pouvoirs,* 683.

17. I am using the term "identity" very loosely in this book to mean the different "hats" printers wore when representing themselves to their communities. Others could be included—for example, printers' religious affiliations, or their important role as employers of labor. Influential here are Stephen Greenblatt, *Renaissance Self-Fashioning: From More to Shakespeare* (Chicago: University of Chicago Press, 1980), and Kristen Neuschel, *Word of Honor: Interpreting Noble Culture in Sixteenth-Century France* (Ithaca: Cornell University Press, 1989).

18. Arlette Farge, *Subversive Words: Public Opinion in Eighteenth-Century France,* trans. Rosemary Morris (University Park: Pennsylvania State University Press, 1995).

19. Very influential in this study are William Beik, *Absolutism and Society in Seventeenth-Century France: State Power and Provincial Aristocracy in Languedoc* (Cambridge: Cambridge University Press, 1985), and Sharon Kettering, *Patrons, Brokers, and Clients in Seventeenth-Century France* (Oxford: Oxford University Press, 1986).

20. Control of printers was a twofold process of offering encouragements to loyalty and punishing disloyalty. On repression, see Daniel Roche, "Censorship and the Publishing Industry," in *Revolution in Print: The Press in France, 1775–1800*, ed. Robert Darnton and Daniel Roche (Berkeley: University of California Press, 1989); Raymond Birn, "La Contrebande et la saisie de livres à l'aube du siècle des Lumières," *Revue d'histoire moderne et contemporaine* 28 (1981): 158–73, and Birn, "Book Production and Censorship in France (1700–1715)," in *Books and Society in History*, ed. Kenneth Carpenter (New York: Bowker, 1983), 145–71. I am currently completing a study of French printers' experiences in the courts in the early modern era.

21. For an overview of this literature, see Jane McLeod, "Provincial Book Trade Inspectors in Eighteenth-Century France," *French History* 12 (1998): 127–31.

22. Raymond Birn has recently studied the censors in *La Censure royale des livres dans la France des Lumières* (Paris: Odile Jacob, 2007). See also Sophia Rosenfeld, "Writing the History of Censorship in the Age of Enlightenment," in *Postmodernism and the Enlightenment: New Perspectives in Eighteenth-Century French Intellectual History*, ed. Daniel Gordon (New York: Routledge, 2001), 117–45.

23. Roger Chartier compares printer control with the control of bread in *The Cultural Origins of the French Revolution*, trans. Lydia Cochrane (Durham: Duke University Press, 1991), 44–46. In 1773 Joseph d'Hémery, the inspector of the book trade in Paris, drew the parallel between the government's policing of printing workers with the navy's tracking sailors (BN FF 22063 #41).

Chapter 1

1. BN FF 21832. Georges Bouchon, *Histoire d'une imprimerie bordelaise, 1600–1900* (Bordeaux: Gounouilhou, 1901), 103; Paul Ducourtieux, *Les Barbou, imprimeurs Lyon-Limoges-Paris* (Limoges: Ducourtieux, 1896), 7–8; AN V⁶ 1122, 28 February 1785. On the significance of origin stories, see Joanne Wright, *Origin Stories in Political Thought: Discourses on Gender, Power, and Citizenship* (Toronto: University of Toronto Press, 2004), 2–23; Paul Chauvet, *Les Ouvriers du livre en France des origines à la Révolution de 1789* (Paris: Presses universitaires de France, 1959), 235–36; Jean Quéniart, *L'Imprimerie et la librairie à Rouen au XVIIIe siècle* (Paris: Klincksieck, 1969), 21; Georges Lepreux, *Gallia typographica ou répertoire biographique et chronologique de tous les imprimeurs de France depuis les origines de l'imprimerie jusqu'à la Révolution* (Paris: Champion, 1909–14), vol. 3, pt. 1, pp. 7–11, 230–31; Alain R. Girard, "Les Incunables rouennais: Imprimerie et culture au XVe siècle," *Revue française d'histoire du livre* 53 (1986): 463–525; Jean-Dominique Mellot, *L'Édition rouennaise et ses marchés (vers 1600–vers 1730): Dynamisme provincial et centralisme parisien* (Paris: École des chartes, 1998), 27–28.

2. Jeanne-Marie Dureau, "Les Premiers Ateliers français," in *Histoire de l'édition française: Le Livre conquérant: Du moyen age au milieu du XVIIe siècle,* ed. Roger Chartier and Henri-Jean Martin (Paris: Fayard, 1989), 186–99. Between 1470 and 1500, printers were established in forty-seven towns (Chauvet, *Les Ouvriers,* 480–481).

3. Girard, "Les Incunables," 488–89.

4. Louis Desgraves, "L'Introduction et la diffusion de l'imprimerie dans le sud-ouest," in his *Études sur l'imprimerie dans le sud-ouest de la France au XVe, XVIe et XVIIe siècles* (Amsterdam: Erasmus, 1968), 5–12, and "L'Introduction de l'imprimerie dans le sud-ouest de la France jusqu'à la fin du XVIe siècle," in *Villes d'imprimerie et moulins à papier du XIVe au XVIe siècle: Aspects économiques et sociaux* (Brussels: Crédit Communale de Belgique, 1976), 39–79.

5. Henri-Jean Martin and Jeanne-Marie Dureau, "Des Années de transition: 1500–1530," in Chartier and Martin, *Histoire de l'édition française: Le Livre conquérant,* 256–67, and, in the same

work, Pierre Aquilon, "Les Réalités provinciales," 436–54, and Natalie Zemon Davis, "Le Monde de l'imprimerie humaniste: Lyon," 303–35; Chauvet, *Les Ouvriers,* 6; Mellot, *L'Édition rouennaise,* 27–28; Natalie Zemon Davis, "Publisher Guillaume Rouillé, Businessman and Humanist," in *Editing Sixteenth-Century Texts,* ed. R. J. Schoeck (Toronto: University of Toronto Press, 1966), 72–112.

6. Elizabeth Eisenstein, *The Printing Press as an Agent of Change: Communications and Cultural Transformations in Early Modern Europe,* 2 vols. (Cambridge: Cambridge University Press, 1979).

7. BN FF 21820, fol. 102.

8. *Récit de ce qui s'est passé à l'égard de la communauté des libraires et imprimeurs* . . . in *Chartrier ou recueil par ordre chronologique de divers titres, pièces concernant les libraires et les imprimeurs jurés de l'université de Bordeaux,* II, Bibliothèque municipale de Bordeaux (hereafter BMBx). For a Montpellier example, see AN V⁶ 1115, 15 September 1783.

9. Dureau, "Les Premiers Ateliers," 196. For other examples of noble patronage of printers, see Hélène Duccini, *Faire voir, faire croire: L'Opinion publique sous Louis XIII* (Paris: Champ Vallon, 2003), 43.

10. Desgraves, "L'Introduction et la diffusion de l'imprimerie dans le sud-ouest," 6; Aquilon, "Les Réalités," 440–41.

11. Desgraves, "L'Introduction et la diffusion de l'imprimerie dans le sud-ouest," 6; Desgraves, "L'Introduction de l'imprimerie," 52–54.

12. Bouchon, *Histoire d'une imprimerie bordelaise,* 39.

13. AN V⁶ 1089, 22 March 1779.

14. AN V⁶ 933, 7 May 1742.

15. AN V⁶ 928, 24 October 1740.

16. AN V⁶ 922, 26 June 1739.

17. Hubert Carrier, *La Presse de la Fronde (1648–1653): Les Mazarinades,* vol. 2, *Les Hommes du livre* (Geneva: Droz, 1991), 362.

18. Carrier, *La Presse,* 2:339–46.

19. Lepreux, *Gallia,* vol. 4, Documenta, pp. 2–11, and vol. 2, pp. 268–73.

20. Amédée Lhote, *Histoire de l'imprimerie à Châlons-sur-Marne* (1894; repr., Nieuwkoop: B. de Graaf, 1969), 21–28.

21. Mellot, *L'Édition rouennaise,* 63. See also Jean-Dominique Mellot, "Rouen and Its Printers from the Fifteenth to the Nineteenth Century," in *Printed Matters: Printing, Publishing, and Urban Culture in Europe in the Modern Period,* ed. Malcolm Gee and Tim Kirk (Aldershot: Ashgate, 2002).

22. Micheline Thoumas-Schapira, "La Bourgeoisie toulousaine à la fin du XVIIe siècle," *Annales du Midi* 67 (1955): 313–29; BN FF 22127 #37–38; Madeleine Ventre, *L'Imprimerie et la librairie en Languedoc au dernier siècle de l'ancien régime, 1700–1789* (Paris: Mouton, 1958), 32–55; Tibulle Desbarreaux-Bernard, "L'Inquisition des livres à Toulouse au XVIIe siècle," *Mémoires de l'Académie des sciences, inscriptions et belles-lettres de Toulouse* (1874): 336–37.

23. Louis Desgraves, "L'Imprimeur bordelais Jacques Mongiron-Millanges (1649–1692)," in *Extrait du bulletin philologique et historique du Comité des travaux historiques et scientifiques* (Paris: Imprimerie nationale, 1958); Bouchon, *Histoire d'une imprimerie bordelaise,* 10.

24. The jurats bought the office of *lieutenant général de police* and were responsible for policing in the town. On the jurats and printers, see Archives municipales de Bordeaux (hereafter AMBx) BB 53, 1 February 1659; *Inventaire sommaire des registres de la Jurade, 1520 à 1783* (Bordeaux, 1947), 8:88–106.

25. Christian Jouhaud, "Écriture et action au XVII siècle: Sur un corpus de Mazarinades," *Annales E.S.C.* 38 (1983): 63; *Inventaire,* 89–91; Bouchon, *Histoire d'une imprimerie bordelaise,* 51–52.

26. Henri-Jean Martin, "Renouvellements et concurrences," in Chartier and Martin, *Histoire de l'édition française: Le Livre conquérant*, 475–77; *Livre, pouvoirs, et société à Paris au XVIIe siècle (1598–1701)* (Geneva: Droz, 1969), 1:420–22; and "Un Grand Éditeur parisien au XVIIe siècle: Sébastien Cramoisy," *Gutenberg Jahrbuch* (1957): 179–88.

27. Martin argues that Vitré was a new sort of printer, more of a technician than a scholar in that he did not engage in his printing projects intellectually the way the scholar-printers of the sixteenth century had ("Renouvellements," 477). Here I am using Robert Darnton's definition of *libelles:* "slanderous attacks on public figures known collectively as 'les grands'" (*The Forbidden Best-Sellers of Pre-Revolutionary France* [London: Fontana, 1997], 198). On patronage and early seventeenth-century printers, see Jeffrey K. Sawyer, *Printed Poison: Pamphlet Propaganda, Faction Politics, and the Public Sphere in Early Seventeenth-Century France* (Berkeley: University of California Press, 1990).

28. On Lyon printers in the sixteenth and seventeenth centuries, see Natalie Zemon Davis, "A Trade Union in Sixteenth-Century France," *Economic History Review,* 2nd ser., 19 (1960): 48–69; "Strikes and Salvation in Lyon," in *Society and Culture in Early Modern France* (Stanford: Stanford University Press, 1975), 1–16; and "Le Monde de l'imprimerie humaniste," 303–35. See also Jacqueline Roubert, "La Situation de l'imprimerie lyonnaise à la fin du XVIIe siècle," in *Cinq Études lyonnaises,* ed. René Fédou et al. (Geneva: Droz, 1966), 77–99.

29. Guy Parguez, "L'Imprimerie à Lyon au temps de Dolet," in *Étienne Dolet (1509–1546),* Collection de l'École normale supérieure des jeunes filles 31, Cahiers V. L. Saulnier 3 (Paris: École normale supérieure des jeunes filles, 1986), 63–77.

30. Martin, "Renouvellements," 494–96.

31. Martin, "Renouvellements," 492–94.

32. Henri-Jean Martin, *Print, Power, and People in Seventeenth-Century France,* trans. David Gerard (Metuchen, N.J.: Scarecrow, 1993), 501–2; Martin, "Renouvellements," 493–94.

33. Steven Kaplan, "Social Stratification and Representation in the Corporate World of Eighteenth-Century France: Turgot's 'Carnival,'" in *Work in France: Representations, Meaning, Organization, and Practice,* ed. Steven Kaplan and Cynthia Koepp (Ithaca: Cornell University Press, 1986), 176–228.

34. See many examples in BN FF 22125–22129; Chauvet, *Les Ouvriers,* 214–55; Ventre, *L'Imprimerie,* 32–57.

35. Lepreux, *Gallia,* vol. 3, pt. 1, pp. 13–14; Chauvet, *Les Ouvriers,* 43–47.

36. Chauvet, *Les Ouvriers,* 252.

37. Émile Pasquier and Victor Dauphin, *Imprimeurs et libraires de l'Anjou* (Angers: Éditions de l'Ouest, 1932), 27.

38. *Règlements pour les imprimeurs de Metz,* dated 29 May 1656, in Albert Isnard and Suzanne Honoré, *Catalogue générale des livres imprimés de la Bibliothèque nationale: Actes royaux* (Paris: Imprimerie nationale, 1938) 2:948.

39. Ventre, *L'Imprimerie,* 57.

40. These generalizations are taken from rules outlined in Bordeaux in 1608, in Paris in 1618, and in Rennes and Toulouse.

41. BN FF 22125 #1–2.

42. Ernest Labadie, *Notices biographiques sur les imprimeurs et les libraires bordelais des XVIe, XVIIe et XVIIIe siècles* (Bordeaux: Mounastre-Picamilh, 1900), xxxiv.

43. BN FF 22125 #115.

44. Labadie, *Notices,* xxvi.

45. Lepreux, *Gallia,* vol. 4, Documenta, pp. 15, 35–37, 169–72.

46. BN FF 22127 #37–38.

47. The following discussion is drawn from Francis Higman, "Le Levain de l'Évangile," and Denis Pallier, "Les Réponses catholiques," in Chartier and Martin, Histoire de l'édition française: Le Livre conquérant, 373–435; the works of Natalie Davis cited above; Louis Desgraves, Les Haultin, 1571–1623 (Geneva: Droz, 1960), and "L'Introduction de l'imprimerie"; Donald R. Kelley, The Beginning of Ideology: Consciousness and Society in the French Reformation (Cambridge: Cambridge University Press, 1981); Chauvet, Les Ouvriers, 63–66; and Aquilon, "Les Réalités," 444.

48. Kelley, The Beginning, 215–44; Eisenstein, The Printing Press as an Agent of Change.

49. Denis Pallier, "Les Victimes de la Saint-Barthélémy dans le monde du livre parisien," in Le Livre et l'historien: Études offertes en l'honneur du professeur Henri-Jean Martin, ed. Frédéric Barbier et al. (Geneva: Droz, 1997), 141–63.

50. Davis, "Le Monde de l'imprimerie humaniste," 330; Higman, "Le Levain," 393. The execution of Dolet is, of course, an exception.

51. Pallier, "Les Victimes de la Saint-Barthélémy," 142–43.

52. J. Michael Hayden, "The Uses of Political Pamphlets: The Example of 1614–1615 in France," Canadian Journal of History 21 (1986): 143–66; Sawyer, Printed Poison, 63–65; Martin, Livre, pouvoirs, 1:366–67.

53. Davis, "A Trade Union"; Chauvet, Les Ouvriers, 2–75; Paul Mellottée, Histoire économique de l'imprimerie: L'Imprimerie sous l'ancien régime (Paris: Hachette, 1905).

54. Chauvet, Les Ouvriers, 214–15.

55. There is a large literature on copyright protection. For an overview of some of it, see Raymond Birn, "The Profits of Ideas: Privilèges en librairie in Eighteenth-Century France," Eighteenth-Century Studies 4 (1971): 131–68. The most recent examinations are Mellot, L'Édition rouennaise, and Robert Dawson, The French Booktrade and the "Permission Simple" of 1777: Copyright and Public Domain (Oxford: Voltaire Foundation, 1992).

56. Roger Chartier, "Pamphlets and Gazettes," in Chartier and Martin, Histoire de l'édition française: Le Livre conquérant, 509–17; Louis Desgraves, "Les Bulletins d'information imprimés à Bordeaux aux XVIe et XVIIe siècles," Bulletin de la Société des bibliophiles de Guyenne (1964): 25.

57. Martin, Livre, pouvoirs; Lepreux, Galia, vol. 3.

58. Sawyer, Printed Poison, 134–45.

59. Sawyer, Printed Poison, 137. On the ordonnance of 1618, see Martin, Livre, pouvoirs, 1:54–57.

60. Quoted in Sawyer, Printed Poison, 137.

61. Quoted in Sawyer, Printed Poison, 140; Martin, Livre, pouvoirs, 1:442–44.

62. Alfred Soman, "Press, Pulpit, and Censorship in France Before Richelieu," Proceedings of the American Philosophical Society 120 (1976): 444; Sawyer, Printed Poison, 134.

63. Quoted in Sawyer, Printed Poison, 64.

64. Henri-Jean Martin and Anne-Marie Lecocq, Livres et lecteurs à Grenoble: Les Registres du libraire Nicolas (1645–1668) (Geneva: Droz, 1977), 1:45–46.

65. Hayden, "The Uses," 157.

66. Soman, "Press, Pulpit," 440.

67. Sawyer, Printed Poison, 124; Soman, "Press, Pulpit," 441.

68. Martin argued for a state with an agenda of control: "De plus en plus, cependant, le souci principal du Pouvoir face à la presse, était de réorganiser les professions du livre afin de les mieux tenir en main et de pouvoir ainsi éviter que se multiplient pamphlets et ouvrages interdits" (Livre, pouvoirs, 1:52). He also claimed that "le désir du Roi de lutter contre les petites imprimeries qui vivaient de l'impression des pamphlets et des livres prohibés, coïncidait avec la volonté des maîtres de limiter la concurrence" (54–55).

69. Chartier, "Pamphlets et gazettes," 524.

70. See many works of Steven Kaplan, including "The Luxury Guilds in Paris in the Eighteenth Century," *Francia* 9 (1981): 257–98.

71. Robert Ian Moore, *The Formation of a Persecuting Society: Power and Deviance in Western Europe, 950–1250* (Oxford: Blackwell, 1987).

Chapter 2

1. BN FF 18600, fols. 649, 693–96. Henri-Jean Martin, *Livre, pouvoirs et société à Paris au XVII siècle (1598–1701)* (Geneva: Droz, 1969), 2:555–70; "Un Projet de réforme de l'imprimerie parisienne en 1645," in *Humanisme actif: Mélanges d'art et de littérature offert à Julien Cain,* ed. Étienne Dennery (Paris: Hermann, 1968), 2:261–64; "Un Grand Éditeur parisien au XVIIe siècle: Sébastien Cramoisy," *Gutenberg Jahrbuch* (1957): 179–88.

2. Hubert Carrier, *La Presse de la Fronde (1648–1653): Les Mazarinades,* 2 vols. (Geneva: Droz, 1989, 1991); Martin, *Livre, pouvoirs,* 2:570–96; Alphonse Feillet, "Une Page de l'histoire de la presse en 1649," in his edition of *Oeuvres du Cardinal Retz* (Paris: Hachette, 1872), 2:660–74.

3. Christian Jouhaud, *Mazarinades: La Fronde des mots* (Paris: Aubier, 1985).

4. Martin, *Livre, pouvoirs,* 2:573–80; Carrier, *La Presse,* 2:125; Bernard Barbiche, "Le Régime de l'édition," in *Histoire de l'édition française: Le Livre conquérant: Du moyen age au milieu du XVIIe siècle,* ed. Roger Chartier and Henri-Jean Martin (Paris: Fayard, 1989), 469–70.

5. Partisans of the new statutes referred to the December 1649 text as "Edit du Roi contenant les nouveaux statuts et réglements pour le fait de l'imprimerie," and those who opposed them called them "Lettres obtenues par aucuns des imprimeurs et libraires de Paris" (Martin, *Livre, pouvoirs,* 2:573–80).

6. Martin, *Livre, pouvoirs,* 2:578–80.

7. Roger Chartier, "Pamphlets et gazettes," in Chartier and Martin, *Histoire de l'édition française: Le Livre conquérant,* 519–20; Carrier, *La Presse,* 2:129; Jouhaud, "Écriture et action au XVIIe siècle: Sur un corpus de Mazarinades," *Annales E.S.C.* 38 (1983): 42–64; Georges Bouchon, *Histoire d'une imprimerie bordelaise, 1600–1900* (Bordeaux: Gounouilhou, 1901), 53.

8. Henri-Jean Martin and Anne-Marie Lecocq, *Livres et lecteurs à Grenoble: Les Registres du libraire Nicolas (1645–1668)* (Geneva: Droz, 1977), 1:95–97.

9. Jean-Dominique Mellot, *L'Édition rouennaise et ses marchés (vers 1600–vers 1730): Dynamisme provincial et centralisme parisien* (Paris: École des chartes, 1998), 68–70, 175–76.

10. More research is needed on the ways in which provincial authorities handled censorship issues.

11. Godefroi Hermant, *Mémoires de Godefroi Hermant sur l'histoire ecclésiastique du XVIIe siècle, 1630–1663,* ed. Augustin Gazier, 6 vols. (Paris: Plon, 1905–10).

12. Hermant, *Mémoires,* 2:49–55.

13. Hermant, *Mémoires,* 3:6–7; Henri-Jean Martin, "Guillaume Desprez, libraire de Pascal et de Port-Royal," *Fédération des sociétés historiques et archéologiques de Paris et de l'Ile-de-France: Mémoires* 2 (1950): 205–28; Hermant, *Mémoires,* 3:6–7, 4:156, 312–15; Charles-Augustin Sainte-Beuve, *Port-Royal,* ed. Maxime Leroy (Paris: Gallimard, 1961–64), 2:79–90; Ernest Jovy, *Le Journal de Monsieur de Saint-Gilles* (Paris: Vrin, 1936), 117–20.

14. On diocesan printing in the eighteenth century, see Michel Péronnet, *Les Évêques de l'ancienne France* (Lille: Reproduction des thèses, 1977), 2:943–62, and "Les Évêques français et le livre au XVIe siècle: Auteurs, éditeurs et censeurs," in *Le Livre dans l'Europe de la Renaissance: Actes du XXVIIIe colloque international d'études humanistes de Tours,* ed. Pierre Aquilon and Henri-Jean Martin (Paris: Promodis, 1988), 159–69. I am indebted to Tim Le Goff for the biographical information on bishops in this book.

15. Hermant, *Mémoires,* 5:165–69.

16. Mellot, *L'Édition rouennaise, 359–67.*

17. Albert Hamscher, *The Parlement of Paris After the Fronde, 1653–1673* (Pittsburgh: University of Pittsburgh Press, 1976), 136.

18. Martin, *Livre, pouvoirs,* 2:678–83; BN FF 22065 #20–21.

19. Martin, *Livre, pouvoirs,* 2:682.

20. Pierre Clément, *Lettres, instructions et mémoires de Colbert* (Paris: Imprimerie nationale, 1868), 5:270–27, 409–10; Martin, *Livre, pouvoirs,* 2:680–81.

21. Hermant, *Mémoires,* 6:183–94.

22. Colbert to La Reynie, 29 May 1679, in Clément, *Lettres, instructions,* 5:395–96; Martin, "Un Grand Éditeur parisien," 183.

23. The most recent work on Colbert suggests he had ambitious plans to control the media (Jacob Soll, *The Information Master: Jean-Baptiste Colbert's Secret State Intelligence System* [Ann Arbor: University of Michigan Press, 2009]). I am grateful for an advance look at a section of this work.

24. BN FF 22061 #118; AN V⁶ 612, 11 April 1674. In the same day two other orders in council were issued, one insisting on implementation in Paris of the reduction in the number of printers in 1666 and 1667 and the other ordering the enforcement of the order of 6 October 1667 in the provinces. (See chapter 3.)

25. Martin, *Livre, pouvoirs,* 2:594–96.

26. Martin, *Livre, pouvoirs,* 2:690–95.

27. There are numerous examples of the Parisians initiating raids in the provinces and requesting that pirating cases be heard by royal councils. For example, in 1672 Denis Thierry was behind raids that discovered prohibited and pirated books in Lyon and Aix (AN V⁶ 608, 18 September 1673).

28. Martin, *Livre, pouvoirs,* 678–98.

29. Martin and Lecocq, *Livres et lecteurs,* and Chartier, "Pamphlets et gazettes," 520–24.

30. Copy of the order in council of 6 October 1667 in AN E 402; BN FF 22065 #22. It also required tri-monthly reports to be made on printing in the towns and specifically denied residents of convents, colleges, or other privileged spaces the right to sell books or engage in printing. The ban was reiterated in two orders in council dated 11 April 1674 (AN V⁶ 612), which ordered all those who had set up as booksellers or printers after 1667 to be closed down and commanded that a survey be done of all printers in the realm. For a description of the political climate in 1667 and an overview of a number of initiatives taken by the king and his ministers in the 1660s to firm up royal power, see Albert Hamscher, "Une Contestation évitée: La Prétendue lettre du Parlement de Paris, 1667," in *Pouvoirs, contestations et comportements dans l'Europe moderne,* ed. Bernard Barbiche, Jean-Pierre Poussou, and Alain Tallon (Paris: Presses de l'université Paris-Sorbonne, 2005), 659–73. Colbert was also envisaging major reforms of the universities in France in 1667; see *L'Éducation en France du XVIe au XVIIIe siècle,* ed. Roger Chartier, Marie-Madeleine Compère, and Dominique Julia (Paris: Société d'édition d'enseignement supérieur, 1976), 251–52, 256–58.

31. Paul Chauvet, *Les Ouvriers du livre en France des origines à la Révolution de 1789* (Paris: Presses universitaires de France, 1959), 206. "Les Imprimeurs et libraires de Lyon n'en tinrent guère compte," according to Jacqueline Roubert; see "La Situation de l'imprimerie lyonnaise à la fin du XVIIe siècle," in *Cinq Études lyonnaises,* ed. René Fédou et al. (Geneva: Droz, 1966), 82. Henri-Jean Martin claimed that because of practical difficulties, "[le Pouvoir] semble n'avoir même pas tenté de se faire obéir hors de Paris"; see *Livre, pouvoirs,* 2:683.

32. The archives of the Privy Council are AN V⁶. For a guide to the activity of the Privy Council in the seventeenth century and to the V⁶ holdings, see Albert Hamscher, *The Conseil*

Privé and the Parlements in the Age of Louis XIV: A Study in French Absolutism (Philadelphia: American Philosophical Society, 1987). I have examined all the licenses in five periods: 1709–14, 1719–24, 1739–44, 1754–60, 1776–80. After collecting 719 orders in council in these periods relating to licensing matters, I then pushed the investigation back into the seventeenth century in a less systematic fashion in order to look at the early stages of the licensing policy. The following discussion is based mainly on 30 orders in council dated 1669 to 1699 and a number of these orders and other documents published in Georges Lepreux, *Gallia typographica ou répertoire biographique et chronologique de tous les imprimeurs de France depuis les origines de l'imprimerie jusqu'à la Révolution*, 7 vols. (Paris: Champion, 1909–14). These were signed by the chancellors (Pierre Séguier, Michel Le Tellier, and Louis Boucherat). On the huge increase in these orders in council on book trade matters in 1703 and the establishment of the Bureau de la librairie, see chapter 3.

33. On printing in Châlons, see Amédée Lhote, *Histoire de l'imprimerie à Châlons-sur-Marne* (1894; repr., Nieuwkoop: B. de Graaf, 1969).

34. Lepreux, *Gallia*, vol. 2, Documenta, pp. 28–30; Lhote, *Histoire*, 188–89. The letters patent for king's printing were registered by the Parlement of Paris in 1663. On members of the Seneuze family, see also Lhote, *Histoire*, 39–41, 43, 50–57, 61, 68–69, 72–73, 84–87, 101–6.

35. 24 April 1670. *Procès-verbal de visite de l'imprimerie de Jean Bouchard à Châlons* (Lepreux, *Gallia*, vol. 2, Documenta, pp. 32–35).

36. Lepreux, *Gallia*, vol. 2, Documenta, p. 40. See *Pour Jacques Seneuze, imprimeur du roi, marchand libraire à Châlons en Champagne, demandeur et deffendeur contre Nicolas Denoux, soi-disant marchand libraire, imprimeur de ladite Ville . . .* , BN FF 22126 #11 (copy in Lepreux, *Gallia*, vol. 2, pp. 246–49).

37. *Procès-verbal des contestations pendantes entre Jacques I Seneuze et Nicolas Denoux, imprimeurs à Châlons-sur-Marne, dressé par l'intendant de Champagne* (Lepreux, *Gallia*, vol. 2, Documenta, pp. 122–24).

38. On the advice of Guillaume De Sève, intendant and first president of the Parlement of Metz, Didier Fanart was granted a license in Verdun (AN V⁶ 733, 16 April 1692).

39. AN V⁶ 556, 3 September 1669. This began with a complaint by the printer Hyp to the *bailli* in Vendôme on 9 March 1669 that Claude Grinet had ignored the 1667 ban and set up a printing establishment in Vendôme. The *bailli*'s sentence on 13 April 1669 referred the case to the king's council.

40. Vialart was a Jansenist and *frondeur* bishop in the entourage of Cardinal Retz. See Richard Golden, *The Godly Rebellion: Parisian Curés and the Religious Fronde, 1652–1662* (Chapel Hill: University of North Carolina Press, 1981), 9.

41. Lepreux, *Gallia*, vol. 2, Documenta, pp. 46–47.

42. Miromesnil had rendered his opinion that the 1667 order be implemented and no printers allowed to set up businesses without the king's permission, but that Denoux could continue in Châlons nevertheless (AN V⁶ 656, 2 August 1680); copy of part of this order in Lepreux, *Gallia*, vol. 2, Documenta, pp. 40–41.

43. AN V⁶ 664, 7 November 1681; V⁶ 664, 25 November 1681. Partial copies in Lepreux, *Gallia*, vol. 2, Documenta, p. 41. There is no indication of who complained of Seneuze's pirating.

44. Seneuze obtained an order in council forbidding Bouchard and two merchants in Vitry from pirating and selling his diocesan printing. The order specified that the printing with the Noailles arms on it had been rightfully seized but, to assess the legality of the seizure of the other items, it sent the parties before the lieutenant general de Châlons and with appeal to the Parlement of Paris (AN V⁶ 679, 1 February 1684; partial copy also in Lepreux, *Gallia*, vol. 2, Documenta, pp. 44–47).

45. Lepreux, *Gallia,* vol. 2, Documenta, p. 48. Pontchartrain also required bishops to have their own writings approved by state-appointed censors. John Woodbridge, "Censure royale et censure épiscopale: Le Conflit de 1702," *Dix-huitième siècle* 8 (1976): 333–55; Raymond Birn, "Book Production and Censorship in France (1700–1715)," in *Books and Society in History,* ed. Kenneth Carpenter (New York: Bowker, 1983), 152.

46. Copy of letter and memorandum in Anne Sauvy, *Livres saisis à Paris entre 1678 et 1701* (The Hague: Martinus Nijhoff, 1972), 423–25. I am assuming that the C. Bouchard from Châlons was the printer Claude Bouchard. On Claude Bouchard (1681–1727), see Lepreux, *Gallia,* vol. 2, pp. 230–32.

47. See chapter 3 for references to works on the royal councils generally.

48. See BN FF 22131, *Minutes d'arrêts de Conseil sur différents objets de librairie, 1700–1708,* for summaries of many orders in council in these years.

49. AN V⁶ 786, 10 and 27 October 1701. Denoux lost his case.

50. Mention of the orders in council dated 4 and 26 June and 16 July 1703 in Lepreux, *Gallia,* vol. 2, Documenta, pp. 62–64; AN V⁶ 796, 3 March 1704 (partial copy also in Lepreux, *Gallia,* vol. 2, Documenta, p. 64).

51. Birn, "Book Production and Censorship in France," 153; Birn, "La Contrebande et la saisie de livres à l'aube du siècle des Lumières," *Revue d'histoire moderne et contemporaine* 28 (1981): 158–73.

52. Lepreux, *Gallia,* vol. 2, Documenta, pp. 50–52.

53. René Taveneaux, *Le Jansénisme en Lorraine, 1640–1789* (Paris: Vrin, 1960), 569.

54. In 1695, Clermont de Chaste de Roussillon was appointed bishop in Laon and employed Rennesson, who had been working for bishops of Laon since his establishment in 1661.

55. AN V⁶ 794, 20 October 1703. This, they claimed, was overt rebellion against royal officers that prevented the discovery of "contraventions très importantes et contraires au bien de l'Etat, aussi bien qu'à l'intérêt des libraires." They wanted Audinot and Godart fined 6,000 livres, the shop closed, and royal orders respected. Audinot and Godart were summoned before the king's council, and in the meantime, their shop was closed.

56. On Caton, see the biographical sketch in Lepreux, *Gallia,* vol. 1, pp. 209–12, and Documenta, pp. 255–60; AN V⁶ 791, 22 January 1703; V⁶ 796, 5 May 1704; V⁶ 798, 1 September and 29 September 1704; V⁶ 815, 27 May 1709; V⁶ 817, 25 November 1709; V⁶ 819, 12 May and 2 June 1710; V⁶ 820, 15 September and 20 October 1710; V⁶ 821, 26 January 1711. On Rennesson, see Lepreux, *Gallia,* vol. 1, pp. 223–26.

57. On the order in council of 1700, see the next chapter on the Bureau de la librairie.

58. Rennesson's postmortem inventory listed printing equipment worth at least 9,000–10,000 livres. Also, the king had given the privilege for diocesan printing to the bishop, who had ceded it to Rennesson for his lifetime and wanted to cede these rights to the nephew François Meunier, whom he wanted licensed as a second printer in Laon—a move that contravened the rules of 1704, which allowed only one printer in the city.

59. See chapter 1.

60. A Privy Council order dated 12 January 1674 admitted Bruyset among the printers in Lyon in the accustomed manner, exempting him from the 1667 ban (AMLyon, HH98). This is the earliest license listed by Lyon printers when they produced documentation on their entitlements in 1709 (AN V⁶ 815, 29 April 1709).

61. AN V⁶ 653, 1 March 1680.

62. See chapter 1; Chauvet, *Les Ouvriers,* 214–31; Roubert, "La Situation de l'imprimerie lyonnaise," 77–111; V⁶ 713, 11 May 1689.

63. Some examples were Benoit Vigneux, Claude Chize, and François Roux.

64. AN V⁶ 664, 7 November 1681; copy in Chauvet, *Les Ouvriers,* 483–85.

65. Chauvet, *Les Ouvriers,* 225–27. Two bookseller applicants interpreted the king's intention as suggesting that he did not want to deprive qualified applicants for licenses but only to choose whom he wanted (AN V⁶ 703, 17 September 1687; V⁶ 723, 23 August 1690).

66. AN V⁶ 721, 31 May 1690.

67. AN V⁶ 723, 9 August 1690.

68. AN V⁶ 794, 15 October 1703. The intendant favored allowing Martin to continue, but Martin did not get a license until 1703.

69. BN FF 22131; AN V⁶ 792, 30 April and 7 May 1703; AN V⁶ 795, 17 December 1703; V⁶ 799, 2 March 1705, and V⁶ 802, 21 October 1705.

70. BN FF 22128 #20 and 21.

71. Some provincial parlements were more cooperative with the government than others. See John Hurt, *Louis XIV and the Parlements: The Assertion of Royal Authority* (Manchester: Manchester University Press, 2002).

72. This is consistent with its attitude toward obtaining permissions and privileges from the Privy Council. See Jean-Dominique Mellot, "Le Régime des privilèges et permissions d'imprimer à Rouen au XVIIe siècle," *Bibliothèque de l'École des chartes* 142 (1984): 137–52.

73. In the 1680s, several printers were accepted (*Inventaire sommaire des registres de la Jurade, 1520 à 1783,* 8 [Bordeaux: Castera, 1947]). It was not until 1713 that the first printer obtained a royal license in Bordeaux.

74. BN FF 22127 #40–41.

75. Lepreux, *Gallia,* vol. 4, Documenta, pp. 16–19. On Hovius, see Lepreux, *Gallia,* vol. 4, pp. 79–86, and Émile Pasquier and Victor Dauphin, *Imprimeurs et libraires de l'Anjou* (Angers: Éditions de l'Ouest, 1932), 329–31. On Garnier, see Lepreux, *Gallia,* vol. 4, pp. 57–63.

76. Jean Marchand, *Une Enquête sur l'imprimerie et la librairie en Guyenne, mars 1701* (Bordeaux: Taffard, 1939), 19–23, 51–52; Ernest Labadie, *Notices biographiques sur les imprimeurs et les libraires bordelais des XVIe, XVIIe et XVIIIe siècles* (Bordeaux: Mounastre-Picamilh, 1900).

77. AN V⁶ 556, 3 September 1669.

78. Lepreux, *Gallia,* vol. 3, pt. 2, Documenta, pp. 209–12. Faced with the Caen guild's application of the 1667 ban against him, the Protestant printer, Jacques Le Bourgeois, appealed to the Privy Council, which decided the issue on 26 August 1670. It quashed the resistance of the Caen masters and ordered that Le Bourgeois be allowed to continue working as a printer and bookseller in Caen.

79. Lepreux, *Gallia,* vol. 3, pt. 2, Documenta, pp. 210–13.

80. Lepreux, *Gallia,* vol. 1, pp. 159–60; Documenta, pp. 251–53.

81. AN V⁶ 570, 23 September 1670. This conflict brought into clear focus the competing courts of appeal for matters concerning the regulation of provincial printers. The printers Nicolas Oudot and Claude Lefevre wanted matters heard by the king's council, and the others wanted the case appealed to the Parlement of Paris, which had thrown out earlier drafts of guild statutes.

82. AN V⁶ 782, 5 July 1700.

83. This claim is made on preliminary research; a full study on repression is needed to substantiate or discount it.

84. Chauvet, *Les Ouvriers;* Roubert, "La Situation de l'imprimerie lyonnais"; Martin, *Livre, pouvoirs.*

Chapter 3

1. AN V⁶ 782, 6 December 1700.

2. For Pontchartrain and book trade matters, see Henri-Jean Martin, *Livre, pouvoirs et société à Paris au XVIIe siècle (1598–1701)* (Geneva: Droz, 1969), 2:757–72; Raymond Birn, "Book

Production and Censorship in France (1700–1715)," in *Books and Society in History*, ed. Kenneth Carpenter (New York: Bowker, 1983), 145–71; Claude Lannette-Claverie, "L'Enquête de 1701 sur l'état de la librairie dans le royaume" (thesis, École des chartes, 1964), 39; *Correspondance administrative sous le règne de Louis XIV,* ed. Georges-Bernard Depping (Paris: Imprimerie impériale, 1850–55), 4 vols. See also the many works by Charles Frostin as well as Sara Chapman, *Private Ambition and Political Alliances: The Phélypeaux de Pontchartrain Family and Louis XIV's Government, 1650–1715* (Rochester: University of Rochester Press, 2004).

3. Birn, "Book Production and Censorship," 153.

4. A number of recent studies have pointed to the last years of the reign of Louis XIV as a period of innovative reform of many aspects of the royal administration. For a summary of this literature, see David Kammerling Smith, "Structuring Politics in Early Eighteenth-Century France: The Political Innovations of the French Council of Commerce," *Journal of Modern History* 74 (2002): 490–537; James Collins, *The State in Early Modern France* (Cambridge: Cambridge University Press, 1995), 142–46.

5. On the inquiry, see Claude Lannette-Claverie, "L'Enquête du 1701," "La Librairie française en 1700," *Revue française d'histoire du livre* 3 (1972): 3–43, and "Les Tours de France des imprimeurs et libraires à la fin du XVII siècle," *Revue française d'histoire du livre* 6 (1973): 207–33; Jean Marchand, *Une Enquête sur l'imprimerie et la librairie en Guyenne, mars 1701* (Bordeaux: Taffard, 1939); Martin, *Livre, pouvoirs,* 761–62; Jean-Dominique Mellot, *L'Édition rouennaise et ses marchés (vers 1600–vers 1730): Dynamisme provincial et centralisme parisien* (Paris: École des chartes, 1998), 468–74. On inquiries generally, and on Bignon, see Christiane Demeulenaere-Douyère and David J. Sturdy, *L'Enquête du Régent 1716–1718: Sciences, techniques et politique dans la France pré-industrielle* (Turnhout: Brepols, 2008), 21–29. Bignon thought that the book trade was docile enough in Paris but out of control in the provinces, where forbidden books were printed and imported from abroad (Martin, *Livre, pouvoirs,* 2:761). Martin, Lannette-Claverie, and Sauvy (*Livres saisis à Paris entre 1678 et 1701* [The Hague: Martinus Nijhoff, 1972]) all say that the survey was done because there was a crisis.

6. Marchand, *Une Enquête,* 17, 81–86.

7. Lannette-Claverie, "L'Enquête," 58.

8. Some of the other major surveys of printers occurred in 1739, 1758, 1764, 1768, and 1775; see Roger Chartier, "L'Imprimerie en France à la fin de l'ancien régime: L'État général des imprimeurs de 1777," *Revue française d'histoire du livre* 6 (1973): 253–79. For a recent study of the 1764 survey, see Thierry Rigogne, *Between State and Market: Printing and Bookselling in Eighteenth-Century France* (Oxford: Voltaire Foundation, 2007).

9. Chartier, "L'Imprimerie," 262. He compares 1701 (360 shops in provinces) with 1764 (248 shops in provinces) and 1777 (254 shops in provinces).

10. Lannette-Claverie and Jean Quéniart (*L'Imprimerie et la librairie à Rouen au XVIIIe siècle* [Paris: Klincksieck, 1969]) stressed stagnation in printing in the provinces, whereas Mellot (*L'Édition rouennaise*) detected dynamism and adaptation in Rouen, something we can only see if the vast clandestine sector is understood. On interpreting survey information and printing capacity, see Rigogne, *Between State and Market.*

11. Lannette-Claverie, "Les Tours de France," 209.

12. BN FF 22127 #61; BN NA 399–400.

13. See Loyau's story in chapter 5.

14. AMBx BB 88.

15. Mellot, *L'Édition rouennaise,* 469–73.

16. The following discussion comes from Marcel Marion, *Dictionnaire des institutions de la France aux XVIIe et XVIIIe siècles* (1923; repr., Paris: Picard, 1989); Hugues de La Bonninière de Beaumont, "L'Administration de la librairie et la censure des livres de 1700 à 1750" (thesis,

École des chartes, 1966); Nicole Herrmann-Mascard, *La Censure des livres à Paris à la fin de l'ancien régime (1750–1789)* (Paris: Presses universitaires de France, 1968); Christian Jouhaud, "Le Conseil du roi, Bordeaux et les bordelais (1579–1610, 1630–1680)," *Annales du Midi* 93 (1981): 377–96; Michel Antoine, *Le Conseil du roi sous le règne de Louis XV* (Geneva: Droz, 1970), 140–45, 151–60; Antoine, *Le Fonds du conseil d'état du roi aux archives nationales* (Paris: Imprimerie nationale, 1955); Albert Hamscher, *The Conseil Privé and the Parlements in the Age of Louis XIV: A Study in French Absolutism* (Philadelphia: American Philosophical Society, 1987); Hélion de Luçay, *Les Origines du pouvoir ministériel en France: Les Secrétaires d'état depuis leur institution jusqu'à la mort de Louis XV* (1881; repr., Geneva: Slatkine, 1976), 452–55, 632–34.

17. Herrmann-Mascard, *La Censure*, 26–30.

18. When the king lost confidence in a chancellor, he appointed a keeper of the seals to fulfill the duties of chief judicial officer of the realm.

19. On the workings of the royal council and on how the royal administration did not separate administrative and judicial business in many of its councils, see John F. Bosher, *French Finances, 1770–1795: From Business to Bureaucracy* (1970; repr., Cambridge: Cambridge University Press, 2008), 26–46.

20. AN V⁶ 733, 29 March 1692.

21. BN FF 22131.

22. La Bonnière de Beaumont, "L'Administration de la librairie," 249.

23. These names occur frequently on the licenses in AN V⁶.

24. La Bonnière de Beaumont, "L'Administration de la librairie," 257.

25. Herrmann-Mascard, *La Censure*, 40.

26. Antoine, *Le Conseil*, 159.

27. La Bonnière de Beaumont, "L'Administration de la librairie," 257–60.

28. BN FF 22114 #68.

29. Archives départementales de la Gironde (hereafter ADG), C 3308, 23 January 1714.

30. The decisions of the bureau were issued as decrees either in the form of *arrêts en commandement* by the Conseil de Dépêches, a superior council where the king and his ministers handled all manner of domestic affairs (mostly found in AN E), or as *arrêts simples* of the Privy Council (mostly in AN V⁶). It should be noted that *arrêts simples* and *arrêts en commandement* both had legal force, but *arrêts en commandement* had more authority and were used in some cases because the matter was more important or more contested. Nevertheless, a number of seemingly minor matters were settled by *arrêt en commandement*, and they were used fairly frequently for book trade matters at the end of the regime.

31. Claude-Marin Saugrain, ed., *Code de la librairie et imprimerie de Paris ou conférence du réglement arrêté au conseil d'état du roi le 28 février 1723 et rendu commun pour tout le royaume, par arrêt du conseil d'état du 24 mars 1744 avec les anciennes ordonnances. . . .* (1744; repr., Westmead: Gregg International, 1971); La Bonnière de Beaumont, "L'Administration de la librairie," 28–55, 261–62.

32. Chrétien-Guillaume de Lamoignon de Malesherbes, *Mémoires sur la librairie et sur la liberté de la presse* (1809; repr., Geneva: Slatkine, 1969), 12–13. Malesherbes believed that orders in council were not sufficiently respected, especially by the judges in the parlements.

33. ADG C 3313, 14 June 1765.

34. This summary of procedures is taken from many orders is AN V⁶; Saugrain, ed., *Code*, 180–211, 191–92; Germain-Louis Chauvelin's *Mémoire* (Archives de la ministère des affaires étrangères, Paris, M et D, France, vol. 1278, fols. 300–317v); Malesherbes' memorandum in BN FF 22114 #68; *Arrêt du conseil qui règle les formalités à observer pour la réception des libraires et imprimeurs*, August 1777, copy in Jourdan, Decrusy, and Isambert, et al., eds., *Recueil général des anciennes lois françaises depuis l'an 420 jusqu'à la Révolution de 1789* (Paris: Belin-Leprieur, 1821–33), 25:117–19, available online at http://cour-de-france.fr/article348.html.

35. Chauvelin, *Mémoire,* third memorandum.

36. *Manuel de l'auteur et du libraire* (Paris: Veuve Duchesne, 1777).

37. See below. After 1777 many provincial booksellers applied for and obtained licenses that are in AN V⁶.

38. Another way was to charge fees for permissions and copyrights. On this see Robert Dawson, *The French Booktrade and the "Permission Simple" of 1777: Copyright and Public Domain* (Oxford: Voltaire Foundation, 1992).

39. Madeleine Ventre, *L'Imprimerie et la librairie en Languedoc au dernier siècle de l'ancien régime, 1700–1789* (Paris: Mouton, 1958), 51–52; Jacques Billioud, *Le Livre en Provence du XVIe au XVIIIe siècle* (Marseille: Saint-Victor, 1962), 37; Émile Pasquier and Victor Dauphin, *Imprimeurs et libraires de l'Anjou* (Angers: Éditions de l'Ouest, 1932), 28–29; Bibliothèque muncipale de Toulouse (hereafter BMToulouse), MS 1010, 17 March 1745: the Toulouse printer Guillemette refused to pay increased fees, objecting to the extension of the 1723 Code to the provinces in 1744. On confusion over the fees in the 1777 decree, see the Toulouse guild register for 1787–1791 (Archives départementales de la Haute Garonne [hereafter ADHG] E 1315, 23 June 1787). For Bordeaux, see *État des sommes* in *Chartrier ou recueil par ordre chronologique de divers titres, pièces concernant les libraires et les imprimeurs jurés de l'université de Bordeaux,* 4, BMBx J 1185.

40. BN FF Joly de Fleury, 1682; Paul Chauvet, *Les Ouvriers du livre en France des origines à la Révolution de 1789* (Paris: Presses universitaires de France, 1959), 295.

41. ADG C 3314; *Arrêt du conseil d'Etat du roi portant nouveau règlement pour l'imprimerie de Bordeaux* (BN FF 22125 #45).

42. On Chauvelin, see Michel Antoine, *Le Gouvernement et l'administration sous Louis XV: Dictionnaire biographique* (Paris: CNRS, 1978), 66–67; John Rogister, "New Light on the Fall of Chauvelin," *English Historical Review* 83 (1968): 314–30.

43. Chauvelin, *Mémoire,* second memorandum.

44. Chauvelin, *Mémoire,* second memorandum.

45. On D'Aguesseau, see Isabelle Storez, *Le Chancelier Henri-François D'Aguesseau (1668–1751): Monarchiste et libéral* (Paris: Publisud, 1996), 341–48.

46. *Arrêt en commandement 31 March 1739 qui fixe le nombre des Imprimeurs dans toutes les Villes du Royaume, et porte reglement pour les places d'imprimeurs vacantes* (Saugrain, ed., *Code,* 203); ADG C 3312.

47. ADG C 3308, 3312–3313.

48. ADG C 3308–3315; 6E 68.

49. On Merlin, see Anne Sauvy, "Un Marginal du livre au XVIIIe siècle: Jacques Merlin," *Revue française d'histoire du livre* 45 (1976): 443–85; ADG C 3308, 3771; BN FF 22125 #53.

50. Antoine, *Le Gouvernement,* 143. Lamoignon was chancellor from 10 December 1750 to 14 September 1768, but he was disgraced in 1763. His son Malesherbes' role in book trade matters attracted much favorable attention from *philosophes* and later historians of the Enlightenment. Some recent works on Malesherbes include John Hardman, *French Politics, 1774–1789: From the Accession of Louis XVI to the Fall of the Bastille* (London: Longman, 1995); Roger Chartier, *The Cultural Origins of the French Revolution,* trans. Lydia Cochrane (Durham: Duke University Press, 1991), and Roger Chartier's edition of Malesherbes' *Mémoires sur la librairie: Mémoire sur la liberté de la presse* (Paris: Imprimerie nationale, 1994).

51. Malesherbes, *Mémoires,* 144.

52. ADG C 3312.

53. Copies of these orders, all dated 12 May 1759, are in BN (*Imprimés*) F 23663. All the decrees began in a similar fashion, outlining previous legislated quotas and lamenting that they were not being respected.

54. Ventre, *L'Imprimerie,* 41.

55. In 1704 two printers were permitted in Saint-Malo, but the number was reduced to one in 1739; see Lucien Sarazin, "Un 'Chalotiste' malouin: Louis-Philippe-Claude Hovius, imprimeur-libraire (1721–1806)," in *Extrait des Annales de la Société historique et archéologique de l'arrondissement de Saint-Malo* (Saint-Servan: J. Haize, 1912). In 1758 the sons of two printers, Le Comte and Delamarre, were investigated by officials for not having licenses, and in 1759 the mayor wrote to the intendant to argue that both printers should be allowed to continue.

56. Georges Lepreux, *Gallia typographica ou répertoire biographique et chronologique de tous les imprimeurs de France depuis les origines de l'imprimerie jusqu'à la Révolution* (Paris: Champion, 1909–14), vol. 4, Documenta, pp. 97–102; AN V^6 991, 19 December 1757; V^6 992, 30 January 1758. See chapter 6.

57. ADG C 3308–3315.

58. Struggles occurred in other towns to keep a printer. In Bourg Saint-Andéol, the license was abolished in 1739 and reestablished in 1767; in Carcassonne, a license was abolished in 1758 and reestablished in 1760 (i.e., the cut was never really implemented); a Beziers license was abolished in 1760, which led to a huge fight and the reestablishment of a printer in 1781.

59. René-Charles de Maupeou took the title of vice-chancellor from 1763 to 1768, and his son René-Nicolas Maupeou was chancellor from 1768 to 1774. For some recent work on Maupeou, see William Doyle, *Venality: The Sale of Offices in Eighteenth-Century France* (Oxford: Clarendon Press, 1996); David Bell, "Lawyers into Demagogues: Chancellor Maupeou and the Transformation of Legal Practice in France, 1771–1789," *Past and Present* 130 (1991): 107–41; and Julian Swann, *Politics and the Parlement of Paris Under Louis XV, 1754–1774* (Cambridge: Cambridge University Press, 1995).

60. Sartine did not like the title of "director" and was angry with the Paris guild for using it, preferring *premier magistrat ou chef de la librairie* (BN FF 22077 #97).

61. For an analysis of the data collected in the 1764 survey, see Rigogne, *Between State and Market.* I would be more inclined than Rigogne to see provincial printers, booksellers, and local officials as capable of strategic maneuvering when they responded to survey questions and of using the opportunity to present the facts in such a way as to serve their ongoing agendas. The printers and the intendants and subdelegates had an interest in exaggerating the lack of regulation—the former to get royal intervention to close down competitors, and the latter, to justify extending their powers over the purportedly incompetent local officials.

62. ADG C 3312. For some copies of letters by both Maupeous on licensing, see François Ritter, *La Police de l'imprimerie et de la librairie à Strasbourg depuis les origines jusqu'à la Révolution français: Extrait de la Revue des bibliothèques* (Paris: Champion, 1922), 24–27. The town of Strasbourg claimed that the terms of its capitulation in 1681 protected it from French censorship legislation. Strasbourg successfully resisted the licensing requirement and would not recognize the book trade inspector.

63. ADG C 3309; AN V^6 1023, 15 September, 1766, V^6 1024, 31 December 1766. Phillippot referred to his *bonne conduite,* the guild's support, and the regularity of his morals.

64. Marie-Thérèse Blanc-Rouquette, "Un Imprimeur toulousain au XVIIIe siècle: Jean-Florent Baour," *Revue française d'histoire du livre* 27 (1980): 297–317.

65. Archives départementales de la Seine-Maritime (hereafter ADSM) J 218.

66. Maupeou's letters are printed in *Archives historiques* 1 (1859): 279–80; *À juger en la cour consulaire de cette ville pour Paul-Anne Pallandre jeune, libraire à Bordeaux contre Antoine Pallandre son frère aîné, aussi libraire de ladite ville* (BMBx); ADG C 3309, 3314.

67. Ventre, *L'Imprimerie,* 41–42.

68. On Miromesnil, see *Correspondance politique et administrative de Miromesnil, premier président du parlement de Normandie,* ed. Pierre Le Verdier, 5 vols. (Rouen: Lestringant, 1899–1903);

Hardman, *French Politics;* Georges de Beaurepaire, *Le Contrôle de la librairie à Rouen à la fin du XVIIIe siècle* (Rouen: A. Lainé, 1929); Dawson, *The French Booktrade;* and Jean Egret, *Louis XV et l'opposition parlementaire, 1715–1774* (Paris: A. Colin, 1970). For a glimpse of Miromesnil's direct role in book trade matters, see the description of the audience he granted to Joseph Fiévée—future journalist, author, and advisor to Napoleon—who needed Miromesnil's protection from the opposition of the Paris printers' and booksellers' guild when he applied to become a printer's apprentice: Joseph Fiévée, *Correspondance et relations de J. Fiévée avec Bonaparte, premier consul et empereur pendant onze années (1802–1813)* (Paris: A. Desrez [etc.], 1836), I:xxviii–xxxii.

69. Whereas elsewhere intendants had the supervision of the book trade, in Rouen, the first president of the parlement had it.

70. ADSM J 217.

71. On Le Camus de Néville, see Sylvie Nicolas, *Les Derniers maîtres des requêtes de l'ancien régime (1771–1789)* (Paris: École des chartes, 1998), 228–30.

72. On 1777, see Raymond Birn, "The Profits of Ideas: *Privilèges en librairie* in Eighteenth-Century France," *Eighteenth-Century Studies* 4 (1971): 131–68; Dawson, *The French Booktrade.*

73. By one account, there were twenty-one vacant places in France in 1778, and printers' guilds were trying to obtain the suppression of some of these (*À juger en la cour consulaire de cette ville pour Paul-Anne Pallandre jeune; Dépôt de pièces,* ADG notary Verdelet, 2 January 1779).

74. Cited in Ventre, *L'Imprimerie,* 48. I am assuming that she meant Miromesnil.

75. Ventre, *L'Imprimerie,* 47–48.

76. This happened in 1780 in Toulouse when the printer Desclassan, a member of an old printing family, requested the place of his cousin, whom he planned to marry (AN V⁶ 1098, 25 September 1780; Ventre, *L'Imprimerie,* 48).

77. ADG C 3310.

78. He found it surprising that one candidate, Garde—one of the poorest booksellers in town, and known for his little knowledge of Latin—turned out to be the one who best succeeded in the composition and correction part of the examination. Second in the ranking was the printer Calamy, whose "ignorance can scarcely be matched" and who had been suspended for a year for engaging in the clandestine trade. There were also inconsistencies in the assessment of the candidate Levieux.

79. ADG C 3310; AN V⁶ 1128, 27 March 1786. On Beaume, see Archives départementales du Gard E Dépôt 36/52, 1774. A Bordeaux chronicler, Augustin Laboubée, noted that Beaume was the protégé of Miromesnil and of the comte de Périgord, gouverneur de Languedoc (*Notes recueillies pour la Bibliothèque historique de la Guyenne,* BMBx MS 712 [2]).

80. AN V⁶ 1070, 11 March 1776. Jean-Baptiste Puynesge had been denounced by the Bordeaux guild in 1775 for Protestant printing there (ADG C 3771; Louis Desgraves, *Dictionnaire des imprimeurs, libraires et relieurs de Bordeaux et de la Gironde (XVe–XVIIIe siècles)* [Baden-Baden: Valentin Koerner, 1995], 245).

81. See above. The bishop Falcombelle de Ponte d'Albaret was more successful than his predecessors and convinced Miromesnil in 1785 that Sarlat should have a printer. The two met several times. Vergennes signed the decree creating the license on 22 September 1785, and Miromesnil handled the *concours.*

82. Administrative documentation such as I have studied here is only one lens through which to see the regulation of the book trade. The documents from a newly created bureau necessarily focus our attention on the modern bureaucratic aspects of the eighteenth-century state. They provide the language and argumentation used by officials, which certainly suggests the presence of a bureaucratic ethos in the later reign of Louis XIV. By their very nature, however, these documents disguise the role of patronage, which we know was important at the end

of the regime and undoubtedly had many regional variations (see chapter 6). On the debates over if, how, and when some of the features of an absolutist or modern state came into play in seventeenth- and eighteenth-century France, see Antoine, *Le Conseil du roi;* Hamscher, *Le Conseil Privé;* John Hurt, *Louis XIV and the Parlements: The Assertion of Royal Authority* (Manchester: Manchester University Press, 2002); Peter R. Campbell, *Politics in Old Regime France, 1720–1745* (London: Routledge, 1996); and Collins, *The State in Early Modern France.*

Chapter 4

1. For the figures for 1700, see Roger Chartier, "L'Imprimerie en France à la fin de l'ancien régime: L'État général des imprimeurs de 1777," *Revue française d'histoire du livre* 6 (1973): 253–79. Those permitted in 1704 are calculated from the *arrêt du conseil* of 21 July 1704 in Claude-Marin Saugrain, ed., *Code de la librairie et imprimerie de Paris ou conférence du réglement arrêté au conseil d'état du roi le 28 février 1723 et rendu commun pour tout le royaume, par arrêt du conseil d'état du 24 mars 1744 avec les anciennes ordonnances* . . . (1744; repr., Westmead: Gregg International, 1971), 201–3. These are the figures for the legal printing houses. For an impressive statistical analysis of the reduction in shops over the eighteenth century, see Thierry Rigogne, *Between State and Market: Printing and Bookselling in Eighteenth-Century France* (Oxford: Voltaire Foundation, 2007), 110–17.

2. The term "purge" is perhaps too strong and too dramatic, because the process often took more than one generation, but it is worth noting that the inspector of the book trade in Lyon used the term in 1763 (BN FF 22128 #99, cited in Louis Trénard, *Commerce et culture: Le Livre à Lyon au XVIIIe siècle* (Lyon: Imprimeries unies, 1953), 24.

3. AN V⁶ 815, 29 April 1709; AN V⁶ 815, 18 March 1709.

4. AN V⁶ 794, 15 October 1703. In March 1703, the printer André Laurent tried to be admitted by applying to the *sénéchaussée* court but was forced to apply to the chancellor. In April 1703 Pierre Thenet was given a preparatory order and got Sajac's license in June, and Laurent was admitted to Phaeton's place. In May, Martin Sibert got a preparatory order for the Jullieron place and, in June, got a license. In August 1703 Philibert Chabanne (a journeyman for thirty years) and Barthélémy Martin got a preliminary order and, in December, Chabanne got a license (BN FF 22131; AN V⁶ 792, 30 April 1703; AN V⁶ 792, 7 May 1703). For biographical information on Lyon printers, see Aimé Vingtrinier, *Histoire de l'imprimerie à Lyon de l'origine jusqu'à nos jours* (Lyon: Adrien Storck, 1894). Musée de l'imprimerie Lyon: http://www.imprimerie.lyon.fr/imprimerie/sections/fr/documentation/somme_typographique.

5. AN V⁶ 813, 17 September 1708.

6. AN V⁶ 815, 29 April 1709.

7. V⁶ 824, 25 January 1712. Of the fifteen printers allowed to be licensed in Lyon, ten had obtained their licenses between 1674 and 1708. The fifteen were André Laurent, Michel Goy, Pierre Thened, Jean Couteros, Simon Pottin, François Barbier, Jean Veyron, Laurent Langlois, Jean Bruyset, Philibert Chabanne, Claude Carteron, Pierre Valfray, François Sarrasin, Marcelin Gautherin, and Barthélémy Martin.

8. AN V⁶ 807, 24 January 1707.

9. Eugène Griselle, "La Contrefaçon en librairie à Lyon vers l'an 1702: Mémoire et lettres autographes du libraire Baritel, premier adjoint de la communauté des libraires et imprimeurs," *Bulletin du bibliophile et du bibliothécaire* (1903): 189.

10. AN V⁶ 827, 5 and 19 December 1712. A Claude Moulu was in trouble for selling Protestant books in 1734 (ADR 1C 253). Vignieu, Moulu, and Chappuis were raided in 1705 (AN V⁶ 799, 16 February 1705).

11. AN V^6 827, 19 December 1712.

12. AN V^6 799, 16 February 1705. See Chappuis' response to this in AN V^6 802, 12 October 1705, and further accusations of piracy in V6 808, 23 May 1707. For the 1702 case, see V^6 790, 6 November 1702.

13. V^6 739, 14 February 1693. Chappuis was convicted in 1683 (with others) of pirating *Histoire du Calvinisme à Lyon* (BN FF 22074 #52–53). Thierry and Desprez cited orders of September 1665, October 1667, and April 1674.

14. AN V^6 790, 6 November 1702; BN FF 22074 #83 and 85.

15. AN V^6 798, 24 November 1704.

16. AN V^6 799, 16 February 1705.

17. AN V^6 802, 12 October 1705.

18. AN V^6 808, 23 May 1707.

19. AN V^6 827, 19 December 1712.

20. AN V^6 831, 8 January 1714.

21. AN V^6 815, 18 March 1709; Georges Lepreux, *Gallia typographica ou répertoire biographique et chronologique de tous les imprimeurs de France depuis les origines de l'imprimerie jusqu'à la Révolution* (Paris: Champion, 1909–14), vol. 3, pt. 2, Documenta, pp. 252–53, 260–66, 276–79; ADSM C145; Georges-Bernard Depping, ed., *Correspondance administrative sous le règne de Louis XIV* (Paris: Imprimerie impériale, 1850–55), 2:358–59; Jean-Dominique Mellot, *L'Édition rouennaise et ses marchés (vers 1600–vers 1730): Dynamisme provincial et centralisme parisien* (Paris: École des chartes, 1998), 476–84; Jean Quéniart, *L'Imprimerie et la librairie à Rouen au XVIIIe siècle* (Paris: Klincksieck, 1969), 45–52.

22. Jean-Dominique Mellot, "Le Régime des privilèges et permissions d'imprimer à Rouen au XVIIe siècle," *Bibliothèque de l'École des chartes* 142 (1984): 137–52.

23. What follows is taken from these orders in council for Caen: AN V^6 792, 7 May 1703; V^6 814, 18 February 1709; V^6 817, 16 December 1709; V^6 819, 23 June 1710; V^6 820, 22 September 1710; V^6 822, 20 April 1711; V^6 824, 26 October 1711 (2 orders); V^6 825, 7 March 1712.

24. Rennes orders in council: AN V^6 814, 28 January 1709; V^6 815, 27 May 1709; AN V^6 817, 23 September 1709; V^6 822, 23 March 1711; V^6 827, 28 November 1712; V^6 828, 29 May 1713; V^6 830, 29 September 1713; V^6 831, 19 March 1714; V^6 831, 26 March 1714; Lepreux, *Gallia,* vol. 4, Documenta, pp. 52–54.

25. Arrêt du Parlement of Brittany, 12 December 1701, in Lepreux, *Gallia,* vol. 4, Documenta, p. 37. Once Hébert was ousted, the Rennes printers began to dip into the lucrative monopoly work that the king's printer enjoyed. In 1717 the Parlement issued a decree forbidding this and fined Sébastien Durand for doing it. A month later it relaxed the penalties against Durand but reiterated that Vatar had the monopoly on the king's printing. Durand— and assuredly other Rennes masters—argued that all printers had the right to official printing. In 1719 Guillaume Vatar was licensed as king's printer (Lepreux, *Gallia,* vol. 4, Documenta, p. 70).

26. Joseph Vatar, a cousin of Guillaume, also had difficulty obtaining a license because there were too many printers in Rennes. He requested a place in 1714 but was refused. In 1718 he was allowed to print, but as a supernumerary whose position was not to continue after his death or resignation (Lepreux, *Gallia,* vol. 4, Documenta, p. 68).

27. AN V^6 826, 27 June 1712; V^6 828, 20 February 1713; V^6 830, 29 September 1713. Between 1709 and 1714 there were only five orders in council governing Bordeaux printing and bookselling matters. Between 1719 and 1724, there were fifteen.

28. Furt and Albespy stayed, and the guild tried to make Furt pay a high fee, but the intendant intervened in 1715 to discharge Furt of the arbitrary imposition. Furt continued to appeal to royal officials about harassment. D'Argenson, D'Aguesseau, and intendant Boucher were all

drawn into the conflict that resulted when the guild tried to argue that Furt, while allowed to print, could not sell books. See Emile Brives-Cazes, *De la police des livres en Guyenne (1713–1785)* (Bordeaux: Gounouilhou, 1883), 9–19. The issue resurfaced when a Bordeaux printer (Séjourné) died and candidates found no vacancy because of the pressure on numbers caused by the Sauvetat positions (*Mémoire pour Paul Caillier-Gobain, demandeur contre . . . le sieur Labottière syndic des imprimeurs et libraires de la ville de Bordeaux, défendeur* [1714]).

29. AN V⁶ 814, 10 December 1708; AN V⁶ 815, 25 June 1709.

30. Orléans: AN V⁶ 799, 9 March 1705; V⁶ 802, 12 October 1705. Toulouse: AN V⁶ 825, 25 April 1712. By this date, the Privy Council had already been involved in printer appointments for some years. In 1705, four booksellers who had set up without authorization were ousted, fined, and had their property seized and sold for the profit of the general hospital in Toulouse. This alone gave others an incentive to apply for a license, as several did between 1705 and 1711. Between 1709 and 1714, the bureau issued nine orders regulating bookselling in Toulouse. The Toulouse guild tried to force booksellers to get licenses. Jean-Pierre Dalles claimed in 1714 that, as he was the son of a bookseller, his admittance to the guild should be automatic, but the guild warden, "sous le pretexte d'un reglement du conseil," was denying him entry (AN V⁶ 833, 17 September 1714). He did not get a bookseller's license before 1719 (AN V⁶ 847, 28 January 1719).

31. AN V⁶ 803, 8 March 1706; V⁶ 807, 21 February 1707. In Limoges there were eight printers in 1704 but, as early as 1700, several printers had been ousted for not respecting the 1667 ban. Three printers who had obtained licenses complained that all the others should be closed down. This led to investigations and an effort to reduce the numbers of printers in the town. One widow and one other woman were expelled and three other printers allowed to work; they were all told that the number must be reduced to four before anyone else would be allowed into the printing business. The ousted women applied, along with a son of one of them, and got bookselling licenses (AN V⁶ 790, 27 November 1702; V⁶ 796, 3 March 1704 [2 orders], 28 April 1704; V⁶ 798, 1 September 1704).

32. *Sentence du sénéchal de Quimper défendant à Jean-Baptiste Duchesne d'exercer l'imprimerie dans cette ville*, 13 September 1707, in Lepreux, *Gallia,* vol. 4, Documenta, pp. 44–46.

33. Rouen stands out in this regard because of the continued solidarity of the guild (Mellot, *L'Édition rouennaise*).

34. Griselle, "Contrefaçon." In 1702 Louis Guérin was in litigation with three Lyon booksellers: Pierre Contanos, Barthélémy Martin, and Pierre Thened (AN V⁶ 794, 26 November 1703).

35. Baritel worried that sons might not be able to follow fathers, but he directed his criticism mainly at the choices made in Lyon; many were totally unacceptable, and good subjects were being rejected. He thought that two who should be excluded for printing pirated and prohibited books were Sarazin and Benoît Vignieu; André Laurent and André Molin were better candidates. In 1707 Baritel himself was expelled from the book trade for furnishing illegal books and pamphlets.

36. John Rule, "Royal Ministers and Government Reform During the Last Decades of Louis XIV's Reign," in *Consortium on Revolutionary Europe, 1750–1850,* ed. Claude Sturgill (Gainesville: University Presses of Florida, 1975), 5. For the story of the Anisson family, see Ernest Coyecque, *Inventaire de la collection Anisson sur l'histoire de l'imprimerie et la librairie principalement à Paris* (1900; repr., New York: Burt Franklin), 1:li–lxx, and Frédéric Barbier, Sabine Juratic, and Annick Mellerio, *Dictionnaire des imprimeurs, libraires et gens du livre à Paris, 1701–1789, A–C* (Geneva: Droz, 2007), 69–82. There is abundant evidence of close ties between Jean Anisson and royal officials after he went to Paris in 1691. He passed on the Imprimerie Royale to his nephew Claude Rigaud and was then on the Council of Commerce. See Thomas J. Schaeper, *The French Council of Commerce, 1700–1715: A Study of Mercantilism After Colbert*

(Columbus: Ohio State University Press, 1983), 40–41, 50, 53. In 1721 the duc de Villeroy, the governor and influential representative of Versailles in Lyon, wrote about Anisson at his death in 1721: "Je regretterai longtemps M. Anisson. C'était un homme d'honneur d'une affection et d'une fidélité qu'on ne peut assez estimer. Pouvez-vous penser que je puisse songer à un étranger pour remplir sa place, et qu'on ose me proposer de jeunes gens sans expérience, quelques bonnes qualités qu'ils aient" (quoted in Maurice Garden, "Formes de contrôle du pouvoir local: Lyon en 1721," in *Pouvoir, ville et société en Europe, 1650–1750: Actes du colloque international du CNRS, octobre 1981*, ed. Georges Livet and Bernard Vogler [Paris: Éditions Ophrys, 1983], 178). There is much less information on Jacques, the brother who stayed in Lyon and worked with associates Rigaud and Posuel.

37. Depping, ed., *Correspondance*, 2:781–82; Anne Sauvy, *Livres saisis à Paris entre 1678 et 1701* (The Hague: Martinus Nijhoff, 1972), 15.

38. See the following sources for interference with guild elections. For Bordeaux in 1723, see ADG C 3308; for the annulment of elections in Nantes in 1718, Lepreux, *Gallia*, vol. 4, Documenta, pp. 69–70. For Lyon, see AMLyon HH 98; AN V⁶ 799, 23 March 1705; V⁶ 802, 12 October 1705; BN FF 22128 #31; BN FF 22128 #32; AN V⁶ 808, 9 May 1707. In Rouen, a Privy Council order not only annulled the elections but also imposed the king's choice as warden: AN V⁶ 810, 21 October 1707; Lepreux, *Gallia*, vol. 3, pt. 1, pp. 15–23, and pt. 2, Documenta, pp. 253–59; V⁶ 814, 3 and 17 December 1708; ADSM C 145; AN V⁶ 819, 16 June 1710; AN V⁶ 822, 15 June 1711. Mellot referred to Lallemant as one of the "enfants chéri du pouvoir" who did not participate in the local communitarian spirit he identified in the Rouen guild (*L'Édition rouennaise*, 79–80). For later examples, see Actes Royaux, BN F 23664 (166–241), 15 July 1764; AN V¹ 549. Until the end of the *ancien régime*, the selection of guild officers in the provincial guilds was closely controlled by officials in Versailles.

39. Sébastien Maréchal tried to block the admission of a certain printer named Bahau to the guild. The case was heard by the *prévôt* of Nantes and then evoked to the Privy Council, which, in 1684, sided with Maréchal and ordered Bahau closed down. Maréchal went on to use the 1667 order and appealed to the king to attempt to close down competitors. When the *prévôt* accepted a certain Heuqueville in 1688, Maréchal appealed this to the king, and the Privy Council agreed to decide the case in 1688. In 1696 Jacques Maréchal (a new guild warden and brother of Sébastien) appealed a similar case to the king. Here he claimed that the intruding printer had "trouvé le moyen et le secret, auprès du prévôt de Nantes" to be admitted as a bookseller. In 1700 Jacques Maréchal was so accustomed to appealing to the king that he got an order to confirm a sentence of the *juges et consuls* of Nantes, issued three months earlier, concerning a sum of money owed him by a bookseller. In January 1704 a Privy Council order decided in Maréchal's favor and closed down two competitors. When his father died in March 1704, Maréchal took no chances and rushed to obtain a license, which was granted in April 1704. In the request he described himself as "seul imprimeur ordinaire de sa majesté et du sieur évêque en la ville et université de Nantes." His other titles would be useless without a printer's license. Thus, "pour prévenir le trouble qui pouvait lui être fait, [il] a recours à Sa Majesté pour la supplier très humblement d'ordonner qu'il sera reçu imprimeur et libraire en la ville de Nantes." On Maréchal, see Lepreux, *Gallia*, vol. 4, pp. 239–45; AN V⁶ 796, 7 April 1704; V⁶ 814, 4 March 1709; V⁶ 817, 16 December 1709; V⁶ 818, 7 April 1710; V⁶ 821, 22 December 1710 and 13 February 1711; BN FF 22131; BN FF 22125 #114, #130.

40. BN FF NA 3546. Maréchal's letter provoked an anonymous memorandum in response (possibly written by Anisson) that clearly suggested that Maréchal was exaggerating things and getting carried away, wanting to "mettre tous les libraires de la province sous sa dépendance." In 1710 royal officials established a set of rules governing the inspection of imported books at ports of entry: *arrêt du conseil*, 11 June 1710, copy in Saugrain, ed., *Code*, 302–3.

41. AN V⁶ 821, 13 February 1711. In 1711 Maréchal complained to the king of unfair accusations made by his enemies—the commandant and the lieutenant of police in Nantes. He attributed their opposition to his zeal in enforcing the rules and his practice of taking all contraventions directly to the royal council rather than to the lieutenant of police.

42. On Ressayre, see the following orders in council: AN V⁶ 807, 24 January and 28 March 1707; V⁶ 808, 18 April 1707 (Parlement decree quashed); V⁶ 810, 30 January 1708 (2 decrees: Migneret got a bookseller's license and Fay got a printer's license); Archives départementales de la Côte d'Or (hereafter ADCD) B2, arrêt du Parlement de Dijon, 12 January 1707; Michel-Hilaire Clément-Janin, *Les Imprimeurs et les libraires dans la Côte-d'Or* (1883; repr., Geneva: Slatkine, 1971), 45–47.

43. BN FF 22065 #71; AN V⁶ 807, 24 January 1707.

44. Jane McLeod, "Provincial Book Trade Inspectors in Eighteenth-Century France," *French History* 12 (1998): 127–48.

45. In 1699 a number of large cities, including Lyon, were forced to create and buy offices of *lieutenants généraux* de police, following the Parisian model. It is not entirely clear how these offices affected the policing in these towns. On this, see Marc Chassaigne, *La Lieutenance générale de police de Paris* (1906; repr., Geneva: Slatkine, 1975), 79–88.

46. AN V⁶ 790, 6 November 1702. See the story of Chappuis above.

47. BN FF 22131.

48. In Toulouse, the *sénéchal* or *juges mages* retained jurisdiction over the printers, and this may partly explain the ineffectiveness of control; the real policing force in the town was the Capitouls. See Michel Taillefer, *Vivre à Toulouse sous l'ancien régime* (Paris: Perrin, 2000), 63–64, 67–84. They played a role in printer competitions and wrote reports on printers. The intendant was based in Montpellier.

49. AN V⁶ 856, 6 September 1721.

50. AN V⁶ 856, 3 September 1721.

51. The printers and booksellers in Lyon wrote a memorandum in 1765 requesting that three printer positions there be abolished (BN FF 21815). The Bordeaux printers pushed for reduction from eight to six in Bordeaux in 1777 (BN FF 21832). The lieutenants of police and others criticized the policy of reducing the number of printers: the booksellers did not support the reduction in the number of printers, arguing that it forced booksellers in the provinces to pay higher prices for provincial editions and gave business to foreign presses. In Toulouse a memorandum written to Sartine in 1767 stated that the public felt that a stop should be made to all the memoranda being sent to the royal council demanding a reduction in the number of printer places: "These were ambitious ideas from individuals who did not have the public good as their goal." A reduction would lead to higher prices and hold up judicial printing (BN FF 22127 #108). The same year, a bookseller in Toulouse blamed the reduction in printer numbers on the Parisian publishers (BN FF 22127 #107).

52. Lepreux, *Gallia*, vol. 2, Documenta, pp. 49–50, and vol. 4, Documenta, pp. 46–49; AN V⁶ 814, 17 December 1708.

53. AN V⁶ 810, 30 January 1708.

54. AN V⁶ 853, 9 September 1720.

55. *Mémoire pour Paul Caillier-Gobain;* on Racle, see chapter 5; AN V⁶ 852, 17 August 1720; V⁶ 856, 3 September and 20 December 1721; V⁶ 859, 6 July 1722. The lieutenant of police did not inform the chancellor that there was a son when he approved another candidate.

56. AN V⁶ 1004, 13 July 1761; AN V⁶ 1011, 20 June 1763. The Galles family had their supporters—the rector of the Vannes seminary, the principal of the college, and the director of the school—who said that the Galles brothers charged the same prices as other provincial booksellers. The king did not quash the police sentence but did order Lamoré closed down and the

lieutenant of police not to admit any printers or booksellers, nor to allow any binders to work without obtaining licenses as booksellers. On Vannes, see Timothy Le Goff, *Vannes and Its Region: A Study of Town and Country in Eighteenth-Century France* (Oxford: Clarendon Press, 1981).

57. ADSM C 145.

58. BN FF 22127 #93–99. Others included printers in Béziers, Le Puy, Mende, and Albi. Pierre François Tonnet in Dole blamed his problems on outsider competition and claimed that the government must help him; see Michel Vernus, "Une Page de l'histoire du livre dans le Jura, les Tonnets, imprimeurs-libraires dolois (1712–1781)," *Revue française d'histoire du livre* 27 (1980): 283.

59. BN FF 22080 #81.

60. Mellot, *L'Édition rouennaise.*

61. McLeod, "Provincial Book Trade Inspectors"; BN FF 22128 #99. Bourgelat, the inspector in Lyon—like other inspectors—offered a perspective that could at times counter the guild's dominant one. In 1762 he suggested that the printers had their own, not the public's, interest at heart when they lobbied for reductions.

62. ADG C 3308. Urbain Guillaume de Lamoignon, comte de Courson, was intendant in Bordeaux from 1709 to 1720. Courson worked as a master of requests in the Bureau de la librairie and would have known Bignon from then.

63. William Beik, *Absolutism and Society in Seventeenth-Century France: State Power and Provincial Aristocracy in Languedoc* (Cambridge: Cambridge University Press, 1985), and *Urban Protest in Seventeenth-Century France: The Culture of Retribution* (Cambridge: Cambridge University Press, 1997); Sharon Kettering, *Patrons, Brokers, and Clients in Seventeenth-Century France* (Oxford: Oxford University Press, 1986).

64. Brives-Cazes, *De la police,* 13. The economic motivations of printers and booksellers have received attention: Robert Darnton, *Édition et sédition: L'Univers de la littérature clandestine au XVIIIe siècle* (Paris: Gallimard, 1991), and Carla Hesse, *Publishing and Cultural Politics in Revolutionary Paris, 1789–1810* (Berkeley: University of California Press, 1991).

65. Rigogne, *Between State and Market,* 98–145.

Chapter 5

1. This chapter draws on some of the material in a larger study of argumentation theory and history currently undertaken by Jane McLeod and Hans V. Hansen. Some results have been presented in their "Argument Density and Argument Diversity in the License Applications of French Provincial Printers, 1669–1781," in *Argumentation in Practice,* ed. Frans H. van Eemeren and Peter Houtlosser (Amsterdam: John Benjamins, 2005). The principal sources here are Privy Council orders in council handling licensing requests (hereafter licenses) for the years 1669 to 1781 in the Archives nationales, AN V[6]. The main sample consists of 350 licenses from the following five-year periods: 1709–1714, 1719–1724, 1739–1744, 1755–1760, and 1776–1781. A few additional licenses were used, including 18 from the years 1669–1703. The text of a license provides a summary of the arguments presented in the original petitions but does not reveal the reasons for a decision. The original petition letters, with very few exceptions, have been destroyed.

2. AN V[6] 556, 3 September 1669.

3. Listed here are references to the principal statutes. Paris 1618: *Lettres patentes sur les nouveaux statuts des libraires, imprimeurs et relieurs de la ville et université de Paris,* June 1618 (see *Recueil général des anciennes lois françaises depuis l'an 420 jusqu'à la Révolution de 1789,* ed. Jourdan,

Decrusy, and Isambert, et al. [Paris: Belin-Leprieur, 1821–33], 16:117–25, available online at http://cour-de-france.fr/article348.html); Paris 1686: *Édit contenant règlement sur les imprimeurs et libraires de Paris*, in *Recueil général*, 20:6–20; Bordeaux 1608: *Règlements et statuts qui doivent être observés et gardés par les imprimeurs et marchands libraires de . . . Bordeaux* (BN FF 22125 #1–2); Bordeaux 1688: *Édit du Roy pour le règlement des imprimeurs et libraires de Bordeaux* (BN FF 22125 #4); Toulouse 1620, 1673, 1687: *Lettres patentes . . .* (BN FF 22127 #38–41); Reims 1623: *Arrêt et règlement pour les imprimeurs, libraires et relieurs de la ville de Reims* (BN FF 22126 #9–10); Rennes 1624, 1678: *Chartres et statuts des imprimeurs et libraires de la ville de Rennes* (BN FF 22125 #115); Lyon 1675: *Règlements et statuts proposés par les maîtres imprimeurs de la ville de Lyon . . . 1675* (AMLyon, HH 98); Lyon 1695: *Déclaration du roi portant règlement pour les libraires et imprimeurs de la ville de Lyon* (BN FF 22173 #77).

4. Claude-Marin Saugrain, ed., *Code de la librairie et imprimerie de Paris ou conférence du régle-ment arrêté au conseil d'état du roi le 28 février 1723 et rendu commun pour tout le royaume, par arrêt du conseil d'état du 24 mars 1744 avec les anciennes ordonnances . . .* (1744; repr., Westmead: Gregg International, 1971), 180–207.

5. For a general discussion of other aspects of the 1744 order extending the 1723 Code to the rest of the realm, see Thierry Rigogne, *Between State and Market: Printing and Bookselling in Eighteenth-Century France* (Oxford: Voltaire Foundation, 2007), 47–53.

6. BN FF 22127 #61.

7. On "talents," see David Bien, "The Army in the French Enlightenment: Reform, Reaction, and Revolution," *Past and Present* 85 (1979): 68–98.

8. AN V^6 849, 15 July 1719.

9. AN V^6 1087, 21 December 1778.

10. Jean-Louis Derrieu in Quimper mentioned Breton (V^6 1091, 16 August 1779): Joseph Antoine in Metz, German (AN V^6 986, 12 January and 23 February 1756); Jean-Balthazar Mouret in Aix, Hebrew (V^6 1086, 30 November 1778).

11. AN V^6 826, 26 October 1712; V^6 816, 2 September 1709; V^6 817, 16 December 1709.

12. AN V^6 833, 27 August 1714.

13. AN V^6 794, 15 October 1703; V^6 792, 30 April 1703; V^6 850, 2 December 1719. Another version of a time-served argument was that offered by Benoît Vignieu, who, when ordered by the guild officers to close his business for lack of a license, exploded with indignation and de-manded to know what these same guild officers were thinking, because he had always paid his share of the guild dues and they had always regarded him as a master and honored the many cer-tificates of training he had provided apprentices over his long career. He was seventy years old, had been printing to the satisfaction of the public for thirty years, had a fully equipped printing house, and was in no position to change his profession at his age (AN V^6 827, 19 December 1712).

14. AN V^6 1069, 18 December 1775; Miromesnil granted the license.

15. AN V^6 850, 2 December 1719; V^6 851, 2 March 1720.

16. AN V^6 850, 2 December 1719; V^6 867, 12 June 1724.

17. AN V^6 820, 1 December 1710.

18. AN V^6 852, 3 August 1720.

19. AN V^6 849, 15 July 1719.

20. AN V^6 834, 31 December 1714.

21. AN V^6 833, 27 August 1714.

22. AN V^6 823, 4 September 1711.

23. AN V^6 857, 31 January 1722.

24. The situation of widow printers is developed in my "Printer Widows and the State in Eighteenth-Century France," in *Earning Women*, ed. Nina Kushner and Daryl Hafter (in preparation).

25. On women in the printing trades, see most recently, Roméo Arbour, *Dictionnaire des femmes libraires en France (1470–1870)* (Geneva: Droz, 2003).

26. See the references to widows in the statutes cited above and Saugrain, ed., *Code,* 212–15.

27. AN V6 814, 31 December 1708.

28. AN V⁶ 847, 30 March 1719; V⁶ 849, 14 August 1719.

29. In 1704 the printer Jean Collignon in Metz wanted to be "maintained in possession of the position which he has occupied since 1692 and been hereditary in his family for sixty years" (AN V⁶ 798, 13 October 1704). To this principal argument he added that he should be granted a license because he was qualified and he had eight children to support.

30. AN V⁶ 827, 19 December 1712.

31. *Cession,* ADG, notary Loche, 14 July 1755 (widow Labottière); *Démission d'imprimeur,* ADG, notary Séjourné, 26 June 1755 (widow Lacourt).

32. AN V⁶ 850, 30 December 1719.

33. AN V⁶ 798, 1 September 1704.

34. AN V⁶ 849, 10 July 1719 (Jean-Baptiste Machuel); V⁶ 865, 7 September 1723 (Guillaume Virot).

35. AN V⁶ 799, 19 January 1705.

36. AN V⁶ 798, 13 October 1704; V⁶ 827, 19 December 1712.

37. AN V⁶ 1077, 21 April 1777.

38. AN V⁶ 1098, 25 September 1780.

39. AN V⁶ 1099, 18 December 1780.

40. AN V⁶ 1086, 30 November 1778.

41. AN V⁶ 1091, 16 August 1779.

42. AN V⁶ 1098, 25 September 1780.

43. As one example, the bishop of Amiens gave a certificate of good life and morals to Jean-Baptiste-Louis-Charles Caron in Amiens in 1777 (AN V⁶ 1079, 18 August 1777).

44. AN V⁶ 1086, 30 November 1778.

45. AN V⁶ 1086, 30 November 1778.

46. ADG C 3309. On Jacques Merlin, see Anne Sauvy, "Un Marginal du livre au XVIIIe siècle: Jacques Merlin," *Revue française d'histoire du livre* 45 (1976): 443–85.

47. AN V⁶ 814, 31 December 1708.

48. The Bordeaux guild, for example, pointed out that far from living in abject poverty, dependent on her son, the applicant Nicolas Phillippot's mother was well off (ADG C 3309).

49. AN V⁶ 849, 10 July 1719.

50. AN V⁶ 819, 26 May 1710; V⁶ 820, 1 December 1710. In his petition, Muguet offered an interpretation of the 1704 ceilings: they were necessary for both the king's service and the public good, because printers who could not obtain enough work might turn to pirating and other sorts of printing that would undermine good order. Pierre Foureau in Angers in 1703 claimed that the 1700 survey was the king's way of stopping abuses and, in 1708, Jean Borde in Orléans said that the 1704 ceilings were created to prevent the abuses that were happening on a daily basis in printing (AN V⁶ 792, 7 May 1703; V⁶ 813, 22 October 1708).

51. AN V⁶ 834, 31 December 1714.

52. AN V⁶ 819, 26 May 1710.

53. In 1753 the municipality of Angers asked for another printer because the mayor feared that, following the death of the eighty-year-old widow Hubault, the two remaining printers would have an excuse to raise prices and to deprive the public of the printing that it needed. The mayor recommended licensing Hernault, whose family had been in the printing business for almost two hundred years. See Émile Pasquier and Victor Dauphin, *Imprimeurs et libraires de l'Anjou* (Angers: Éditions de l'Ouest, 1932), 19.

54. AN V⁶ 864, 20 July 1723.

55. Archives départementales des Bouches du Rhône: Aix-en-Provence C 1347.

56. Archives départementales du Gard. E. dépôt 36/52, 1774.

57. Political factors could play a role. In Nîmes, the number of printers was increased during the Maupeou years in part because the town was to be the site of one of Maupeou's superior courts.

58. The petitioners did not regard the criteria of family, talent, and character as distinct or separate. In Metz, two printers competed for a position just after the imposition of the 1704 ceilings and produced a mix of all these arguments. One candidate, named Jean Collignon, feared losing his place and offered a three-part argument in his favor. First, he was competent in Latin and Greek and had experience: he had trained in several cities, including Paris, and took his father's place in 1692, and since then he had been following the rules and carrying on the profession of printer. Second, he also had a hereditary claim: he was a descendant of a line of king's printers in Metz. He based his third argument on need; he was responsible for the feeding, clothing, and education of eight small children. He believed that in the process of obtaining royal licenses, the right to print might be stolen (*ravir*) from him because of the machinations of his enemies. The other candidate, Brice Antoine, claimed that he had always carried on the profession of printer in Metz in accordance with the edicts, decrees, and rules. He had done so with honor and probity and to the satisfaction of his superiors and the public, which he could prove with affidavits from the bishop, the intendant, and the attorney general of Metz. He also claimed that he was the king's printer. Both candidates provided all the arguments they could muster (AN V⁶ 798, 13 October 1704; V⁶ 799, 16 February 1705).

59. Bien, "The Army."

60. Royal officials had always rejected family rights arguments, but printers encouraged the idea of stressing family background as a form of merit argument. The intendant in Pau recommended a nephew of an honorable printer who observed the rules because the nephew had been raised *near* his uncle and would be like him (AN V⁶ 1000, 24 November 1760).

61. Jean-Bertrand Auger in Dijon in 1707 was a foreigner and a bookbinder who had never apprenticed and barely knew how to read (AN V⁶ 807, 24 January 1707). Other interlopers in Dijon included a barrister, a dancer, a tailor, secondhand dealers, a drummer, and a haberdasher. The mention of a barrister was extremely unusual, but the other descriptions were typical. In La Rochelle a surgeon and his wife were denounced for printing without authorization along with their worker, a widow and a former Protestant (AN V⁶ 803, 8 March 1706).

62. On factums, see Sarah Maza, *Private Lives and Public Affairs: The Causes Célèbres of Prerevolutionary France* (Berkeley: University of California Press, 1993).

63. *Mémoire pour Pierre Phillippot . . . contre Michel Racle, ci-devant dentiste et bachelier en médicine,* BMBx Factum. On the Racle affair: ADG C 3314; *Mémoire à Monseigneur de Maupeou chancelier et garde des sceaux* (ADG C 3309); *procuration,* ADG notary Séjourné, 14 July 1769. Racle rented the printer Jean-Baptiste Lacornée's equipment in 1769; see the reference to *police passée entre ledit Lacornée et Racle par laquelle le sieur Lacornée lui loue ses ustensiles d'imprimerie pour un an, sauf à eux proroger,* at 1,000 livres a year, signed 1 November 1769, in Lacornée's *inventaire après décès,* ADG notary Baron, 13 April 1772. He also appears to have taken over Lacornée's bookselling business: see *police de ferme sous seing privé* dated 1769, but registered in the *contrôle des actes,* ADG, QB 208, 5 July 1781; *contrat de mariage,* ADG, notary Séjourné, 7 September 1766. Racle was allowed to continue unofficially until he obtained a full license in 1770. On the status of dentists in the eighteenth century, see Colin Jones, "Pulling Teeth in Eighteenth-Century Paris," *Past and Present* 166 (2000): 100–145.

64. *Mémoire pour Pierre Phillippot.*

65. See chapter 6.

66. Chrétien-Guillaume de Lamoignon de Malesherbes, *Mémoires sur la librairie et sur la liberté de la presse* (1809; repr., Geneva: Slatkine, 1969), 131.

67. Bien, "The Army."

Chapter 6

1. AN V^1 549, 25 August 1788.

2. Many historians provide a very negative reading of the printers' and booksellers' guilds. Some examples include Paul Chauvet, *Les Ouvriers du livre en France des origines à la Révolution de 1789* (Paris: Presses universitaires de France, 1959), and Robert Darnton, "Reading, Writing, and Publishing," in *The Literary Underground of the Old Regime* (Cambridge, Mass.: Harvard University Press, 1982), 197–99. A notable exception is Jean-Dominique Mellot, *L'Édition rouennaise et ses marchés (vers 1600–vers 1730: Dynamisme provincial et centralisme parisien* (Paris: École des chartes, 1998). Influential in the following chapter are Michael Sonenscher's argument that the corporate idiom in the eighteenth century has been overstressed in our understanding of the artisanal world ("The Sans-Culottes of the Year II: Rethinking the Language of Labour in Revolutionary France," *Social History* 9 [1984]: 301–28) and Gail Bossenga's views about the flexibility and adaptability of corporate institutions (*The Politics of Privilege: Old Regime and Revolution in Lille* (Cambridge: Cambridge University Press, 1991). Also influential regarding institutional loyalty and corporate identity is Julian Swann's *Politics and the Parlement of Paris Under Louis XV, 1754–1774* (Cambridge: Cambridge University Press, 1995).

3. BMDijon, MS 745 *Communauté des imprimeurs-libraires de Dijon: Registre des délibérations (10 mai 1772–22 fevrier 1790), 1 December 1788.*

4. Many examples: AN V^6 1130, 13 October 1786; V^6 1134, 2 July 1787; V^6 1126, 19 December 1785. In 1781 the widow Giroud in Grenoble got permission to allow her son a license while she continued. Because of the importance of the license to her family, she could not take a chance on a competition (AN V^6 1103, 6 August 1781).

5. AN V^6 1085, 10 August 1778.

6. AN V^6 1112, 17 March 1783.

7. AN V^6 1128, 22 May 1786. Besongne's departure may have been connected to the financial ruin of his firm; see ADSM 201 BP 552 and Georges Lepreux, *Gallia typographica ou répertoire biographique et chronologique de tous les imprimeurs de France depuis les origines de l'imprimerie jusqu'à la Révolution* (Paris: Champion, 1909–14), vol. 3, pt. 1, pp. 82–83. His wife was to take care of her mother-in-law, Marie-Madelaine-Joseph Gruchet.

8. AN V^1 551, May 1789.

9. This assumption underlies Thierry Rigogne's *Between State and Market: Printing and Bookselling in Eighteenth-Century France* (Oxford: Voltaire Foundation, 2007). Rigogne places printers and booksellers "between" the market and the state bureaucracy, which he regards as very modern, with a coherent, enlightened viewpoint. I would argue for a greater place for clientage, factions, and lobbying.

10. David Kammerling Smith, "Structuring Politics in Early Eighteenth-Century France: The Political Innovations of the French Council of Commerce," *Journal of Modern History* 74 (2002): 490–537.

11. Bruyset first tried to obtain a license in 1672, but the guild cited the 6 October 1667 ban. He got a license in January 1674, which he had signified to the guild warden before being sworn in (AMLyon HH 98; ADR BP 3615). On the Bruyset family, see Dominique Varry, "Une Famille de libraires lyonnais turbulents: Les Bruyset," *La Lettre clandestine* 11 (2003): 105–27;

Aimé Vingtrinier, *Histoire de l'imprimerie à Lyon de l'origine jusqu'à nos jours* (Lyon: Adrien Storck, 1894), 376, 394 and 421–24.

12. Louis' share was worth 128,000 livres in his will, and Jacques' business was worth 100,000 livres (*testaments,* ADR, notary Soupat, 11 April 1740 and 9 June 1742).

13. *Contrat de mariage,* ADR, notary Soupat, 7 February 1743.

14. AN V⁶ 990, 9 May 1757; V⁶ 992, 27 February 1758.

15. Louis Trénard, *Commerce et culture: Le Livre à Lyon au XVIIIe siècle* (Lyon: Imprimeries unies, 1953), 13. For Jean-Marie Bruyset's publications and new evidence of his clandestine activities, see Varry, "Une Famille."

16. BN FF 22128 #39–40. They began their memorandum by saying that the extension of the 1723 Code to Lyon would be "as difficult for Lyon as it was useful for Paris."

17. BN FF 22128 #86.

18. BN FF 22128 #92. Bruyset explained that peddlers from the mountains had been tolerated until the Parisian guild deputy David made a tour through the south and got the intendants of Languedoc and Dauphiné to ban them.

19. On these, see Darnton, "Reading, Writing, and Publishing," 191–99.

20. BN FF 21833, February and March 1784. Vergennes sent his copy of the memo to Miromesnil, saying that it contained good counsel.

21. Léon Moulé, "Correspondance de Claude Bourgelat fondateur des écoles vétérinaires," *Bulletin de la Société centrale de médecine vétérinaire* (1911–12): 115–16.

22. This was entitled *Oeuvres du Philosophe de Sans-Souci,* a work that Malesherbes was hesitant to allow to circulate without the express permission of Frederick (Varry, "Une Famille," 188–22).

23. Moulé, "Correspondance," 193–94.

24. See the letter quoted in Dominique Varry, "Jean-Baptiste Reguilliat, imprimeur-libraire lyonnais destitutué en 1767," *La Lettre clandestine* 12 (2003): 207.

25. BN FF 22128 #99.

26. On the career of Henri-Léonard-Jean-Baptiste Bertin (1720–1792), see Michel Antoine, *Le Gouvernement et l'administration sous Louis XV: Dictionnaire biographique* (Paris: CNRS, 1978), 34.

27. BN FF NA 3344, fols. 294–311; BN FF 22075 #127–29.

28. BN FF 22128 #46 and 47; BN FF 22078 #128.

29. BN FF 22128 #46. The informant's name was Parent, who may have been the Lyonnais who was *conseiller à la cour des monnaies* and *premier commis* of Bertin (Moulé, "Correspondance," 550). In 1766–68 Bertin was involved in a similar attempt to replace the king's printer in Caen, who was accused of spending all his time in the country (Lepreux, *Gallia,* vol. 3, pt. 1, pp. 477–81).

30. BN FF 22128 #47. Probably d'Hémery. Bruyset and d'Hémery had a personal friendship (Varry, "Une Famille," 107).

31. King's printer positions in the provinces were, however, transferred between individuals for large sums of money. In Dijon the printer Louis-Nicolas Frantin valued his at 30,000 livres, a sum that included his printing equipment (*contrat de mariage,* ADR, notary Menu, 13 February 1775). When the Lyon printer Pierre Valfray transferred his business to Aimé Delaroche in 1767, the value was reduced by 10,000 livres when the king's printer rights were removed (ADR 1C 221). See below.

32. BN FF 22128 #47.

33. BN FF 22128 #100–110.

34. Bruyset planned to write to La Barborie to provide instructions on drafting the provisions and to clarify that he was to be the only king's printer in Lyon.

35. He sent to him a blank power of attorney to be passed on to a barrister and suggested a certain Brou, rue de Rosiers au Marais, about whom he had heard good things.

36. BN FF 22128 #104.

37. The archbishop of Lyon was Antoine de Malvin de Montazet (1758–88).

38. Bruyset's information is corroborated by the application for a license of Jean-Louis Marteau, an employee of Delaroche (AN V⁶ 1022, 21 July 1766). Later Delaroche described the plan drawn up in 1749 for him to buy Valfray's business and license for 165,000 livres (ADR 1C 221). The printing equipment sold in 1767 for only 30,000 livres, rather than the original sum of 40,000, because of Bruyset's claim on the king's printer rights (ADR 1C 221).

39. ADR 1C 221.

40. On the Millanois family, see Maurice Garden, *Lyon et les lyonnais au XVIIIe siècle* (Paris: Société d'Édition "Les Belles-Lettres," 1970), 516.

41. On Antoine Jean Terray, intendant of Lyon from 1784 to 1790, see Sylvie Nicolas, *Les Dernières maîtres des requêtes de l'ancien régime (1771–1789)* (Paris: École des chartes, 1998), 289–92.

42. AN V¹ 549, August–September 1788. Royal officials also made it their business to protect his interests. In August 1786 the Toulouse guild was informed of a pirated Geneva edition of *Dictionnaire historique par un société de gens de lettres* for which Bruyset had the privilege—and that Vidaud de la Tour, director of the book trade, wanted kept out of the realm (BM Toulouse, MS 1011).

43. AN V⁶ 1142, 13 October 1788.

44. The elder son's (also named Jean-Marie Bruyset) license: AN V⁶ 1114, 23 June 1783.

45. Françoise Bayard, *Vivre à Lyon sous l'ancien régime* (Paris: Perrin, 1997), 295. On Delaroche, see Vingtrinier, *Histoire de l'imprimerie,* 396–98, and Nelly Dumont, "Aimé Delaroche, imprimeur lyonnais du XVIIIe siècle et la presse locale" (master's thesis, École nationale et supérieure de bibliothécaires, Villeurbanne, 1982); Michèle Gasc, "La Naissance de la presse périodique locale à Lyon: *Les Affiches de Lyon, annonces et avis divers,*" *Études sur la presse* 3 (1978): 74. He was deputy warden from 1743 to 1748 and from 1766 to 1768.

46. *Ventes,* ADR, notary Durand, 25 September 1749.

47. ADR 1C 221.

48. Dumont, "Aimé Delaroche," 25.

49. Moulé, "Correspondance," 227.

50. AN V⁶ 1097, 17 July 1780.

51. ADR 1C 221. According to Delaroche, the clique that Bruyset deceived into supporting him included de Salornay (Valfray's brother and executor, a *maître d'hôtel du roi*), abbé Girard (who later changed camps to support Delaroche), and Fay de Sathonay, whose secretary was Couturier, Bruyset's nephew.

52. ADR 1C 221.

53. The following account of his journalism is from Dumont, "Aimé Delaroche."

54. Jean-Marie Bruyset's relatives through his sister's marriage included Jacques Imbert-Colomès, *premier échevin* and a major leader of Lyon society, who was entering the nobility and working with the governor, duc de Villeroy, the intendant Terray, and the *prévôt* Tolozan. Another branch of the family was Bruyset de Manevieux, one of whom was a *trésorier de France.* See ADR, *contrat de mariage,* notary Soupat, 9 December 1742; Louis Trénard, *Lyon de l'Encyclopédie au préromantisme* (Paris: Presses universitaires de France, 1958), 1:58; Varry, "Une Famille"; and Garden, *Lyon et les lyonnais,* 548.

55. For a discussion of the wider critique of guild organization in the reign of Louis XVI and the suggestion that some of it came from the masters themselves, see Steven Kaplan, "Social Stratification and Representation in the Corporate World of Eighteenth-Century France:

Turgot's 'Carnival,'" in *Work in France: Representations, Meaning, Organization, and Practice,* ed. Steven Kaplan and Cynthia Koepp (Ithaca: Cornell University Press, 1986), 176–228.

56. AN V¹ 552, 28 June 1789. On Mossy, see Jacques Billioud, *Le Livre en Provence du XVI au XVIIIe siècle* (Marseille: Saint-Victor, 1962), 21–22. Jean Mossy was the son of Etienne Mossy, a plumber, and Catherine Martouret from Lisbon. He worked for the widow Brebian in 1747; by 1755, he was working as a bookseller, and in 1767 Mossy's business was located in the Arsenal de la Marine. In 1768 Mossy obtained a license for the first vacant place but, in the meantime, was allowed to work as a printer. In 1771 he had a large shop with ten workers and five presses and was guild warden from 1779 to 1782. For his correspondence with the Société Typographique de Neuchâtel and the books he ordered, see Robert Darnton, *Édition et sédition: L'Univers de la littérature clandestine au XVIIIe siècle* (Paris: Gallimard, 1991), 128–30, 228.

57. Jean Sgard, ed., *Dictionnaire des journaux, 1600–1789* (Paris: Universitas, 1991), 1:35, 2:685.

58. Darnton, *Édition,* 264.

59. René Gérard, *Un Journal de province sous la Révolution: Le "Journal de Marseille" de Ferréol Beaugeard (1781–1797)* (Paris: Société des études robespierristes, 1964), 122.

60. A full study of the Vatar family would be very valuable. On the family, see Lepreux, *Gallia,* vol. 4, pp. 110–27; Arthur de La Borderie, "Histoire de l'imprimerie en Bretagne: Les Races typographiques: Les Vatar, imprimeurs à Rennes et à Nantes," *Revue de Bretagne, de Vendée et d'Anjou* 10 (1893): 405–21; and Patricia Sorel, *La Révolution du livre et de la presse en Bretagne (1780–1830)* (Rennes: Presses universitaires de Rennes, 2004), 47–49. The following discussion is limited to licensing issues, but there are many others to be explored, including the family's role as legal printers, king's printers, newspaper printers, and political activists. On the journalist René Vatar, see Isser Woloch, *Jacobin Legacy: The Democratic Movement Under the Directory* (Princeton: Princeton University Press, 1970).

61. Sorel, *La Révolution du livre,* 13–36; Lepreux, *Gallia,* vol. 4, p. 127.

62. AN V⁶ 844, 25 June 1718. He cited support from several well-known barristers in the Parlement.

63. Archives départementales d'Ille-et-Vilaine (hereafter ADI-et-V) C 1463.

64. She claimed that the subdelegate was a close friend of the guild warden Brun and closely connected to the widow Maréchal's lawyer, neither of whom was in her camp.

65. Six years later, the issue was not dead: when the widow Vatar resigned in favor of her son Joseph-Nicolas, the lieutenant of police seems to have seen the choice of Vatar as automatic and not opened a competition, but his recommendation was annulled when Maupeou, D'Aguesseau, and Bertier de Sauvigny agreed with complaints from the guild about a breach of proper form in the competition. Joseph-Nicolas Vatar eventually got his license six months later (AN V⁶ 1022, 7 July 1766; Lepreux, *Gallia,* vol. 4, Documenta, p. 106).

66. ADI-et-V C 1463; Lepreux, *Gallia,* vol. 4, Documenta, p. 93. In 1757 there were three licenses in Vatar family hands (Gilles-Joseph, Julien-Jean, and Guillaume), one in the Garnier family, and one in the Audran family. In 1748 Julien-Charles had wanted to replace his father, Julien-Jean, but was held back because the number of printers was too high. When his uncle Gilles-Joseph died in 1757, he applied for that license, arguing that his claim was older and therefore stronger than those of Gilles-Joseph's own children.

67. ADI-et-V C1462. Lamoignon said that there were two possible solutions. The first would be to suppress a place and work out an indemnity to be paid to the losing family by those printers who carried on; alternatively, officials could declare one license to be for a lifetime only. The indemnity to the children of the family who lost out would be paid by the children of the surviving families and by other printers in town, who benefited from the reduction in number and from the assurance that their printing houses would not be suppressed.

68. Lepreux, *Gallia,* vol. 4, Documenta, pp. 98–99.

69. Frédéric Saulnier, *Le Parlement de Bretagne 1554–1790,* 2nd ed. (Mayenne: Imprimerie de la Manutention, 1991), 2:843–44.

70. Lepreux, *Gallia,* vol. 4, Documenta, pp. 101–2. For the marriage to Delaroche, see above.

71. AN V⁶ 1079, 26 August 1777.

72. ADI-et-V C1467; AN E 2513, 30 December 1775. Marie made a good case against the gender discrimination and knew well what to say: at fifty-six, she had spent her life in the bookselling business, devoted to her elderly parents who had just died without being able to leave her a fortune because they had refused to sell evil books.

73. On Lallemant, see Jean Quéniart, *L'Imprimerie et la librairie à Rouen au XVIIIe siècle* (Paris: Klincksieck, 1969), esp. 248–50; Georges de Beaurepaire, *Le Contrôle de la librairie à Rouen à la fin du XVIIIe siècle* (Rouen: A. Lainé, 1929); ADSM J 217–18; AN V¹ 551, May 1789; V¹ 553, 22 May 1789.

74. Quoted in Quéniart, *L'Imprimerie,* 72.

75. Miromesnil found no need to mention that just a year earlier, he had written to Maupeou because he had found three copies of *Recherches sur l'origine du despotisme* in one of Lallemant's book shipments, a work he suspected was dangerous—and Maupeou agreed (ADSM J 218). Two years before, he had discovered in another of Lallemant's shipments twenty-four copies of *Examen du ministère du Mr. Pitt* and four copies of *Lettres à un seigneur anglais.* Maupeou ordered the first sent back to Holland and sections showing disrespect for the king and the nation removed from the latter (ADSM J 217). Neither did he mention the curt note he had sent to Lallemant in December 1765 asking by what permission he had printed *Reflexions sur l'arrest rendu contre les Receveurs des Consignations le 16 Août 1765* (ADSM J 218).

76. BN FF 22063 #68. On Miromesnil, Le Camus de Néville, and the 1777 reforms, see the wealth of information in Robert Dawson, *The French Booktrade and the "Permission Simple" of 1777: Copyright and Public Domain* (Oxford: Voltaire Foundation, 1992).

77. Gabriel Debien, ed., *Correspondance de Félix Faulcon* (Poitiers: Société des archives historiques du Poitou, 1939), 1:2. The son was a future *conseiller du roi au présidial* of Poitiers and future deputy to the Estates General.

78. Ernest Labadie, *La Presse bordelaise pendant la Révolution* (Bordeaux: Y. Cadoret, 1910), 18.

79. Debien, *Correspondance,* 1:138, 146–47, 154–55; AN V⁶ 1114, 23 June 1783.

80. ADG C 3315; BN FF 21870 #362.

81. ADG C 3310.

82. BN FF 21867.

83. ADG C 3310.

84. ADG C 3309.

85. BN FF 22075.

86. AN V¹ 550.

87. On these archives, see the many works of Robert Darnton as well as *Le Rayonnement d'une maison d'édition dans l'Europe des Lumières: La Société typographique de Neuchâtel, 1769–1789,* ed. Robert Darnton and Michel Schlup (Neuchâtel: Gilles Attinger, 2005); Elizabeth Eisenstein, *Grub Street Abroad: Aspects of the French Cosmopolitan Press from the Age of Louis XIV to the French Revolution* (Oxford: Clarendon Press, 1992), 25.

88. Jane McLeod, "Provincial Book Trade Inspectors in Eighteenth-Century France," *French History* 12 (1998): 141–42.

89. McLeod, "Provincial Book Trade Inspectors," 142.

90. ADHG E 1315, 2 May 1789. The guild agreed to register the decree of 31 January 1789 that nullified the guild elections in Nancy.

91. There are many examples of provincial printers traveling to Paris. The Poitiers printer Félix Faulcon, for instance, made two business trips to Paris in June and August 1777, and the Troyes guild sent members to Paris on several occasions (Rigogne, *Between State and Market,* 72).

92. The Lyon printer André Périsse had a son, Louis-Henri, who married and went to live in Paris in 1780 and worked as an agent for his brothers (AN V⁶ 1115, 15 September 1783). The Dijon printer Frantin was the nephew of the Parisian publisher widow Coignard (see the marriage contract in note 31 above). The Briasson family had members in both Paris and Lyon (AN V⁶ 867, 12 June 1724). A son of the Labotttière family in Bordeaux was a bookseller in Paris (*testament* of Marie Darbis, widow Labottière, ADG notary Dejeneau, 24 May 1724; Paul Delalain, *L'Imprimerie et la librairie à Paris de 1789 à 1813* [Paris: Delalain frères, 1899], 97, 189). The Barbou family had members in Paris and Limoges; see Paul Ducourtieux, *Les Barbou, imprimeurs Lyon-Limoges-Paris* (Limoges: Ducourtieux, 1896).

93. The guilds often considered the wider national and international scene in their lobbying. In 1759, in a struggle between Lyon and Paris printers over copyright renewals, the Lyonnais used a memo on the subject written by the Rouennais to D'Aguesseau (BN FF 22128 #93). The guild warden in Lyon, Duplain, wrote a memorandum on copyright in 1774 and mentioned a decision of the English House of Lords that had just favored the Scots against the London Stationers Company (BN FF 22073 #140). The provincial guilds cited each other in their opposition to the creation of bookseller *brevets* in 1767 (*A Monseigneur le vice-chancelier . . .* BMBx, MS 1546). In 1773 members of the Toulouse guild decided to adopt the strategy of the Bordeaux guild in resisting efforts to make them perform night watch, and in 1779 they reported on consultation with the guild wardens in Paris, Rouen, Lyon, and Bordeaux on this issue. The Lyon guild had a deputy in Paris at the time, Benoît Duplain, representing its interests in 1773 and it offered his services to the Toulouse guild. Its members also sought information on king's printer positions in other towns. These actions might meaningfully be compared to the efforts to form a nationwide association of members of financial courts identified by Bossenga in *The Politics of Privilege,* 67.

94. For a list of twenty-one provincial printers who were editors of provincial newspapers, see Stephen Auerbach, "'Encourager le commerce et répandre les lumières': The Press, the Provinces, and the Origins of the Revolution in France, 1750–1789" (Ph.D. diss., University of Louisiana, 2001), 30.

95. Colin Jones, "The Great Chain of Buying: Medical Advertisement, the Bourgeois Public Sphere, and the Origins of the French Revolution," *American Historical Review* 101 (1996): 13–40; Auerbach, "'Encourager le commerce'"; Jack Censer, *The French Press in the Age of Enlightenment* (London: Routledge, 1994). There are also a number of local studies: see Marie-Thérèse Blanc-Rouquette, *La Presse et l'information à Toulouse, des origines à 1789* (Toulouse: Faculté des lettres et sciences humaines, 1967), and Labadie, *La Presse bordelaise.* On the *Affiches dijonnaises,* see Marcel Bouchard, *De l'Humanisme à l'Encyclopédie: L'Esprit public en Bourgogne sous l'ancien régime* (Paris: Hachette, 1930), 921–24.

96. Blanc-Rouquette, *La Presse,* 202.

97. Colin Lucas, "Nobles, Bourgeois, and the Origins of the French Revolution," in *French Society and the Revolution,* ed. Douglas Johnson (Cambridge: Cambridge University Press, 1976), 88–131.

98. Gilbert Shapiro and John Markoff, *Revolutionary Demands: A Content Analysis of the Cahiers de Doléances of 1789* (Stanford: Stanford University Press, 1998), 278–79.

Chapter 7

1. On the growth in the demand for print, see Henri-Jean Martin, "À la veille de la Révolution: Crise et réorganisation de la librairie," in *Histoire de l'édition française: Le Livre triomphant, 1660–1830,* ed. Roger Chartier and Henri-Jean Martin (Paris: Fayard, 1990), 681–93. For some

first results of a new collaborative research project on French provincial printers, see Frédéric Barbier, *Lumières du nord: Imprimeurs, libraires et "gens du livre" dans le nord au XVIIIe siècle (1701–1789): Dictionnaire prosopographique* (Geneva: Droz, 2002). For data showing no decline in the printing capacity in the provinces in the eighteenth century despite the imposition of quotas, see Thierry Rigogne, *Between State and Market: Printing and Bookselling in Eighteenth-Century France* (Oxford: Voltaire Foundation, 2007), 127–32. In fact in four larger provincial centers— Rouen, Bordeaux, Troyes, and Strasbourg—the average printing house doubled the number of presses.

2. See Jane McLeod, "Social Status and the Politics of Printers in Eighteenth-Century Bordeaux," *Histoire sociale—Social History* 23 (1990): 301–23.

3. Aimé Vingtrinier, *Histoire de l'imprimerie à Lyon de l'origine jusqu'à nos jours* (Lyon: Adrien Storck, 1894); Roger Chartier, "Livre et espace: Circuits commerciaux et géographie culturelle de la librairie lyonnaise au XVIIIe siècle," *Revue française d'histoire du livre* 1 (1971): 77–108; Jeanne-Marie Dureau, "À propos de quelques sources lyonnaises de l'histoire du livre et de la lecture à Lyon," in *Mélanges d'histoire lyonnaise offerts par ses amis à Monsieur Henri Hours* (Lyon: Éditions lyonnaises d'art et d'histoire, 1990): 135–51.

4. In 1764 Aimé Delaroche married Anne Clement, who brought a dowry of 6,000 livres (*contrôle des actes*, ADR, 10C 65, 9 August 1764). In 1749 he made arrangements to buy the Valfray business in 1749 for 165,000 livres (ADR 1C 221); see also Nelly Dumont, "Aimé Delaroche, imprimeur lyonnais du XVIIIe siècle et la presse locale" (master's thesis, École nationale et supérieure de bibliothécaires, Villeurbanne, 1982). When his daughter died in 1783, the property she held with her husband (analysed by both Chartier and Dumont) was worth 96,216 livres, and of this 86,867 was invested in the business.

5. BN FF 22078 #128; ADR 1C 221: Delaroche referred to 10,000 livres *rente* that he paid the widow Valfray. Valfray was *échevin de Lyon,* ennobled, and seigneur de Salornay (Vingtrinier, *Histoire de l'imprimerie,* 385–86).

6. In 1764 Jean-Marie Barrêt's marriage indicates modest wealth: his bride, Clemence Charles Jaquard, brought a dowry of 1,600 livres (*contrôle des actes,* ADR 10C 66, 29 December 1764). But the succession in 1786 (ADR BP 2294) indicates a significant but fragile business worth of 188,230 livres (Dureau, "À propos," 146).

7. Chartier, "Livre et espace."

8. Maurice Garden, *Lyon et les lyonnais au XVIIIe siècle* (Paris: Société d'Édition "Les Belles-Lettres," 1970), 463; ADR, *table de marriages,* 58Q9, 18 December 1784. In 1807 this son, then working in partnership with Bruynaud, went bankrupt (ADR, Série U). The assets were 902,474 and liabilities, 810,608; of this, 597,000 represented books and printing equipment. He had houses worth 210,000 livres.

9. Garden, *Lyon et les lyonnais,* 516–22; *Etats,* ADR 1L 535; ADR 1Q 640.

10. AMLyon, I² 26; brother's *contrat de mariage,* ADR, notary Perrodon, 1 December 1780. On Périsse Duluc, see Timothy Tackett, *Becoming a Revolutionary: The Deputies of the French National Assembly and the Emergence of a Revolutionary Culture (1789–1790)* (Princeton: Princeton University Press, 1996).

11. *Contrat de mariage,* ADR, notary Faucheux, 27 September 1767.

12. *Contrat de mariage,* notary Chastelus, 8 September 1781.

13. *Extrait des registres de la sénéchaussée de Lyon,* ADR 7C 59. Movable property was estimated at 4,413 livres, and the wife's dowry at marriage in 1731 was 29,015 livres; see Dureau, "À propos," 146.

14. I have no information on the wealth of five printers in Lyon: Barbier, Cutty, Chavance, Buisson, and Regnault. The Vialon family at midcentury seems to have lived in modest circumstances, but the two licenses it controlled had, by the 1780s, been passed on to Jean-Baptiste

Delamollière and Claude-André Faucheux (both relatives) who had large prosperous establish-ments by the Revolution (AN V⁶1103, 6 August 1781; *contrat de mariage,* ADR, notary Soupat, 1 February 1758; Faucheux and Delamollière marriages cited above; Vingtrinier, *Histoire de l'imprimerie,* 405–12). In 1761 Joseph Vialon had printing equipment and books worth 18,072 livres (Dureau, "À propos," 146) and, in 1778, Pierre Vialon's succession was worth 28,217 livres (Chartier, "Livre et espace"). See also Pierre Vialon in "La Somme typographique en ligne" on the Musée de l'imprimerie Lyon website, http://www.imprimerie.lyon.fr/imprimerie/sections/fr/documentation/somme_typographique.

15. Jean Quéniart, *L'Imprimerie et la librairie à Rouen au XVIIIe siécle* (Paris: Klincksieck, 1969), 19–36, 103–5, 233–50; Georges de Beaurepaire, *Le Contrôle de la librairie à Rouen à la fin du XVIIIe siècle* (Rouen: A. Lainé, 1929), 7–9. In 1764 there were eighty-nine workers in Rouen and thirty-nine presses. Exact figures on wealth are available for Lallemant in 1797, Machuel in 1742, Besongne (in 1753 and 1784), and Behourt in 1759. Fiscal sources help place Oursel and Dumesnil among the families with wealth. Miromesnil reported in 1764 that while there were some poor booksellers, many printers who engaged in bookselling enjoyed "d'une fortune forte honnête." Unlike Quéniart, I am making generalizations here about the license-holding printers in the later eighteenth century, whereas he was interested a larger group that included journeymen and booksellers. The profile of the Rouen printers and booksellers was very different in the seventeenth century, when there was a large guild of closely tied men and women of modest wealth (Jean-Dominique Mellot, "Clés pour un essor provincial: Le Petit siècle d'or de l'édition rouennaise (vers 1600–vers 1670)," *Annales de Normandie* 45 (1995): 265–300.

16. Madeleine Ventre, *L'Imprimerie et la librairie en Languedoc au dernier siècle de l'ancien régime, 1700–1789* (Paris: Mouton, 1958), 226–44. Ventre was overly influenced by the guild's own self-presentation in its ongoing dialogue with administrators when she stressed the mod-esty of the wealth of printers in Languedoc in a section entitled "Pauvreté des imprimeurs et les libraires." If we consider only the licensed printers of the second half of the eighteenth cen-tury, the story is different.

17. *Contrat de mariage,* ADHG, notary Arnaud, 4 July 1773; *accords,* notary Arnaud, 1 Jan-uary and 9 September 1780.

18. Marie-Thérèse Blanc-Rouquette, "Un Imprimeur toulousain au XVIIIe siècle: Jean-Florent Baour," *Revue française d'histoire du livre* 27 (1980): 317.

19. *Contrat de mariage,* ADHG, notary Arnaud, 17 February 1780.

20. *Contrats de mariage,* ADHG, notary Arnaud, 9 April 1786, and notary Vidal, 16 April 1787. On this family, see Jean-François and Pierre Douladoure, *Une Vieille Famille de maîtres-imprimeurs toulousains* (Toulouse: Les Frères Douladoure, 1937).

21. Ventre, *L'Imprimerie,* 236.

22. *Table de contrats de mariage,* ADHG, 1766–1787; Martyn Lyons, *Revolution in Toulouse: An Essay on Provincial Terrorism* (Bern: Peter Lang, 1978), 169.

23. Michel-Hilaire Clément-Janin, *Les Imprimeurs et les libraires dans la Côte-d'Or* (1883; repr., Geneva: Slatkine, 1971), 45–47, 63–67, 69–77. On Frantin, see Larry Lee Baker, "Politics, Privilege, and Political Culture: Dijon During the French Revolution" (Ph.D. diss., University of Illinois at Chicago, 2002), 52; *contrat de mariage,* ADCD, notary Menu, 13 February 1775 (Frantin); *contrat de mariage,* ADCD, notary Bouché, 9 April 1769 (Defay daughter); *contrat de mariage,* ADCD, notary Lemoine, 4 November 1745 (Defay nephew).

24. Ventre, *L'Imprimerie,* 228–29.

25. *Contrat de mariage,* Archives départementales du Gard, notary Darlac, 6 January 1776.

26. BN FF 21832.

27. Jacques Billioud, *Le Livre en Provence du XVIe au XVIIIe siècles* (Marseille: Saint-Victor, 1962), 20, 22, 47.

28. *Etat et bilan,* ADBR Marseille 13 B 533, 1725.

29. Three exceptions are the widow Besongne and son in Rouen in 1784 (ADSM 201 BP 552), Lemmens in Lille in 1786 (Barbier, *Lumières du nord,* 367), and Tonnet in Dole in 1775, who had particularly bad luck: a fire destroyed his home and business in 1765, and six years later, the Cour des comptes was transferred out of town (Michel Vernus, "Une Page de l'histoire du livre dans le Jura, les Tonnet, imprimeurs-libraires dolois [1712–1781]," *Revue française d'histoire du livre* 27 [1980]: 271–95). When bankruptcy threatened the Oursel family in 1763, many highly placed people—the archbishop of Rouen, the first president of the Parlement of Rouen, the comte de Saint-Florentin, Le Sens de Folleville, the princesse de Conti—came to his assistance. Conti explained to Oursel how to proceed, noting the limits of her influence with the queen; she was not approaching the queen as frequently as in the past and did not like to ask favors from the king's ministers (ADSM J 217). On women at court, see Kathryn Norberg, "Women of Versailles, 1682–1789," in *Servants of the Dynasty: Palace Women in World History,* ed. Anne Walthall (Berkeley: University of California Press, 2008), 191–214.

30. In a rather eccentric book in 1789, Los Rios, who sold secondhand books in Lyon, compared his modest country house with the grand ones possessed by the town's booksellers on the outskirts of town. He also presented a glowing picture of the Lyon book trade in 1789. See Jean François de Los Rios, *Oeuvres de François de Los Rios libraire à Lyon, contenant plusieurs descriptions et observations sur des objets curieux ou particuliers, aventures, voyages etc.* (London [Lyon]: Molin, 1789).

31. ADG C 3771; ADSM C 145.

32. The high level of dynastic continuity among printers contrasts with the much lower levels in other trades. See Michael Sonenscher, *Work and Wages: Natural Law, Politics, and the Eighteenth-Century French Trades* (Cambridge: Cambridge University Press, 1989), 108–9.

33. AN V^6 1143, 16 March 1789; AN V^1 550, 6 March 1789.

34. For Bellegarique, see AN V^6 1138, 3 March 1788; for Sens, see AN V^6 1123, 2 May 1785, ADHG C147. Noel-Etienne Sens competed in the *concours* for the Guillemette license. He was the son of the bookseller Michel Sens, had done an apprenticeship, and worked for the widow Herissant in Paris (BM Toulouse, MS 1011).

35. McLeod, "Social Status."

36. The remaining two uncles were a *bourgeois* and an engraver, and the two other brothers or brothers-in-law became a *bourgeois* and clerk.

37. In Bordeaux these links were not all concentrated in one or two families. Of the nine families with relatives about whom we know something, all but three had at least one *négociant* in the family, and these three, along with three others, all had family members in the legal professions or nobility. Six of the families had a brother or a child in the Church—most often a *docteur en theologie.*

38. McLeod, "Social Status"; *vente d'office,* ADG, 3E 12681, 3 October 1757. Larré later sold this office and Nicolas Lacourt was at a later date *lieutenant général honoraire du sénéchal de Bazas.* His son was a judge in the Cour des aides of Guyenne fom 1787 to 1790. See Denise Bège, "Une Compagnie à la recherche de sa raison d'être: La Cour des aides de Guyenne et ses magistrats, 1553–1790" (doctoral thesis, Université de Paris I, 1974). Larré's father was a *bourgeois et chirurgien.*

39. For Pijon, see Marie-Thérèse Blanc-Rouquette, "Une Dynastie d'imprimeurs toulousains, XVIIe, XVIIIe siècles," *Histoire du Languedoc: Actes du 110e Congrès national des sociétés savantes: Section d'histoire moderne et contemporaine* 2 (1985): 123. For Frantin, see above.

40. Le Marquis de Granges de Surgères, "Contribution à l'histoire de l'imprimerie en France: Notes sur les anciens imprimeurs nantais (XVe à XVIIIe siècles)," *Bulletin du bibliophile et du bibliothécaire* (1897): 416, 569. Brun had five presses and an additional title of *garde à cheval des plaisirs de Sa Majesté;* Émile Pasquier and Victor Dauphin, *Imprimeurs et libraires de l'Anjou*

(Angers: Éditions de l'Ouest, 1932), 157. Audran's son was Audran de Montenay (Georges Lepreux, *Gallia typographica ou répertoire biographique et chronologique de tous les imprimeurs de France depuis les origines de l'imprimerie jusqu'à la Révolution* [Paris: Champion, 1909–14], vol. 4, p. 19).

41. Quéniart, *L'Imprimerie*, 250; his son was Lallemant de Couteray (AN V¹ 551, 22 May 1789).

42. Valfray's brother was Valfray de Salornay (ADR 1C 221). See also Dominique Varry, "Lyons' Printers and Booksellers from the Fifteenth to the Nineteenth Century," in *Printed Matters: Printing, Publishing, and Urban Culture in Europe in the Modern Period,* ed. Malcolm Gee and Tim Kirk (Aldershot: Ashgate, 2002), 41–42.

43. *Contrat de mariage,* ADR, notary Soupat, 9 December 1742. Jean-Marie Bruyset's son-in-law was Jean-François Buynaud des Echelles (Vintringier, *Histoire de l'imprimerie,* 424).

44. ADR, 1C 221. Both husbands of Delaroche's daughter were *écuyers* (Jacques-Julien Vatar and Millanois de Timbaudière).

45. Edna Hindie Lemay, *Dictionnaire des constituants, 1789–1791* (Paris: Universitas, 1991), 2:668.

46. William Doyle, *Venality: The Sale of Offices in Eighteenth-Century France* (Oxford: Clarendon Press, 1996), 153–54; Auguste Kuscinski, *Dictonnaire des conventionnels* (1916; repr., Brueil-en-Vexin: Éditions du Vexin Français, 1973), 206.

47. *Quittance,* ADG, notary Baron, 25 May 1778; *contrats de mariage,* ADG, notary Rauzan, 10 September 1782 (son); Rauzan, 19 November 1781 (daughter).

48. AN V⁶ 867, 3 May 1724.

49. Quéniart, *L'Imprimerie,* 248.

50. AN V⁶ 1139, 17 March 1788.

51. AN V⁶ 1120, 30 August 1784.

52. Frédéric Saulnier, *Le Parlement de Bretagne 1554–1790,* 2nd ed. (Mayenne: Imprimerie de la Manutention, 1991), 2:843–44.

53. Charles Buirette, *Histoire de la ville de Saint-Ménehould* (1837; repr., Paris: Office de l'édition du livre d'histoire, 1997), 435.

54. Lemay, *Dictionnaire des constituants,* 2:668.

55. Michel Vernus, *La Vie comtoise au temps de l'ancien régime* (Lons-le-Saunier: Éditions Marque-Maillard, 1985), 2:178.

56. Printers who were barristers included Pijon, Guillemette, Robert, Henault, Desclassan, Causse, David, Tarbé, Vignancourt, Gibelin, Faure de Beauregard, Willerval, Mourot, and Levrault.

57. On Faulcon, see below.

58. Vernus, *La Vie comtoise,* 178.

59. On the Albespy family, see McLeod, "Social Status," 316–17.

60. Lemay, *Dictionnaire des constituants,* 2:668.

61. On professional families, see Christine Adams, *A Taste for Comfort and Status: A Bourgeois Family in Eighteenth-Century France* (University Park: Pennsylvania State University Press, 2000). On attitudes of barristers in Toulouse, see Lenard Berlanstein, *The Barristers of Toulouse in the Eighteenth Century, 1740–1793* (Baltimore: Johns Hopkins University Press, 1975).

62. AN V⁶ 1077, 21 April 1777.

63. For some examples in Lille, see Barbier, *Lumières du nord,* 104–5.

64. Gabriel Debien, ed., *Correspondance de Félix Faulcon* (Poiters: Société des archives historique du Poitou, 1939), 1, 3–7, 110–11; quotation on page 4.

65. AN V⁶ 826, 27 June 1712; V⁶ 828, 20 February 1713.

66. Grange de Surgères, "Contribution à l'histoire de l'imprimerie en France: Notes sur les anciens imprimeurs nantais (XVe à XVIIIe siècles)," *Bulletin du bibliophile et du bibliothécaire* (1897): 414–16.

67. Other examples include the Desclassan family in Toulouse; they sent a son to Castre (BMToulouse MSS 1010, 11 September 1740; MSS 1011, 3 September 1780; and *contrat de mariage,* ADHG, notary Arnaud, 17 February 1780). Claude Labottière in Bordeaux set up one son, Etienne, as a printer in Bayonne (*testament,* ADG, notary Dejenault, 24 May 1724); AN V⁶ 803, 22 February 1706.

68. ADG C 3308.

69. Pierre Bernadau, "Tablettes contemporaines, historiques et cryptographiques de l'Ecouteur bordelais ou mémoires secrètes pour servir à l'histoire générale et anecdotique du temps qui court," BMBx MS 713, 2 October 1788.

70. *Catalogue des livres qui se trouvent chez Pierre Phillippot libraire-imprimeur sur les fossés de l'hôtel de ville et dans son cabinet littéraire, Grand-Salle du Palais* [1780s].

71. Arthur LeMoy, *Le Parlement de Bretagne et le pouvoir royale au XVIIIe siècle* (1909; repr., Geneva: Megariotis, 1981), 43, 68.

72. Jean Egret, *Le Parlement du Dauphiné et les affaires publiques dans la deuxième moitié du XVIIIe siècle* (Roanne: Éditions Horvath, 1999), 1:304–5.

73. *Inventaire,* ADG, notary Loche, 10 October 1754. Research on book buying suggests that the nobles were frequent clients of printers and booksellers; see Robert Darnton, *The Business of Enlightenment: A Publishing History of the Encyclopédie, 1775–1800* (Cambridge, Mass.: Harvard University Press, 1979); Henri-Jean Martin and Anne-Marie Lecocq, *Livres et lecteurs à Grenoble: Les Registres du libraire Nicolas (1645–1668)* (Geneva: Droz, 1977).

74. Cited in Garden, *Lyon et les lyonnais,* 463.

75. On the clandestine book trade, see (among his many works) Robert Darnton, *Édition et sédition: L'Univers de la littérature clandestine au XVIIIe siècle* (Paris: Gallimard, 1991), and *The Forbidden Best-Sellers of Pre-Revolutionary France* (London: Fontana, 1997); Catherine Maire, *De la cause de dieu à la cause de la nation: Le Jansénisme au XVIIIe siècle* (Paris: Gallimard, 1998), 137–62; Dominique Varry, "La Diffusion sous le manteau: La Société typographique de Neuchâtel et les lyonnais," in *L'Europe et le livre: Réseaux et pratiques du négoce de librairie XVIe–XIXe siècles,* ed. Frédéric Barbier, Sabine Juratic, and Dominique Varry (Paris: Klincksieck, 1996), 309–32; Varry, "Le Livre clandestin à Lyon au XVIIIe siècle," *La Lettre clandestine* 6 (1997): 243–52; and Varry, "Batailles de libelles à Lyon à l'occasion de la suppression de la Compagnie de Jésus (années 1760–1775)," *Histoire et civilisation du livre* 2 (2006):135–68. There is a rich literature on French-language publishing outside the realm for the French market. Some recent examples include Darnton, *The Business of Enlightenment,* and Elizabeth Eisenstein, *Grub Street Abroad: Aspects of the French Cosmopolitan Press from the Age of Louis XIV to the French Revolution* (Oxford: Clarendon Press, 1992).

76. Robert Darnton, "The Science of Piracy: A Crucial Ingredient in Eighteenth-Century Publishing," in *Studies on Voltaire and the Eighteenth Century* 12 (Oxford: Voltaire Foundation, 2003), 3–29.

77. On printers' participation in Jansenist networks, see Maire, *De la cause de dieu.* In his earlier work, Darnton suggested that *libelles* were produced and read by outsiders to the privileged world of eighteenth-century society, claiming that "the gutters overflowed in the reign of Louis 16" and that books "severed the decency that bound public to rulers" ("Reading, Writing, and Publishing," 201–8). Research in the following decades has changed our view of pamphlet literature so that it is now seen more as the product of elites, marketed to elites, and commonly an instrument in elite power struggles; see Christian Jouhaud, *Mazarinades: La Fronde des mots* (Paris: Aubier, 1985); Jeremy Popkin, "Pamphlet Journalism at the End of the Old Regime," *Eighteenth-Century Studies* 22 (1989): 351–67.

78. Explored here is opposition printing, but the printing of pro-ministry pamphlets during the Maupeou years could also be explored. According to the *Mercure dijonnais,* in 1771 "Il

court . . . une infinité de brochures sous différents titres pour servir de réponse aux remonstrances et arrêtés des Parlements, où ces Messieurs sont très peu ménagés et où on met tous leurs torts dans au grand jour." Cited in Marcel Bouchard, *De l'Humanisme à l'Encyclopédie: L'Esprit public en Bourgogne sous l'ancien régime* (Paris: Hachette, 1930), 911.

79. On the printing of parlementary remonstrances in the later eighteenth century, see William Doyle, *Origins of the French Revolution,* 2nd ed. (Oxford: Oxford University Press, 1988), 81–82, and *The Parlement of Bordeaux at the End of the Old Regime, 1771–1790* (New York: St. Martin's Press, 1974), 205, 215, 273.

80. This taken from Keith Baker, "French Political Thought at the Accession of Louis XVI," *Journal of Modern History* 50 (1978): 279–303.

81. Joël Félix, *Finances et politique au siècle des Lumières: Le Ministère L'Averdy, 1763–1768* (Paris: Comité pour l'histoire économique et financière de la France, 1999), 5–31; Guy Chaussinaud-Nogaret, *Choiseul (1719–1785): Naissance de la gauche* (Paris: Perrin, 1998), 180–81.

82. BN FF 22068 #48.

83. For a good overview of censorship, see Daniel Roche, "Censorship and the Publishing Industry," in *Revolution in Print: The Press in France, 1775–1800,* ed. Robert Darnton and Daniel Roche (Berkeley: University of California Press, 1989), 3–26. For a reexamination of the role of the parlements, see Barbara de Negroni, *Lectures interdites: Le Travail des censeurs au XVIIIe siècle, 1723–1774* (Paris: Albin Michel, 1995), 163–94.

84. The parlements began to advocate freedom of the press, a position that fits poorly with their previous history of advocating tough censorship and decrying royal incompetence in this area. Some regarded printing as important in bringing an end to the Maupeou era: in 1786 the barrister pleading for Le Maître—accused of clandestine printing—claimed that the types that had been used to combat the Maupeou revolution should be venerated. See André Doyon, *Un Agent royaliste pendant la Révolution: Pierre-Jacques Le Maître (1790–1795)* (Paris: Société des études robespierristes, 1969), 51. On Lemaître, see Popkin, "Pamphlet Journalism."

85. In Bordeaux the demand for print was particularly high when the courts were in session, normally between January and September. For the importance of the Parlement to printers in Rouen, see Jean-Dominique Mellot, "La Librairie du palais sous l'ancien régime: Splendeur et décadence de l'exception rouennaise du livre," in *Les Parlements et la vie de la cité (XVIe–XVIIIe siècle),* ed. Olivier Chaline and Yves Sassier (Rouen: Publications de l'Université de Rouen, 2004), 111–33.

86. Francis de Chanteau, "De la corporation des imprimeurs-libraires de la ville de Metz," *Mémoires de la Société d'archéologie et d'histoire de la Moselle* 8 (1866): 178.

87. Popkin, "Pamphlet Journalism," 362. The Imprimerie polytype de Hoffmann, located in the *palais royale,* printed pamphlets for the duc d'Orléans and at least seven pamphlets in the Kornmann case in the summer of 1787. In 1787 the government tried to have these protected printing houses scrutinized by book trade inspectors.

88. AN V⁶ 798, 13 October 1704; Rigogne, *Between State and Market,* 85.

89. AN V⁶ 990, 16 May 1757. In Marseille a protected area was l'Arsenal de la marine. Mossy was successful there, and the guild tried to oust him, saying that they could not do inspections (Jacques Billioud, *Le Livre en Provence du XVIe au XVIIIe siècle* [Marseille: Saint-Victor, 1962], 40–41). In Bordeaux, colporteurs and merchants sold books and pamphlets in the Hôtel de la Bourse, eluding the guild officers and the police, especially during the fairs of October and March (ADG C 3314).

90. BN FF 22127 #108.

91. ADSM J 218.

92. Rigogne, *Between State and Market,* 85.

93. Lepreux, *Gallia,* vol. 3, pt. 1, pp. 82–83, and pt. 2, Documenta, p. 363; ADSM J 217; Quéniart, *L'Imprimerie,* 224.

94. ADG C 3314; AN E 2538, 25 May 1777. The title was *Très humbles et très respectueuses remonstrances de la cour des aides et finances de Guyenne au sujet des lettres patentes du roi du 24 november 1776 concernant les octrois de la ville de Bordeaux.*

95. Monique Cuillieron, *Contribution à l'étude de la rébellion des cours souveraines sous le règne de Louis XVI: Le Cas de la cour des aides et finances de Montauban* (Paris: Presses universitaires de France, 1983), 80–81.

96. Julian Swann, *Provincial Power and Absolute Monarchy: The Estates General of Burgundy, 1661–1790* (Cambridge: Cambridge University Press, 2003), 262–94, and "Power and Provincial Politics in Eighteenth-Century France: The Varenne Affair, 1757–1763," *French Historical Studies* 21 (1998): 441–74; Clément-Janin, *Les Imprimeurs,* 60–62; Bouchard, *De l'Humanisme à l'Encyclopèdie,* 870–77; AN V⁶ 940, 24 February 1744 and 30 March 1744. *Le Parlement outragé* was a response to Varenne's defense of the prerogatives of the Estates of Burgundy in the conflict over these with the Parlement of Burgundy. On 7 June 1762 the Parlement had Varenne's second *mémoire* publicly burned in front of large crowds. Hucherot, the son of a notary and the son-in-law of a printer, got a license in 1744. After his arrest he returned to printing, in which he was followed by his son. His grandson bought the office of *conseiller-auditor à la chambre des comptes de Bourgogne* in 1782.

97. Léon Moulé, "Correspondance de Claude Bourgelat fondateur des écoles vétérinaires," *Bulletin de la Société centrale de médecine vétérinaire* (1911–12): 227; Clément-Janin, *Les Imprimeurs,* 124; Buisson's license: AN V⁶ 983, 20 January 1755.

98. For recent examinations of the Brittany Affair, see Félix, *Finances et politique,* 305–60; Julian Swann, *Politics and the Parlement of Paris Under Louis XV, 1754–1774* (Cambridge: Cambridge University Press, 1995), 250–83.

99. For both sides of the conflict, pamphlet production, publications of *arrêts* and *remonstrances,* and efforts to suppress them, see Barthélemy Pocquet, *Le Duc d'Aiguillon et La Chalotais* (Paris: Perrin, 1900), 1:281–83, 296–99, 442–43, 470–71; see also Marcel Marion, *La Bretagne et le duc d'Aiguillon, 1753–1770* (Paris: Fontémoing, 1898). The *Requête de Normandie,* a clandestine pamphlet by Lemaître, was sponsored by leading aristocrats—including Miromesnil, who protected Lemaître early in his career (Popkin, "Pamphlet Journalism"). The printer in Alençon and the bookseller Manoury in Caen were arrested in 1771 for printing anti-ministerial pamphlets (Darnton, *Édition,* 87–91).

100. The term "taking to the streets" is from Dale Van Kley, "The Jansenist Constitutional Legacy in the French Prerevolution, 1750–1789," in *The Political Culture of the Old Régime,* ed. Keith Baker, vol. 1 of *The French Revolution and the Creation of Modern Political Culture* (Oxford: Pergamon Press, 1987), 181.

101. Lucien Sarazin, "Un 'Chalotiste' malouin: Louis-Philippe-Claude Hovius, imprimeur-libraire (1721–1806)," in *Extrait des Annales de la Société historique et archéologique de l'arrondissement de Saint-Malo* (Saint-Servan: J. Haize, 1912); Lepreux, *Gallia,* vol. 4, pp. 40–41, 79–86, 107–10; Bernard Lebeau, "Une Dynastie d'imprimeurs et de maires: Les Hovius," *Bulletin et mémoires de la Société archéologique du département d'Ille-et-Vilaine* 88 (1986): 103–29. The number of licenses in Saint-Malo had been set at two in 1704 and later cut to one. Because of local support, there were still two printers in 1752 and, in 1758, Jean-Baptiste Le Conte and Sébastien Delamare were fighting over the single license, prompting the mayor to ask the intendant in 1759 to persuade chancellor Lamoignon to license both printers. Lamoignon refused, but typically put off the matter by ordering that the position of the first printer to die be extinguished. Three years later, a Saint-Malo bookseller, Louis-Philippe-Claude Hovius—whose request for a license had been rejected in 1754—subcontracted the printing rights of both printers. This was

the situation at the beginning of the Brittany Affair. In 1750, Hovius, born 5 December 1721 to Guillaume-René Hovius and Marie-Anne Couturier, married Hélène Clouet, the daughter of a merchant. Hovius had seven children in the 1750s and their godparents tended to be people of some station.

102. AN V⁶ 1028, 27 September and 1 December 1767. When Hovius was banned from printing, Le Conte took back his place and ceded it for six hundred livres' pension to Valais. Delamare also tried to claim it, and there were disputes about the arrangements between the three men.

103. Marion, *La Bretagne,* 492–93; Sarazin, "Un 'Chalotiste.'" According to Marion, Valais was an "imprimeur en quelque sorte officiel, celui qui prêtait ses presses aux ouvrages favorables aux puissances." Valais complained that Hovius continued to interfere with his business by printing and selling books using supposed names, by "infecting the public with all sorts of evil books attacking religion, the state and good morals," and by initiating suits against him before the Saint-Malo judges.

104. Lepreux, *Gallia,* vol. 4, Documenta, pp. 116–19. The *arrêt en commandement,* dated 24 February 1769, stated that the king had been made aware that, despite the 25 April 1767 order banning him from the printing business, Hovius was continuing through his wife or Lecoq to sell "toutes sortes de livres et souvent les ouvrages aussi dangereux que ceux dont l'impression avait occasionné sa destitution." As such flagrant disobedience to the king's wishes and to the rules of the book trade could not be tolerated, Hovius and his wife were forbidden to engage in any aspect of the book trade, directly or indirectly, and anyone who fronted for him would lose his license. On 3 August 1770 a list of some twenty prohibited books in Hovuis' shop was sent to the intendant, along with a letter informing him of certain suspicions that, despite the seal, books had been removed.

105. Sarazin, "Un 'Chalotiste'"; Lepreux, *Gallia,* vol. 4, p. 85; Darnton, *Édition,* 88–90.

106. During his interrogation in Caen, Hovius informed the subdelegate, "Vous devez être bien heureux que votre exempt n'ait pas été arrêté en Bretagne avec votre ordre; car ma capture fait la plus grande sensation" (quoted in Sarazin, "Un 'Chalotiste,'" 43). When his books were auctioned off, the subdelegate reported that they should have moved the sale to Rennes, because Hovius' friends in Saint-Malo prevented anyone from buying the books.

107. AN E 2519, 4 August 1775; E 2516, 1 October 1775.

108. These three licenses were all issued by order of the Conseil de Dépêches, copies in Lepreux, *Gallia,* vol. 4, Documenta, pp. 142–44, 150–53; Sarazin, "Un 'Chalotiste,'" 50–51. The intendant (Molleville) proposed a compromise: he suggested suppressing the printing house of the young Hovius, but letting him have a bookselling business. Hovius seems to have continued printing in St. Malo with his Dol license. See Patricia Sorel, *La Révolution du livre et de la presse en Bretagne (1780–1830)* (Rennes: Presses universitaires de Rennes, 2004), 21–23.

109. Henri Fréville, *L'Intendance de Bretagne (1689–1790)* (Rennes: Plihon, 1953), 2:208–11. Ravaud's bookshop was also under surveillance.

110. On Vatar, see Arthur de La Borderie, "Histoire de l'imprimerie en Bretagne: Les Races typographiques: Les Vatar, imprimeurs à Rennes et à Nantes," *Revue de Bretagne, de Vendée et d'Anjou* 10 (1893): 405–21; Lepreux, *Gallia,* vol. 4, pp. 110–27. The Vatar family was a very old and established printing family in Rennes; its members had been printers for the Parlement of Brittany since 1653 and king's printers since 1673, and they had followed the Parlement into exile to Vannes in 1675.

111. Lepreux, *Gallia,* vol. 4, pp. 62–63. Pierre-François-Marie Garnier was convicted of printing "des pièces qui auraient exigé une autorisation particulière," but unfortunately we do not know more. In his application for a license he said that his father had had a long career behind him and had printed "à la satisfaction des magistrats et du public" (AN V⁶ 991, 19

December 1757; V⁶ 992, 27 February 1758). According to Marion, Garnier's wife belonged to those publicly devoted to the Chalotais party, whose boutique was the "rendez-vous ordinaire d'une foule de conseillers et de procureurs, était le quartier général de toute l'armée parlementaire" (*La Bretagne,* 568–69).

112. Lepreux, *Gallia,* vol. 4, Documenta, pp. 125–28.

113. Lepreux, *Gallia,* vol. 4, Documenta, pp. 128–34.

114. BN FF 22070 #22. I am assuming that the letter is to Maupeou.

115. On Audran, see Lepreux, *Gallia,* vol. 4, pp. 18–19. His son, Nicolas-Xavier Audran de Montenay, got a license in 1784.

116. In his request to recover the profession of his ancestors, Vatar claimed that "secret declarations" had been the cause of his ruin and that of his children. He had been carrying out his profession with probity and distinction, enjoying the respect of the magistrates and the approval of his fellow citizens, when "secret enemies, jealous of his good fortune," spread damaging rumors that he had printed the Parlement of Brittany's protest against the edict of December 1770 abolishing the offices in the court and creating others to replace them. Like Hovius, Vatar included novel language in his request: if the return of his license would not compensate him entirely for the losses and the disgrace he had endured "pour les affaires qui lui étaient étrangères et dans lesquelles il n'a pu prendre part que par obéissance," it would, nevertheless, soften the bitterness and give him hope to transmit his profession to his children (Lepreux, *Gallia,* vol. 4, Documenta, pp. 137–41).

117. Augustin Cochin, *Les Sociétés de pensée et la Révolution en Bretagne (1788–1789)* (Paris: Champion, 1925), 2:219, 259; AN V⁶ 1121, 15 November 1784. René-François-Charles Vatar got a bookselling license in Rennes in 1784 (AN V⁶ 1119, 19 July 1784). On his future career as a Jacobin journalist and publisher of the *Journal des hommes libres,* see Isser Woloch, *Jacobin Legacy: The Democratic Movement Under the Directory* (Princeton: Princeton University Press, 1970).

118. Marcel Marion, *Le Garde des sceaux Lamoignon et la réforme judiciaire de 1788* (Paris: Hachette, 1905), 204–27. For a good overview of pamphlet production between 1787 and 1789, see Jeremy D. Popkin and Dale Van Kley, "Section 5: The Pre-Revolutionary Debate," in *The French Revolution Research Collection,* ed. Colin Lucas (Oxford: Pergamon Press, 1990), 1–17. Eugène Hatin, *Histoire politique et littéraire de la presse en France* (Paris: Poulet-Malassis et de Broise, 1860), 4:22.

119. Billioud, *Le Livre en Provence,* 67.

120. BN FF 21867.

121. For a new examination of ideas about freedom of the press in the eighteenth century, see Charles Walton, *Policing Public Opinion in the French Revolution: The Culture of Calumny and the Problem of Free Speech* (New York: Oxford University Press, 2009), 51–93.

122. Julian Swann makes this point more generally in *Provincial Power.*

123. The following account is taken from Amable Floquet, *Histoire du parlement de Normandie* (Rouen: Édouard Frère, 1840–42), 7:196–260, and Olivier Chaline, *Godart de Belbeuf: Le Parlement, le roi et les normands* (Luneray: Éditions Bertout, 1996), 457–74. In Rouen the presidial court was elevated to the status of grand bailliage, one of Lamoignon's new (plenary) courts. Louis-Charles-Alexandre Boullenger was named lieutenant general of the grand bailliage of Rouen in August 1787.

124. BN FF 21869.

125. Quoted in Chaline, *Godart,* 469.

126. AN E 2651, 18 July 1788.

127. On Le Boullenger, see Lepreux, *Gallia,* vol. 3, pt. 1, pp. 233–39. In 1766 Jacques-Joseph-Jean-Baptiste Le Boullenger got his father's license (AN V⁶ 1022, 9 June and 14 July 1766) and

became king's printer. Until 1763 the family printed for the Jesuits and afterwards continued a major business in classics and scholarly works. The capitation was thirty-two livres (Mellot, "La Librairie du palais," 125). In 1791 Le Boullenger took the title of *Imprimeur du département de la Seine-Inférieure.*

128. Floquet, *Histoire du Parlement,* 225.

129. Charges of abuse of power during the summer were made in a case against a number of officials, including Havas, who feared being called to testify. Unsure of what to say, he consulted the director of the book trade, Maissemy, who transmitted orders from Barentin that he was to justify his conduct by saying that he was following orders (AN V^1 549, several letters between November 1788 and January 1789; AN E 2652, 8 October 1788). On the revenge taken against those who supported the grand bailliage in Rouen, see Chaline, *Godart,* 475–80.

130. *La Cour plénière, Héroi-tragi-comédie* [1788].

131. On Louis-Joseph Oursel, see *Gallia,* vol. 3, pt. 1, pp. 350–51. He had been warden before Le Boullenger, and when Le Boullenger had to be replaced in January 1789, Pontcarré suggested that Oursel be put back in the position (AN V^1 549, 16 January 1789).

132. *Testament de DesBrugnières* (1788). On the Kornmann case, see Sarah Maza, *Private Lives and Public Affairs: The Causes Célèbres of Prerevolutionary France* (Berkeley: University of California Press, 1993), 295–311.

133. BN FF 21869.

134. BN FF 21869. Frantin and Jean Cortot had worked together in the past and shared political views in 1788–89. I am assuming that this Cortot is the barrister and supporter of the Parlement mentioned in Swann, *Provincial Power,* 382.

135. BN FF 21867. There is a note in the register that this order was not carried out.

136. BN FF 22070 #73–74; BN FF 21869. Claude Lamort in Nancy was banned on 5 July 1788. The bookseller Dominique Bontoux was banned on 20 June 1788. Vignancourt and Daumont in Pau were banned.

137. BN FF 21867; 21869.

138. See the numerous entries in Bernadau, "Tablettes contemporaines," BMBx MS 713, especially 9 December 1787 and 13 and 26 January, 19 February, 2 March, 8 June, and 20–21 October 1788; McLeod, "Social Status," 321.

139. In Lyon, the brother of printer Charles-François Millanois made a moderate speech expressing his dedication to the cause of the Parlement. See Lemay, *Dictionnaire des constituants,* 2:668.

140. BN FF 21869.

141. BN FF 21937.

142. BN FF 21869.

143. BN FF 21869.

144. AN V^1 549. Letter from Bellegarique, 18 January 1789.

145. BN FF 21937.

146. BN FF 216869.

147. Probably *Mémoire sur les états-généraux* (November, 1788). See Kenneth Margerison, *Pamphlets and Public Opinion: The Campaign for a Union of Orders in the Early French Revolution* (West Lafayette: Purdue University Press, 1998), 27.

148. AN V^1 549, 16 January 1789.

149. "Rhetorical dissimulation" is John Hurt's term in *Louis XIV and the Parlements: The Assertion of Royal Authority* (Manchester: Manchester University Press, 2002).

150. Recent work suggests that the judicial world was itself very divided over many constitutional issues (Swann, *Provincial Power,* 411).

151. Robert Darnton has written about how the regime classed *libelles* and high Enlightenment literature together; see "High Enlightenment and the Low-Life of Literature," in *The Literary Underground of the Old Regime* (Cambridge, Mass.: Harvard University Press, 1982), 1–40.

Conclusion

1. Carla Hesse, *Publishing and Cultural Politics in Revolutionary Paris, 1789–1810* (Berkeley: University of California Press, 1991).

2. The Napoleonic era saw explicit comparisons between the regulation of printers and bakers; see M. le Baron Locré, *Discussions sur la liberté de la presse: La censure, la propriété littéraire, l'imprimerie et la librairie qui ont eu lieu dans le Conseil d'État, pendant les années 1808, 1809, 1810, et 1811* (Paris, 1819).

3. Three examples are Robert Darnton, *The Forbidden Best-Sellers of Pre-Revolutionary France* (London: Fontana, 1997); Elizabeth Eisenstein, *Grub Street Abroad: Aspects of the French Cosmopolitan Press from the Age of Louis XIV to the French Revolution* (Oxford: Clarendon Press, 1992); and Roger Chartier, *The Cultural Origins of the French Revolution,* trans. Lydia Cochrane (Durham: Duke University Press, 1991).

4. Among the many works on the constitutional crises in the provinces, see William Doyle, *The Parlement of Bordeaux at the End of the Old Regime, 1771–1790* (New York: St. Martin's Press, 1974), and Julian Swann, *Provincial Power and Absolute Monarchy: The Estates General of Burgundy, 1661–1790* (Cambridge: Cambridge University Press, 2003).

5. On increased dialogue between the commercial and manufacturing sector and state officials more broadly, see Pierre-Claude Reynard, "Early Modern State and Enterprise: Shaping the Dialogue Between the French Monarchy and Paper Manufacturers," *French History* 13 (1999): 1–15; David Kammerling Smith, "Structuring Politics in Early Eighteenth-Century France: The Political Innovations of the French Council of Commerce," *Journal of Modern History* 74 (2002): 490–537.

6. William Beik, "The Absolutism of Louis XIV as Social Collaboration," *Past and Present* 188 (2005): 195–224.

7. Frédéric Barbier and Catherine Bertho Lavenir, *Histoire des médias: De Diderot à internet,* 3rd ed. (Paris: Armand Colin, 2003).

Bibliography

Manuscript Sources

The main sources for this study were the *arrêts du conseil privé* in the Archives nationales, dated from 1669 to 1791 (V^6 556–1151), and the notarial documents in the departmental archives of the provincial towns. These are too numerous to list here.

Archives de la ministère des affaires étrangères, Paris (AE)

AE M et D France, vol. 1278, fols. 300–317v.

Archives nationales de France, Paris (AN)

CONSEIL DU ROI

E 402 (1667)	Arrêts simples en finance
E 2477 (1772)	Arrêts en commandement
E 2513 (1775)	Arrêts en commandement
E 2516 (1775)	Arrêts en commandement
E 2519 (1775)	Arrêts en commandement
E 2538 (1777)	Arrêts en commandement
E 2543 (1778)	Arrêts en commandement
E 2651 (1788)	Arrêts en commandement
E 2652 (1788)	Arrêts en commandement
V^1 549–553	Documents divers sur l'imprimerie et la librairie à la fin de l'ancien régime

Bibliothèque nationale, Paris (BN)

BN FF 6683	Siméon-Prosper Hardy, "Mes Loisirs, ou Journal d'événemens telsqu'ils parviennent à ma connoissance," entry of 3 January 1779
BN FF 18600	Recueil de pièces provenant de la collection Séguier-Coislin
BN Joly de Fleury 1682	Libraires, imprimeurs et censure de livres (1507–1786)

ARCHIVES DE LA CHAMBRE SYNDICALE DE LA LIBRAIRIE ET DE L'IMPRIMERIE DE PARIS

BN FF 21815	Bureau de la librairie. Mémoires divers.
BN FF 21820	Bureau de la librairie. Mémoires divers.
BN FF 21832	Bureau de la librairie. Etat général des imprimeurs du royaume en 1777.

BN FF 21833   Bureau de la librairie. Mémoires divers

BN FF 21867   Registre contenant les extraits des réponses faites tant aux différents particuliers qu'aux personnes de l'administration, 1 octobre 1787–5 décembre 1788

BN FF 21868   Répertoire des lettres reçues et répondues, décembre 1785–octobre 1787

BN FF 21869   Répertoire alphabétique des personnes qui ont demandé des privilèges, permissions, dispenses, etc., concernant la librairie-imprimerie, 1788

BN FF 21870   Registre de la librairie contentieuse: Demandes de réception d'imprimeurs et d'établissements d'imprimeries en province, avec les décisions prises en marge de 1767 à 1787

BN FF 21937   Registre de la librairie sous la direction de M. de Villedeuil, 1784–1787

ACTES ROYAUX

BN F 23663   Actes royaux, 1759

BN F 23664   Actes royaux, 1764

ARCHIVES DE LA DIRECTION DE LA LIBRAIRIE (COLLECTION ANISSON)

BN FF 22063   Règlements généraux de la librairie (1728–99)

BN FF 22065   Réceptions d'imprimeurs et libraires (1586–1750)

BN FF 22066   Réceptions d'imprimeurs et libraires (1723–77)

BN FF 22068   Règlements de la librairie et de l'imprimerie (1551–1768)

BN FF 22070   Règlements de la librairie et de l'imprimerie (1769–89)

BN FF 22073   Privilèges et permissions (1729–89)

BN FF 22074   Livres contrefaits (1551–1749)

BN FF 22075   Livres contrefaits (1731–87)

BN FF 22077–78   Imprimeurs du roi

BN FF 22080   Inspecteurs de la librairie (1687–1787)

BN FF 22094   Libelles diffamatoires et autres livres prohibés (1759–60)

BN FF 22114   Marchands privilégiés suivant la Cour, etc. (1544–1773)

BN FF 22124   Libraires Imprimeurs des différentes villes rangées par généralités: Aix-Auvergne (1617–1778)

BN FF 22125   Libraires Imprimeurs des différentes villes rangées par généralités: Bordeaux-Corse (1560–1785)

BN FF 22126   Libraires Imprimeurs des différentes villes rangées par généralités (1623–1788) Caen-Franche-Comté (1623–1788)

BN FF 22127   Libraires Imprimeurs des différentes villes rangées par généralités: Grenoble-Lorraine (1618–1789)

BN FF 22128	Libraires Imprimeurs des différentes villes rangées par généralités: Lyon-Orléans (1542–1787)
BN FF 22129	Libraires Imprimeurs des différentes villes rangées par généralités: Paris-Tours (1565–1788)
BN FF 22131	Minutes d'arrêts de Conseil sur différents objets de librairie, 1700–1708
BN FF 22173	Règlement de la librairie (1665–1703)
BN FF NA 399–400	État de la Librairie en France sous M. Le Chancelier Pontchartrain
BN FF NA 3344	Librairie sous M. de Malesherbes
BN FF NA 3546	Receuil de documents sur l'histoire de la librairie (1703–53)
BN FF NA 11820	Correspondance

Bibliothèque de l'Arsenal, Archives de la Bastille, Paris

| MS 1229 | Dossier Trebosq |

Archives départementales du Bouches du Rhône, Aix (ADBR)

| C 1347 | Correspondance |

Archives départementales de la Gironde, Bordeaux (ADG)

2B 58–59	Cour des aides
7B 1450 Registre	Livre journal, Ducot
10B 56	Jurisdiction des monnaies. Dossier de procédure
12B 357	Jurats de Bordeaux, Plainte et Informations
12B 386–389	Jurats de Bordeaux, Plainte et Informations
C 301	Correspondance avec les subdélégués
C 2912	Capitation
C 3308–3315	Imprimerie et Librairie
C 3771	Instruction publique et librairie
2E 1203	Droits de familles
2E 1616	Lacourt
6E 68	Imprimeurs-Libraires, 1582–XVIIIe

Archives municipales de Bordeaux (AMBx)

AA 26	Etats généraux
BB 53, 88, 127	Registres de la Jurade: Serments des imprimeurs et de libraires devant les Jurats
GG 667	Parish registers
HH 98	Corporation des Imprimeurs et Libraires

Bibliothèque municipale de Bordeaux (BMBx)

J 1185	*Chartrier ou recueil par ordre chronologique de divers titres, pièces concernant les libraires et les imprimeurs jurés de l'université de Bordeaux*, 2 vols.
MS 712	Augustin Laboubée, *Notes recueillies pour la Bibliothèque historique de la Guyenne ou mémoires pour servir à l'histoire de sciences, des lettres et des arts de cette province*
MS 713	Pierre Bernadau, "Tablettes contemporaines, historiques et cryptographiques de l'Ecouteur bordelais ou mémoires secrètes pour servir à l'histoire générale et anecdotique du temps qui court"
MS 1545–1548	Chartrier des libraires-imprimeurs de Bordeaux, 1500–1789, 4 vols.

Archives départmentales du Côte d'Or, Dijon (ADCD)

B2	Arrêt du parlement de Dijon, 12 January 1707
C 380	Intendance, Imprimerie, librairie, 1721–86
C 381	Intendance, Estampillage et colportage, 1779–80

Bibliothèque de Dijon (BMDijon)

MS 745	Communauté des imprimeurs-libraires de Dijon: Registre de déliberations (10 mai 1772–22 février 1790)
MS 1431	Correspondance Fontette

Archives départementales du Rhône, Lyon (ADR)

BP 2294	Succession Barret, 1786
BP 3615	Imprimeurs et libraires (assemblés, réceptions, règlements etc. XVIe–XVIIIe siècle)
1C 221	Imprimeur du Roi à Lyon
1C 252	Procédure extraordinaire faite par commission du Conseil contre Donat et Faucheux
7C	Consignations du produit des biens meubles et immeubles: Dossiers individuels

7C 59   Declaustre
7C 166   Vialon

Archives municipales de Lyon (AMLyon)

HH 98–103   Commerce et Industrie

Archives départmentales du Bouches de Rhône, Marseille (ADBR)

13B 533   Bilans, 1725 (Mallard)
240E 54   Libraires et imprimeurs de Marseille

Archives départementales du Gard

E Dépot 36/52   Requête de Pierre Beaume, 1774

Archives départementales d'Ille-et-Vilaine, Rennes (ADI-et-V)

C 1461–1471   Intendance de Bretagne: Imprimeurs, libraires

Archives départementales de la Seine Maritime, Rouen (ADSM)

201 BP 552   Faillites: Etat de Veuve Besonge et fils marchands à Rouen, 1784
C 145   Correspondance et papiers relatifs aux imprimeurs et libraires de Rouen
J 217–18   Papiers Miromesnil

Archives départementales de la Haute Garonne, Toulouse (ADHG)

C 146   La Librairie à Toulouse, 1745–1788
C 147   L'Imprimerie et la librairie à Toulouse et en Languedoc, 1756–1789
E 1315   Livre de la communauté, 1787–1791

Bibliothèque municipale de Toulouse (BMToulouse)

MS 1010   Livre de la communauté des imprimeurs, 1733–1769
MS 1011   Livre de la communauté des imprimeurs, 1770–1787

Published Sources

Primary Sources

À juger en la cour consulaire de cette ville pour Paul-Anne Pallandre jeune, libraire à Bordeaux contre Antoine Pallandre son frère aîné, aussi libraire de ladite ville.

Arrêts du conseil du roi: Règne de Louis XVI: Inventaire analytique des arrêts en commandement. Vol. 1, *10 mai 1774–12 mai 1776 (ministère Turgot),* by Danielle Gallet-Guerne. Paris: Archives nationales, 1978. Vol. 2, *12 mai 1776–31 décembre 1778,* by Brigitte Schmauch. Paris: Archives nationales, 1991.

Catalogue des livres qui se trouvent chez Pierre Phillippot libraire-imprimeur sur les fossés de l'hôtel de ville et dans son cabinet littéraire, Grand-Salle du Palais. [1780s.]

Clément, Pierre. *Lettres, instructions et mémoires de Colbert.* Vol. 5. Paris: Imprimerie nationale, 1868.

La Cour Plénière: Héroi-tragi-comédie. [1788.]

Debien, Gabriel, ed. *Correspondance de Félix Faulcon.* 2 vols. Poitiers: Société des archives historique du Poitou, 1939.

Depping, Georges-Bernard, ed. *Correspondance administrative sous le règne de Louis XIV.* 4 vols. Paris: Imprimerie impériale, 1850–55.

Feillet, Alphonse. *Oeuvres du Cardinal Retz.* Paris: Hachette, 1872.

Fiévée, Joseph. *Correspondance et relations de J. Fiévée avec Bonaparte, premier consul et empereur pendant onze années (1802–1813).* 3 vols. Paris: A. Desrez [etc.], 1836.

Griselle, Eugène. "La Contrefaçon en librairie à Lyon vers l'an 1702: Mémoire et lettres autographes du libraire Baritel, premier adjoint de la communauté des libraires et imprimeurs." *Bulletin du bibliophile et du bibliothécaire* (1903): 181–96, 245–53.

Hermant, Godefroi. *Mémoires de Godefroi Hermant sur l'histoire ecclésiastique du XVIIe siècle, 1630–1663.* Edited by Augustin Gazier. 6 vols. Paris: Plon, 1905–10.

Jourdan, [Athanase-Jean-Léger], Decrusy, and [François-André] Isambert, et al., eds. *Recueil général des anciennes lois françaises depuis l'an 420 jusqu'à la Révolution de 1789.* Paris: Belin-Leprieur, 1821–33. [Available online at http://cour-de-france.fr/article 348.html.]

Jovy, Ernest. *Le Journal de Monsieur de Saint-Gilles.* Paris: Vrin, 1936.

Los Rios, Jean François de. *Oeuvres de François de Los Rios libraire à Lyon, contenant plusieurs descriptions et observations sur des objets curieux ou particuliers, aventures, voyages etc.* London [Lyon]: Molin, 1789.

Malesherbes, Chrétien-Guillaume de Lamoignon de. *Mémoires sur la librairie et sur la liberté de la presse.* 1809. Reprint, Geneva: Slatkine, 1969.

———. *Mémoires sur la librairie: Mémoire sur la liberté de la presse.* Edited by Roger Chartier. Paris: Imprimerie nationale, 1994.

Manuel de l'auteur et du libraire. Paris: Veuve Duchesne, 1777.

Mémoire à Monseigneur de Maupeou chancelier et garde des sceaux. . . . [1766.]

Mémoire pour Paul Caillier-Gobain, demandeur contre . . . le sieur Labottière syndic des imprimeurs et libraires de la ville de Bordeaux, défendeur. [1714.]

Mémoire pour Pierre Phillippot et Joseph Brulle, au nom et comme syndic et adjoint des Imprimeurs et Libraires jurés de l'université de Bordeaux, ses membres et suppôts contre Michel Racle, ci-devant dentiste et bachelier en médecine. [1770.]

Mémoire pour sieur Arnaud-Antoine Pallandre aîné, . . . contre sieur François Pelusset, ancien procureur à l'Hôtel de Ville. 1783.

Moulé, Léon. "Correspondance de Claude Bourgelat fondateur des écoles vétérinaires." *Bulletin de la Société centrale de médecine vétérinaire* (1911–12): 58–64, 115–20, 216–32, 342–47, 548–53.

Réclamation de M. Phillippot, imprimeur du parlement de Bordeaux, contre une de calumnies consignées dans un écrit du sieur Bernadau. [1789.]

Sainte-Beuve, Charles-Augustin. *Port-Royal.* Edited by Maxime Leroy. 3 vols. Paris: Gallimard, 1961–64.

Saugrain, Claude-Marin, ed. *Code de la librairie et imprimerie de Paris ou conférence du réglement arrêté au conseil d'état du roi le 28 février 1723 et rendu commun pour tout le royaume, par arrêt du conseil d'état du 24 mars 1744 avec les anciennes ordonnances. . . .* 1744. Reprint, Westmead: Gregg International, 1971.

Verdier, Pierre Le, ed. *Correspondance politique et administrative de Miromesnil, premier président du parlement de Normandie.* 5 vols. Rouen: Lestringant, 1899–1903.

Selected Secondary Sources

Adams, Christine. *A Taste for Comfort and Status: A Bourgeois Family in Eighteenth-Century France.* University Park: Pennsylvania State University Press, 2000.

Andréani, Roland. "Une Famille d'imprimeurs à Montpellier de Louis XVI à Napoléon III: Les Tournel." *Actes du 106e Congrès national des sociétés savantes, Perpignan, 1981: Section d'histoire moderne et contemporaine: Histoire du Roussillon et questions diverses* 2 (1984): 117–27.

Antoine, Michel. *Le Conseil du roi sous le règne de Louis XV.* Geneva: Droz, 1970.

———. *Le Fonds du conseil d'état du roi aux archives nationales.* Paris: Imprimerie nationale, 1955.

———. *Le Gouvernement et l'administration sous Louis XV: Dictionnaire biographique.* Paris: CNRS, 1978.

Aquilon, Pierre. "Les Réalités provinciales." In Chartier and Martin, *Histoire de l'édition française: Le Livre conquérant,* 436–54.

Arbour, Roméo. *Dictionnaire des femmes libraires en France (1470–1870).* Geneva: Droz, 2003.

Auerbach, Stephen. "'Encourager le commerce et répandre les lumières': The Press, the Provinces, and the Origins of the Revolution in France, 1750–1789." Ph.D diss., University of Louisiana, 2001.

Baker, Keith Michael. "French Political Thought at the Accession of Louis XVI." *Journal of Modern History* 50 (1978): 279–303.

———, ed. *The Political Culture of the Old Régime.* Vol. 1 of *The French Revolution and the Creation of Modern Political Culture.* Oxford: Pergamon Press, 1987.

Baker, Larry Lee. "Politics, Privilege, and Political Culture: Dijon During the French Revolution." Ph.D diss., University of Illinois at Chicago, 2002.

Barbiche, Bernard. "Le Régime de l'édition." In Chartier and Martin, *Histoire de l'édition française: Le Livre conquérant,* 457–71.

Barbiche, Bernard, Jean-Pierre Poussou, and Alain Tallon, eds. *Pouvoirs, contestations et comportements dans l'Europe moderne.* Paris: Presses de l'université Paris-Sorbonne, 2005.

Barbier, Frédéric. "Les Henry, imprimeurs et libraires à Valenciennes au XVIIIe siècle." *Mémoires du cercle archeologique et historique de Valenciennes au XVIIIe siècle* 10 (1987): 61–80.

———. *Histoire du livre.* Paris: Armand Colin, 2000.

———. *Lumières du nord: Imprimeurs, libraires et "gens du livre" dans le nord au XVIIIe siècle (1701–1789): Dictionnaire prosopographique.* Geneva: Droz, 2002.

———. *Trois cents ans de librairie et d'imprimerie: Berger-Levrault, 1676–1830.* Geneva: Droz, 1979.

Barbier, Frédéric, and Catherine Bertho Lavenir. *Histoire des médias: De Diderot à internet*. 3rd ed. Paris: Armand Colin, 2003.

Barbier, Frédéric, and Sabine Juratic. "Autopsie d'une famille: Les Desaint." *Revue française d'histoire du livre* 98–99 (1998): 189–98.

Barbier, Frédéric, Sabine Juratic, and Annick Mellerio. *Dictionnaire des imprimeurs, libraires et gens du livre à Paris, 1701–1789, A–C*. Geneva: Droz, 2007.

Barbier, Frédéric, Sabine Juratic, and Dominique Varry, eds. *L'Europe et le livre: Réseaux et pratiques du négoce de librairie XVIe–XIXe siècles*. Paris: Klincksieck, 1996.

Barbier, Frédéric, et al., eds. *Le Livre et l'historien: Études offertes en l'honneur du professeur Henri-Jean Martin*. Geneva: Droz, 1997.

Bayard, Françoise. *Vivre à Lyon sous l'ancien régime*. Paris: Perrin, 1997.

Beaurepaire, Georges de. *Le Contrôle de la librairie à Rouen à la fin du XVIIIe siècle*. Rouen: A. Lainé, 1929.

Bège, Denise. "Une Compagnie à la recherche de sa raison d'être: La Cour des aides de Guyenne et ses magistrats, 1553–1790." Doctoral thesis, Université de Paris I, 1974.

Beik, William. *Absolutism and Society in Seventeenth-Century France: State Power and Provincial Aristocracy in Languedoc*. Cambridge: Cambridge University Press, 1985.

———. "The Absolutism of Louis XIV as Social Collaboration." *Past and Present* 188 (2005): 195–224.

———. *Louis XIV and Absolutism: A Brief Study with Documents*. Boston: Bedford/St. Martin's, 2000.

Bell, David. "Lawyers into Demagogues: Chancellor Maupeou and the Transformation of Legal Practice in France, 1771–1789." *Past and Present* 130 (1991): 107–41.

Berlanstein, Lenard. *The Barristers of Toulouse in the Eighteenth Century, 1740–1793*. Baltimore: Johns Hopkins University Press, 1975.

Bien, David. "The Army in the French Enlightenment: Reform, Reaction, and Revolution." *Past and Present* 85 (1979): 68–98.

Billioud, Jacques. *Le Livre en Provence du XVIe au XVIIIe siècle*. Marseille: Saint-Victor, 1962.

Birn, Raymond. "Book Production and Censorship in France (1700–1715)." In *Books and Society in History*, edited by Kenneth Carpenter, 145–71. New York: Bowker, 1983.

———. *La Censure royale des livres dans la France des Lumières*. Paris: Odile Jacob, 2007.

———. "La Contrebande et la saisie de livres à l'aube du siècle des Lumières." *Revue d'histoire moderne et contemporaine* 28 (1981): 158–73.

———. "Malesherbes and the Call for a Free Press." In Darnton and Roche, *Revolution in Print*, 50–66.

———. "The Profits of Ideas: *Privilèges en librairie* in Eighteenth-Century France." *Eighteenth-Century Studies* 4 (1971): 131–68.

———. "Religious Toleration and Freedom of Expression." In *The French Idea of Freedom: The Old Regime and the Declaration of Rights of 1789*, edited by Dale Van Kley, 265–99. Stanford: Stanford University Press, 1994.

Blanc-Rouquette, Marie-Thérèse. "Une Dynastie d'imprimeurs toulousains, XVIIe, XVIIIe siècles." *Histoire du Languedoc: Actes du 110e Congrès national des sociétés savantes: Section d'histoire moderne et contemporaine* 2 (1985): 115–27.

———. "Un Imprimeur toulousain au XVIIIe siècle: Jean-Florent Baour." *Revue française d'histoire du livre* 27 (1980): 297–317.

———. *La Presse et l'information à Toulouse, des origines à 1789.* Toulouse: Faculté des lettres et sciences humaines, 1967.

Bosher, John F. *French Finances, 1770–1795: From Business to Bureaucracy.* 1970. Reprint, Cambridge: Cambridge University Press, 2008.

Bossenga, Gail. *The Politics of Privilege: Old Regime and Revolution in Lille.* Cambridge: Cambridge University Press, 1991.

Bouchard, Marcel. *De l'Humanisme à l'Encyclopédie: L'Esprit public en Bourgogne sous l'ancien régime.* Paris: Hachette, 1930.

Bouchon, Georges. *Histoire d'une imprimerie bordelaise, 1600–1900.* Bordeaux: Gounouilhou, 1901.

Brives-Cazes, Emile. *De la police des livres en Guyenne (1713–1785).* Bordeaux: Gounouilhou, 1883.

Buirette, Charles. *Histoire de la ville de Sainte-Ménehould.* 1837. Reprint, Paris: Office de l'édition du livre d'histoire, 1997.

Campbell, Peter R. *Politics in Old Regime France, 1720–1745.* London: Routledge, 1996.

Carré, Henri. *La Fin des parlements (1788–1790).* Paris: Hachette, 1912.

Carrier, Hubert. *La Presse de la Fronde (1648–1653): Les Mazarinades.* Vol. 1, *La Conquête de l'opinion.* Geneva: Droz, 1989.

———. *La Presse de la Fronde (1648–1653): Les Mazarinades.* Vol. 2, *Les Hommes du livre.* Geneva: Droz, 1991.

Censer, Jack. *The French Press in the Age of Enlightenment.* London: Routledge, 1994.

Chaline, Olivier. *Godart de Belbeuf: Le Parlement, le roi et les normands.* Luneray: Éditions Bertout, 1996.

Chanteau, Francis de. "De la corporation des imprimeurs-libraires de la ville de Metz." *Mémoires de la Société d'archéologie et d'histoire de la Moselle* 8 (1866): 143–80.

Chapman, Sara. *Private Ambition and Political Alliances: The Phélypeaux de Pontchartrain Family and Louis XIV's Government, 1650–1715.* Rochester: University of Rochester Press, 2004.

Chartier, Roger. *The Cultural Origins of the French Revolution.* Translated by Lydia Cochrane. Durham: Duke University Press, 1991.

———. "L'Imprimerie en France à la fin de l'ancien régime: L'État général des imprimeurs de 1777." *Revue française d'histoire du livre* 6 (1973): 253–79.

———. "Livre et espace: Circuits commerciaux et géographie culturelle de la librairie lyonnaise au XVIIIe siècle." *Revue française d'histoire du livre* 1 (1971): 77–108.

———. "Pamphlets and Gazettes." In Chartier and Martin, *Histoire de l'édition française: Le Livre conquérant,* 503–26.

———. "Trajectoires et tensions culturelles de l'ancien régime." In *Les Formes de la culture,* edited by André Burguière, 307–92. Paris: Seuil, 1993.

Chartier, Roger, Marie-Madeleine Compère, and Dominique Julia, eds. *L'Éducation en France du XVIe au XVIIIe siècle.* Paris: Société d'édition d'enseignement supérieur, 1976.

Chartier, Roger, and Henri-Jean Martin, eds. *Histoire de l'édition française.* Vol. 1, *Le Livre conquérant: Du moyen age au milieu du XVIIe siècle.* Vol. 2, *Le Livre triomphant, 1660–1830.* Paris: Fayard, 1989, 1990.

Chassaigne, Marc. *La Lieutenance générale de police de Paris.* 1906. Reprint, Geneva: Slatkine, 1975.

Chaussinaud-Nogaret, Guy. *Choiseul (1719–1785): Naissance de la gauche.* Paris: Perrin, 1998.

Chauvet, Paul. *Les Ouvriers du livre en France des origines à la Révolution de 1789.* Paris: Presses universitaires de France, 1959.

Clément-Janin, Michel-Hilaire. *Les Imprimeurs et les libraires dans la Côte-d'Or.* 1883. Reprint, Geneva: Slatkine, 1971.

Cochin, Augustin. *Les Sociétés de pensée et la Révolution en Bretagne (1788–1789).* Paris: Champion, 1925.

Collins, James. *The State in Early Modern France.* Cambridge: Cambridge University Press, 1995.

Coyecque, Ernest. *Inventaire de la collection Anisson sur l'histoire de l'imprimerie et la librairie principalement à Paris.* 2 vols. 1900. Reprint, New York: Burt Franklin, 1964.

Crook, Malcolm. *Toulon in War and Revolution: From the Ancien Régime to the Restoration.* Manchester: Manchester University Press, 1991.

Cuillieron, Monique. *Contribution à l'étude de la rébellion des cours souveraines sous le règne de Louis XVI: Le Cas de la cour des aides et finances de Montauban.* Paris: Presses universitaires de France, 1983.

Darnton, Robert. *The Business of Enlightenment: A Publishing History of the Encyclopédie, 1775–1800.* Cambridge, Mass.: Harvard University Press, 1979.

———. *The Corpus of Clandestine Literature in France, 1769–1789.* New York: Norton, 1995.

———. *Édition et sédition: L'Univers de la littérature clandestine au XVIIIe siècle.* Paris: Gallimard, 1991.

———. *The Forbidden Best-Sellers of Pre-Revolutionary France.* London: Fontana, 1997.

———. *The Literary Underground of the Old Regime.* Cambridge, Mass.: Harvard University Press, 1982.

———. "Reading, Writing, and Publishing." In *The Literary Underground of the Old Regime,* 167–208. Cambridge, Mass.: Harvard University Press, 1982.

———. "The Science of Piracy: A Crucial Ingredient in Eighteenth-Century Publishing." In *Studies on Voltaire and the Eighteenth Century* 12 (Oxford: Voltaire Foundation, 2003), 3–29.

Darnton, Robert, and Daniel Roche, eds. *Revolution in Print: The Press in France, 1775–1800.* Berkeley: University of California Press, 1989.

Darnton, Robert, and Michel Schlup, eds. *Le Rayonnement d'une maison d'édition dans l'Europe des Lumières: La Société typographique de Neuchâtel, 1769–1789.* Neuchâtel: Gilles Attinger, 2005.

Davis, Natalie Zemon. "Le Monde de l'imprimerie humaniste: Lyon." In Chartier and Martin, *Histoire de l'édition française: Le Livre conquérant,* 303–35.

———. "Publisher Guillaume Rouillé, Businessman and Humanist." In *Editing Sixteenth-Century Texts,* edited by R. J. Schoeck, 72–112. Toronto: University of Toronto Press, 1966.

———. "A Trade Union in Sixteenth-Century France." *Economic History Review,* 2nd ser., 19 (1960): 48–69.

Dawson, Robert. *The French Booktrade and the "Permission Simple" of 1777: Copyright and Public Domain.* Oxford: Voltaire Foundation, 1992.

De Baecque, Antoine. "Le Commerce de libelle interdit à Paris (1790–1791)." *Dix-huitième siècle* 21 (1989): 233–46.

Delalain, Paul. *L'Imprimerie et la librairie à Paris de 1789 à 1813.* Paris: Delalain frères, 1899.

Demeulenaere-Douyère, Christiane, and David J. Sturdy. *L'Enquête du Régent 1716–1718: Sciences, techniques et politique dans la France pré-industrielle.* Turnhout: Brepols, 2008.

Desbarreaux-Bernard, Tibulle. "L'Inquisition des livres à Toulouse au XVIIe siècle." *Mémoires de l'Académie des sciences, inscriptions et belles-lettres de Toulouse* (1874): 330–81.

Desgraves, Louis. "Les Bulletins d'information imprimés à Bordeaux au XVIe et XVIIe siècles." *Bulletin de la Société des bibliophiles de Guyenne* (1964): 13–52.

———. *Dictionnaire des imprimeurs, libraires et relieurs de Bordeaux et de la Gironde (XVe–XVIIIe siècles).* Baden-Baden: Valentin Koerner, 1995.

———. *Études sur l'imprimerie dans le sud-ouest de la France aux XVe, XVIe et XVIIe siècles.* Amsterdam: Erasmus, 1968.

———. "L'Imprimeur bordelais Jacques Mongiron-Millanges (1649–1692)." In *Extrait du Bulletin philologique et historique de Comité des travaux historiques et scientifiques.* Paris: Imprimerie nationale, 1958.

———. "L'Introduction de l'imprimerie dans le sud-ouest de la France jusqu'à la fin du XVIe siècle." In *Villes d'imprimerie et moulins à papier du XIVe au XVIe siècle: Aspects économiques et sociaux,* 39–80. Brussels: Crédit Communale de Belgique, 1976.

Douladoure, Jean-François, and Pierre Douladoure. *Une Vieille Famille de maîtres-imprimeurs toulousains.* Toulouse: Les Frères Douladoure, 1937.

Doyle, William. *Origins of the French Revolution.* 2nd ed. Oxford: Oxford University Press, 1988.

———. *The Parlement of Bordeaux at the End of the Old Regime, 1771–1790.* New York: St. Martin's Press, 1974.

———. *Venality: The Sale of Offices in Eighteenth-Century France.* Oxford: Clarendon Press, 1996.

Doyon, André. *Un Agent royaliste pendant la Révolution: Pierre-Jacques Le Maître (1790–1795).* Paris: Société des études robespierristes, 1969.

Duccini, Hélène. *Faire voir, faire croire: L'Opinion publique sous Louis XIII.* Paris: Champ Vallon, 2003.

Ducourtieux, Paul. *Les Barbou, imprimeurs Lyon-Limoges-Paris.* Limoges: Ducourtieux, 1896.

Dumont, Nelly. "Aimé Delaroche, imprimeur lyonnais du XVIIIe siècle et la presse locale." Master's thesis, École nationale et supérieure de bibliothécaires, Villeurbanne, 1982.

Dureau, Jeanne-Marie. "À propos de quelques sources lyonnaises de l'histoire du livre et de la lecture à Lyon." In *Mélanges d'histoire lyonnaise offerts par ses amis à Monsieur Henri Hours,* 135–51. Lyon: Éditions lyonnaises d'art et d'histoire, 1990.

———. "Les Premiers Ateliers français." In Chartier and Martin, *Histoire de l'édition française: Le Livre conquérant,* 186–99.

Éboli, Gilles. "Les David, imprimeurs-libraires à Aix-en-Provence." In Chartier and Martin, *Histoire de l'édition française: Le Livre triomphant,* 368–69.

Edmonds, William. *Jacobinism and the Revolt of Lyon, 1789–1793.* Oxford: Clarendon Press, 1990.

Egret, Jean. *Louis XV et l'opposition parlementaire, 1715–1774.* Paris: A. Colin, 1970.

———. *Le Parlement du Dauphiné et les affaires publiques dans la deuxième moitié du XVIIIe siècle.* 2 vols. Roanne: Éditions Horvath, 1942.

Eisenstein, Elizabeth. *Grub Street Abroad: Aspects of the French Cosmopolitan Press from the Age of Louis XIV to the French Revolution.* Oxford: Clarendon Press, 1992.

———. *The Printing Press as an Agent of Change: Communications and Cultural Transformations in Early Modern Europe.* 2 vols. Cambridge: Cambridge University Press, 1979.

Farge, Arlette. *Subversive Words: Public Opinion in Eighteenth-Century France*. Translated by Rosemary Morris. University Park: Pennsylvania State University Press, 1995.

Fédou, René, et al., eds. *Cinq Études lyonnaises*. Geneva: Droz, 1966.

Félix, Joël. *Finances et politique au siècle des Lumières: Le Ministère L'Averdy, 1763–1768*. Paris: Comité pour l'histoire économique et financière de la France, 1999.

Floquet, Amable. *Histoire du parlement de Normandie*. 7 vols. Rouen: Édouard Frère, 1840–42.

Fortuny, Claudette. "Les Éditions lyonnaises de *l'Histoire des deux Indes* de l'abbé Raynal." *Histoire et civilisation du livre* 2 (2006): 169–85.

Fréville, Henri. *L'Intendance de Bretagne (1689–1790)*. 3 vols. Rennes: Plihon, 1953.

Garden, Maurice. "Formes de contrôle du pouvoir local: Lyon en 1721." In *Pouvoir, ville et société en Europe, 1650–1750: Actes du colloque international du CNRS, octobre 1981*, edited by Georges Livet and Bernard Vogler, 173–82. Paris: Éditions Ophrys, 1983.

———. *Lyon et les lyonnais au XVIIIe siècle*. Paris: Société d'Édition "Les Belles-Lettres," 1970.

Gasc, Michèle. "La Naissance de la presse périodique locale à Lyon: Les *Affiches de Lyon, annonces et avis divers*." *Études sur la presse* 3 (1978): 61–80.

Gee, Malcolm, and Tim Kirk, eds. *Printed Matters: Printing, Publishing, and Urban Culture in Europe in the Modern Period*. Aldershot: Ashgate, 2002.

Girard, Alain R. "Les Incunables rouennais: Imprimerie et culture au XVe siècle." *Revue française d'histoire du livre* 53 (1986): 463–525.

Golden, Richard. *The Godly Rebellion: Parisian Curés and the Religious Fronde, 1652–1662*. Chapel Hill: University of North Carolina Press, 1981.

Granges de Surgères, le marquis de. "Contribution à l'histoire de l'imprimerie en France: Notes sur les anciens imprimeurs nantais (XVe à XVIIIe siècles)." *Bulletin du bibliophile et du bibliothécaire* (1897): 240–46, 414–22, 472–79, 525–33, 562–70.

Greenblatt, Stephen. *Renaissance Self-Fashioning: From More to Shakespeare*. Chicago: University of Chicago Press, 1980.

Hamscher, Albert. *The Conseil Privé and the Parlements in the Age of Louis XIV: A Study in French Absolutism*. Philadelphia: American Philosophical Society, 1987.

———. "Une Contestation évitée: La Prétendue lettre du Parlement de Paris, 1667." In Barbiche, Poussou, and Tallon, *Pouvoirs, contestations et comportements dans l'Europe moderne*, 659–73.

———. *The Parlement of Paris After the Fronde, 1653–1673*. Pittsburgh: University of Pittsburgh Press, 1976.

Hardman, John. *French Politics, 1774–1789: From the Accession of Louis XVI to the Fall of the Bastille*. London: Longman, 1995.

———. *Louis XVI*. New Haven: Yale University Press, 1993.

Hatin, Eugène. *Histoire politique et littéraire de la presse en France*. Vol. 4. Paris: Poulet-Malassis et de Broise, 1860.

Hayden, J. Michael. "The Uses of Political Pamphlets: The Example of 1614–15 in France." *Canadian Journal of History* 21 (1986): 143–66.

Herrmann-Mascard, Nicole. *La Censure des livres à Paris à la fin de l'ancien régime (1750–1789)*. Paris: Presses universitaires de France, 1968.

Hesse, Carla. *Publishing and Cultural Politics in Revolutionary Paris, 1789–1810*. Berkeley: University of California Press, 1991.

Higman, Francis. "Le Levain de l'Évangile." In Chartier and Martin, *Histoire de l'édition française: Le Livre conquérant,* 373–403.

Hurt, John J. *Louis XIV and the Parlements: The Assertion of Royal Authority.* Manchester: Manchester University Press, 2002.

Isnard, Albert, and Suzanne Honoré. *Catalogue générale des livres imprimés de la Bibliothèque nationale: Actes royaux.* 7 vols. Paris: Imprimerie nationale, 1910–60.

Jones, Colin. "The Great Chain of Buying: Medical Advertisement, the Bourgeois Public Sphere, and the Origins of the French Revolution." *American Historical Review* 101 (1996): 13–40.

———. "Pulling Teeth in Eighteenth-Century Paris." *Past and Present* 166 (2000): 100–145.

Jouhaud, Christian. "Le Conseil du roi, Bordeaux et les bordelais (1579–1610, 1630–1680)." *Annales du Midi* 93 (1981): 377–96.

———. *Mazarinades: La Fronde des mots.* Paris: Aubier, 1985.

Kammerling Smith, David. "Structuring Politics in Early Eighteenth-Century France: The Political Innovations of the French Council of Commerce." *Journal of Modern History* 74 (2002): 490–537.

Kaplan, Steven. "The Luxury Guilds in Paris in the Eighteenth Century." *Francia* 9 (1981): 257–98.

———. "Social Stratification and Representation in the Corporate World of Eighteenth-Century France: Turgot's 'Carnival.'" In *Work in France: Representations, Meaning, Organization, and Practice,* edited by Steven Kaplan and Cynthia Koepp, 176–228. Ithaca: Cornell University Press, 1986.

Kelley, Donald R. *The Beginning of Ideology: Consciousness and Society in the French Reformation.* Cambridge: Cambridge University Press, 1981.

Kettering, Sharon. *Patrons, Brokers, and Clients in Seventeenth-Century France.* Oxford: Oxford University Press, 1986.

Labadie, Ernest. *Notices biographiques sur les imprimeurs et les libraires bordelais des XVIe, XVIIe et XVIIIe siècles.* Bordeaux: Mounastre-Picamilh, 1900.

La Bonninière de Beaumont, Hugues de. "L'Administration de la librairie et la censure des livres de 1700 à 1750." Thesis, École des chartes, 1966.

La Borderie, Arthur de. "Histoire de l'imprimerie en Bretagne: Les Races typographiques: Les Vatar, imprimeurs à Rennes et à Nantes." *Revue de Bretagne, de Vendée et d'Anjou* 10 (1893): 405–21.

Laffont, Jean-Luc. "La Production réglementaire des Capitouls de Toulouse sous l'ancien régime." *Bibliothèque de l'École des chartes* 156 (1998): 481–536.

Lannette-Claverie, Claude. "L'Enquête de 1701 sur l'état de la librairie dans le royaume." Thesis, École des chartes, 1964.

———. "La Librairie française en 1700." *Revue française d'histoire du livre* 3 (1972): 3–43.

———. "Les Tours de France des imprimeurs et libraires à la fin du XVIIe siècle." *Revue française d'histoire du livre* 6 (1973): 207–33.

Lebeau, Bernard. "Une Dynastie d'imprimeurs et de maires: Les Hovius." *Bulletin et mémoires de la Société archéologique du département d'Ille-et-Vilaine* 88 (1986): 103–29.

Lefebvre-Teillard, Anne. *La Population de Dole au XVIIIe siècle.* Paris: Presses universitaires de France, 1969.

Le Goff, Timothy. *Vannes and Its Region: A Study of Town and Country in Eighteenth-Century France.* Oxford: Clarendon Press, 1981.

Lemay, Edna Hindie. *Dictionnaire des constituants, 1789–1791*. 2 vols. Paris: Universitas, 1991.

LeMoy, Arthur. *Le Parlement de Bretagne et le pouvoir royale au XVIIIe siècle*. 1909. Reprint, Geneva: Megariotis, 1981.

Lepreux, Georges. *Gallia typographica ou répertoire biographique et chronologique de tous les imprimeurs de France depuis les origines de l'imprimerie jusqu'à la Révolution*. 7 vols. Paris: Champion, 1909–14.

Lhote, Amédée. *Histoire de l'imprimerie à Châlons-sur-Marne*. 1894. Reprint, Nieuwkoop: B. de Graaf, 1969.

Lucas, Colin. "Nobles, Bourgeois, and the Origins of the French Revolution." In *French Society and the Revolution*, edited by Douglas Johnson, 88–131. Cambridge: Cambridge University Press, 1976.

Luçay, Hélion de. *Les Origines du pouvoir ministériel en France: Les Secrétaires d'état depuis leur institution jusqu'à la mort de Louis XV*. 1881. Reprint, Geneva: Slatkine, 1976.

Maire, Catherine. *De la cause de dieu à la cause de la nation: Le Jansénisme au XVIIIe siècle*. Paris: Gallimard, 1998.

Marchand, Jean. *Une Enquête sur l'imprimerie et la librairie en Guyenne, mars 1701*. Bordeaux: Taffard, 1939.

Margerison, Kenneth. *Pamphlets and Public Opinion: The Campaign for a Union of Orders in the Early French Revolution*. West Lafayette: Purdue University Press, 1998.

Marion, Marcel. *La Bretagne et le duc d'Aiguillon, 1753–1770*. Paris: Fontémoing, 1898.

———. *Dictionnaire des institutions de la France aux XVIIe et XVIIIe siècles*. 1923. Reprint, Paris: Picard, 1989.

———. *Le Garde des sceaux Lamoignon et la réforme judiciaire de 1788*. Paris: Hachette, 1905.

Martin, Henri-Jean. "Un Grand Éditeur parisien au XVIIe siècle: Sébastien Cramoisy." *Gutenberg Jahrbuch* (1957): 179–88.

———. "Guillaume Desprez, libraire de Pascal et de Port-Royal." *Fédération des sociétés historiques et archéologiques de Paris et de l'Ile-de-France: Mémoires* 2 (1950): 205–28.

———. *Livre, pouvoirs et société à Paris au XVIIe siècle (1598–1701)*. 2 vols. Geneva: Droz, 1969.

———. *Print, Power, and People in Seventeenth-Century France*. Translated by David Gerard. Metuchen, N.J.: Scarecrow, 1993.

———. "Un Projet de réforme de l'imprimerie parisienne en 1645." In *Humanisme actif: Mélanges d'art et de littérature offerts à Julien Cain*, edited by Étienne Dennery, 2:261–64. Paris: Hermann, 1968.

———. "Renouvellements et concurrences." In Chartier and Martin, *Histoire de l'édition française: Le Livre conquérant*, 472–99.

Martin, Henri-Jean, and Jeanne-Marie Dureau. "Des Années de transition: 1500–1530." In Chartier and Martin, *Histoire de l'édition française: Le Livre conquérant*, 256–67.

Martin, Henri-Jean, and Anne-Marie Lecocq. *Livres et lecteurs à Grenoble: Les Registres du libraire Nicolas (1645–1668)*. 2 vols. Geneva: Droz, 1977.

Maza, Sarah. *Private Lives and Public Affairs: The Causes Célèbres of Prerevolutionary France*. Berkeley: University of California Press, 1993.

———. *Servants and Masters in Eighteenth-Century France: The Uses of Loyalty*. Princeton: Princeton University Press, 1983.

McLeod, Jane. "Provincial Book Trade Inspectors in Eighteenth-Century France." *French History* 12 (1998): 127–48.

———. "Social Status and the Politics of Printers in Eighteenth-Century Bordeaux." *Histoire sociale—Social History* 23 (1990): 301–23.

McLeod, Jane, and Hans V. Hansen. "Argument Density and Argument Diversity in the License Applications of French Provincial Printers, 1669–1781." In *Argumentation in Practice*, edited by Frans H. Van Eemeren and Peter Houtlosser, 321–36. Amsterdam: John Benjamins, 2005.

Mellot, Jean-Dominique. "Clés pour un essor provincial: Le Petit siècle d'or de l'édition rouennaise (vers 1600–vers 1670)." *Annales de Normandie* 45 (1995): 265–300.

———. *L'Édition rouennaise et ses marchés (vers 1600–vers 1730): Dynamisme provincial et centralisme Parisien*. Paris: École des chartes, 1998.

———. "La Librairie du palais sous l'ancien régime: Splendeur et décadence de l'exception rouennaise du livre." In *Les Parlements et la vie de la cité (XVIe–XVIIIe siècle)*, edited by Olivier Chaline and Yves Sassier, 111–33. Rouen: Publications de l'Université de Rouen, 2004.

———. "Librairie et cadre corporatif en France à l'age classique." In Barbier, Juratic, and Varry, *L'Europe et le livre*, 61–77.

———. "Le Régime des privilèges et permissions d'imprimer à Rouen au XVIIe siècle." *Bibliothèque de l'École des chartes* 142 (1984): 137–52.

———. "Rouen and Its Printers from the Fifteenth to the Nineteenth Century." In Gee and Kirk, *Printed Matters*, 8–29.

Mellot, Jean-Dominique, and Élisabeth Queval. *Répértoire d'imprimeurs/libraires (vers 1500–vers 1810)*. Paris: Bibliothèque nationale, 2004.

Mellottée, Paul. *Histoire économique de l'imprimerie: L'Imprimerie sous l'ancien régime*. Paris: Hachette, 1905.

Moore, Robert Ian. *The Formation of a Persecuting Society: Power and Deviance in Western Europe, 950–1250*. Oxford: Blackwell, 1987.

Morin, Louis. "Les Febvre, imprimeurs et libraires à Troyes, à Bar-sur-Aube(?) et à Paris." *Bulletin du bibliophile* (1901): 394–428.

Negroni, Barbara de. *Lectures interdites: Le Travail des censeurs au XVIIIe siècle, 1723–1774*. Paris: Albin Michel, 1995.

Neuschel, Kristen. *Word of Honor: Interpreting Noble Culture in Sixteenth-Century France*. Ithaca: Cornell University Press, 1989.

Nicolas, Sylvie. *Les Derniers maîtres des requêtes de l'ancien régime (1771–1789)*. Paris: École des chartes, 1998.

Norberg, Kathryn. "Women of Versailles, 1682–1789." In *Servants of the Dynasty: Palace Women in World History*, edited by Anne Walthall, 191–214. Berkeley: University of California Press, 2008.

Orieux, Madeleine, and Jean-Dominique Mellot. *Répertoire d'imprimeurs/libraires, XVIe–XVIIe siècles: État au 31 Décembre 1990*. Paris: Bibliothèque nationale, 1991.

Page, Ivan. "Claude-Gilles Lecamus et sa famille, imprimeurs du clergé de Toulouse." *Revue française d'histoire du livre* 74–75 (1992): 77–101.

Pallier, Denis. "Les Réponses catholiques." In Chartier and Martin, *Histoire de l'édition française: Le Livre conquérant*, 404–35.

———. "Les Victimes de la Saint-Barthélémy dans le monde du livre parisien." In Barbier et al., *Le Livre et l'historien*, 141–63.

Parent, Françoise. "De Nouvelles pratiques de lecture." In Chartier and Martin, *Histoire de l'édition française: Le Livre triomphant*, 801–18.

Parguez, Guy. "L'Imprimerie à Lyon au temps de Dolet." In *Étienne Dolet (1509–1546)*, 63–77. Collection de l'École normale supérieure des jeunes filles 31. Cahiers V. L. Saulnier 3. Paris: École normale supérieure des jeunes filles, 1986.

Pariset, François-Georges, ed. *Bordeaux au XVIIIe siècle*. Bordeaux: Fédération historique du sud-ouest, 1968.

Pasquier, Émile, and Victor Dauphin. *Imprimeurs et libraires de l'Anjou*. Angers: Éditions de l'Ouest, 1932.

Péronnet, Michel. *Les Évêques de l'ancienne France*. 2 vols. Lille: Reproduction des thèses, 1977.

———. "Les Évêques français et le livre au XVI siècle: Auteurs, éditeurs et censeurs." In *Le Livre dans l'Europe de la Renaissance: Actes du XXVIIIe colloque international d'études humanistes de Tours*, edited by Pierre Aquilon and Henri-Jean Martin, 159–69. Paris: Promodis, 1988.

Pocquet, Barthélemy. *Le Duc d'Aiguillon et La Chalotais*. 2 vols. Paris: Perrin, 1900.

Popkin, Jeremy D. "Pamphlet Journalism at the End of the Old Regime." *Eighteenth-Century Studies* 22 (1989): 351–67.

Popkin, Jeremy D., and Dale Van Kley. "Section 5: The Pre-Revolutionary Debate." In *French Revolution Research Collection*, edited by Colin Lucas, 1–17. Oxford: Pergamon Press, 1990.

Quéniart, Jean. *L'Imprimerie et la librairie à Rouen au XVIIIe siècle*. Paris: Klincksieck, 1969.

Rebillon, Armand. *Les États de Bretagne de 1661 à 1789*. Paris: Picard, 1932.

Reynard, Pierre-Claude. "Early Modern State and Enterprise: Shaping the Dialogue Between the French Monarchy and Paper Manufacturers." *French History* 13 (1999): 1–15.

Rigogne, Thierry. *Between State and Market: Printing and Bookselling in Eighteenth-Century France*. Oxford: Voltaire Foundation, 2007.

Ritter, François. *La Police de l'imprimerie et de la librairie à Strasbourg depuis les origines jusqu'à la Révolution française: Extrait de la Revue des bibliothèques*. Paris: Champion, 1922.

Roche, Daniel. "Censorship and the Publishing Industry." In Darnton and Roche, *Revolution in Print,* 3–26.

Rogister, John. "New Light on the Fall of Chauvelin." *English Historical Review* 83 (1968): 314–30.

Rosenfeld, Sophia. "Writing the History of Censorship in the Age of Enlightenment." In *Postmodernism and the Enlightenment: New Perspectives in Eighteenth-Century French Intellectual History*, edited by Daniel Gordon, 117–45. New York: Routledge, 2001.

Roubert, Jacqueline. "La Situation de l'imprimerie lyonnaise à la fin du XVIIe siècle." In *Cinq Études lyonnaises,* edited by René Fédou et al., 77–111. Geneva: Droz, 1966.

Rule, John C. "Royal Ministers and Government Reform During the Last Decades of Louis XIV's Reign." In *Consortium on Revolutionary Europe, 1750–1850*, edited by Claude Sturgill, 1–13. Gainesville: University Presses of Florida, 1975.

Sarazin, Lucien. "Un 'Chalotiste' malouin: Louis-Philippe-Claude Hovius, imprimeur-libraire (1721–1806)." In *Extrait des Annales de la Société historique et archéologique de l'arrondissement de Saint-Malo*. Saint-Servan: J. Haize, 1912.

Saulnier, Frédéric. *Le Parlement de Bretagne 1554–1790*. 2nd ed. Vol. 2. Mayenne: Imprimerie de la Manutention, 1991.

Sauvy, Anne. *Livres saisis à Paris entre 1678 et 1701*. The Hague: Martinus Nijhoff, 1972.

————. "Un Marginal du livre au XVIIIe siècle: Jacques Merlin." *Revue française d'histoire du livre* 45 (1976): 443–85.

Sawyer, Jeffrey K. *Printed Poison: Pamphlet Propaganda, Faction Politics, and the Public Sphere in Early Seventeenth-Century France.* Berkeley: University of California Press, 1990.

Schaeper, Thomas J. *The French Council of Commerce, 1700–1715: A Study of Mercantilism After Colbert.* Columbus: Ohio State University Press, 1983.

Schneider, Robert A. "Crown and Capitoulat: Municipal Government in Toulouse, 1500–1789." In *Cities and Social Change in Early Modern France*, edited by Philip Benedict, 195–220. London: Unwin Hyman, 1989.

Sentou, Jean. *Fortunes et groupes sociaux à Toulouse sous la Révolution (1789–1799): Essai d'histoire statistique.* Toulouse: Privat, 1969.

Sgard, Jean, ed. *Dictionnaire des journaux, 1600–1789.* 2 vols. Paris: Universitas, 1991.

Shapiro, Gilbert, and John Markoff. *Revolutionary Demands: A Content Analysis of the Cahiers de Doléances of 1789.* Stanford: Stanford University Press, 1998.

Smith, David. "Helvétius, Voltaire, and a French Pirate: Michelin of Provins." *Australian Journal of French Studies* 7 (1970): 289–98.

Soll, Jacob. *The Information Master: Jean-Baptiste Colbert's Secret Intelligence System.* Ann Arbor: University of Michigan Press, 2009.

Soman, Alfred. "Press, Pulpit, and Censorship in France Before Richelieu." *Proceedings of the American Philosophical Society* 120 (1976): 439–63.

Sonenscher, Michael. "The Sans-Culottes of the Year II: Rethinking the Language of Labour in Revolutionary France." *Social History* 9 (1984): 301–28.

————. *Work and Wages: Natural Law, Politics, and the Eighteenth-Century French Trades.* Cambridge: Cambridge University Press, 1989.

Sorel, Patricia. *La Révolution du livre et de la presse en Bretagne (1780–1830).* Rennes: Presses universitaires de Rennes, 2004.

Storez, Isabelle. *Le Chancelier Henri-François D'Aguesseau (1668–1751): Monarchiste et libéral.* Paris: Publisud, 1996.

Swann, Julien. *Politics and the Parlement of Paris Under Louis XV, 1754–1774.* Cambridge: Cambridge University Press, 1995.

————. "Power and Provincial Politics in Eighteenth-Century France: The Varenne Affair, 1757–1763." *French Historical Studies* 21 (1998): 441–74.

————. *Provincial Power and Absolute Monarchy: The Estates General of Burgundy, 1661–1790.* Cambridge: Cambridge University Press, 2003.

Tackett, Timothy. *Becoming a Revolutionary: The Deputies of the French National Assembly and the Emergence of a Revolutionary Culture (1789–1790).* Princeton: Princeton University Press, 1996.

Taillefer, Michel. *Vivre à Toulouse sous l'ancien régime.* Paris: Perrin, 2000.

Taveneaux, René. *Le Jansénisme en Lorraine, 1640–1789.* Paris: Vrin, 1960.

Thévenin, Léon. "Un Libraire de Port-Royal: André Pralard." *Bulletin du bibliophile et du bibliothécaire* 45 (1961): 18–38.

Thoumas-Schapira, Micheline. "La Bourgeoisie toulousaine à la fin du XVIIe siècle." *Annales du Midi* 67 (1955): 313–29.

Trénard, Louis. *Commerce et culture: Le Livre à Lyon au XVIIIe siècle.* Lyon: Imprimeries unies, 1953.

————. *Lyon de l'Encyclopédie au préromantisme.* 2 vols. Paris: Presses universitaires de France, 1958.

Van Kley, Dale. "The Jansenist Constitutional Legacy in the French Prerevolution, 1750–1789." In Baker, *The Political Culture of the Old Regime,* 169–201.

Varry, Dominique. "Batailles de libelles à Lyon à l'occasion de la suppression de la Compagnie de Jésus (années 1760–1775)." *Histoire et civilisation du livre* 2 (2006): 135–68.

———. "De la Bastille à Bellecour: Une 'canaille littéraire,' Taupin Dorval." In Barbier et al., *Le Livre et l'historien,* 571–82.

———. "La Diffusion sous le manteau: La Société typographique de Neuchâtel et les lyonnais." In Barbier, Juratic, and Varry, *L'Europe et le livre,* 309–32.

———. "Une Famille de libraires lyonnais turbulents: Les Bruyset." *La Lettre clandestine* 11 (2003): 105–27.

———. "Gens du livre à Lyon au XVIIIe siècle: Quelques Résultats d'une enquête prosopographique en cours." In *The Enlightenment in Europe,* edited by Werner Schneiders, 287–309. Berlin: Berliner Wissenschafts-Verlag, 2003.

———. "L'Imprimerie et la librairie à Lyon au XIXe siècle." In *Le Commerce de la librairie en France au XIXe siècle,* edited by Jean-Yves Mollier, 61–69. Paris: Éditions de la Maison des sciences de l'homme, 1997.

———. "Jean-Baptiste Reguilliat, imprimeur-libraire lyonnais destitué en 1767." *La Lettre clandestine* 12 (2003): 202–17.

———. "Le Livre clandestin à Lyon au XVIIIe siècle." *La Lettre clandestine* 6 (1997): 243–52.

———. "Lyons' Printers and Booksellers from the Fifteenth to the Nineteenth Century." In Gee and Kirk, *Printed Matters,* 30–47.

Ventre, Madeleine. *L'Imprimerie et la librairie en Languedoc au dernier siècle de l'ancien régime, 1700–1789.* Paris: Mouton, 1958.

Vernus, Michel. "Une Page de l'histoire du livre dans le Jura, les Tonnet, imprimeurs-libraires dolois (1712–1781)." *Revue française d'histoire du livre* 27 (1980): 271–95.

———. "A Provincial Perspective." In Darnton and Roche, *Revolution in Print,* 124–38.

———. *La Vie comtoise au temps de l'ancien régime.* Vol. 2. Lons-le-Saunier: Éditions Marque-Maillard, 1985.

Vingtrinier, Aimé. *Histoire de l'imprimerie à Lyon de l'origine jusqu'à nos jours.* Lyon: Adrien Storck, 1894.

Walton, Charles. *Policing Public Opinion in the French Revolution: The Culture of Calumny and the Problem of Free Speech.* New York: Oxford University Press, 2009.

Woloch, Isser. *Jacobin Legacy: The Democratic Movement Under the Directory.* Princeton: Princeton University Press, 1970.

Woodbridge, John. "Censure royale et censure épiscopale: Le Conflit de 1702." *Dix-huitième siècle* 8 (1976): 333–55.

Wright, Joanne. *Origin Stories in Political Thought: Discourses on Gender, Power, and Citizenship.* Toronto: University of Toronto Press, 2004.

Index

Page numbers in *italics* refer to tables.

www.ingramcontent.com/pod-product-compliance
Lightning Source LLC
Chambersburg PA
CBHW021851020426
42334CB00013B/283